CERES™
Celestial Legend
Volume 12: Tôya

STORY & ART BY YUU WATASE

Editor's Note: At the author's request, the spelling of Ms. Watase's first name has been changed from "Yû,"
as it has appeared on previous VIZ publications, to "Yuu."

English Adaptation/Gary Leach

Translation/Lillian Olsen
Touch-Up Art & Lettering/Melanie Lewis
Cover & Graphic Design/Hidemi Sahara
Editor/Avery Gotoh
Supervising Editor/Frances E. Wall

Managing Editor/Annette Roman
Director of Production/Noboru Watanabe
Vice President of Publishing/Alvin Lu
Sr. Director of Acquisitions/Rika Inouye
Vice President of Sales & Marketing/Liza Coppola
Publisher/Hyoe Narita

Printed in Canada

Published by VIZ, LLC
P.O. Box 77010 • San Francisco CA 94107

Shôjo Edition

10 9 8 7 6 5 4 3 2 1

First printing, July 2005

www.viz.com

store.viz.com

VIZ GRAPHIC NOVEL

CERES
Celestial Legend
Vol. 12: Tôya

Story and Art by
Yuu Watase

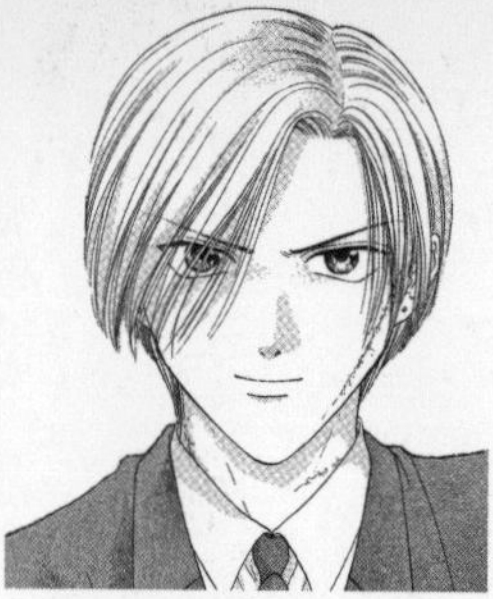

TÔYA: His former memories regained (and, thankfully, all his new ones still intact), Tôya has always felt that his existence required something he couldn't name. Since the moment he first drew breath, Tôya has been seeking something...and, once he found it, he knew its name—<u>her</u> name—was Aya.

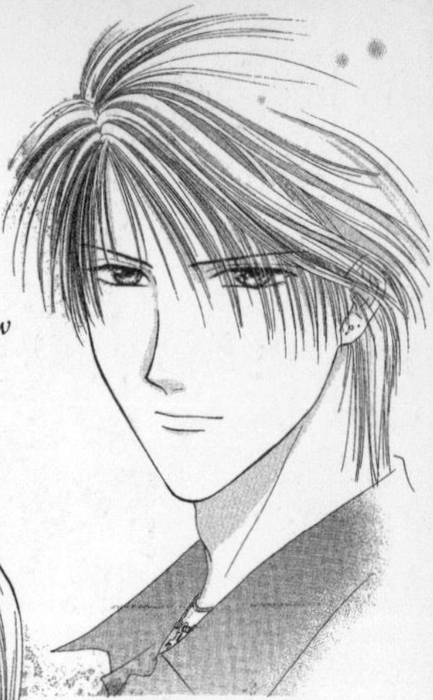

AKI MIKAGE: Aya's twin brother and host to (or hostage of, more like) the angry, Ceres-obsessed "Progenitor." Although Aya still believes that, somewhere deep inside, her brother still exists, the longer he is exposed to the insane love of the Progenitor for Ceres (who of course inhabits Aya), the less the real Aki remains.

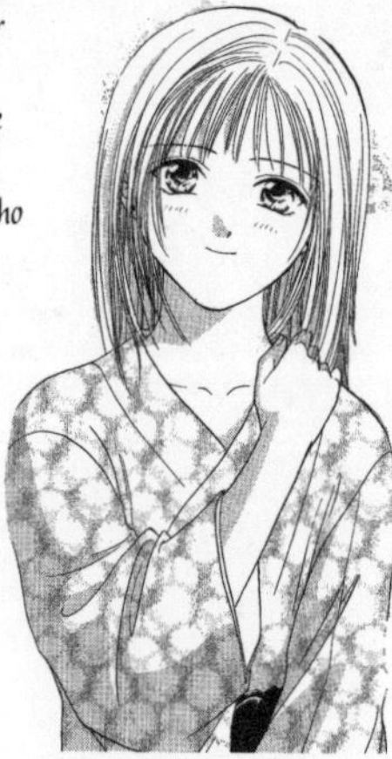

AYA MIKAGE: Fated to be together since they first met—back on Hachijô Island, when Aya was only eight—Aya and Tôya are both very different, yet...no matter what separates them, no matter how their memories may come and go, their love is the one thing that neither of them will ever forget.

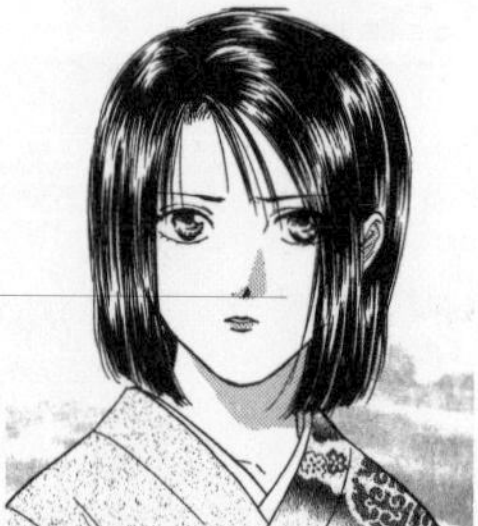

SUZUMI AOGIRI: Current head of the Aogiri household (after her husband, Yûhi's half-brother, passed away) and possessor of some *ten'nyo* or "celestial" blood herself. A "big sister" figure to both Yûhi and to Aya, from the start Suzumi's protection and support has meant a great deal...maybe even the difference between Aya's life and death.

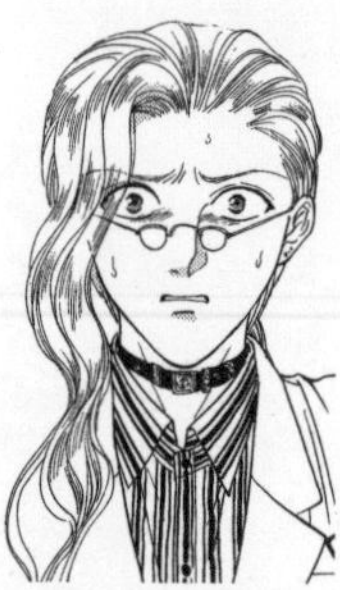

HOWELL: A brilliant research scientist working in the Mikage labs directly accountable to Kagami himself, Alexander Howell ("Alec") spends what little time he doesn't spend in the lab watching anime, playing video games, collecting action figures...a real *otaku*, in other words.

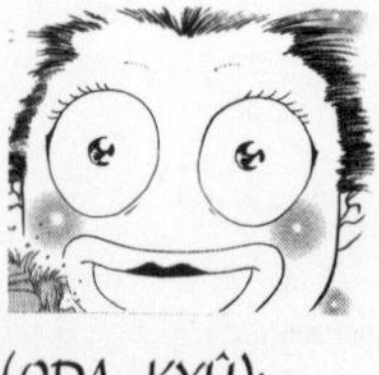

MRS. Q (ODA-KYÛ): Eccentric yet loyal-to-a-fault servant (?) to the Aogiri household...and not without a few secret powers of her own.

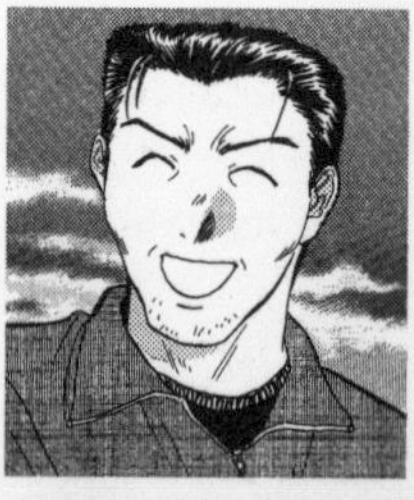

DR. KUROZUKA: A gruff-talking country doctor who's also endlessly kind, "Kurozuka-*sensei*" is there with open arms to welcome both Tôya and Aya into their new lives as a self-supporting couple...or mostly self-supporting, anyway.

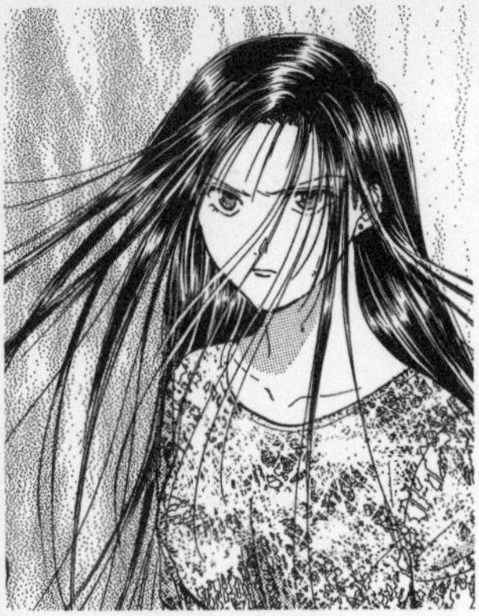

CERES: A *ten'nyo* or "celestial being" prevented from returning to the heavens after her *hagoromo* or "celestial robes" were stolen, Ceres bears little love for the descendants born of her forced union with a mortal male—the being known as "the Progenitor."

KAGAMI MIKAGE: Scion of the family empire and founder of the nefarious "C-Project." His passion mistaken by Aki/The Progenitor as lust for Ceres, the true purpose behind Kagami's search for Ceres' *hagoromo* is slowly being revealed.

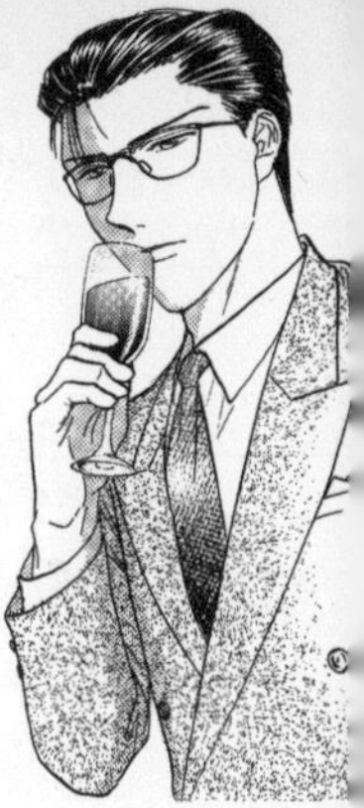

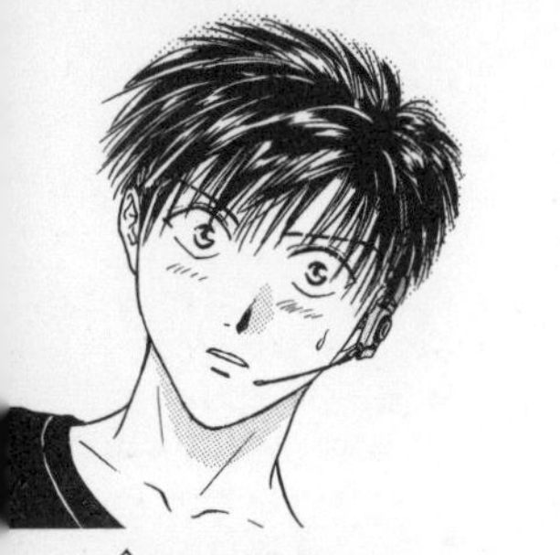

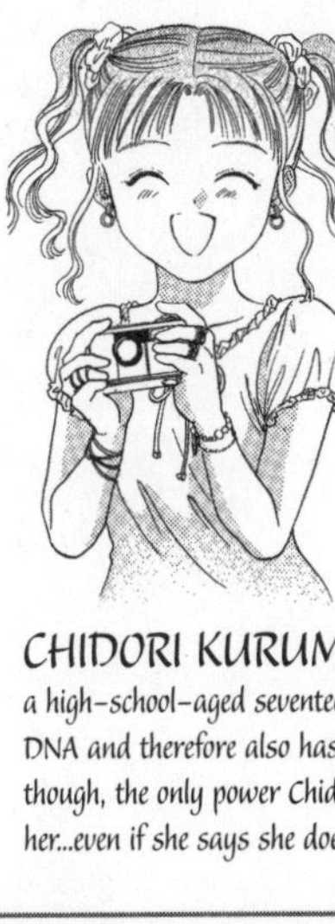

SHURO: A woman who once passed as a man (as part of the wildly popular Japanese pop duo GeSANG), Shuro is yet another conflicted celestial, ambiguous not only about her powers, but also her sexuality.

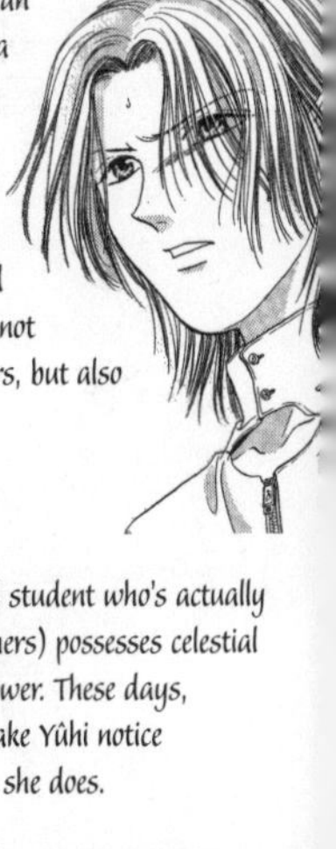

YÛHI AOGIRI: Once it hurt just to look at her, but gradually Yûhi is learning to accept (if not understand) the love Aya bears for his rival, Tôya. Another benefit? The knowledge that he can still care for and love—without necessarily being *in* love with—someone.

CHIDORI KURUMA: A seeming grade-school student who's actually a high-school-aged seventeen years old, Chidori (like others) possesses celestial DNA and therefore also has some amount of celestial power. These days, though, the only power Chidori wants is the power to make Yûhi notice her...even if she says she doesn't, which naturally means she does.

You may have noticed some unfamiliar people and things mentioned in CERES. VIZ left these Japanese pop-culture references as they originally appeared in the manga series. Here's an explanation for those who may not be so J-Pop savvy:

Page 43: ***"YOU'RE RUNNING A FEVER!"*** In the U.S., baby books reassure anxious new parents that fevers below 102 Fahrenheit are no cause for panic and yet, in Japan, fevers of any degree over "normal" seem to elicit considerable concern. Even in the absence of any other symptoms, in anime and manga, any mention of "fever" (*netsu*) is meant to be taken very seriously, indeed.

Page 74: ***NORIKA FUJIWARA*** Well-known Japanese celebrity (TV, movies, commercials, etc.) who, in 1992, was also crowned "Miss Japan."

Page 77: ***MIKURA ISLAND*** One of the seven "Izu islands," Mikura Island is located approximately 90 km (56 miles) north of Japan's real-life Hachijô Island (200 km [124 miles] south of Tokyo), and is known for its wild dolphin population.

Page 169: ***POST PET*** "Virtual" pet that, once trained with the correct settings, is also a kind of e-mail delivery service—both on the computer, and on certain cell phones.

Page 169: ***NAVONA*** Popular cream-filled sponge pastry from famous Japanese confectionary Kame-ya ("Turtle House").

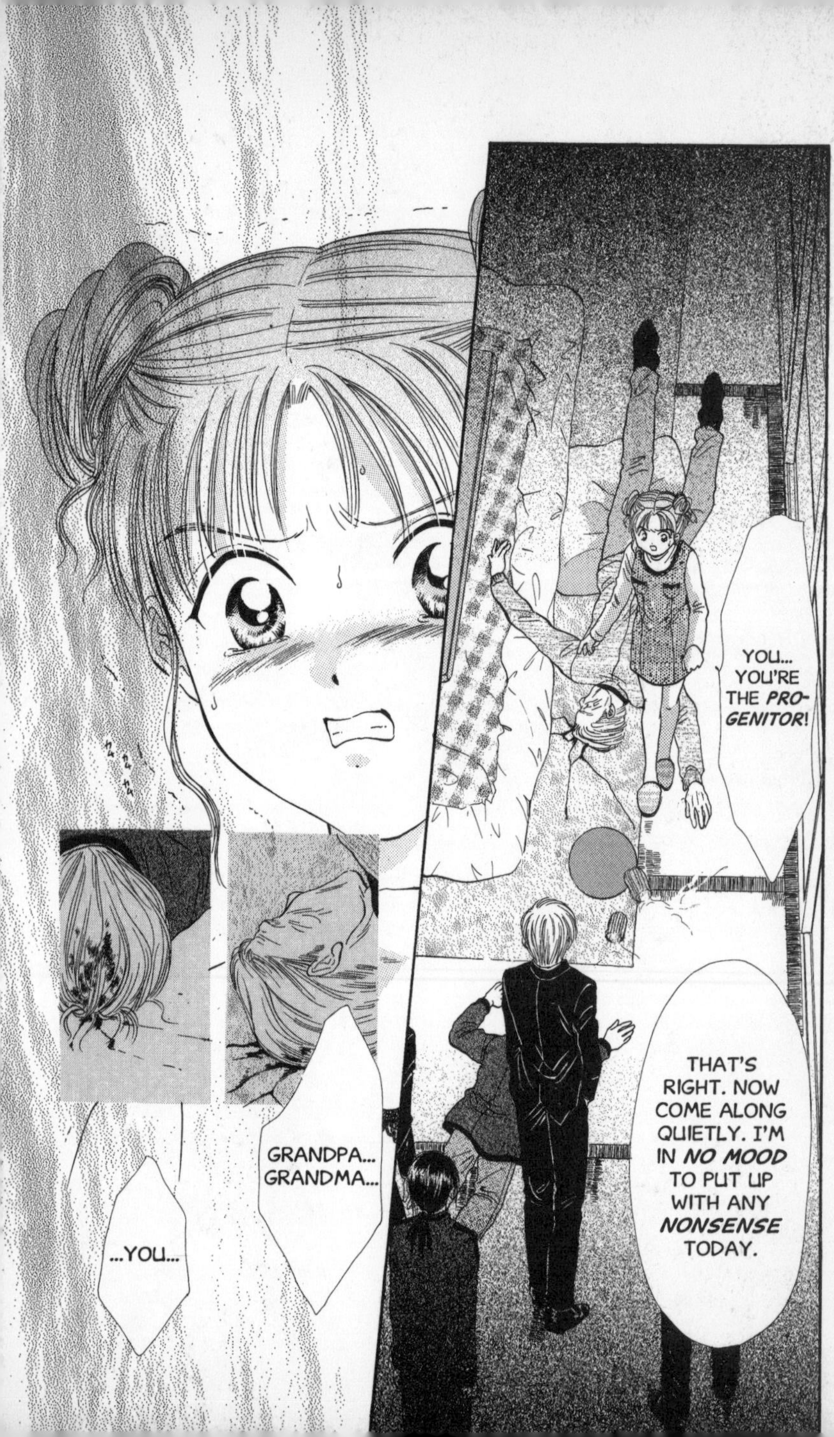
YOU... YOU'RE THE *PRO-GENITOR*!
THAT'S RIGHT. NOW COME ALONG QUIETLY. I'M IN ***NO MOOD*** TO PUT UP WITH ANY ***NONSENSE*** TODAY.
GRANDPA... GRANDMA...
...YOU...

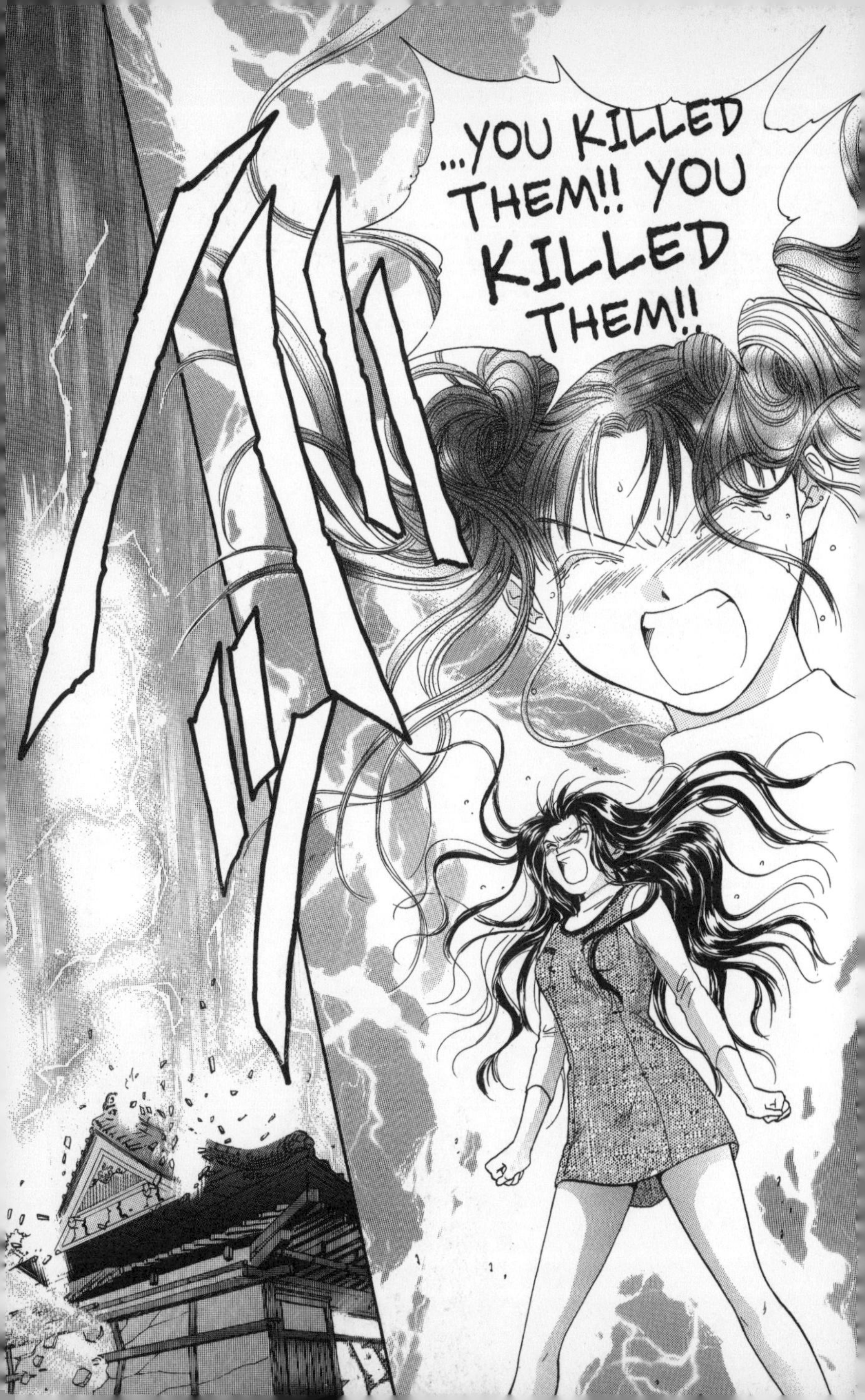
...YOU KILLED THEM!! YOU KILLED THEM!!

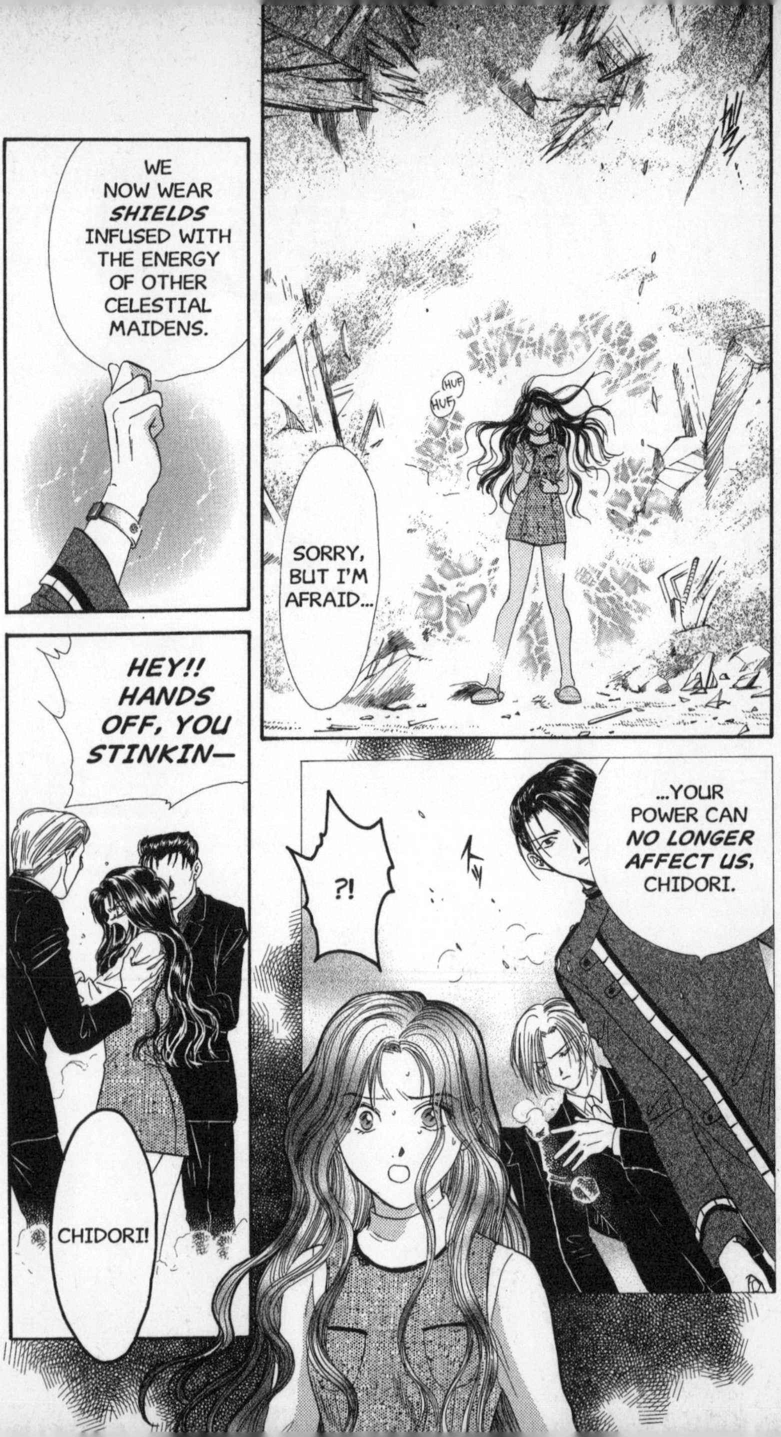
HUF
HUF
SORRY, BUT I'M AFRAID...
WE NOW WEAR SHIELDS INFUSED WITH THE ENERGY OF OTHER CELESTIAL MAIDENS.
...YOUR POWER CAN NO LONGER AFFECT US, CHIDORI.
?!
HEY!! HANDS OFF, YOU STINKIN—
CHIDORI!

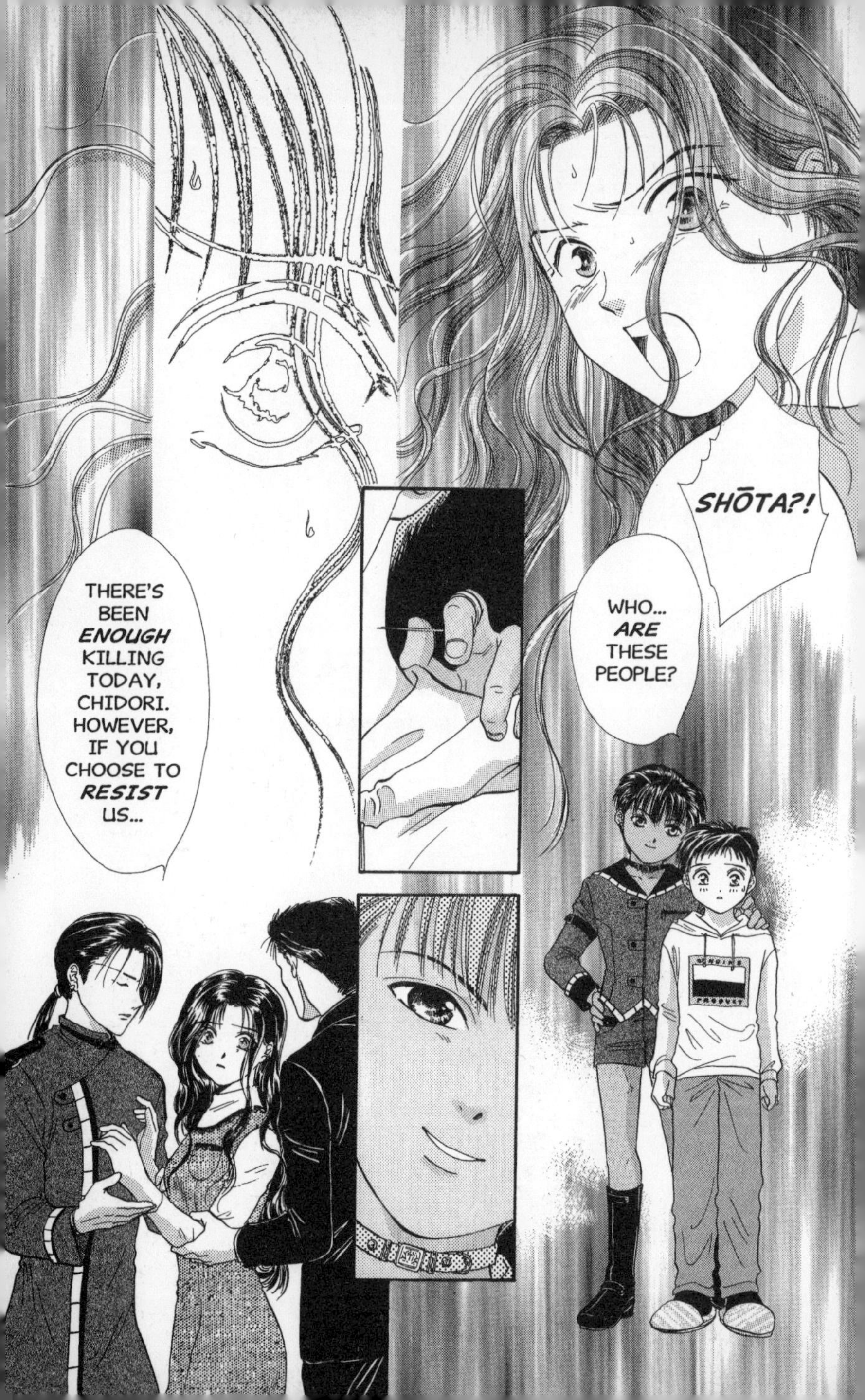
SHŌTA?!
WHO... ARE THESE PEOPLE?
THERE'S BEEN ENOUGH KILLING TODAY, CHIDORI. HOWEVER, IF YOU CHOOSE TO RESIST US...

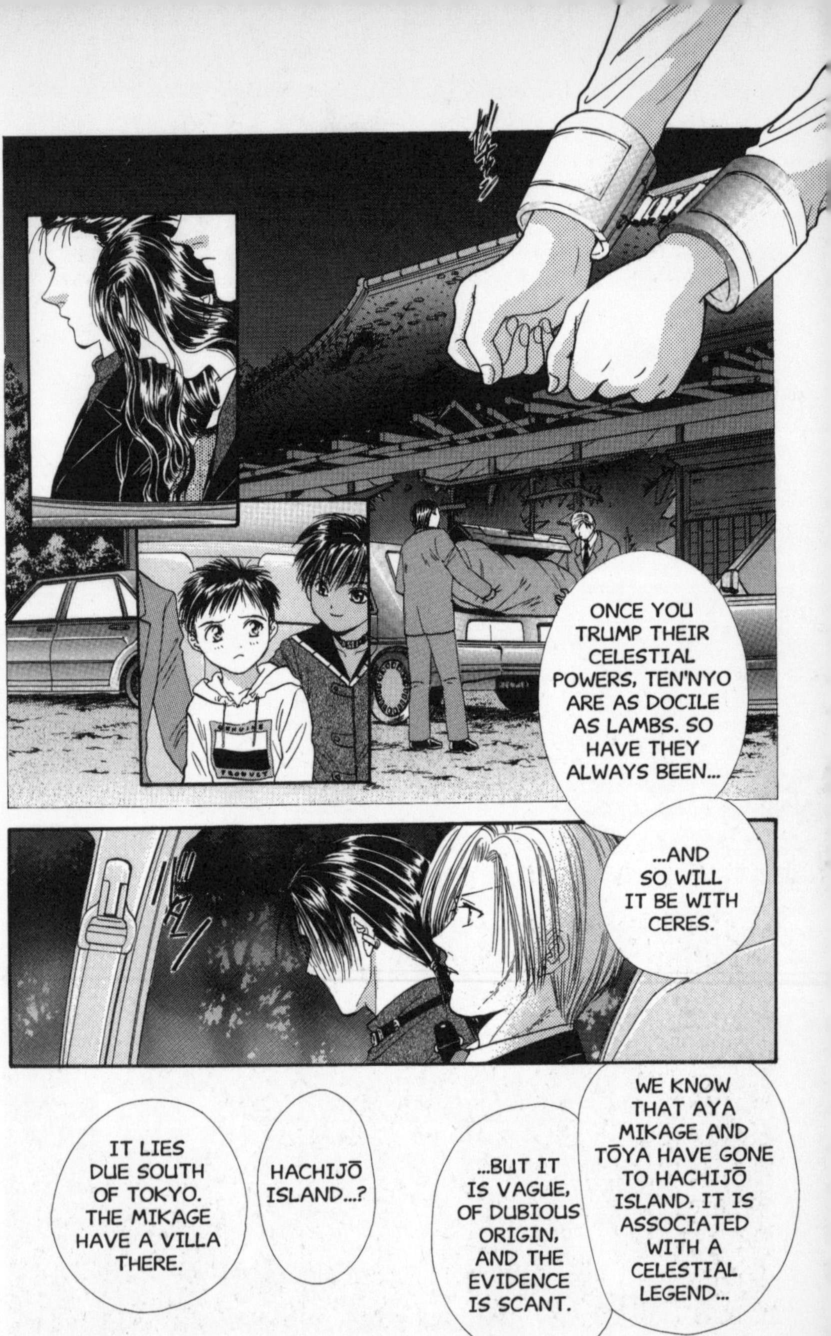
ONCE YOU TRUMP THEIR CELESTIAL POWERS, TEN'NYO ARE AS DOCILE AS LAMBS. SO HAVE THEY ALWAYS BEEN...
...AND SO WILL IT BE WITH CERES.
WE KNOW THAT AYA MIKAGE AND TŌYA HAVE GONE TO HACHIJŌ ISLAND. IT IS ASSOCIATED WITH A CELESTIAL LEGEND...
...BUT IT IS VAGUE, OF DUBIOUS ORIGIN, AND THE EVIDENCE IS SCANT.
HACHIJŌ ISLAND...?
IT LIES DUE SOUTH OF TOKYO. THE MIKAGE HAVE A VILLA THERE.

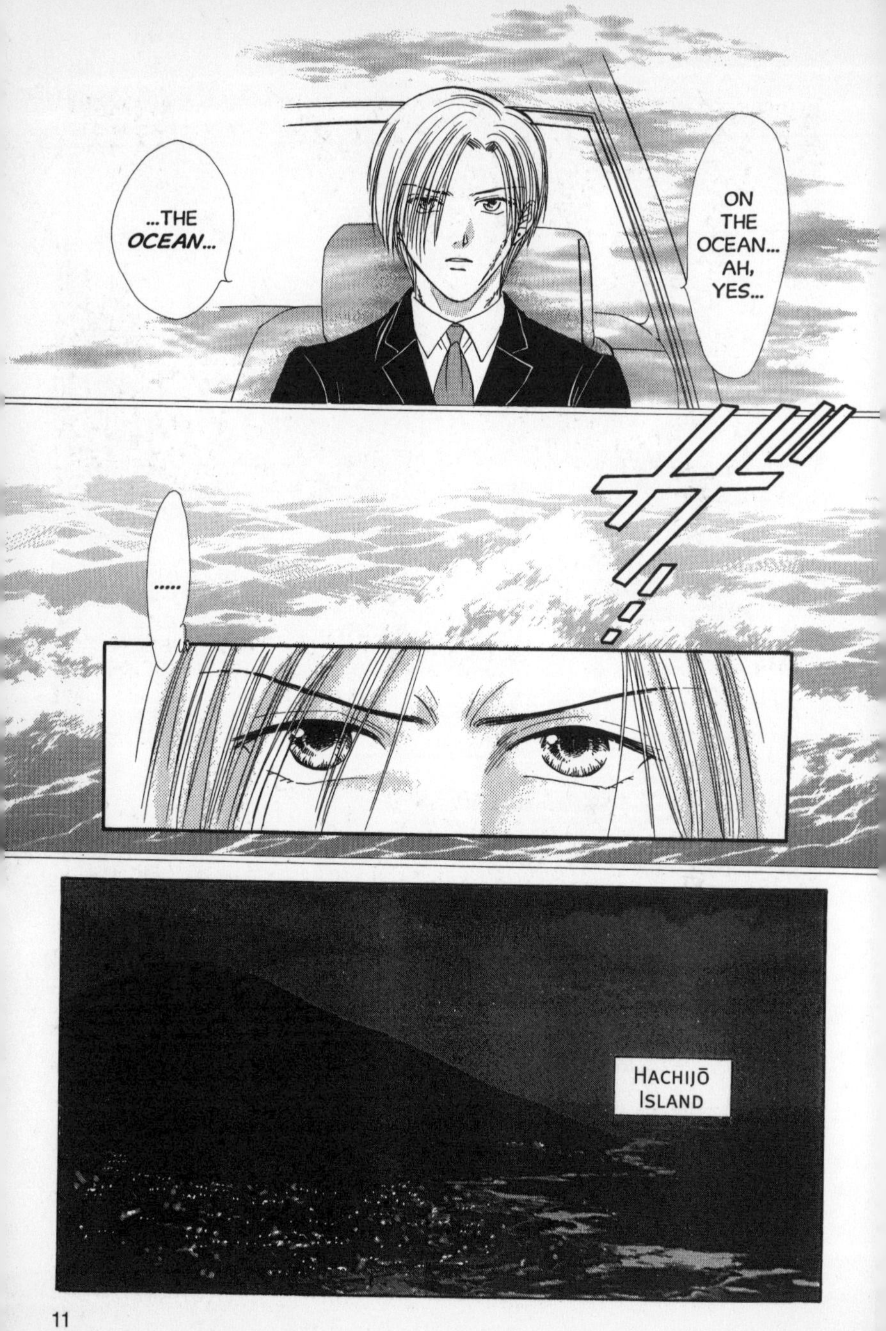
ON THE OCEAN... AH, YES...
...THE *OCEAN*...
......
HACHIJŌ ISLAND

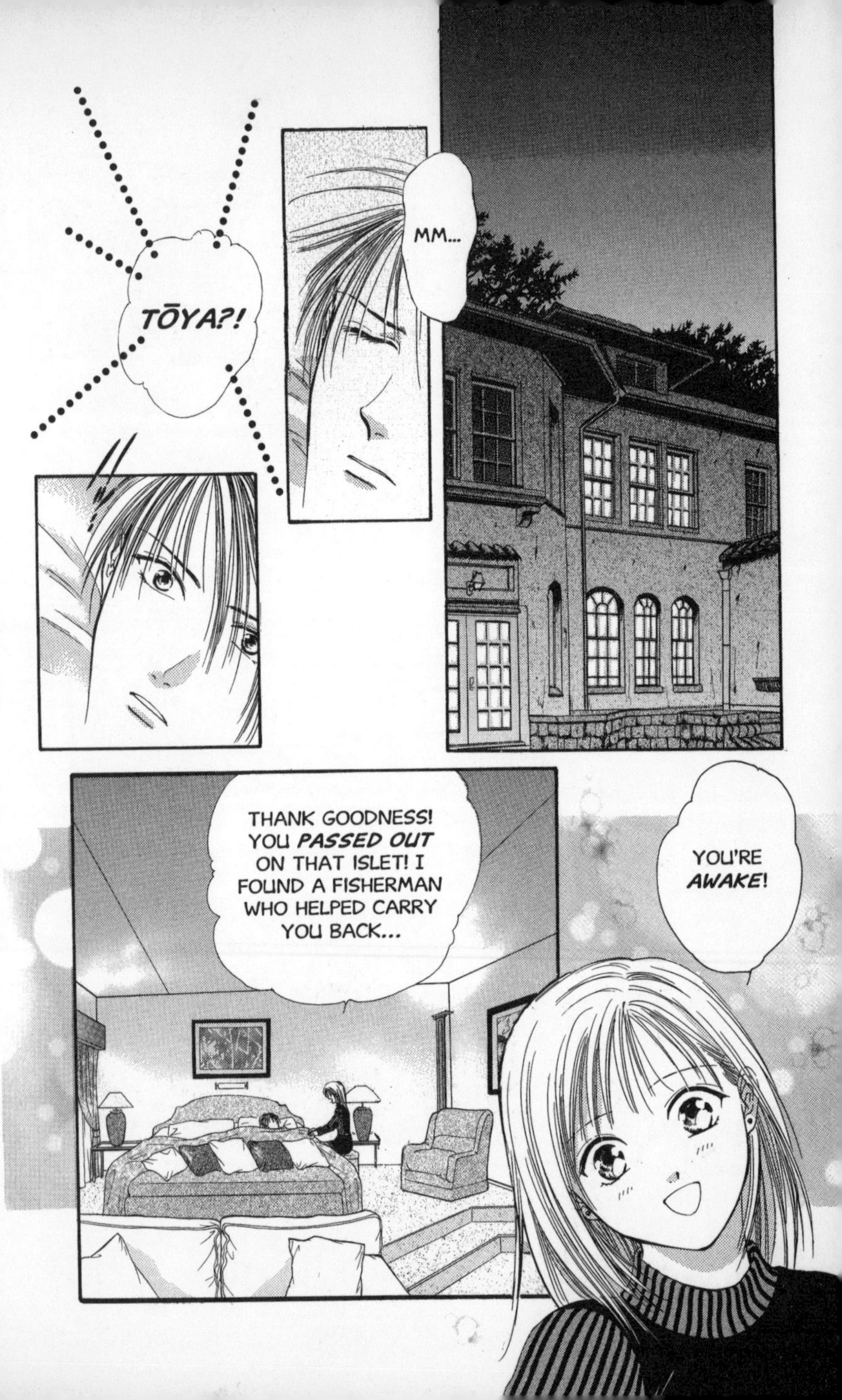
MM...
TŌYA?!
YOU'RE AWAKE!
THANK GOODNESS! YOU PASSED OUT ON THAT ISLET! I FOUND A FISHERMAN WHO HELPED CARRY YOU BACK...

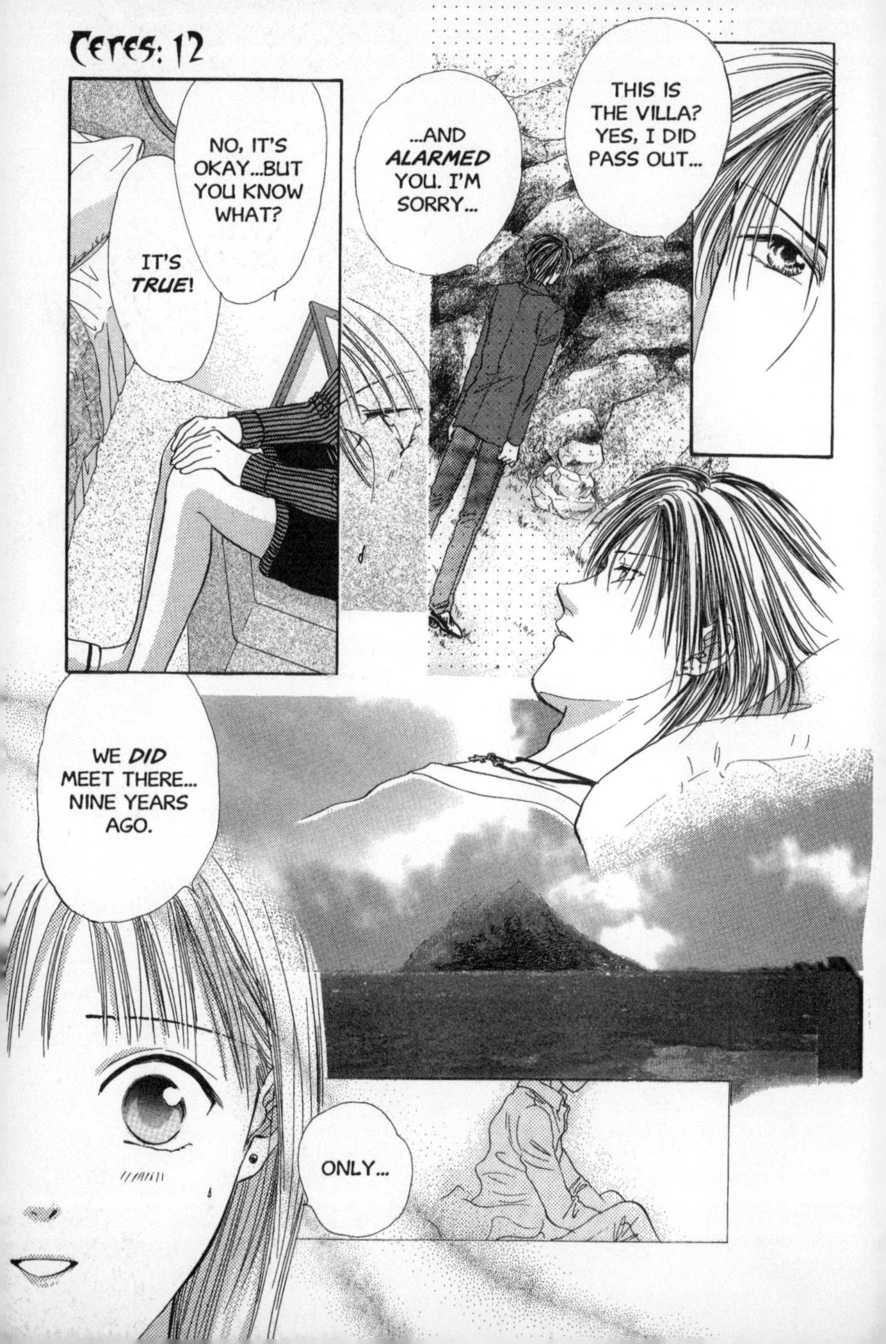
THIS IS THE VILLA? YES, I DID PASS OUT...
...AND *ALARMED* YOU. I'M SORRY...
NO, IT'S OKAY...BUT YOU KNOW WHAT?
IT'S *TRUE*!
WE *DID* MEET THERE... NINE YEARS AGO.
ONLY...

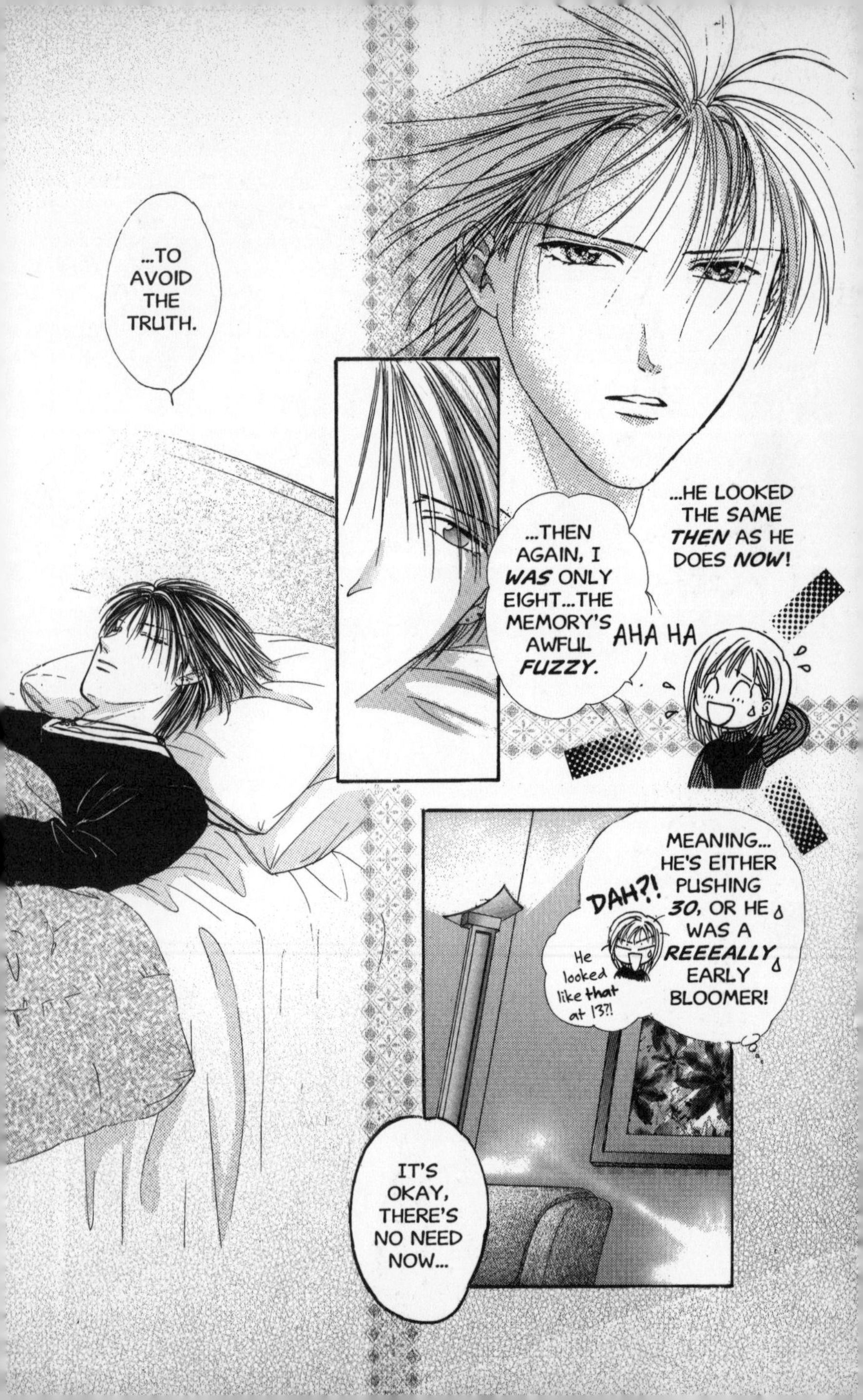

...HE LOOKED THE SAME *THEN* AS HE DOES *NOW*!
...THEN AGAIN, I *WAS* ONLY EIGHT...THE MEMORY'S AWFUL *FUZZY*.
AHA HA
MEANING... HE'S EITHER PUSHING *30*, OR HE WAS A *REEEALLY* EARLY BLOOMER!
DAH?!
He looked like that at 13?!
IT'S OKAY, THERE'S NO NEED NOW...
...TO AVOID THE TRUTH.

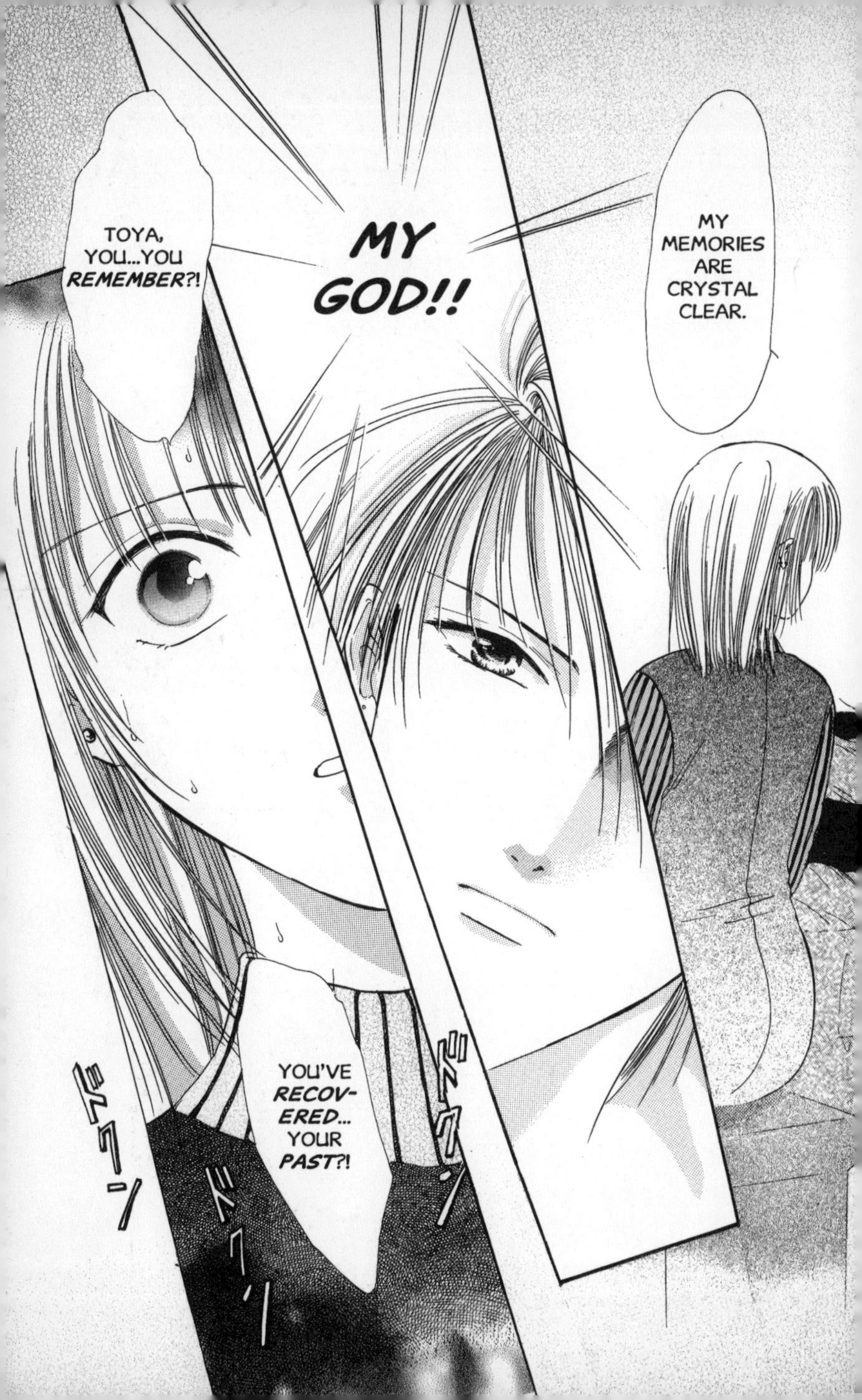
MY MEMORIES ARE CRYSTAL CLEAR.
MY GOD!!
TOYA, YOU...YOU *REMEMBER*?!
YOU'VE *RECOVERED*... YOUR *PAST*?!

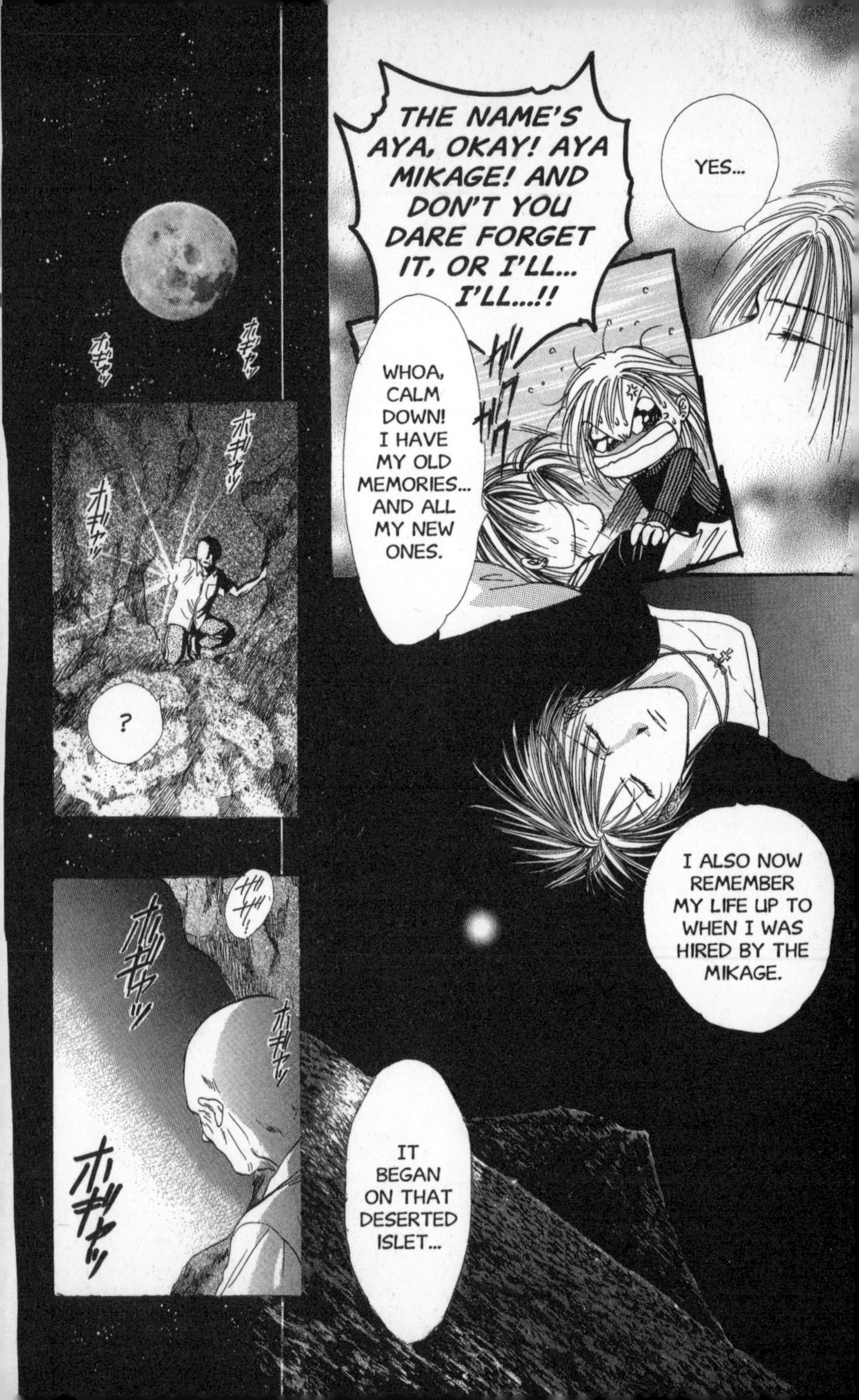

YES...
THE NAME'S AYA, OKAY! AYA MIKAGE! AND DON'T YOU DARE FORGET IT, OR I'LL... I'LL...!!
WHOA, CALM DOWN! I HAVE MY OLD MEMORIES... AND ALL MY NEW ONES.
I ALSO NOW REMEMBER MY LIFE UP TO WHEN I WAS HIRED BY THE MIKAGE.
IT BEGAN ON THAT DESERTED ISLET...
?

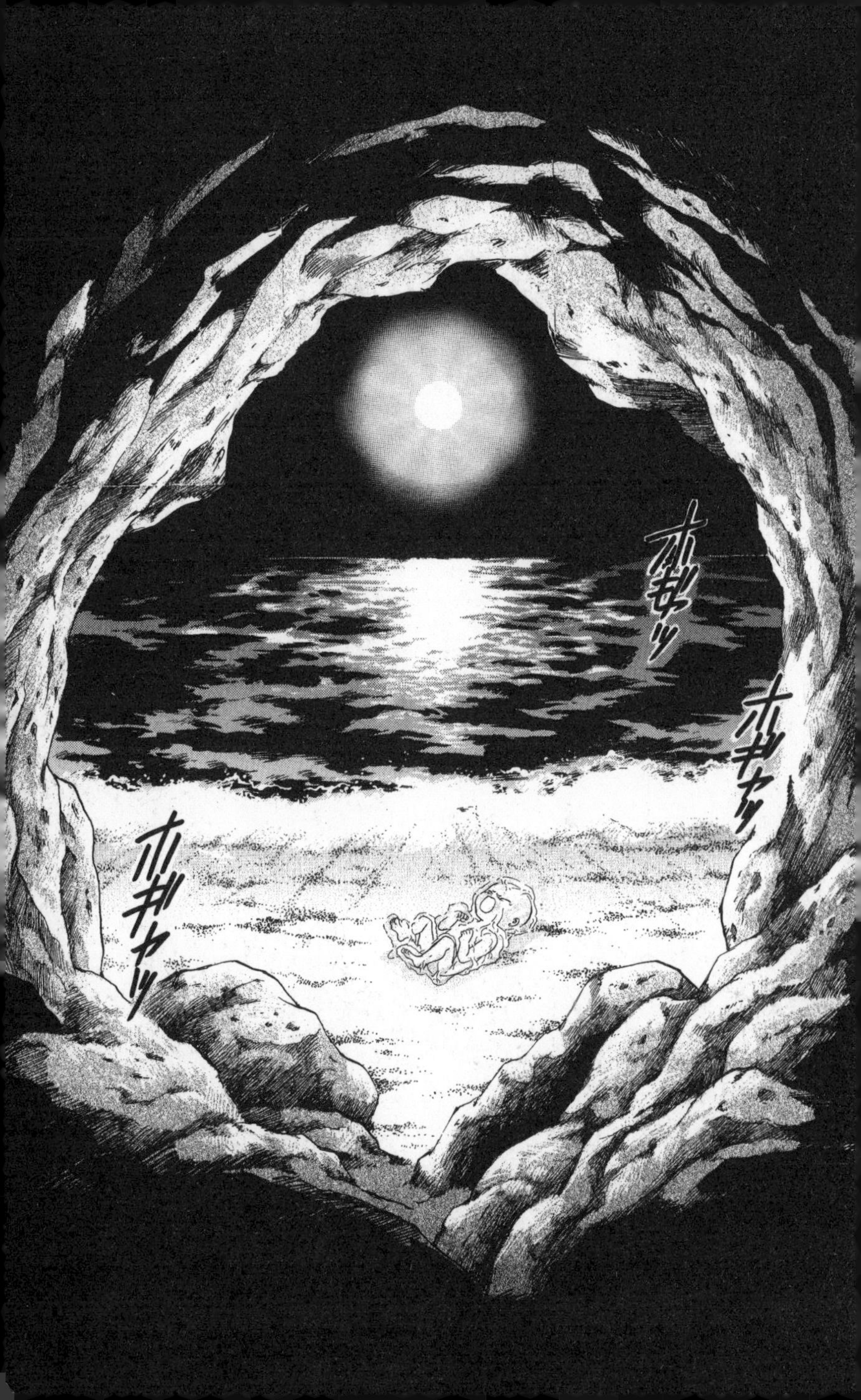
ホギャッ
ホギャッ
ホギャッ

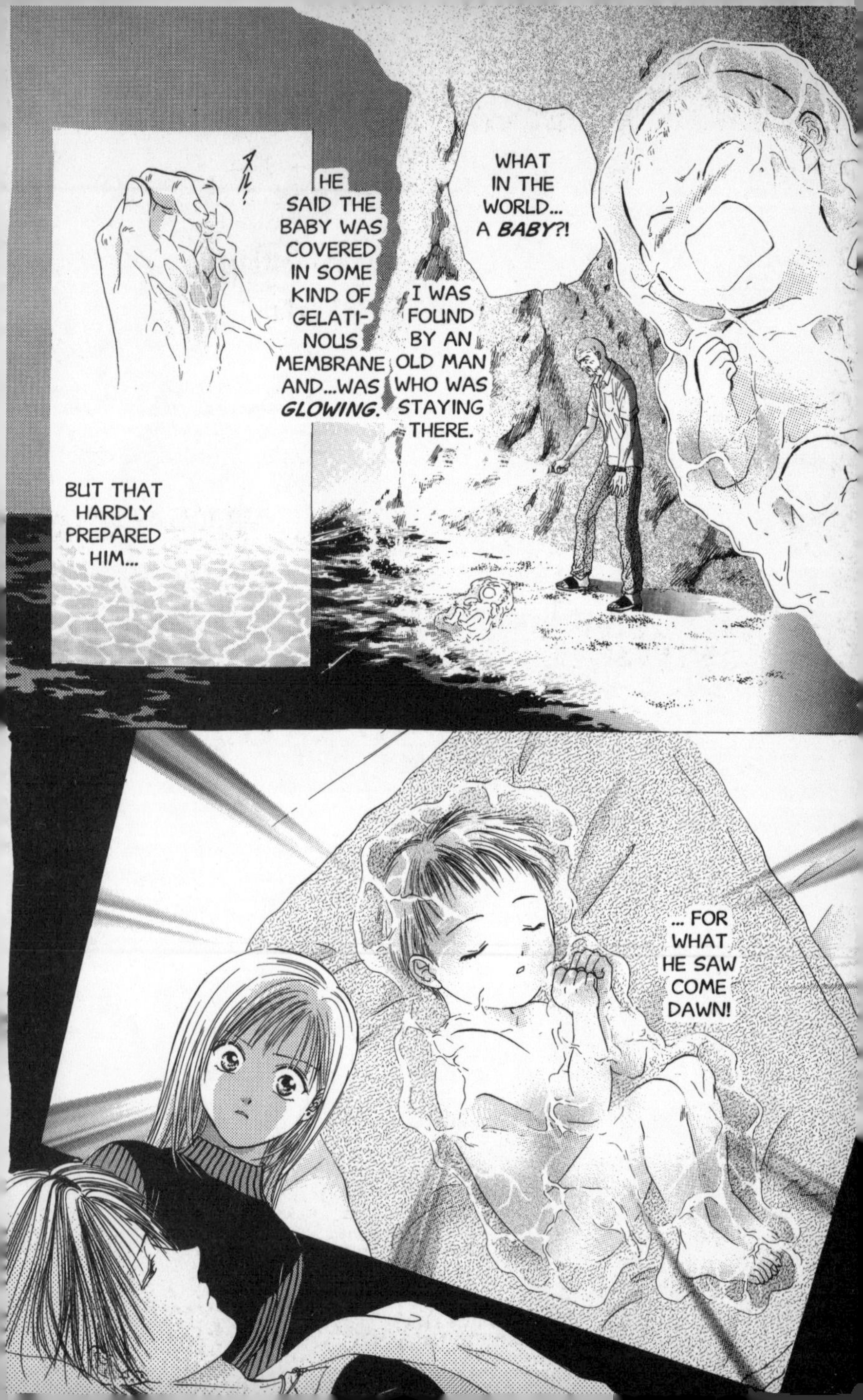
WHAT IN THE WORLD... A *BABY*?!
I WAS FOUND BY AN OLD MAN WHO WAS STAYING THERE.
HE SAID THE BABY WAS COVERED IN SOME KIND OF GELATI- NOUS MEMBRANE AND...WAS *GLOWING.*
ヌル!
BUT THAT HARDLY PREPARED HIM...
... FOR WHAT HE SAW COME DAWN!

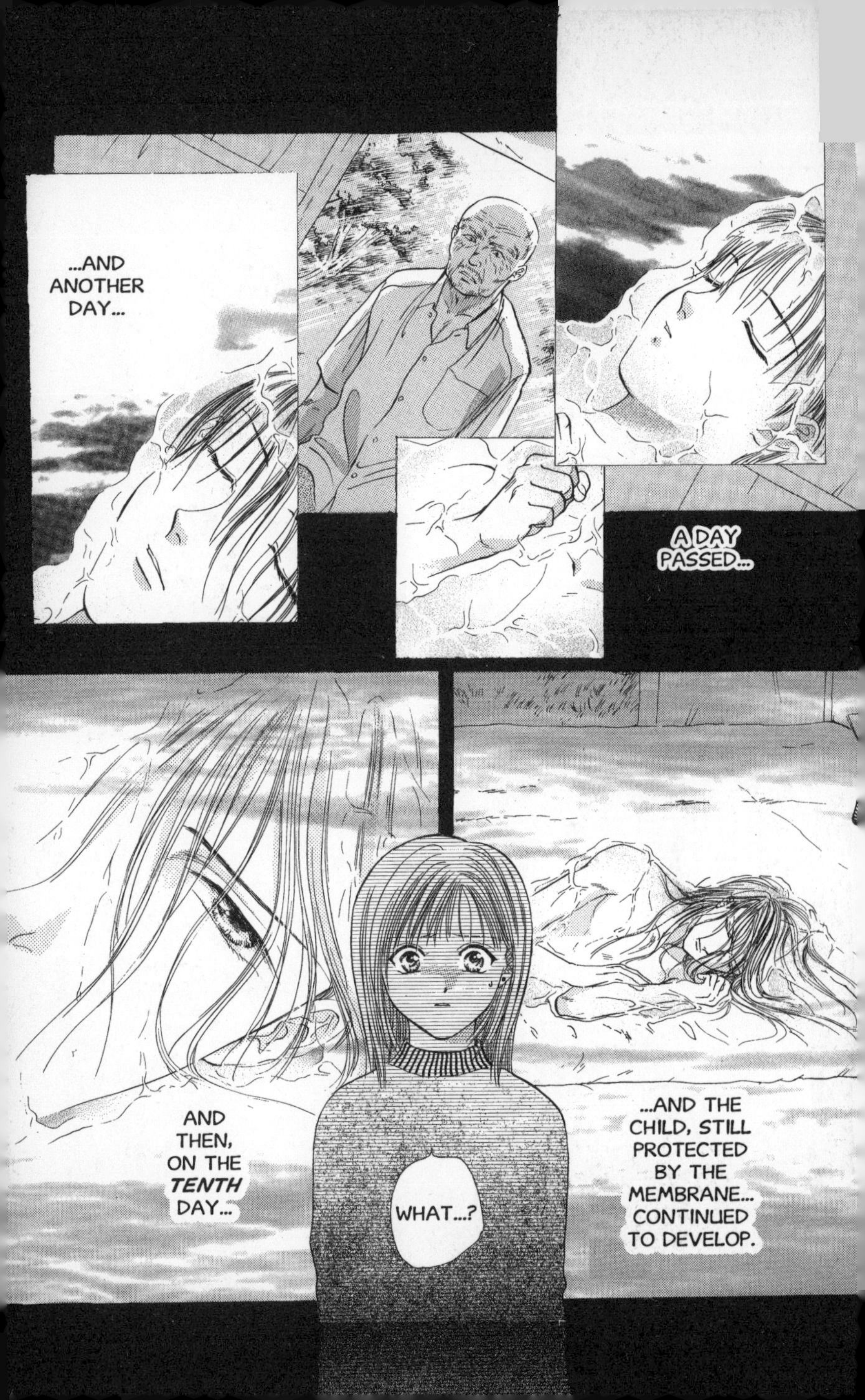
A DAY PASSED...
...AND ANOTHER DAY...
...AND THE CHILD, STILL PROTECTED BY THE MEMBRANE... CONTINUED TO DEVELOP.
AND THEN, ON THE *TENTH* DAY...
WHAT...?

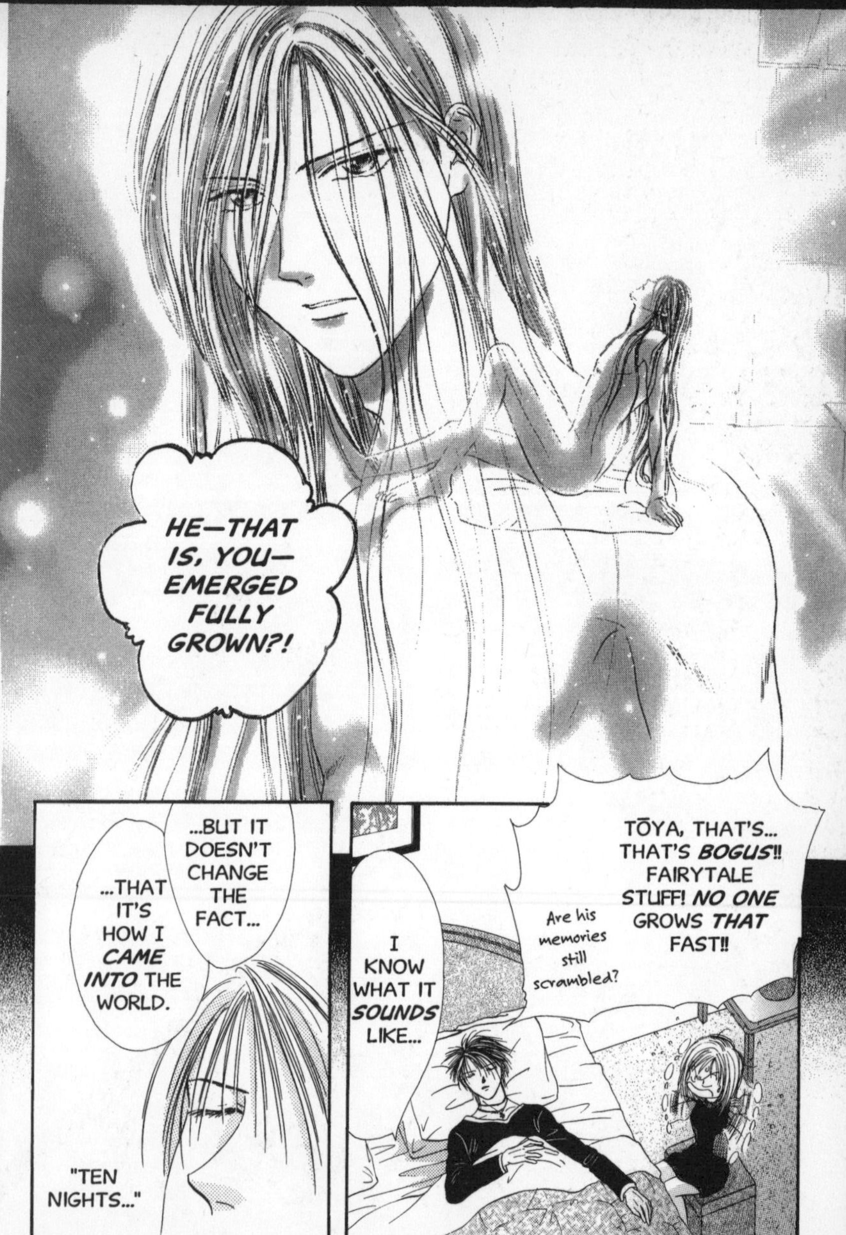
HE—THAT IS, YOU—EMERGED FULLY GROWN?!
TŌYA, THAT'S... THAT'S BOGUS!! FAIRYTALE STUFF! NO ONE GROWS THAT FAST!!
Are his memories still scrambled?
I KNOW WHAT IT SOUNDS LIKE...
...BUT IT DOESN'T CHANGE THE FACT...
...THAT IT'S HOW I CAME INTO THE WORLD.
"TEN NIGHTS..."

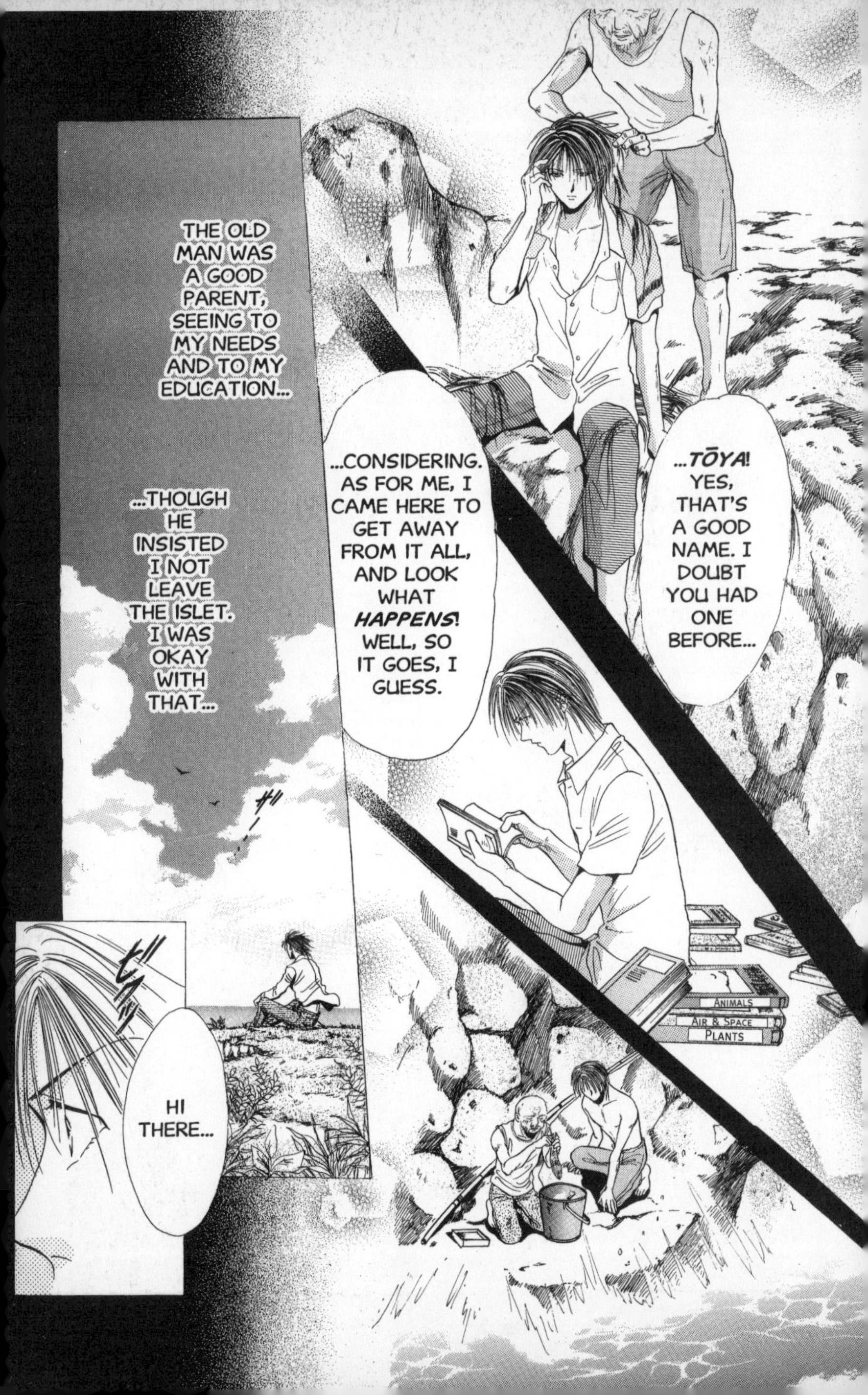
...*TŌYA*! YES, THAT'S A GOOD NAME. I DOUBT YOU HAD ONE BEFORE...
...CONSIDERING. AS FOR ME, I CAME HERE TO GET AWAY FROM IT ALL, AND LOOK WHAT *HAPPENS*! WELL, SO IT GOES, I GUESS.
ANIMALS
AIR & SPACE
PLANTS
THE OLD MAN WAS A GOOD PARENT, SEEING TO MY NEEDS AND TO MY EDUCATION...
...THOUGH HE INSISTED I NOT LEAVE THE ISLET. I WAS OKAY WITH THAT...
HI THERE...

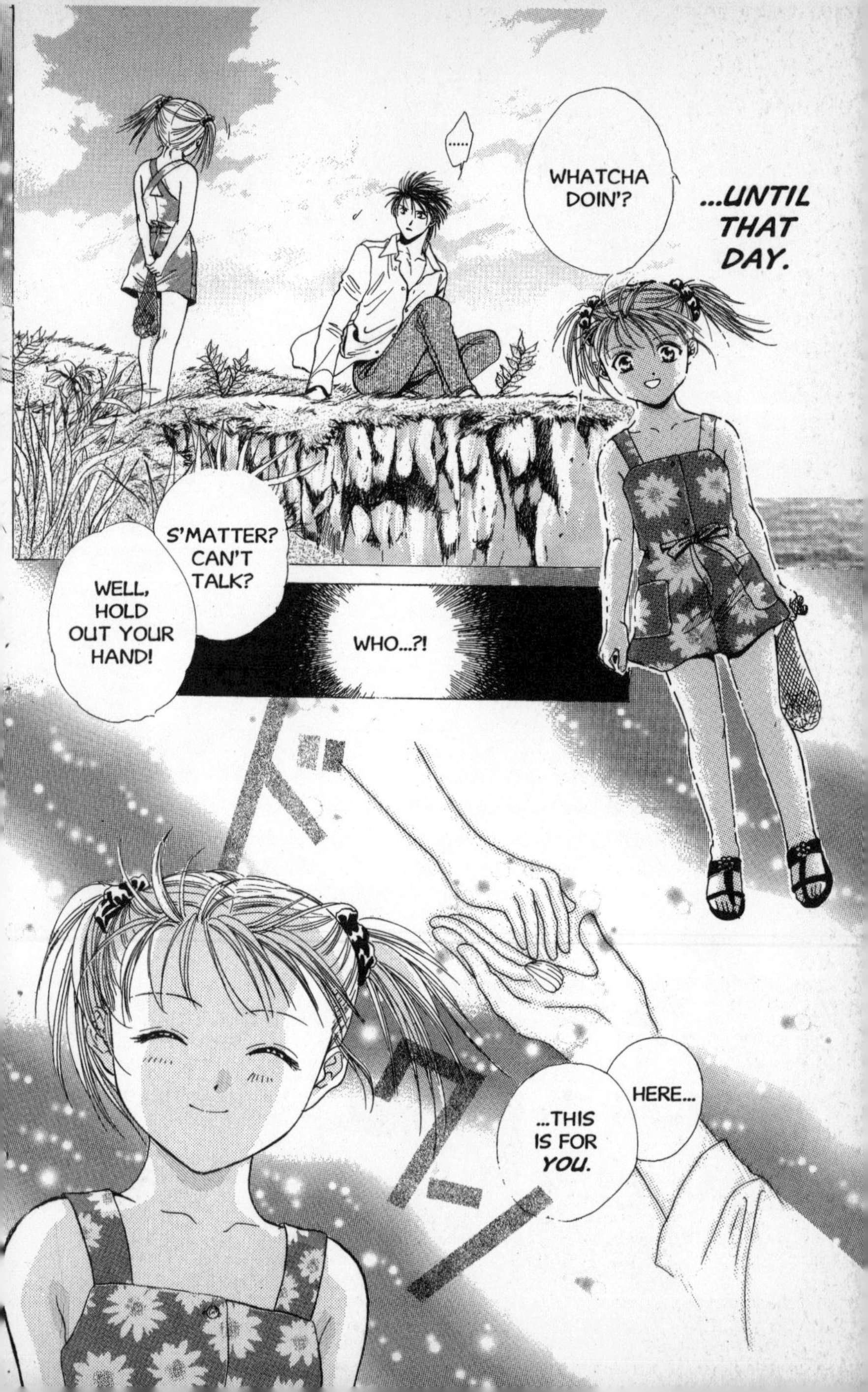
...UNTIL THAT DAY.
WHATCHA DOIN'?
......
WHO...?!
S'MATTER? CAN'T TALK?
WELL, HOLD OUT YOUR HAND!
HERE...
...THIS IS FOR *YOU*.

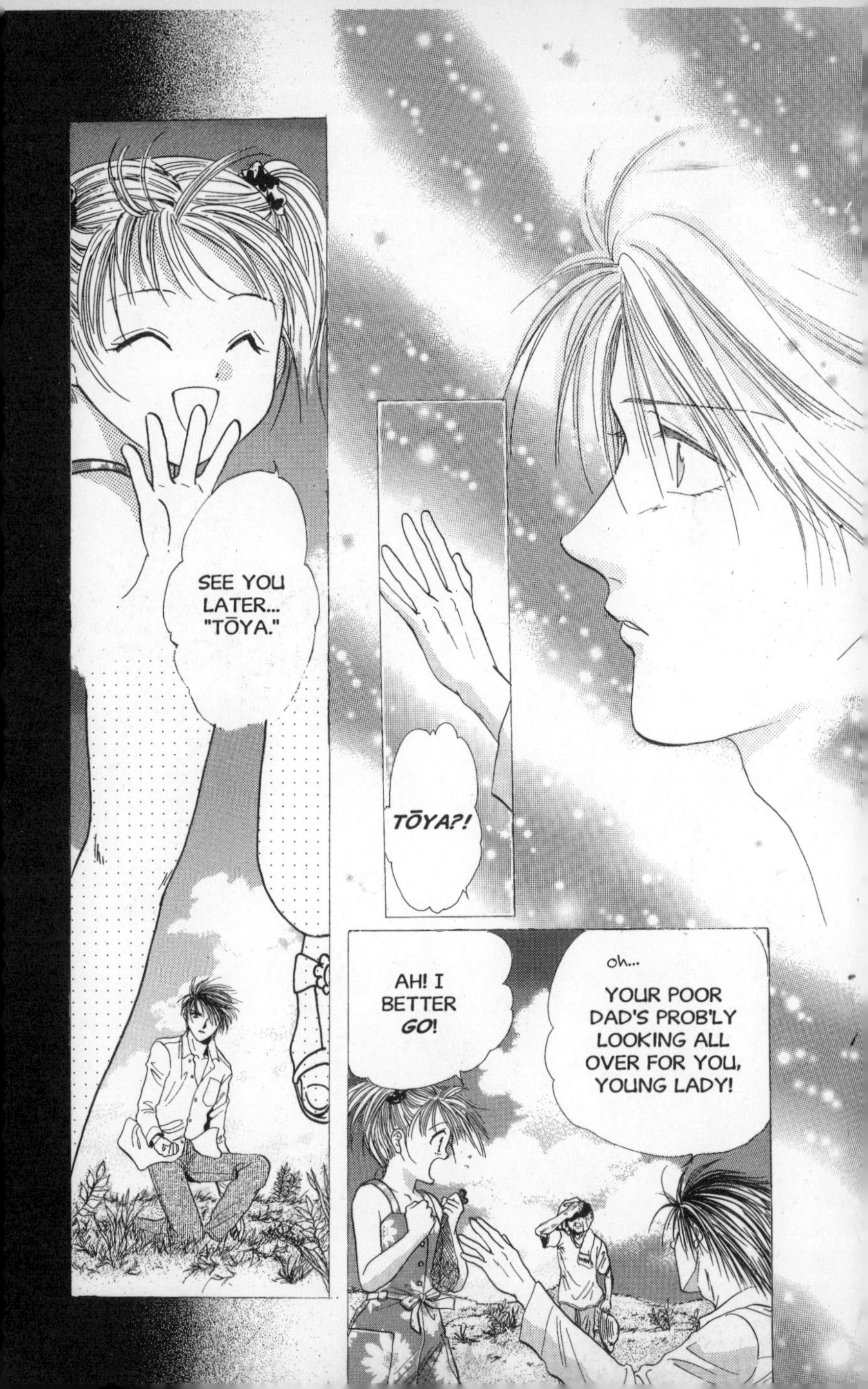
TŌYA?!
oh... YOUR POOR DAD'S PROB'LY LOOKING ALL OVER FOR YOU, YOUNG LADY!
AH! I BETTER GO!
SEE YOU LATER... "TŌYA."

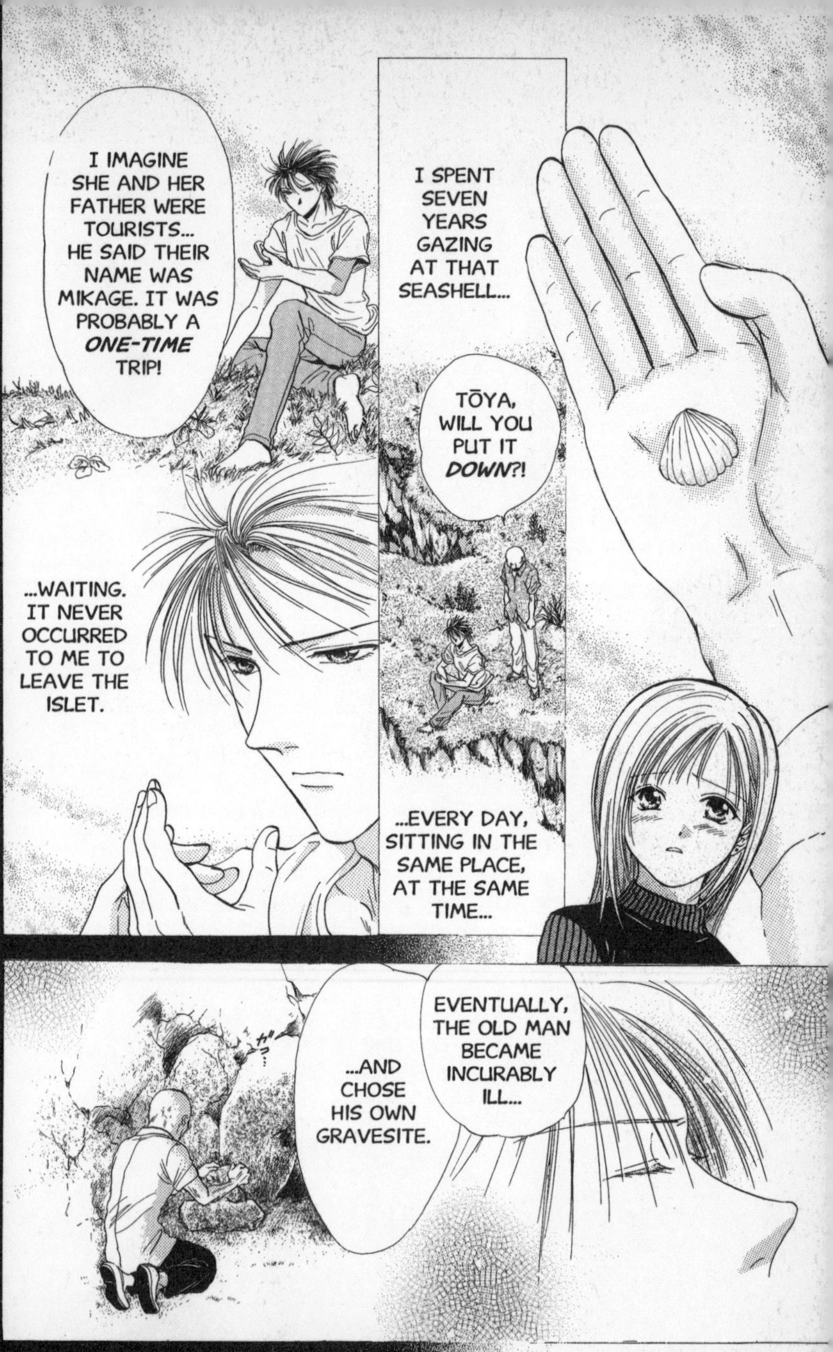
I SPENT SEVEN YEARS GAZING AT THAT SEASHELL...
TŌYA, WILL YOU PUT IT *DOWN*?!
...EVERY DAY, SITTING IN THE SAME PLACE, AT THE SAME TIME...
I IMAGINE SHE AND HER FATHER WERE TOURISTS... HE SAID THEIR NAME WAS MIKAGE. IT WAS PROBABLY A *ONE-TIME* TRIP!
...WAITING. IT NEVER OCCURRED TO ME TO LEAVE THE ISLET.
EVENTUALLY, THE OLD MAN BECAME INCURABLY ILL...
...AND CHOSE HIS OWN GRAVESITE.
ガッ

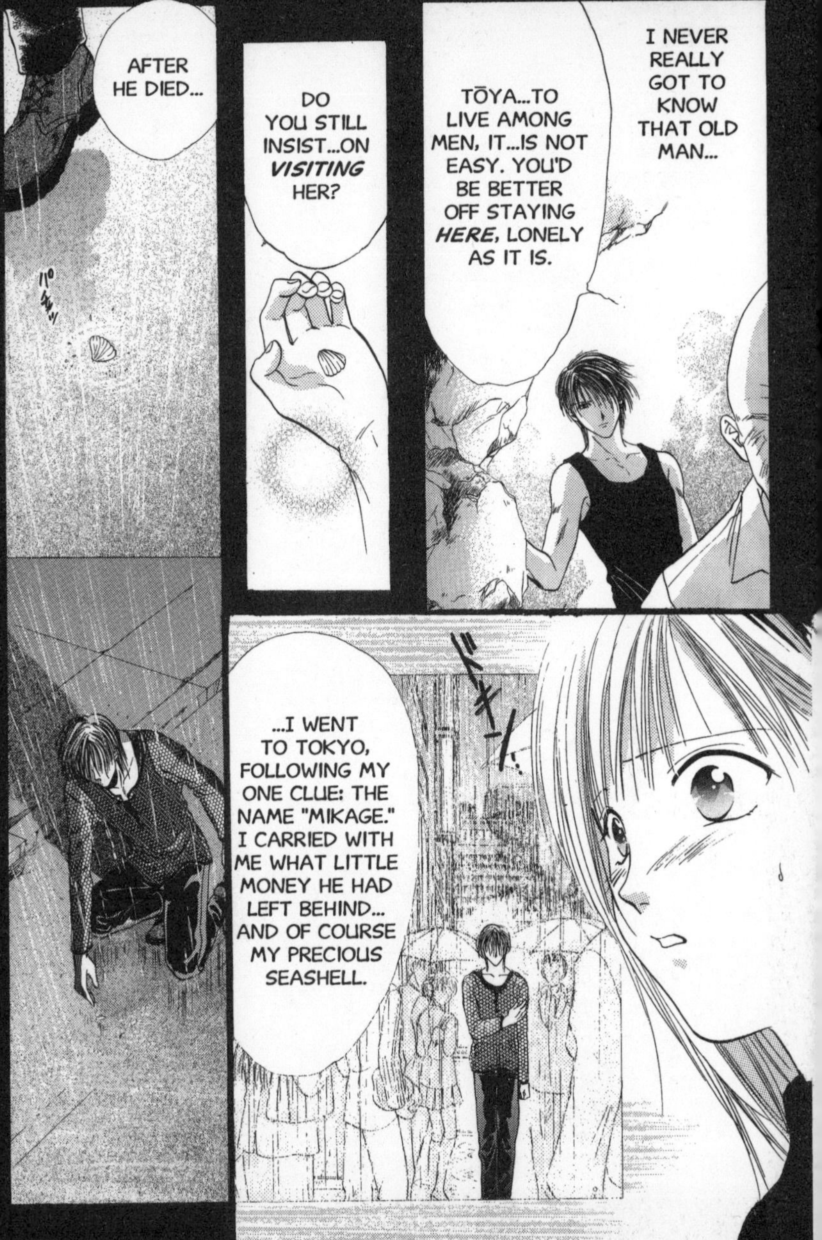
I NEVER REALLY GOT TO KNOW THAT OLD MAN...
TŌYA...TO LIVE AMONG MEN, IT...IS NOT EASY. YOU'D BE BETTER OFF STAYING *HERE*, LONELY AS IT IS.
DO YOU STILL INSIST...ON *VISITING* HER?
AFTER HE DIED...
パシャッ
ドキーン!!
...I WENT TO TOKYO, FOLLOWING MY ONE CLUE: THE NAME "MIKAGE." I CARRIED WITH ME WHAT LITTLE MONEY HE HAD LEFT BEHIND... AND OF COURSE MY PRECIOUS SEASHELL.

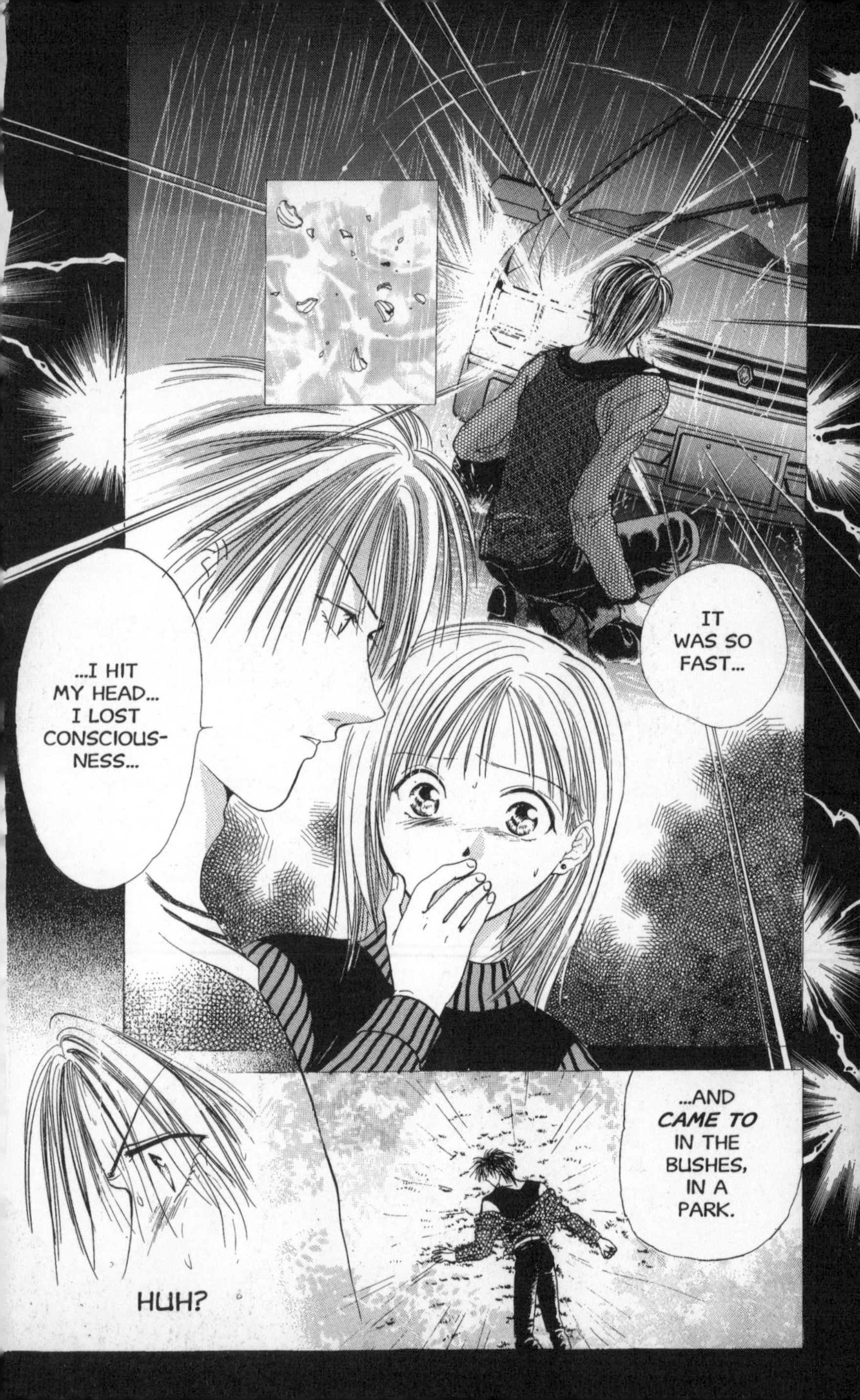
IT WAS SO FAST...
...I HIT MY HEAD... I LOST CONSCIOUS-NESS...
...AND *CAME TO* IN THE BUSHES, IN A PARK.
HUH?

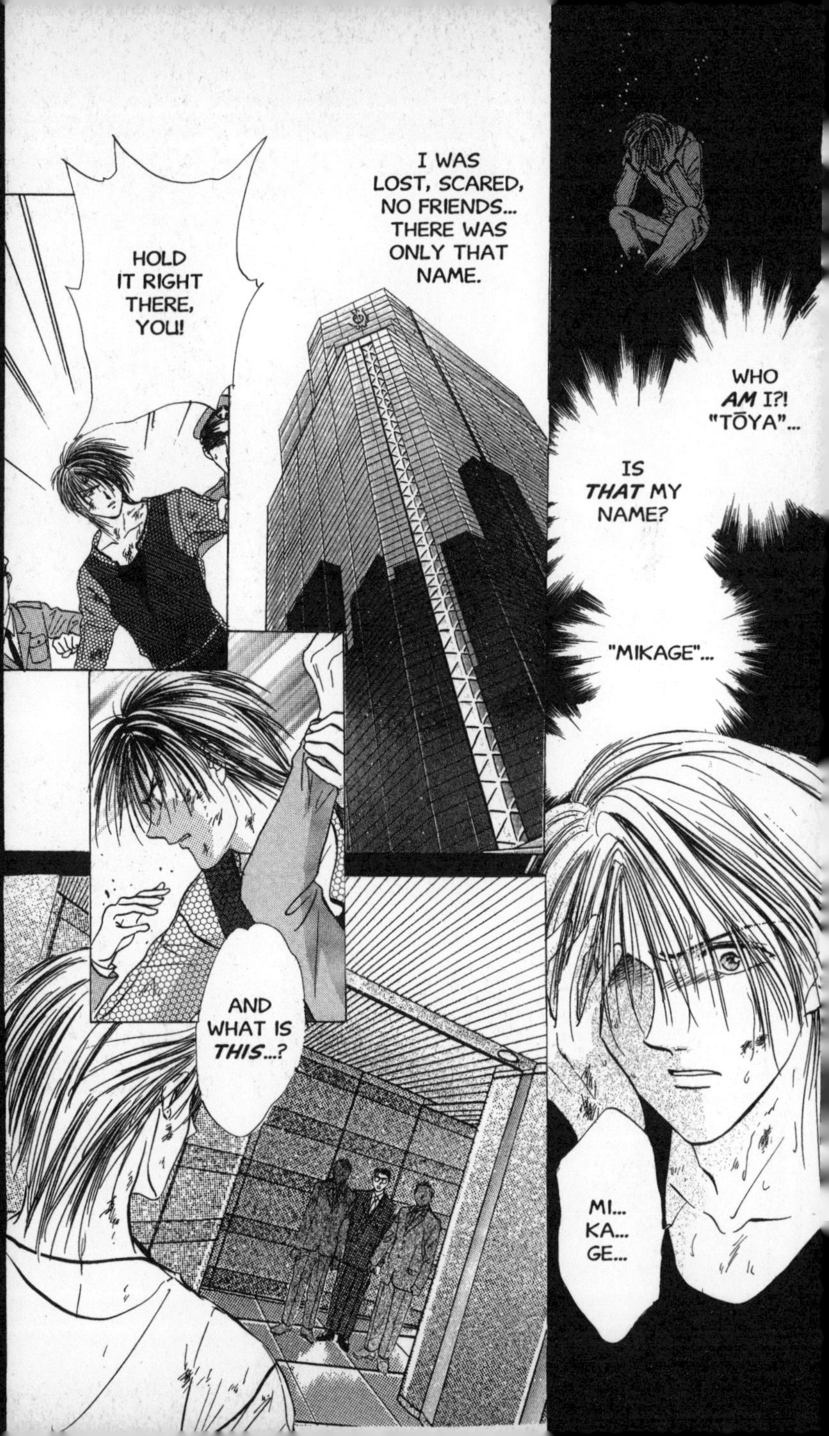
WHO AM I?! "TŌYA"...
IS THAT MY NAME?
"MIKAGE"...
MI... KA... GE...
I WAS LOST, SCARED, NO FRIENDS... THERE WAS ONLY THAT NAME.
HOLD IT RIGHT THERE, YOU!
AND WHAT IS THIS...?

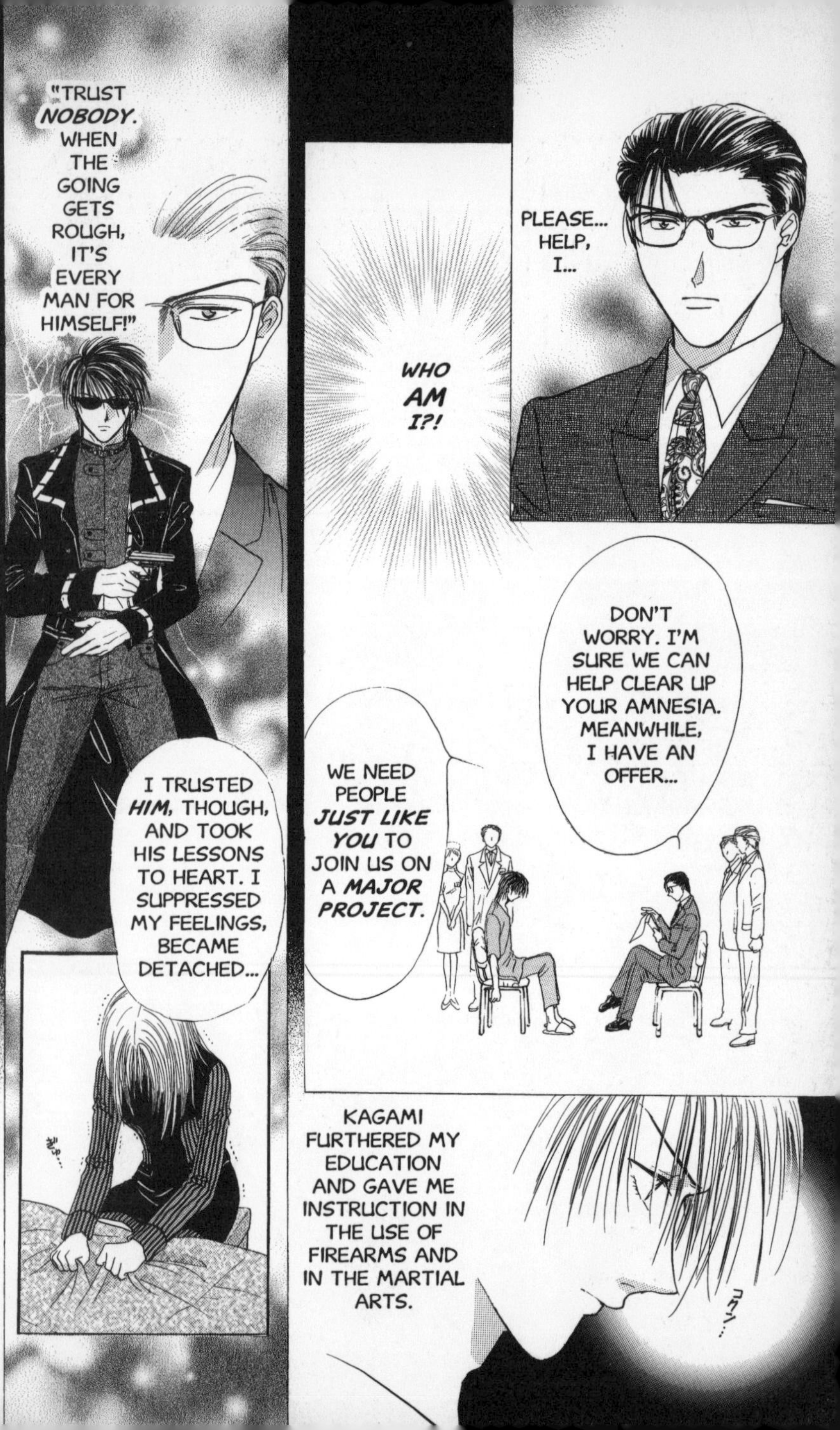
PLEASE... HELP, I...
WHO AM I?!
DON'T WORRY. I'M SURE WE CAN HELP CLEAR UP YOUR AMNESIA. MEANWHILE, I HAVE AN OFFER...
WE NEED PEOPLE *JUST LIKE YOU* TO JOIN US ON A *MAJOR PROJECT*.
KAGAMI FURTHERED MY EDUCATION AND GAVE ME INSTRUCTION IN THE USE OF FIREARMS AND IN THE MARTIAL ARTS.
"TRUST *NOBODY*. WHEN THE GOING GETS ROUGH, IT'S EVERY MAN FOR HIMSELF!"
I TRUSTED *HIM*, THOUGH, AND TOOK HIS LESSONS TO HEART. I SUPPRESSED MY FEELINGS, BECAME DETACHED...

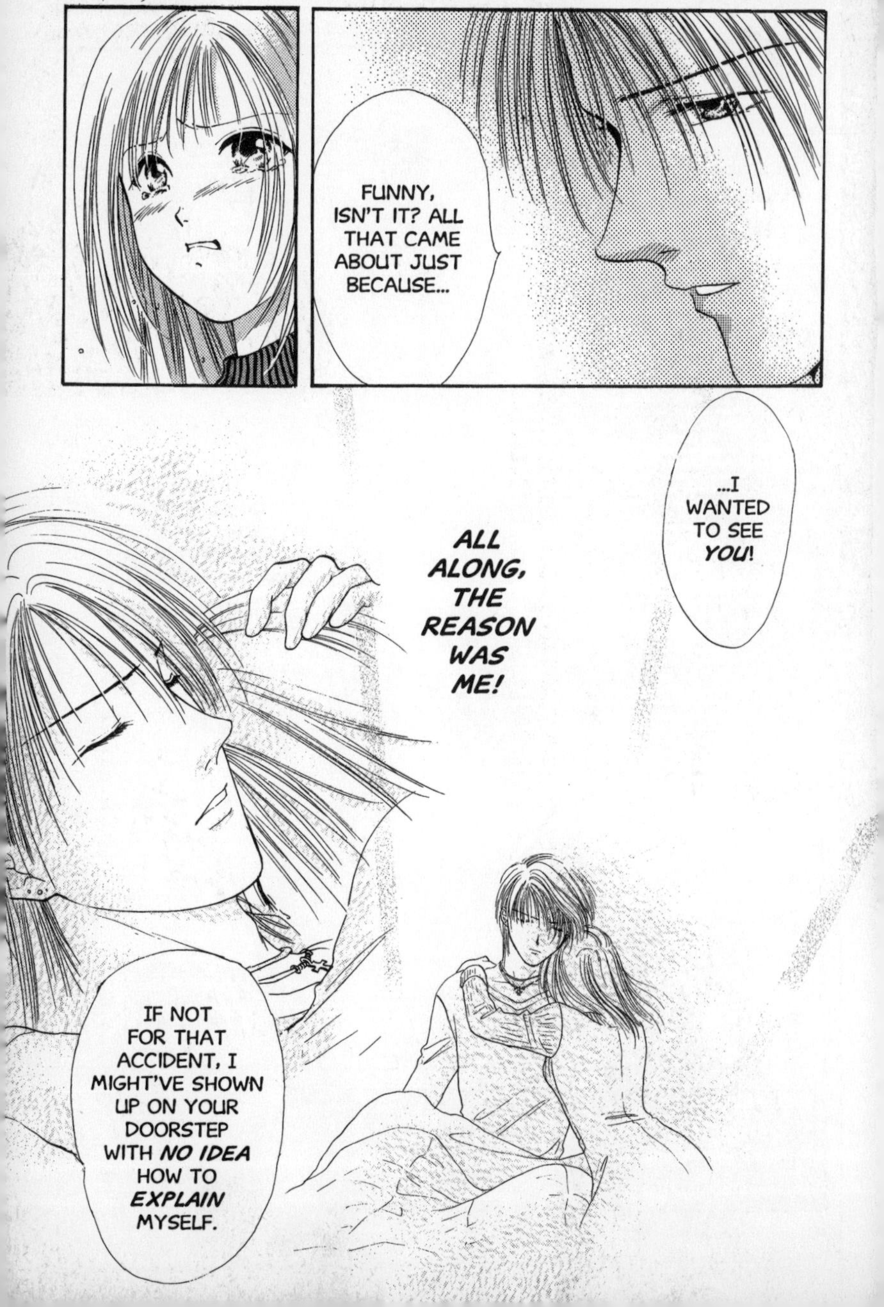
FUNNY, ISN'T IT? ALL THAT CAME ABOUT JUST BECAUSE...
...I WANTED TO SEE *YOU*!
ALL ALONG, THE REASON WAS ME!
IF NOT FOR THAT ACCIDENT, I MIGHT'VE SHOWN UP ON YOUR DOORSTEP WITH *NO IDEA* HOW TO *EXPLAIN* MYSELF.

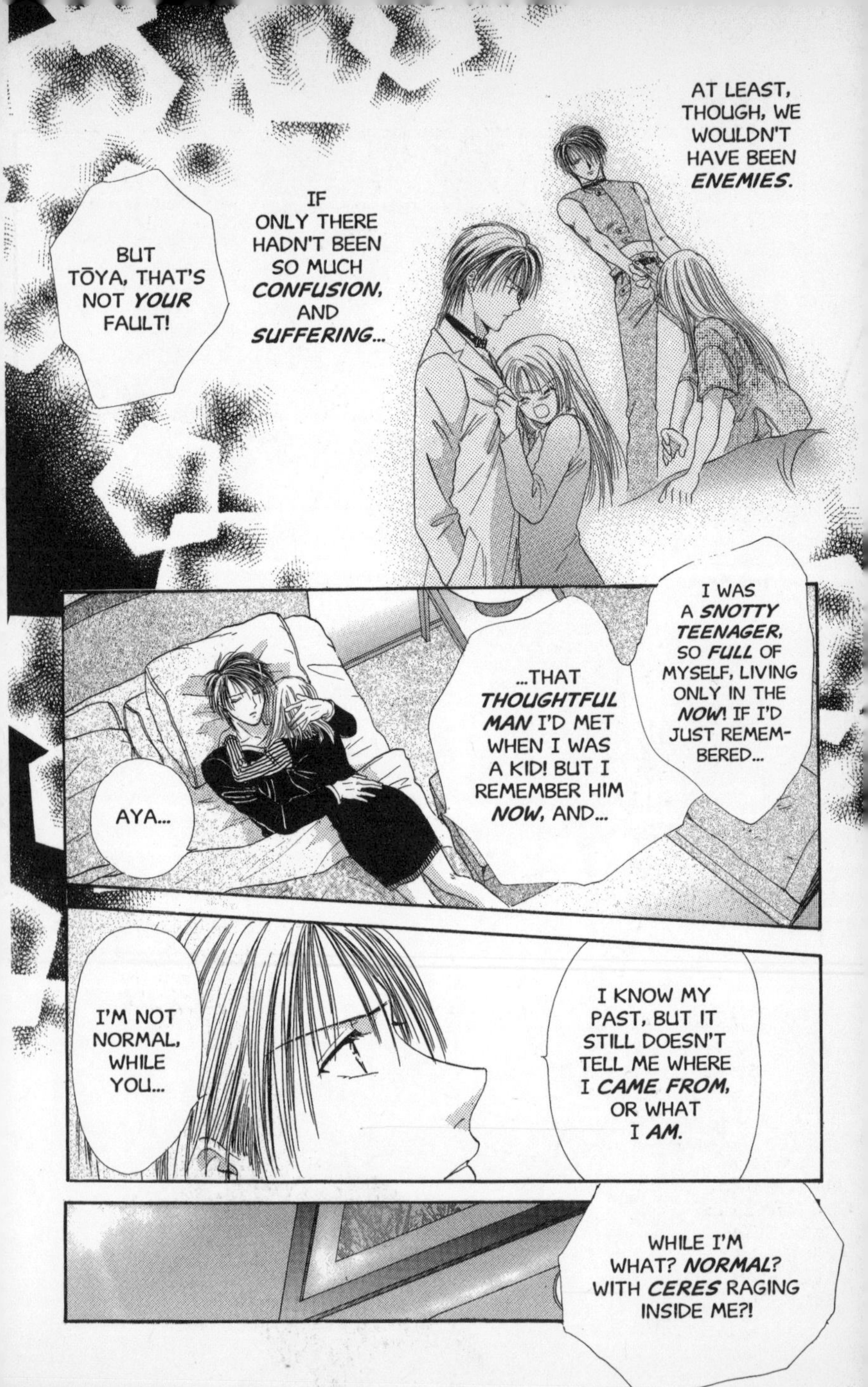
AT LEAST, THOUGH, WE WOULDN'T HAVE BEEN ENEMIES.
IF ONLY THERE HADN'T BEEN SO MUCH CONFUSION, AND SUFFERING...
BUT TŌYA, THAT'S NOT YOUR FAULT!
I WAS A SNOTTY TEENAGER, SO FULL OF MYSELF, LIVING ONLY IN THE NOW! IF I'D JUST REMEMBERED...
...THAT THOUGHTFUL MAN I'D MET WHEN I WAS A KID! BUT I REMEMBER HIM NOW, AND...
AYA...
I KNOW MY PAST, BUT IT STILL DOESN'T TELL ME WHERE I CAME FROM, OR WHAT I AM.
I'M NOT NORMAL, WHILE YOU...
WHILE I'M WHAT? NORMAL? WITH CERES RAGING INSIDE ME?!

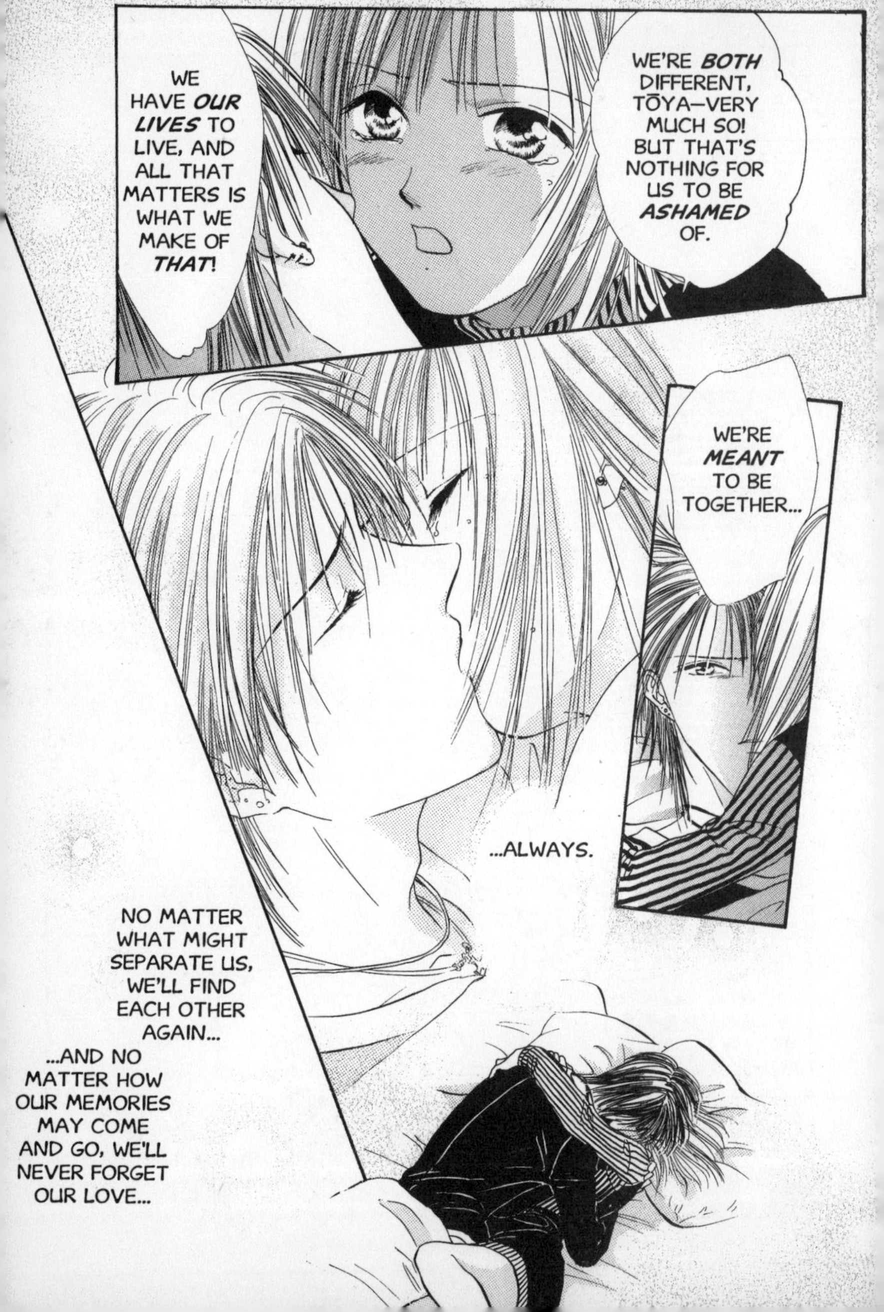
WE'RE *BOTH* DIFFERENT, TŌYA—VERY MUCH SO! BUT THAT'S NOTHING FOR US TO BE *ASHAMED* OF.
WE HAVE *OUR LIVES* TO LIVE, AND ALL THAT MATTERS IS WHAT WE MAKE OF *THAT*!
WE'RE *MEANT* TO BE TOGETHER...
...ALWAYS.
NO MATTER WHAT MIGHT SEPARATE US, WE'LL FIND EACH OTHER AGAIN...
...AND NO MATTER HOW OUR MEMORIES MAY COME AND GO, WE'LL NEVER FORGET OUR LOVE...

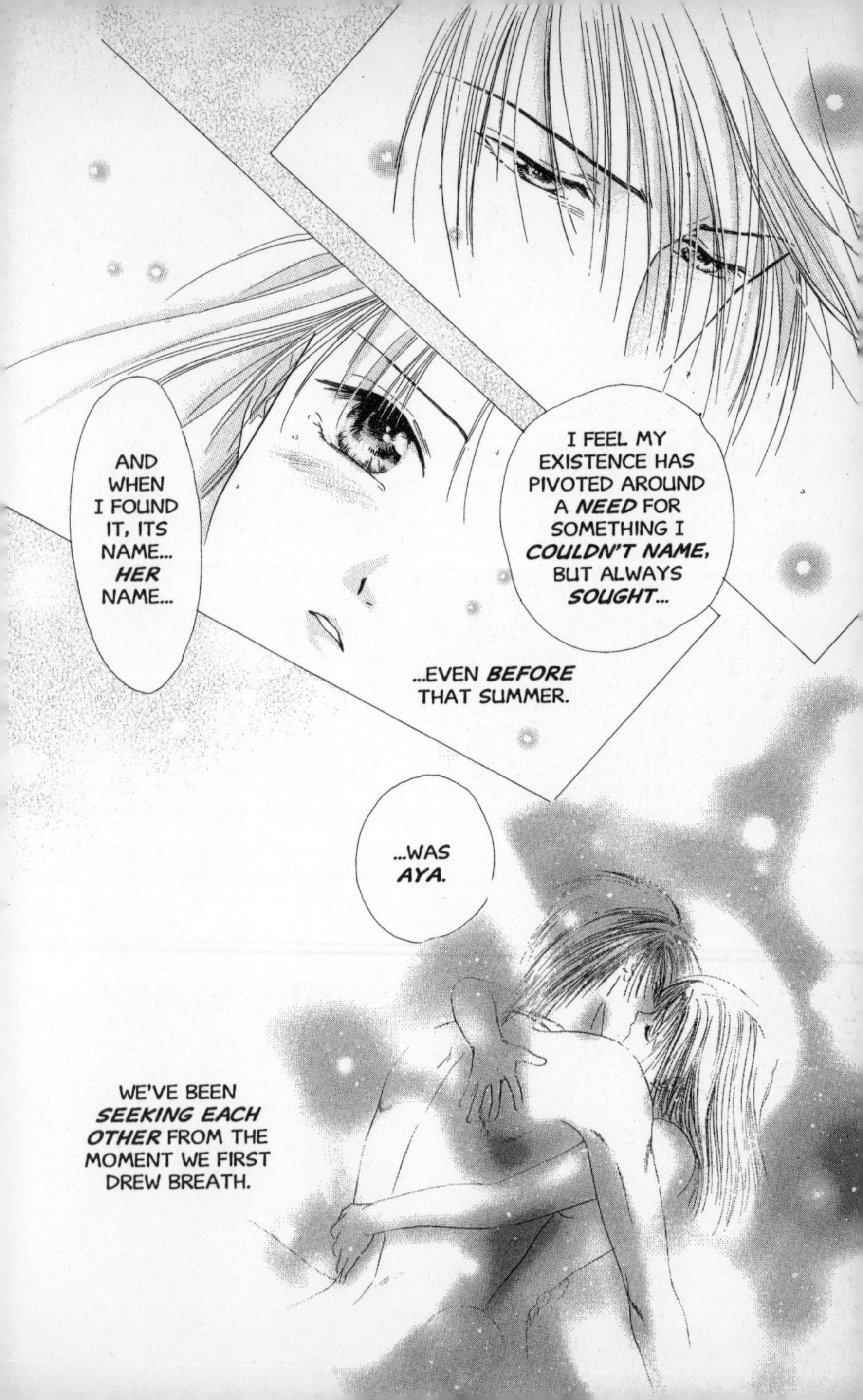
I FEEL MY EXISTENCE HAS PIVOTED AROUND A *NEED* FOR SOMETHING I *COULDN'T NAME,* BUT ALWAYS *SOUGHT...*
...EVEN *BEFORE* THAT SUMMER.
AND WHEN I FOUND IT, ITS NAME... *HER* NAME...
...WAS *AYA.*
WE'VE BEEN *SEEKING EACH OTHER* FROM THE MOMENT WE FIRST DREW BREATH.

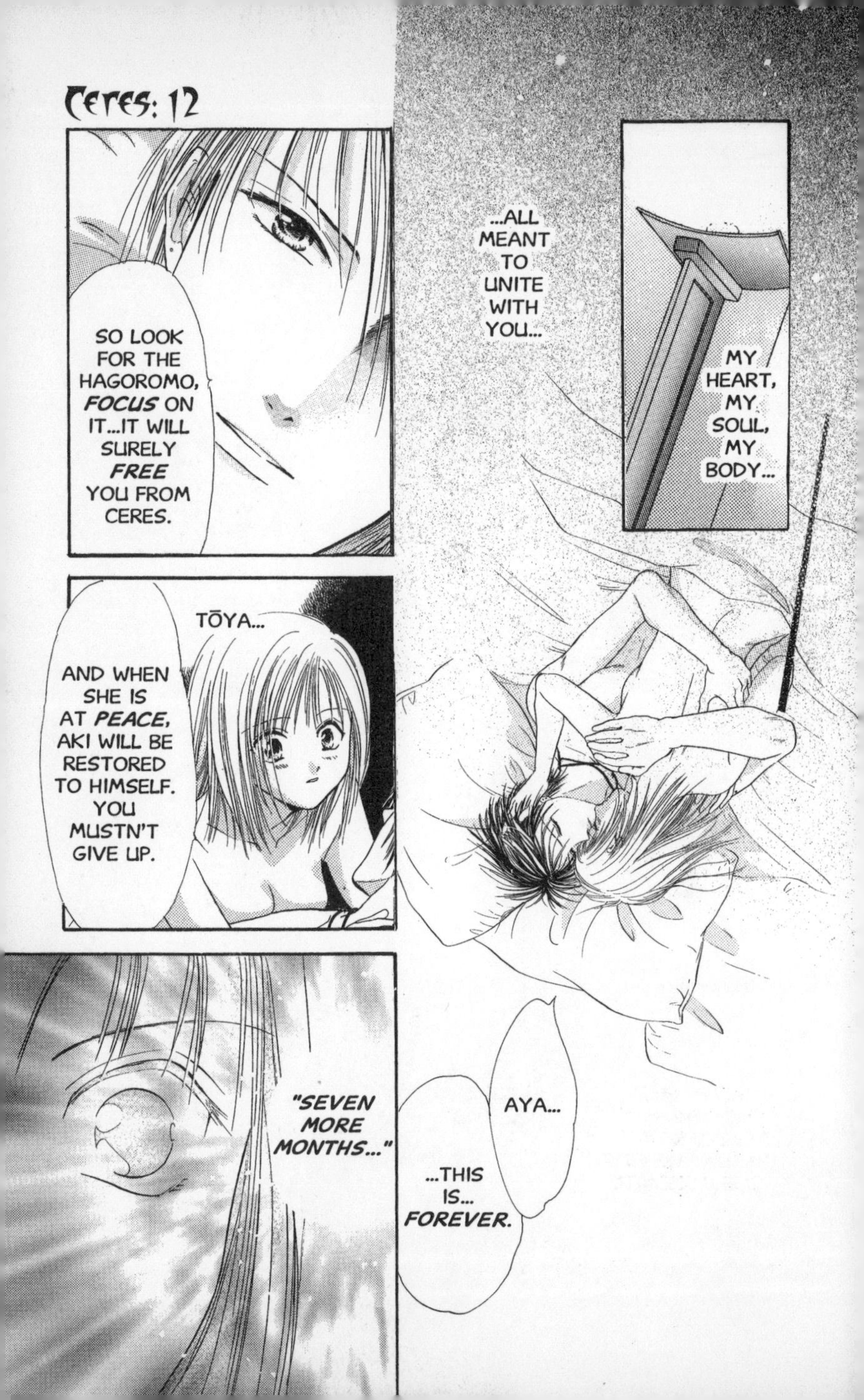
MY HEART, MY SOUL, MY BODY...
...ALL MEANT TO UNITE WITH YOU...
AYA...
...THIS IS... *FOREVER.*
SO LOOK FOR THE HAGOROMO, *FOCUS* ON IT...IT WILL SURELY *FREE* YOU FROM CERES.
TŌYA...
AND WHEN SHE IS AT *PEACE*, AKI WILL BE RESTORED TO HIMSELF. YOU MUSTN'T GIVE UP.
"SEVEN MORE MONTHS..."

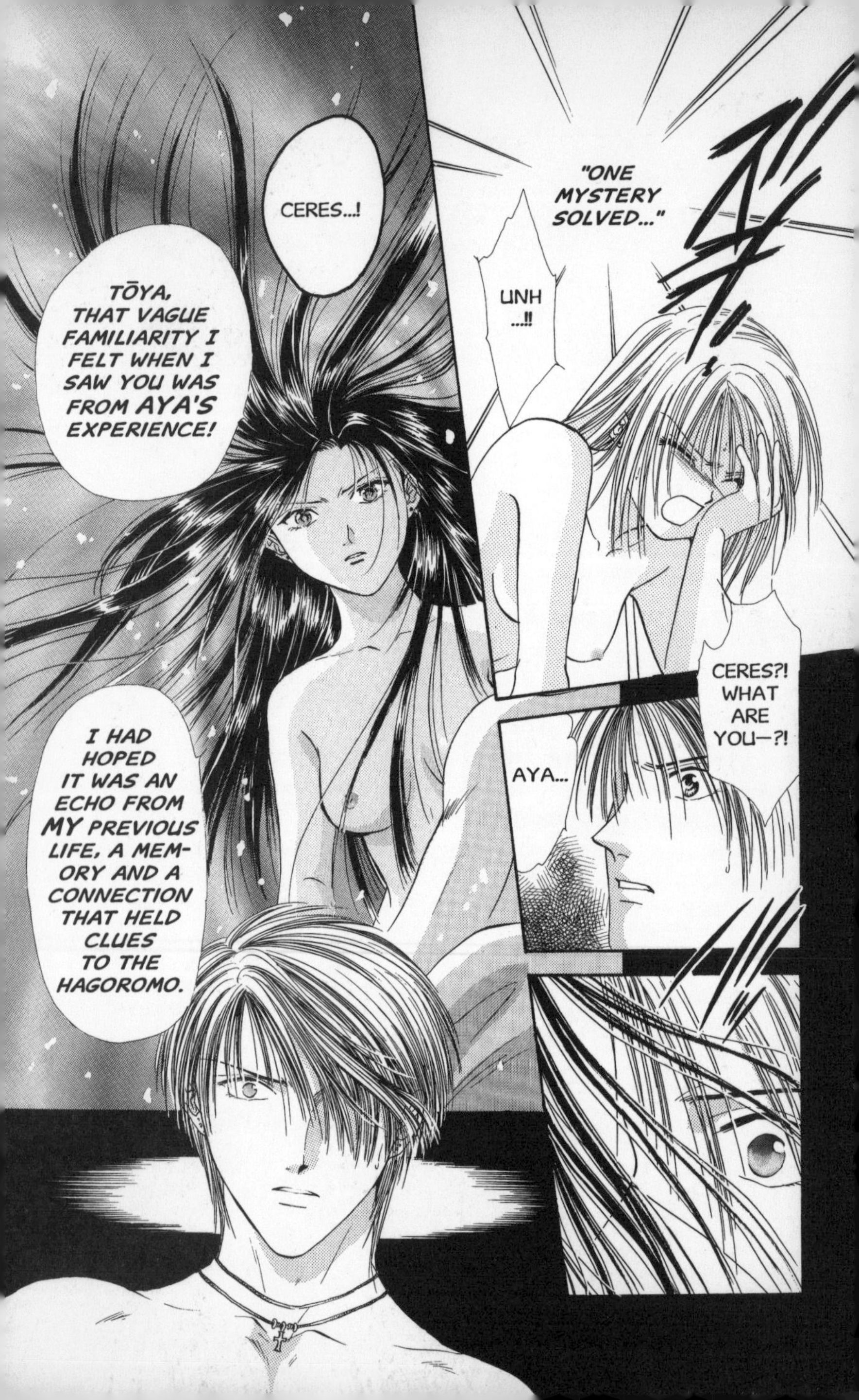
"ONE MYSTERY SOLVED..."
UNH ...!!
CERES?! WHAT ARE YOU—?!
AYA...
CERES...!
TŌYA, THAT VAGUE FAMILIARITY I FELT WHEN I SAW YOU WAS FROM AYA'S EXPERIENCE!
I HAD HOPED IT WAS AN ECHO FROM MY PREVIOUS LIFE, A MEMORY AND A CONNECTION THAT HELD CLUES TO THE HAGOROMO.

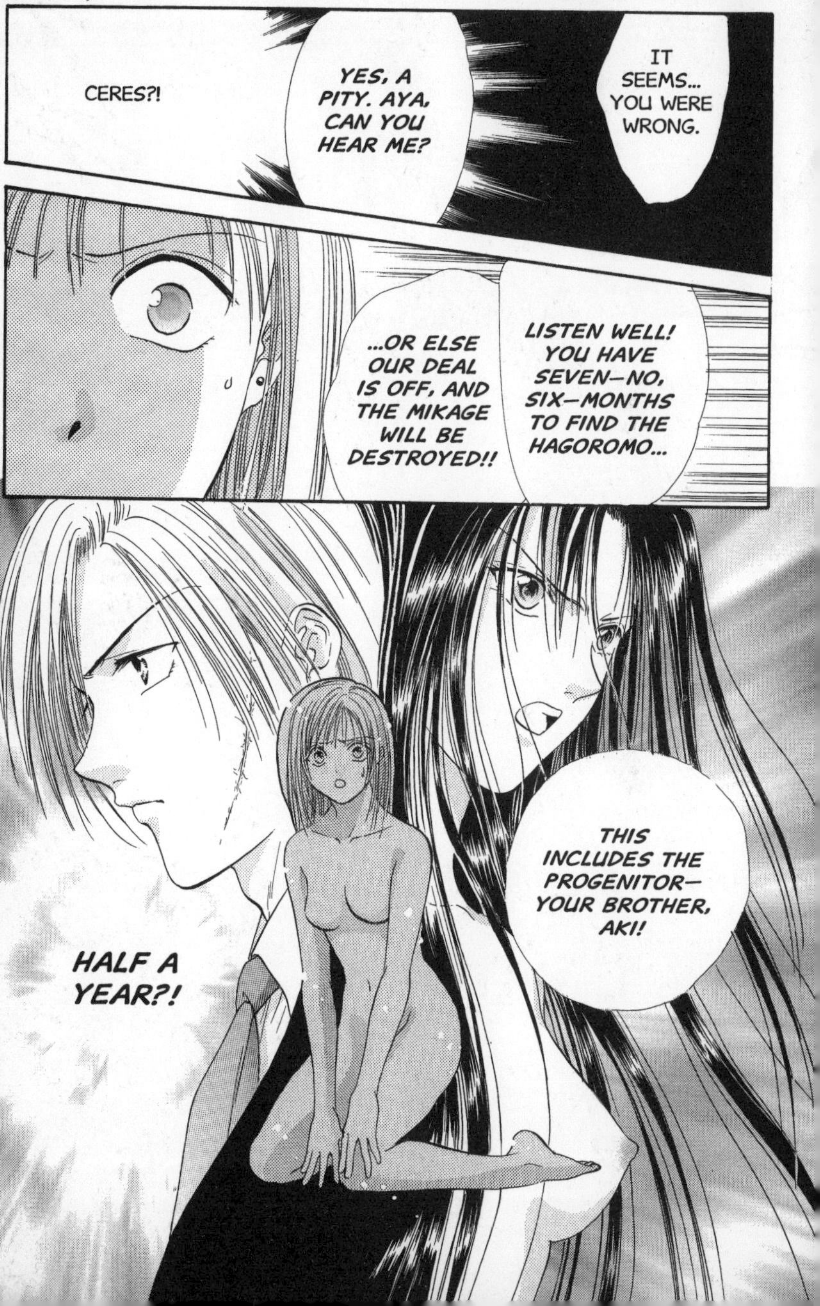
IT SEEMS... YOU WERE WRONG.
YES, A PITY. AYA, CAN YOU HEAR ME?
CERES?!
LISTEN WELL! YOU HAVE SEVEN—NO, SIX—MONTHS TO FIND THE HAGOROMO...
...OR ELSE OUR DEAL IS OFF, AND THE MIKAGE WILL BE DESTROYED!!
THIS INCLUDES THE PROGENITOR—YOUR BROTHER, AKI!
HALF A YEAR?!

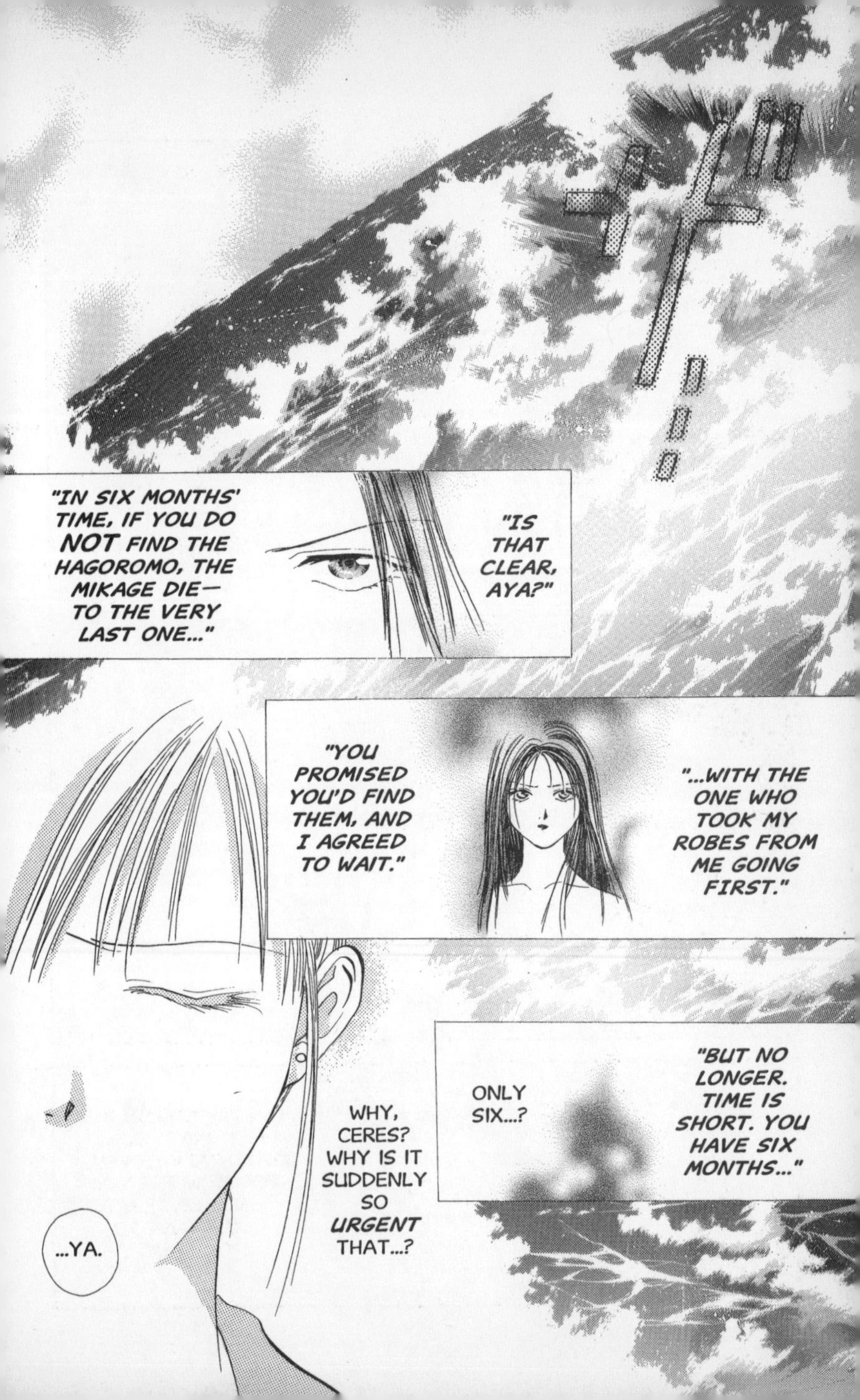
"IS THAT CLEAR, AYA?"
"IN SIX MONTHS' TIME, IF YOU DO NOT FIND THE HAGOROMO, THE MIKAGE DIE— TO THE VERY LAST ONE..."
"...WITH THE ONE WHO TOOK MY ROBES FROM ME GOING FIRST."
"YOU PROMISED YOU'D FIND THEM, AND I AGREED TO WAIT."
"BUT NO LONGER. TIME IS SHORT. YOU HAVE SIX MONTHS..."
ONLY SIX...?
WHY, CERES? WHY IS IT SUDDENLY SO URGENT THAT...?
...YA.

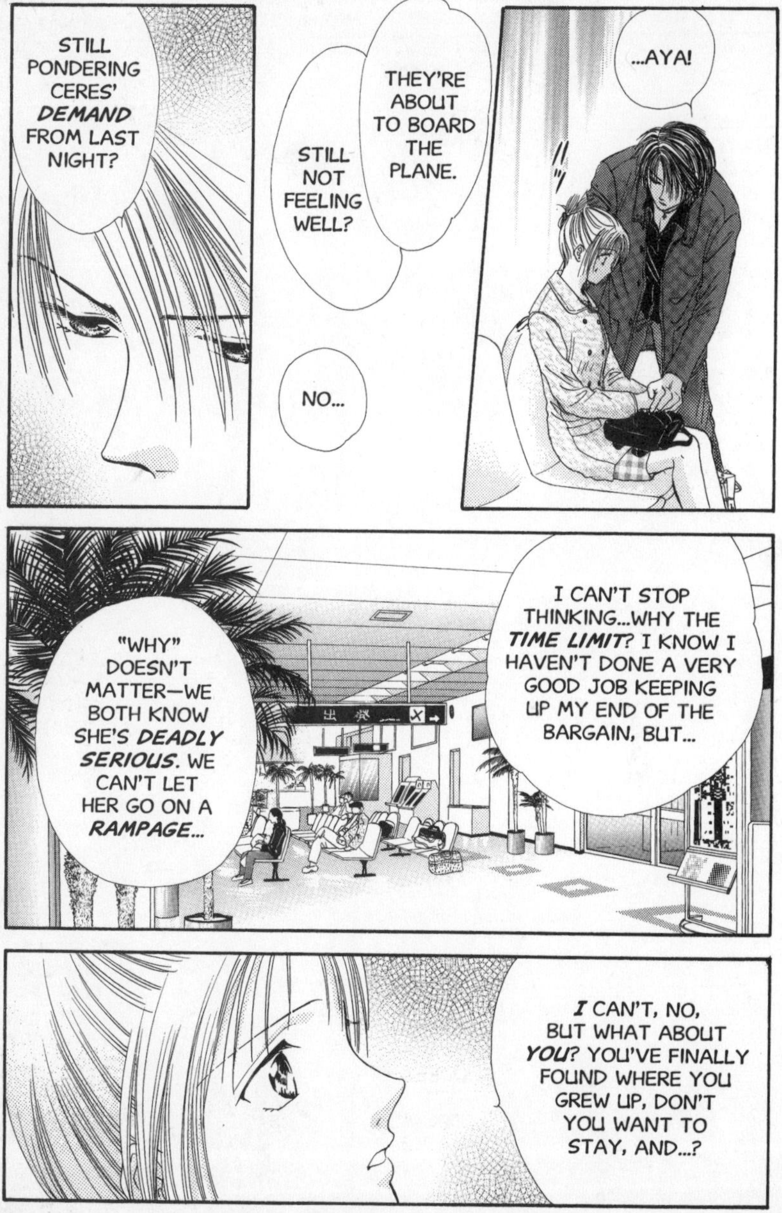
...AYA!
THEY'RE ABOUT TO BOARD THE PLANE.
STILL NOT FEELING WELL?
NO...
STILL PONDERING CERES' *DEMAND* FROM LAST NIGHT?
I CAN'T STOP THINKING...WHY THE *TIME LIMIT*? I KNOW I HAVEN'T DONE A VERY GOOD JOB KEEPING UP MY END OF THE BARGAIN, BUT...
"WHY" DOESN'T MATTER—WE BOTH KNOW SHE'S *DEADLY SERIOUS*. WE CAN'T LET HER GO ON A *RAMPAGE*...
I CAN'T, NO, BUT WHAT ABOUT *YOU*? YOU'VE FINALLY FOUND WHERE YOU GREW UP, DON'T YOU WANT TO STAY, AND...?

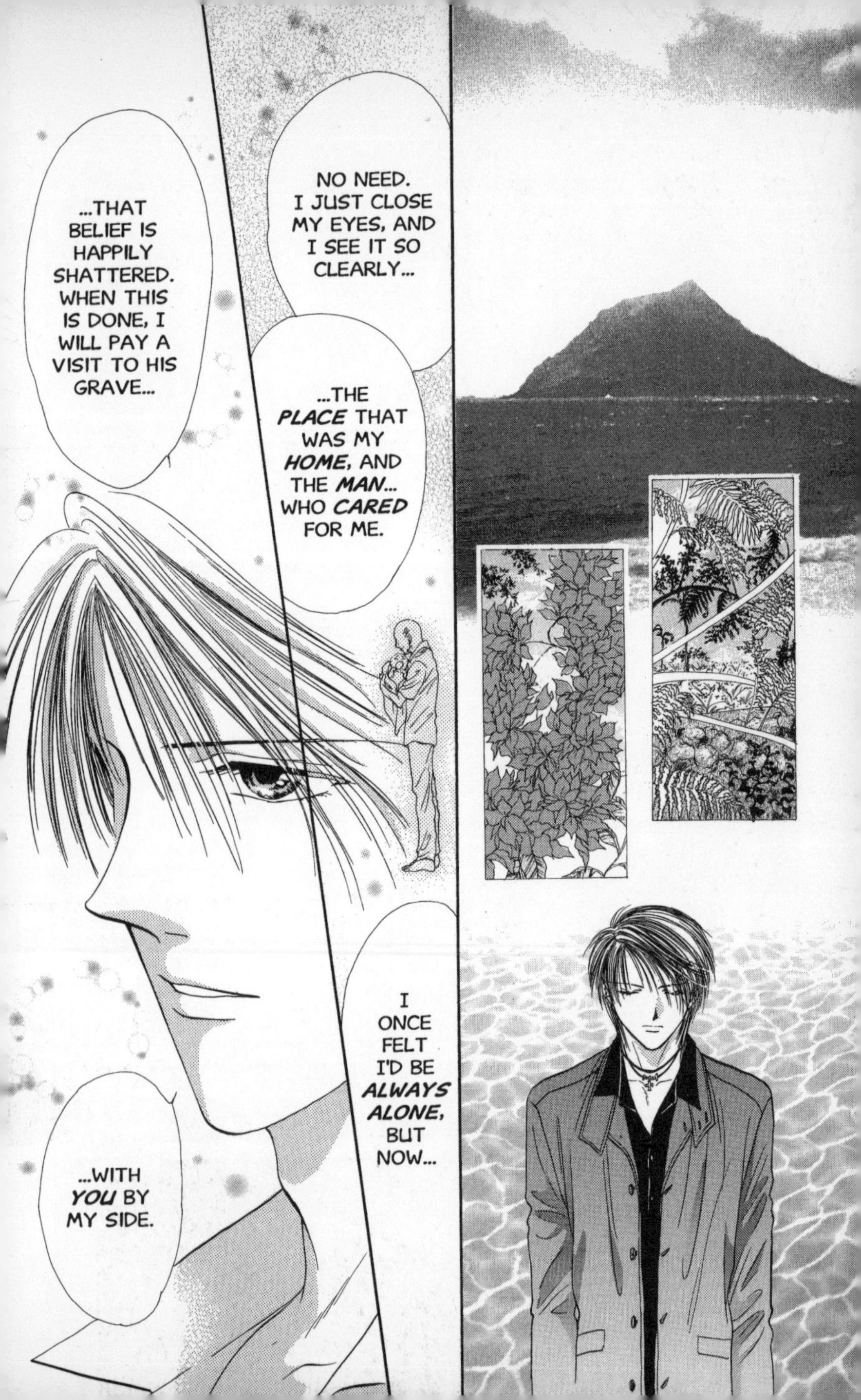
NO NEED. I JUST CLOSE MY EYES, AND I SEE IT SO CLEARLY...
...THE *PLACE* THAT WAS MY *HOME*, AND THE *MAN*... WHO *CARED* FOR ME.
I ONCE FELT I'D BE *ALWAYS ALONE*, BUT NOW...
...THAT BELIEF IS HAPPILY SHATTERED. WHEN THIS IS DONE, I WILL PAY A VISIT TO HIS GRAVE...
...WITH *YOU* BY MY SIDE.

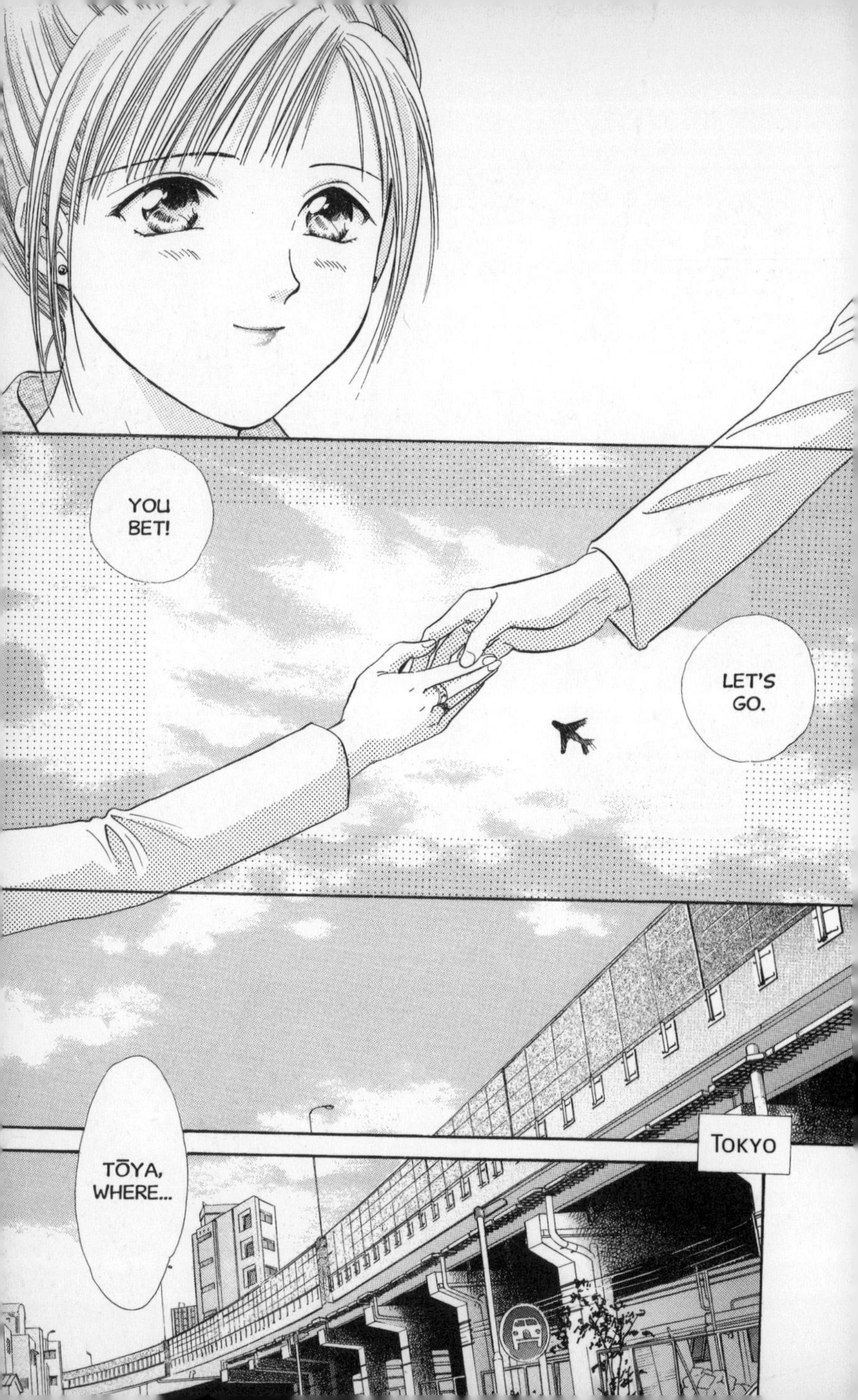
LET'S GO.
YOU BET!
TOKYO
TŌYA, WHERE...

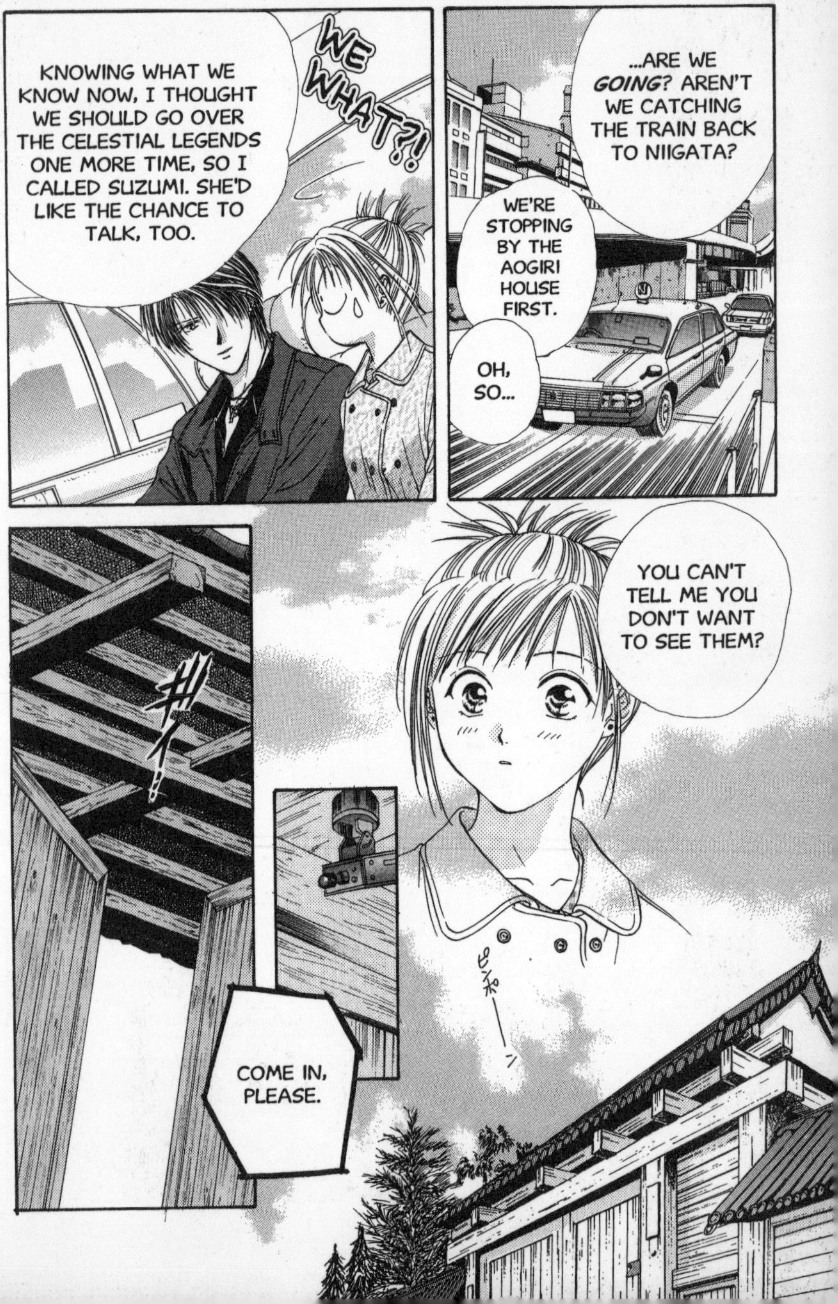
...ARE WE *GOING*? AREN'T WE CATCHING THE TRAIN BACK TO NIIGATA?
WE'RE STOPPING BY THE AOGIRI HOUSE FIRST.
OH, SO...
WE WHAT?!
KNOWING WHAT WE KNOW NOW, I THOUGHT WE SHOULD GO OVER THE CELESTIAL LEGENDS ONE MORE TIME, SO I CALLED SUZUMI. SHE'D LIKE THE CHANCE TO TALK, TOO.
YOU CAN'T TELL ME YOU DON'T WANT TO SEE THEM?
ピンポーン
COME IN, PLEASE.

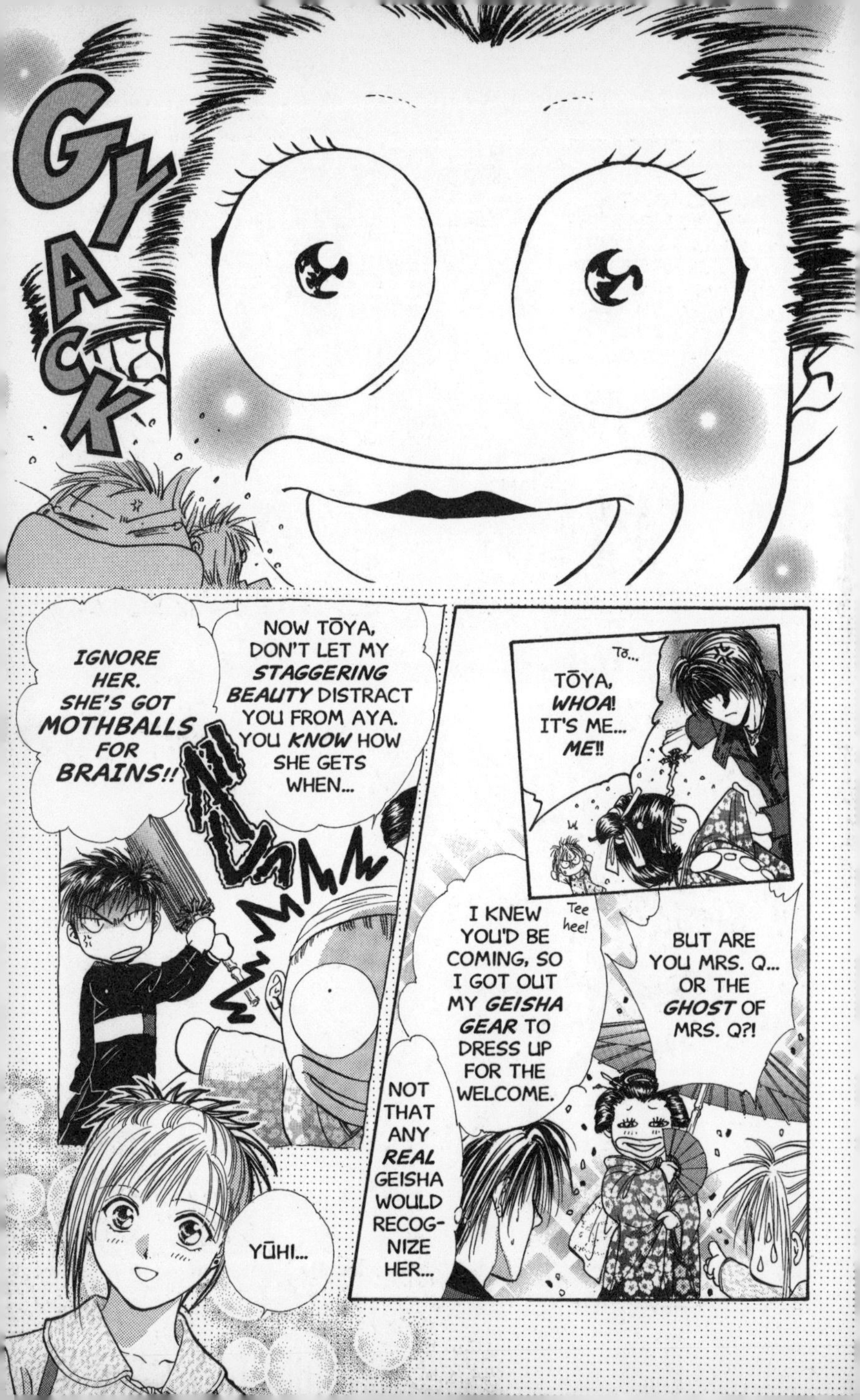
GYACK
Tō...
TŌYA, WHOA! IT'S ME... ME!!
BUT ARE YOU MRS. Q... OR THE GHOST OF MRS. Q?!
Tee hee!
I KNEW YOU'D BE COMING, SO I GOT OUT MY GEISHA GEAR TO DRESS UP FOR THE WELCOME.
NOT THAT ANY REAL GEISHA WOULD RECOGNIZE HER...
NOW TŌYA, DON'T LET MY STAGGERING BEAUTY DISTRACT YOU FROM AYA. YOU KNOW HOW SHE GETS WHEN...
IGNORE HER. SHE'S GOT MOTHBALLS FOR BRAINS!!
YŪHI...

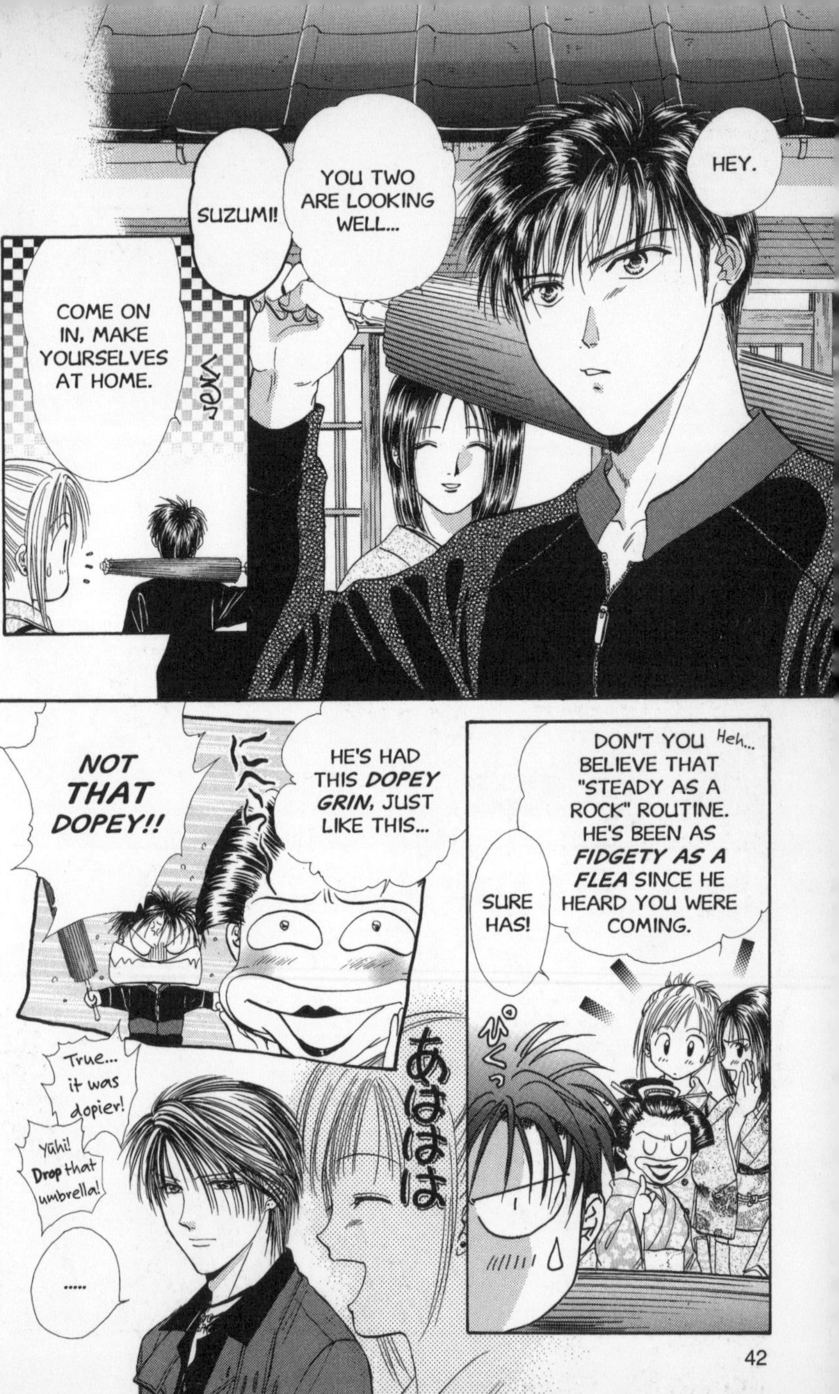
HEY.
YOU TWO ARE LOOKING WELL...
SUZUMI!
COME ON IN, MAKE YOURSELVES AT HOME.
DON'T YOU BELIEVE THAT "STEADY AS A ROCK" ROUTINE. HE'S BEEN AS *FIDGETY AS A FLEA* SINCE HE HEARD YOU WERE COMING.
Heh...
SURE HAS!
HE'S HAD THIS *DOPEY GRIN*, JUST LIKE THIS...
NOT THAT DOPEY!!
あははは
True... it was dopier!
Yūhi! **Drop** that umbrella!
.....

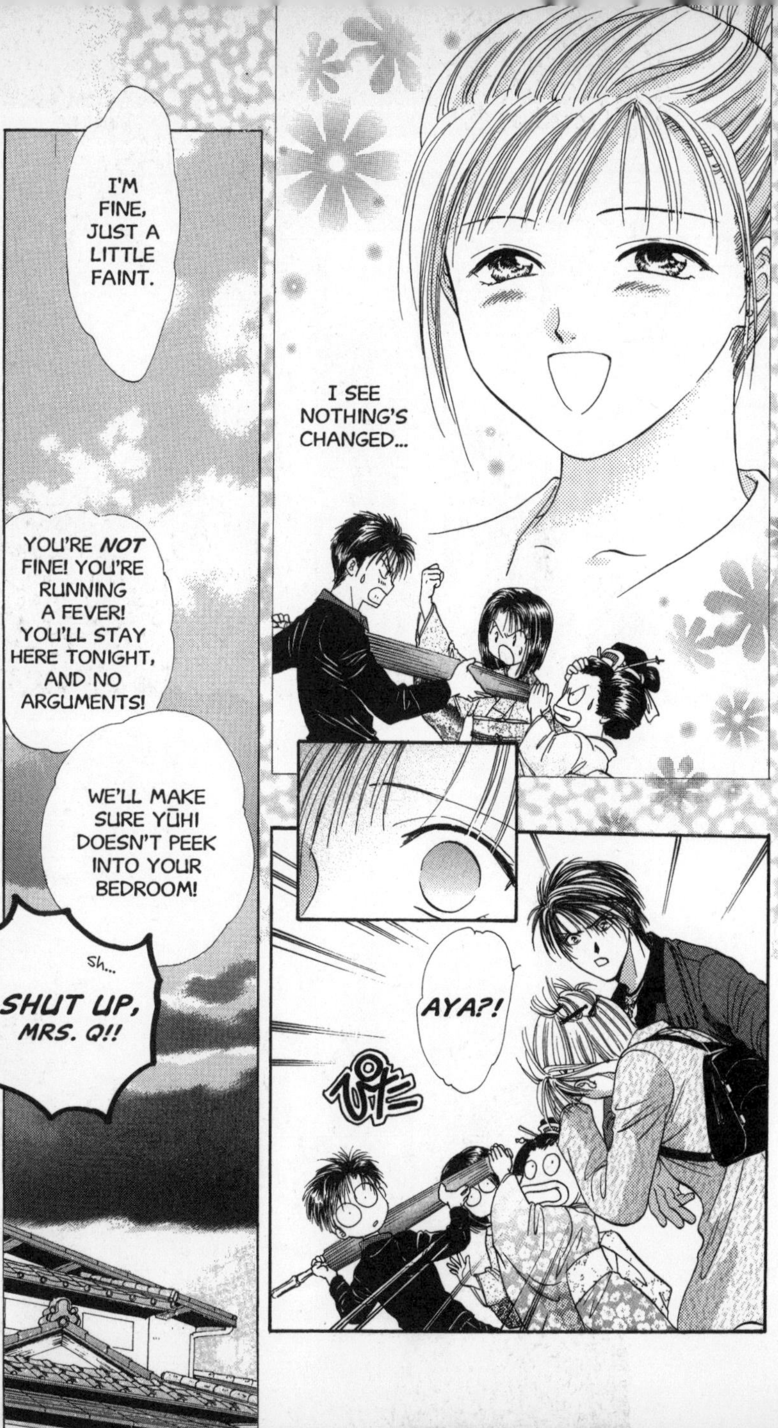
I SEE NOTHING'S CHANGED...
AYA?!
I'M FINE, JUST A LITTLE FAINT.
YOU'RE *NOT* FINE! YOU'RE RUNNING A FEVER! YOU'LL STAY HERE TONIGHT, AND NO ARGUMENTS!
WE'LL MAKE SURE YŪHI DOESN'T PEEK INTO YOUR BEDROOM!
Sh...
SHUT UP, MRS. Q!!

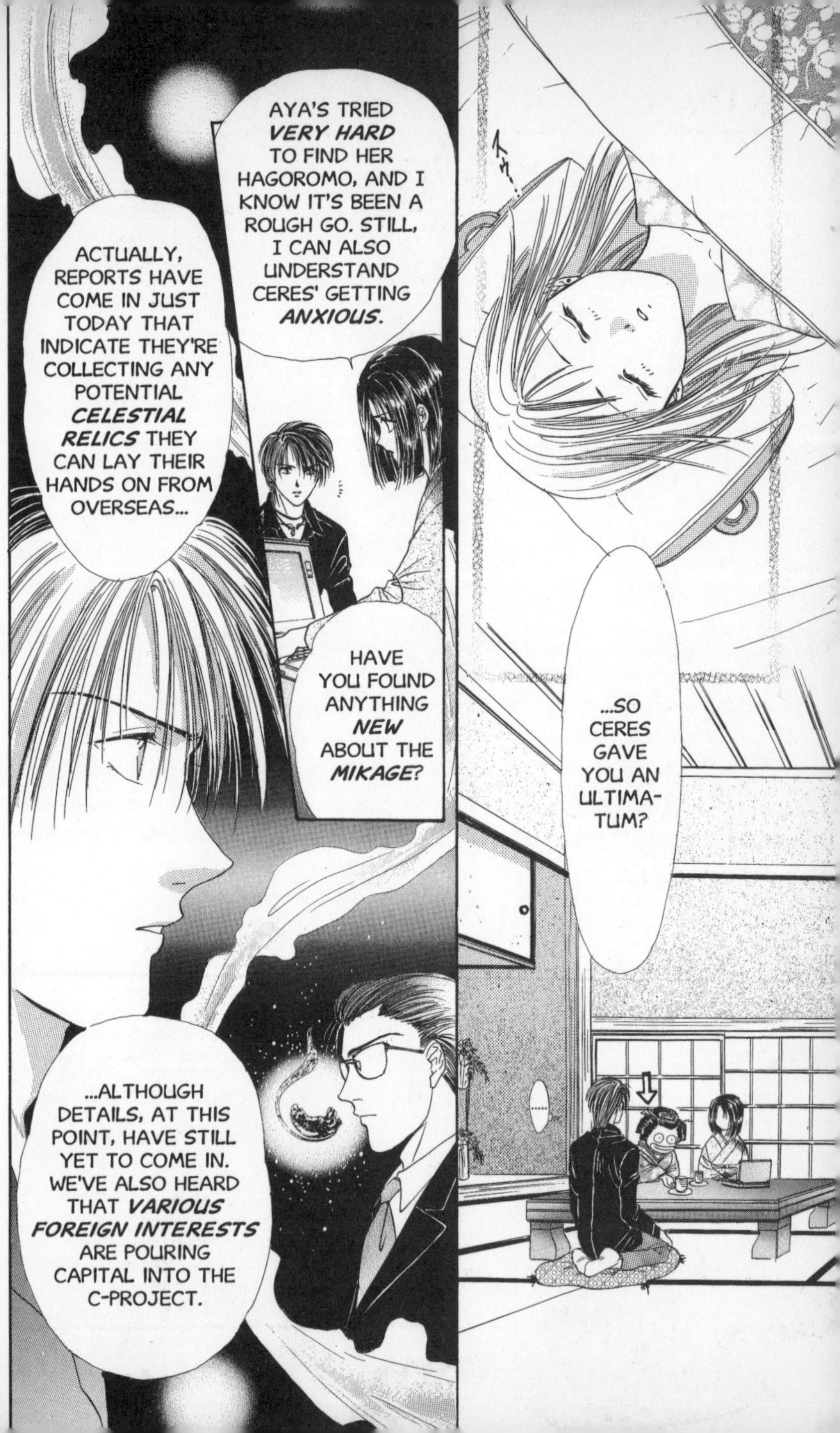
...SO CERES GAVE YOU AN ULTIMATUM?
......
AYA'S TRIED *VERY HARD* TO FIND HER HAGOROMO, AND I KNOW IT'S BEEN A ROUGH GO. STILL, I CAN ALSO UNDERSTAND CERES' GETTING *ANXIOUS*.
HAVE YOU FOUND ANYTHING *NEW* ABOUT THE *MIKAGE*?
ACTUALLY, REPORTS HAVE COME IN JUST TODAY THAT INDICATE THEY'RE COLLECTING ANY POTENTIAL *CELESTIAL RELICS* THEY CAN LAY THEIR HANDS ON FROM OVERSEAS...
...ALTHOUGH DETAILS, AT THIS POINT, HAVE STILL YET TO COME IN. WE'VE ALSO HEARD THAT *VARIOUS FOREIGN INTERESTS* ARE POURING CAPITAL INTO THE C-PROJECT.

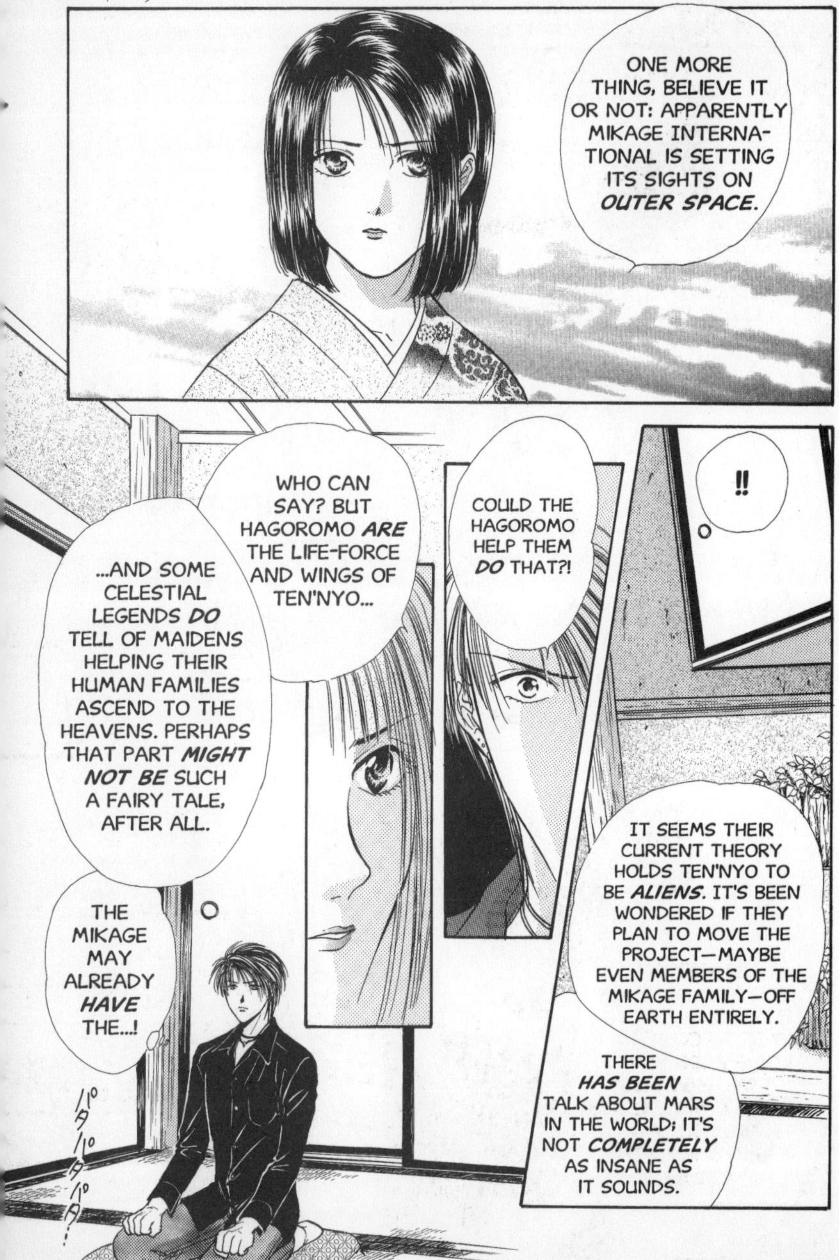
ONE MORE THING, BELIEVE IT OR NOT: APPARENTLY MIKAGE INTERNATIONAL IS SETTING ITS SIGHTS ON *OUTER SPACE.*
!!
COULD THE HAGOROMO HELP THEM *DO* THAT?!
WHO CAN SAY? BUT HAGOROMO *ARE* THE LIFE-FORCE AND WINGS OF TEN'NYO...
...AND SOME CELESTIAL LEGENDS *DO* TELL OF MAIDENS HELPING THEIR HUMAN FAMILIES ASCEND TO THE HEAVENS. PERHAPS THAT PART *MIGHT NOT BE* SUCH A FAIRY TALE, AFTER ALL.
IT SEEMS THEIR CURRENT THEORY HOLDS TEN'NYO TO BE *ALIENS.* IT'S BEEN WONDERED IF THEY PLAN TO MOVE THE PROJECT—MAYBE EVEN MEMBERS OF THE MIKAGE FAMILY—OFF EARTH ENTIRELY.
THERE *HAS BEEN* TALK ABOUT MARS IN THE WORLD; IT'S NOT *COMPLETELY* AS INSANE AS IT SOUNDS.
THE MIKAGE MAY ALREADY *HAVE* THE...!
パタパタパタ…

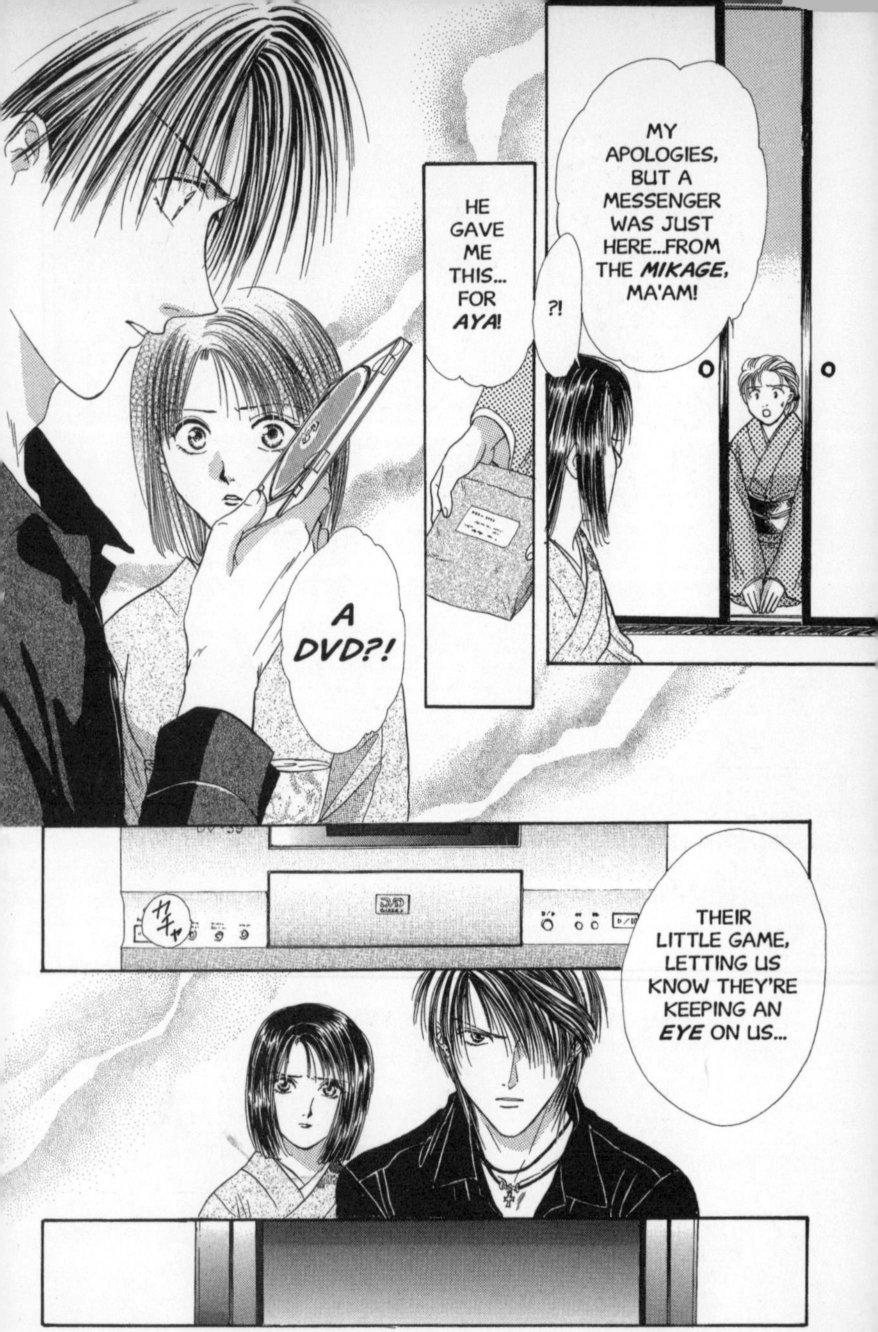
MY APOLOGIES, BUT A MESSENGER WAS JUST HERE...FROM THE *MIKAGE*, MA'AM!
?!
HE GAVE ME THIS... FOR *AYA*!
A DVD?!
カチャ
THEIR LITTLE GAME, LETTING US KNOW THEY'RE KEEPING AN *EYE* ON US...

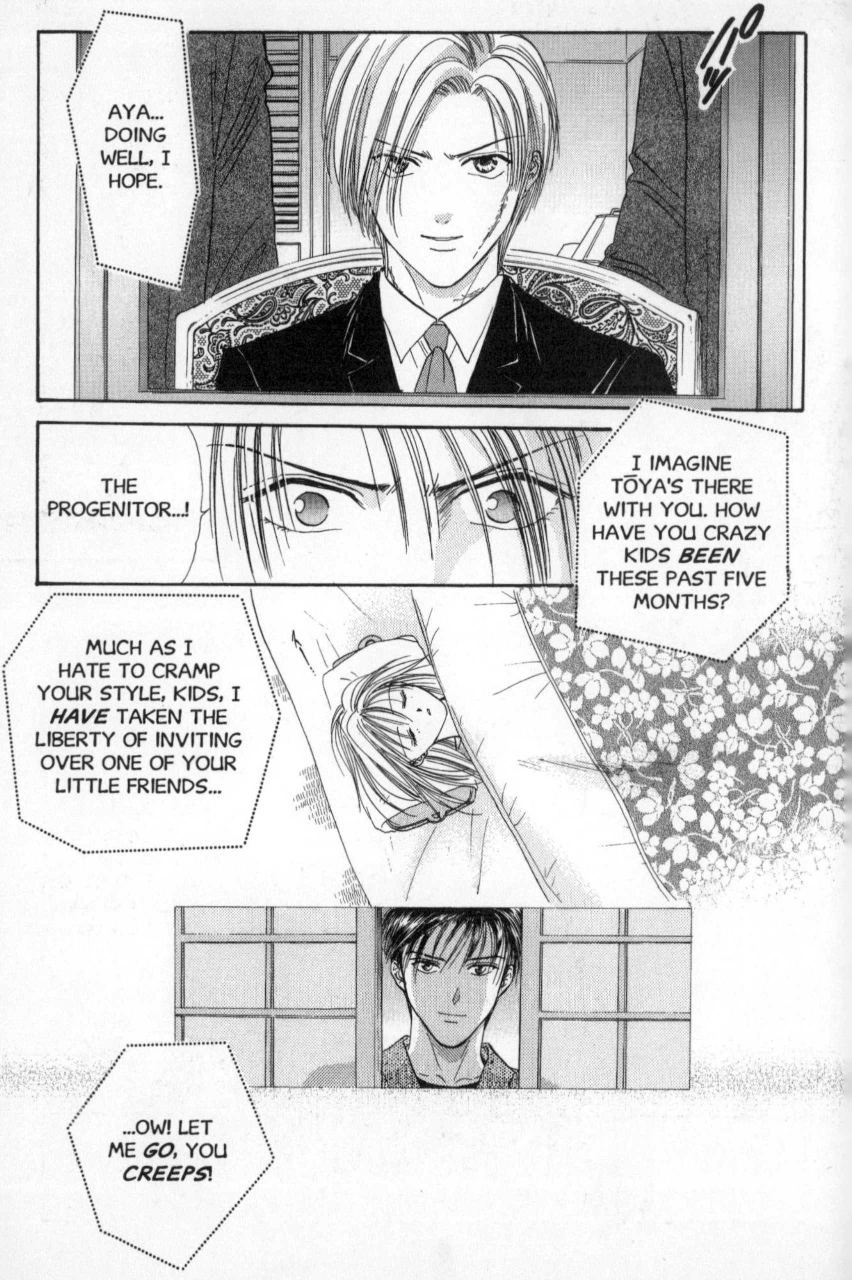
AYA... DOING WELL, I HOPE.
I IMAGINE TŌYA'S THERE WITH YOU. HOW HAVE YOU CRAZY KIDS *BEEN* THESE PAST FIVE MONTHS?
THE PROGENITOR...!
MUCH AS I HATE TO CRAMP YOUR STYLE, KIDS, I *HAVE* TAKEN THE LIBERTY OF INVITING OVER ONE OF YOUR LITTLE FRIENDS...
...OW! LET ME *GO*, YOU *CREEPS*!

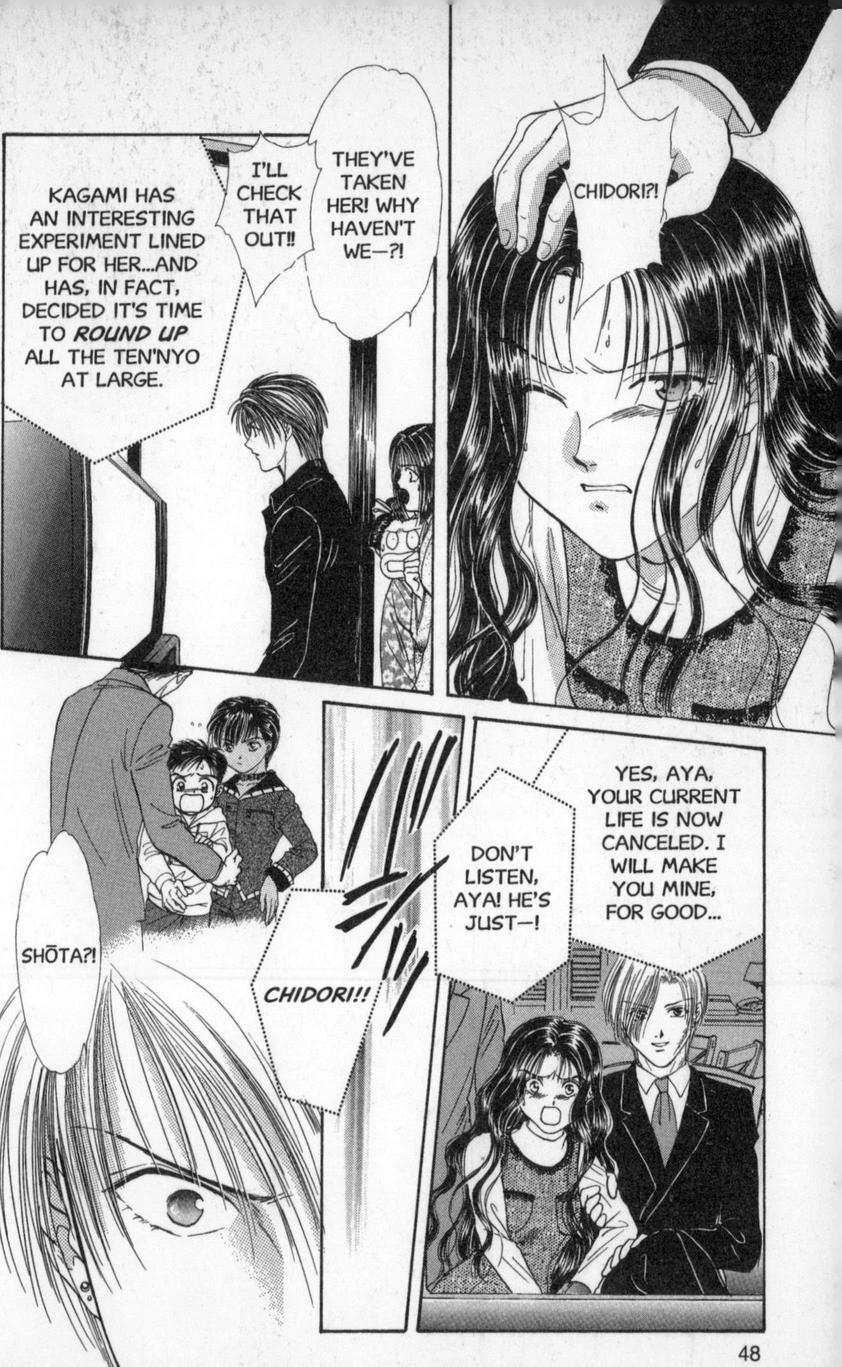
CHIDORI?!
THEY'VE TAKEN HER! WHY HAVEN'T WE—?!
I'LL CHECK THAT OUT!!
KAGAMI HAS AN INTERESTING EXPERIMENT LINED UP FOR HER...AND HAS, IN FACT, DECIDED IT'S TIME TO *ROUND UP* ALL THE TEN'NYO AT LARGE.
YES, AYA, YOUR CURRENT LIFE IS NOW CANCELED. I WILL MAKE YOU MINE, FOR GOOD...
DON'T LISTEN, AYA! HE'S JUST—!
CHIDORI!!
SHŌTA?!

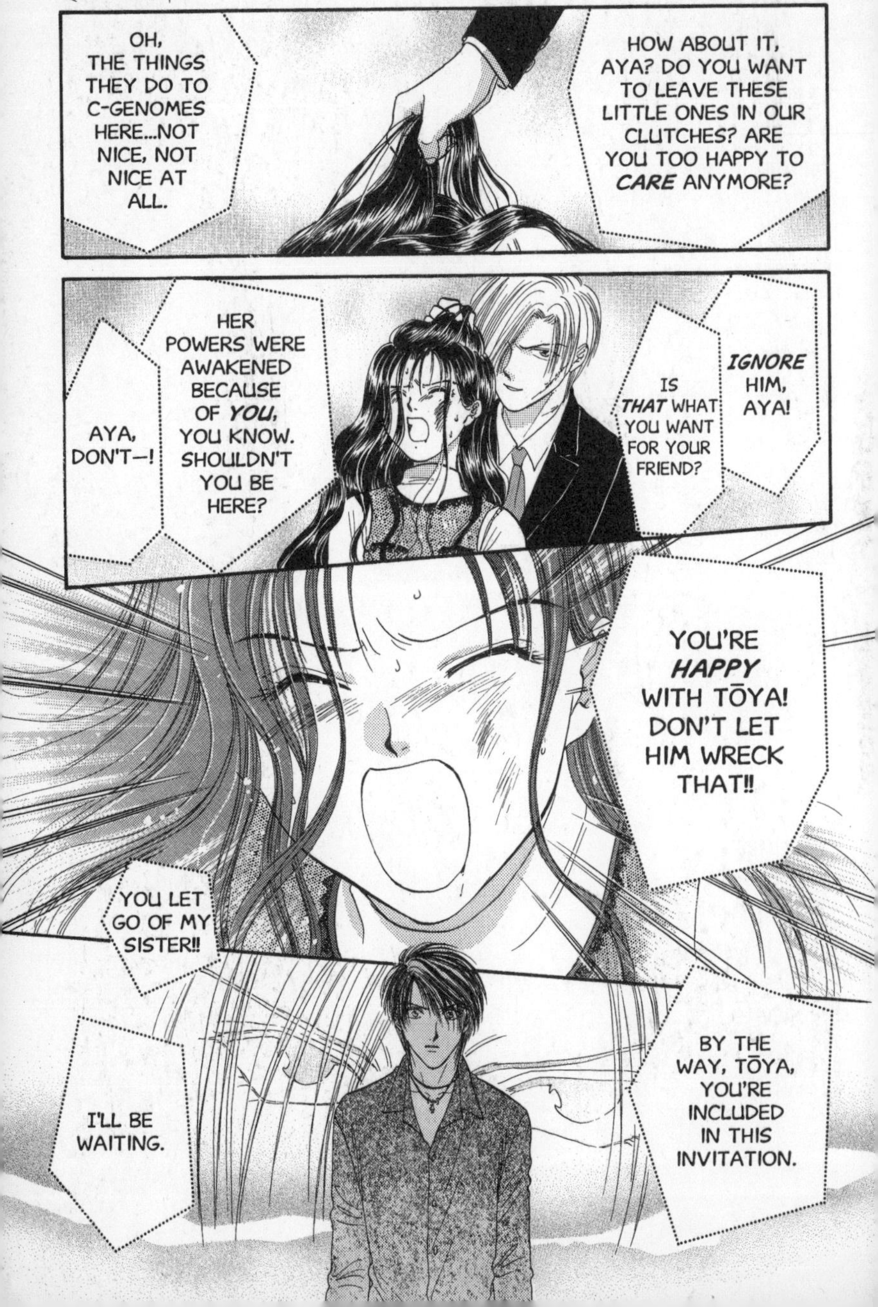
HOW ABOUT IT, AYA? DO YOU WANT TO LEAVE THESE LITTLE ONES IN OUR CLUTCHES? ARE YOU TOO HAPPY TO *CARE* ANYMORE?
OH, THE THINGS THEY DO TO C-GENOMES HERE...NOT NICE, NOT NICE AT ALL.
IGNORE HIM, AYA!
IS *THAT* WHAT YOU WANT FOR YOUR FRIEND?
HER POWERS WERE AWAKENED BECAUSE OF *YOU*, YOU KNOW. SHOULDN'T YOU BE HERE?
AYA, DON'T—!
YOU'RE *HAPPY* WITH TŌYA! DON'T LET HIM WRECK THAT!!
YOU LET GO OF MY SISTER!!
BY THE WAY, TŌYA, YOU'RE INCLUDED IN THIS INVITATION.
I'LL BE WAITING.

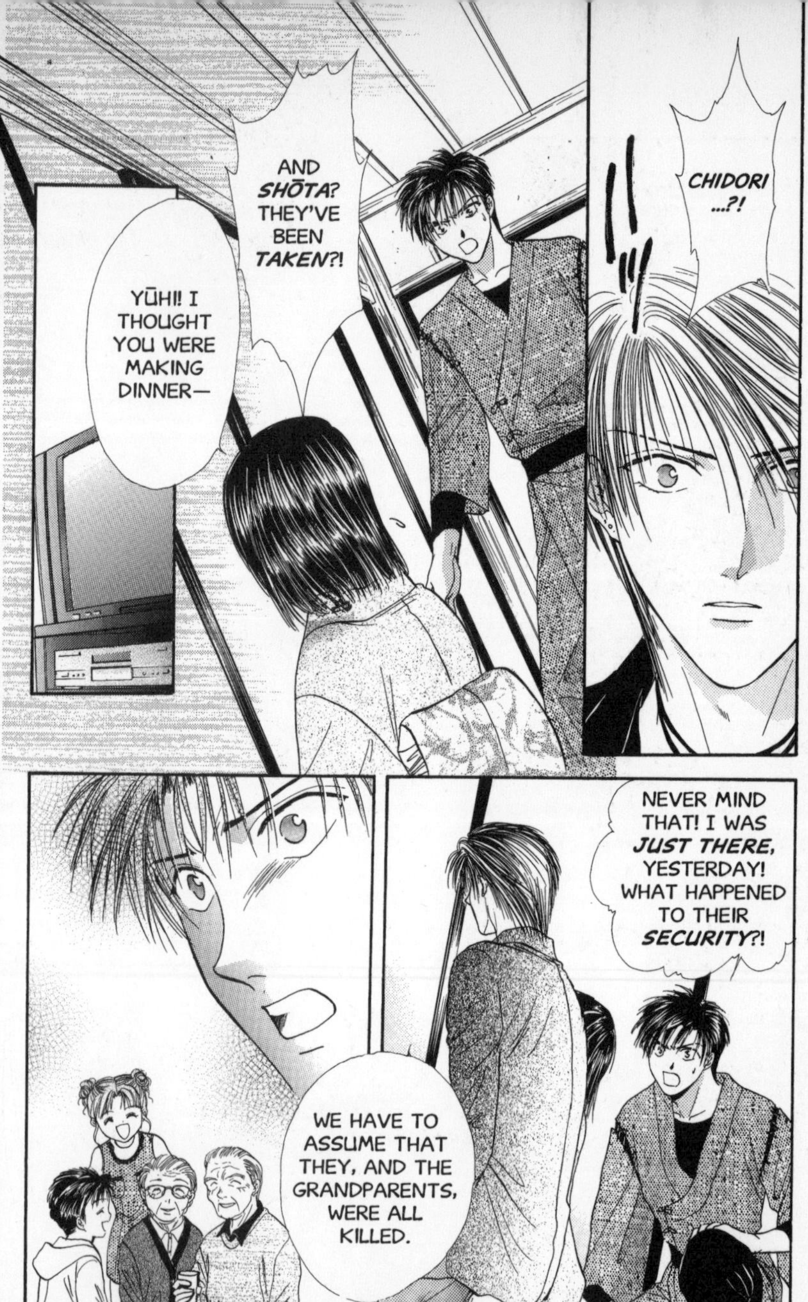
CHIDORI ...?!
AND SHŌTA? THEY'VE BEEN TAKEN?!
YŪHI! I THOUGHT YOU WERE MAKING DINNER—
NEVER MIND THAT! I WAS JUST THERE, YESTERDAY! WHAT HAPPENED TO THEIR SECURITY?!
WE HAVE TO ASSUME THAT THEY, AND THE GRANDPARENTS, WERE ALL KILLED.

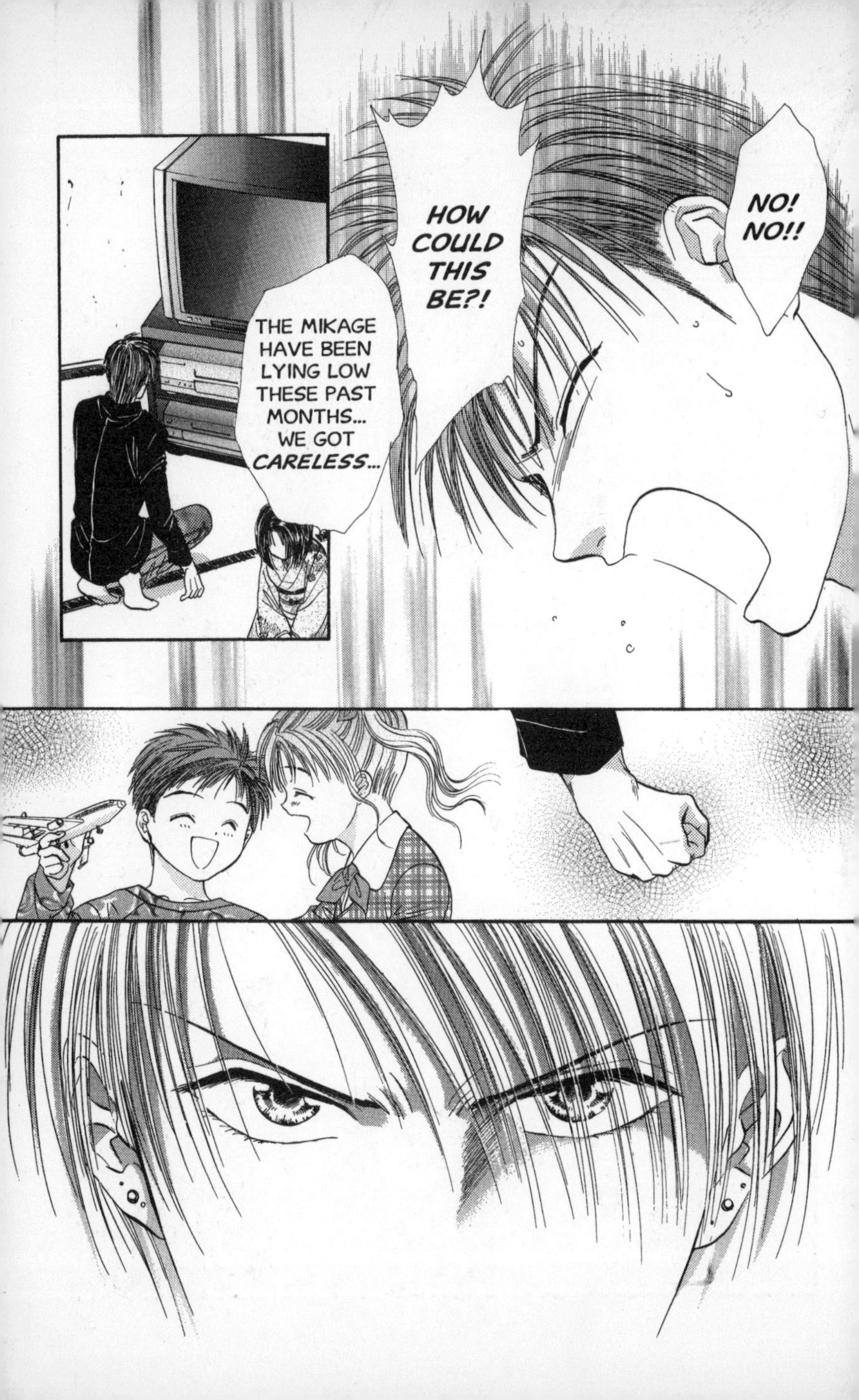
NO! NO!!
HOW COULD THIS BE?!
THE MIKAGE HAVE BEEN LYING LOW THESE PAST MONTHS... WE GOT *CARELESS*...

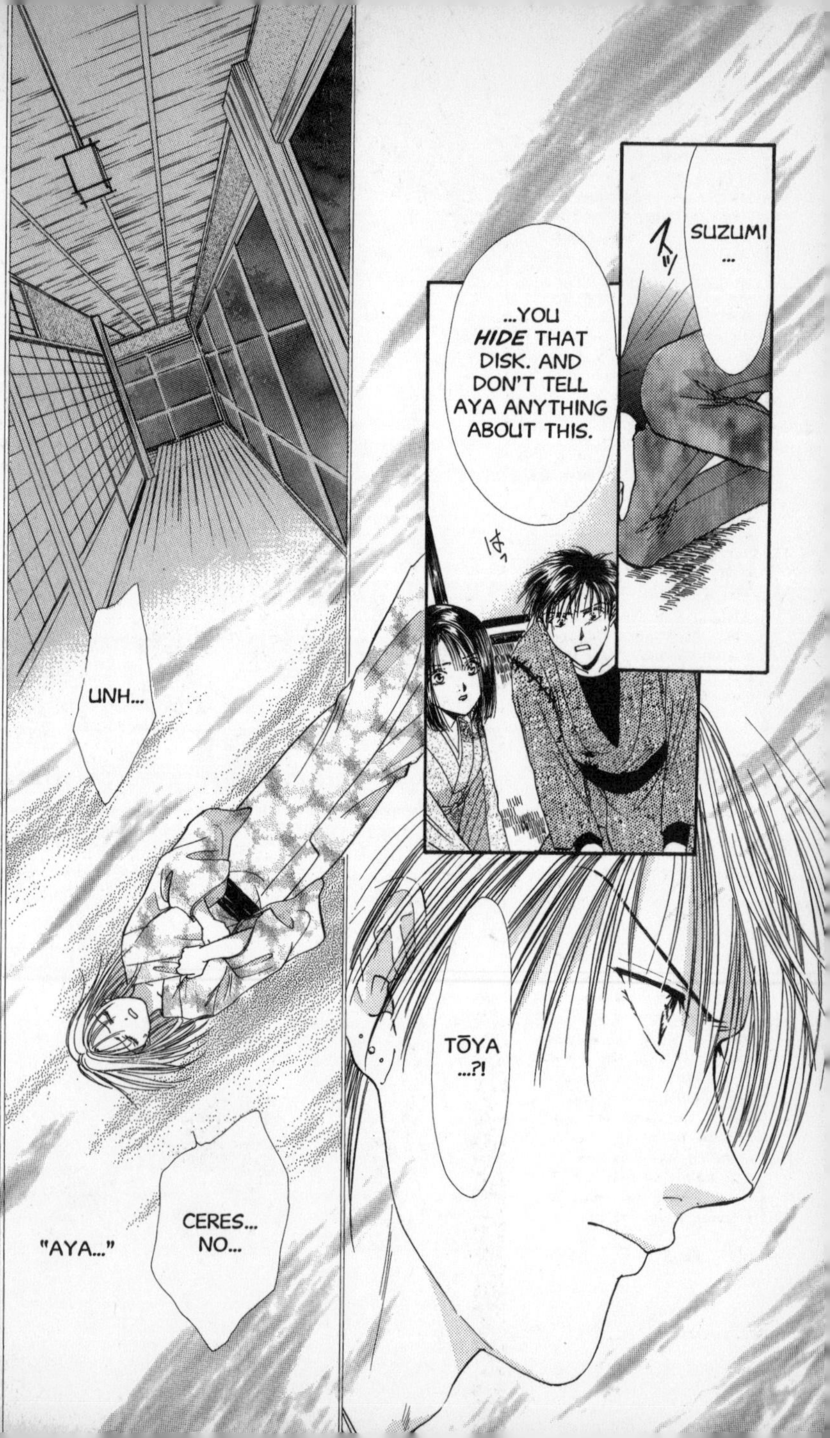
ズッ
SUZUMI ...
...YOU HIDE THAT DISK. AND DON'T TELL AYA ANYTHING ABOUT THIS.
はっ
TŌYA ...?!
UNH...
CERES... NO...
"AYA..."

◆ TŌYA ◆

Hey, Watase here. I caught a summer cold, which means I'm coughing and sniffling. Then again, my nose is sensitive, so I don't always know what's wrong....

Onward! Hachijō Island has been featured in this arc and, the thing is, I actually went there to research it. It was a nice place—so tropical!—though we had bad luck with the weather. I did read that average temperatures are about the same as (south-of-mainland-Japan) Kagoshima, so I suppose it wasn't **too** hot... although, then again, it **was** only May when we went.

I also went on my first-ever "discover scuba" adventure! I'd always had an interest, but never the chance. The ocean comes up a lot in Ceres, so I figured it was only right I have first-hand experience. I put on a "drysuit" (my editor had brought his own!) over my jeans, and in we went. Again, though, the weather wasn't good, and the waves were choppy, and it was starting to drizzle...and don't forget that I'm not a very good swimmer to begin with! Oh, I was so nervous. The waves, crashing into my face. The water, so salty! We put on oxygen tanks once we were in the water and practiced breathing...those glasses-like things slide around a lot. I learned how to breathe, and how to equalize the pressure in my ears, but just as we were about to dive under-water, the waves practically knocked us over! I was so scared, I clung to the instructor for dear life...I wasn't trying to drown her, I swear I wasn't! ὂὂ

Sorry about that.

To be continued.

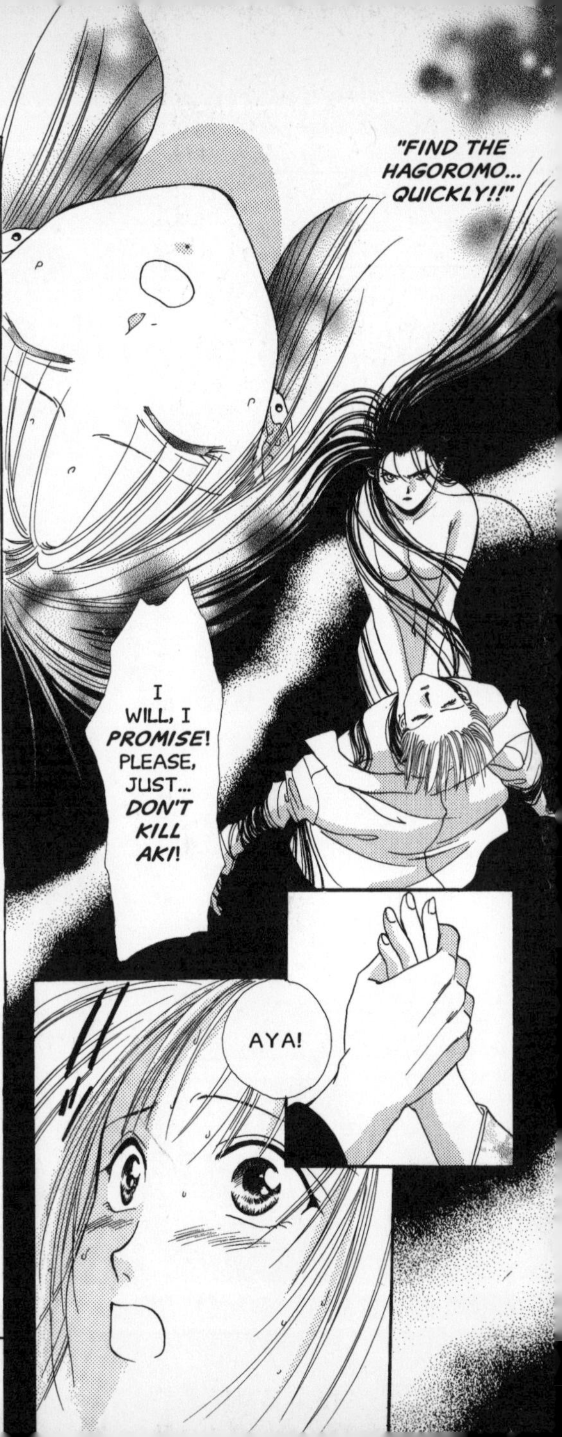
"FIND THE HAGOROMO... QUICKLY!!"
I WILL, I PROMISE! PLEASE, JUST... DON'T KILL AKI!
AYA!

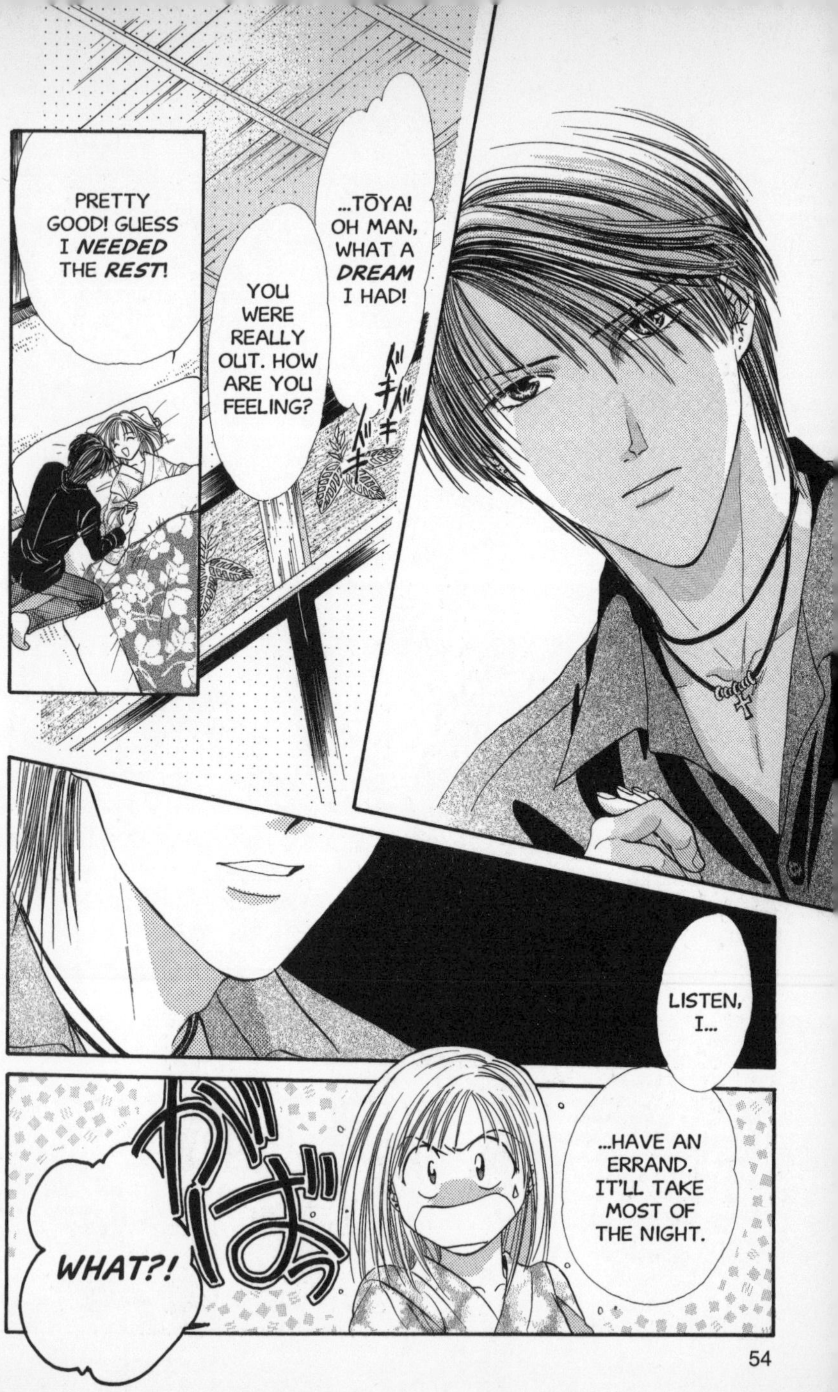

...TŌYA! OH MAN, WHAT A DREAM I HAD!
ズキズキズキ
YOU WERE REALLY OUT. HOW ARE YOU FEELING?
PRETTY GOOD! GUESS I NEEDED THE REST!
LISTEN, I...
...HAVE AN ERRAND. IT'LL TAKE MOST OF THE NIGHT.
WHAT?!

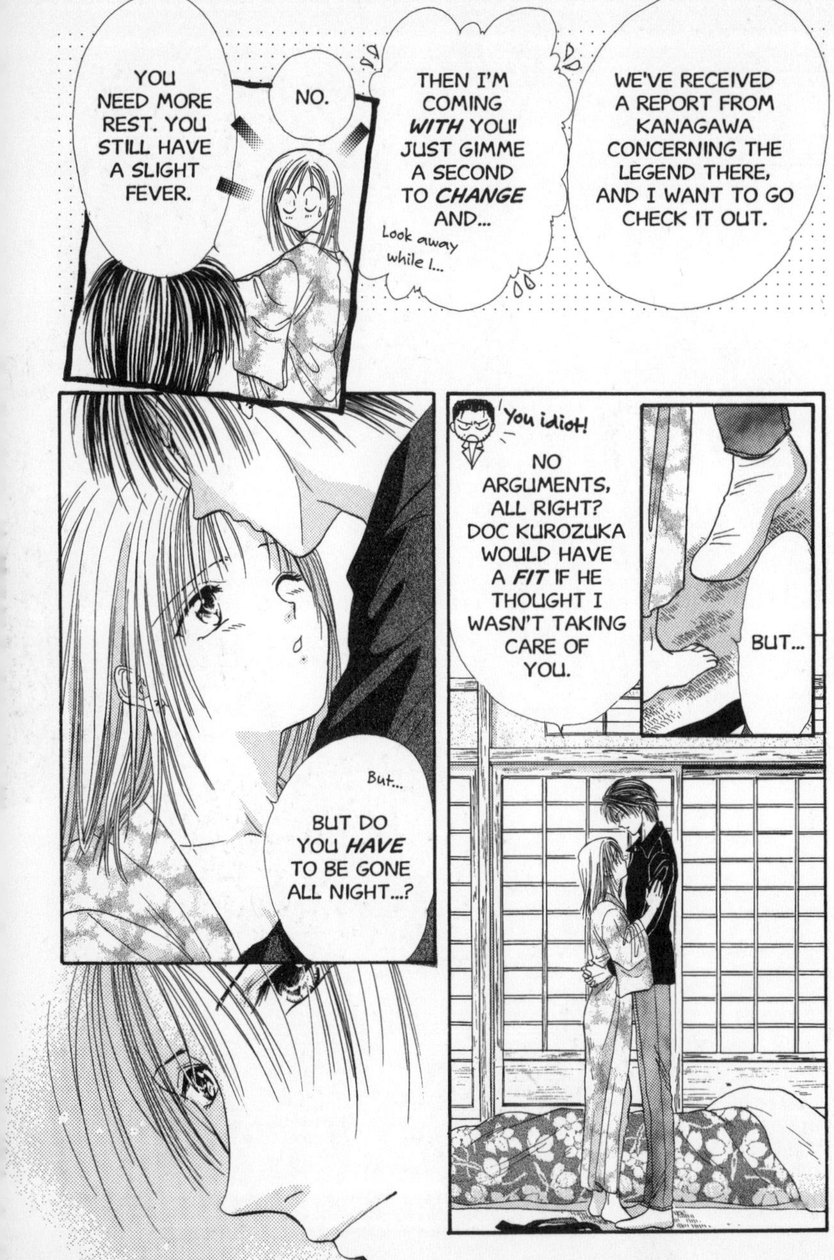
WE'VE RECEIVED A REPORT FROM KANAGAWA CONCERNING THE LEGEND THERE, AND I WANT TO GO CHECK IT OUT.
THEN I'M COMING *WITH* YOU! JUST GIMME A SECOND TO *CHANGE* AND...
Look away while I...
NO.
YOU NEED MORE REST. YOU STILL HAVE A SLIGHT FEVER.
BUT...
You idiot!
NO ARGUMENTS, ALL RIGHT? DOC KUROZUKA WOULD HAVE A *FIT* IF HE THOUGHT I WASN'T TAKING CARE OF YOU.
But...
BUT DO YOU *HAVE* TO BE GONE ALL NIGHT...?

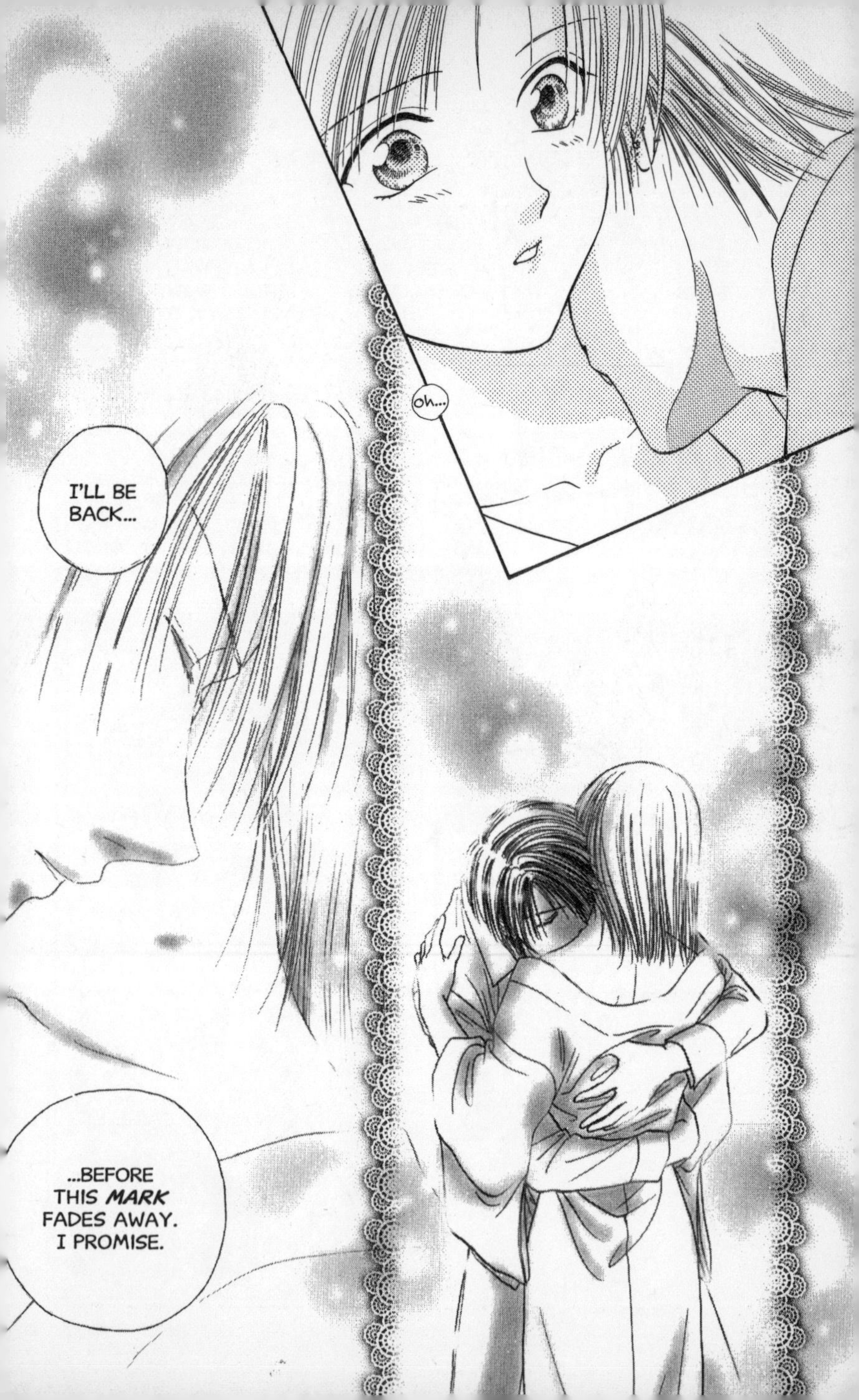
Oh...
I'LL BE BACK...
...BEFORE THIS *MARK* FADES AWAY. I PROMISE.

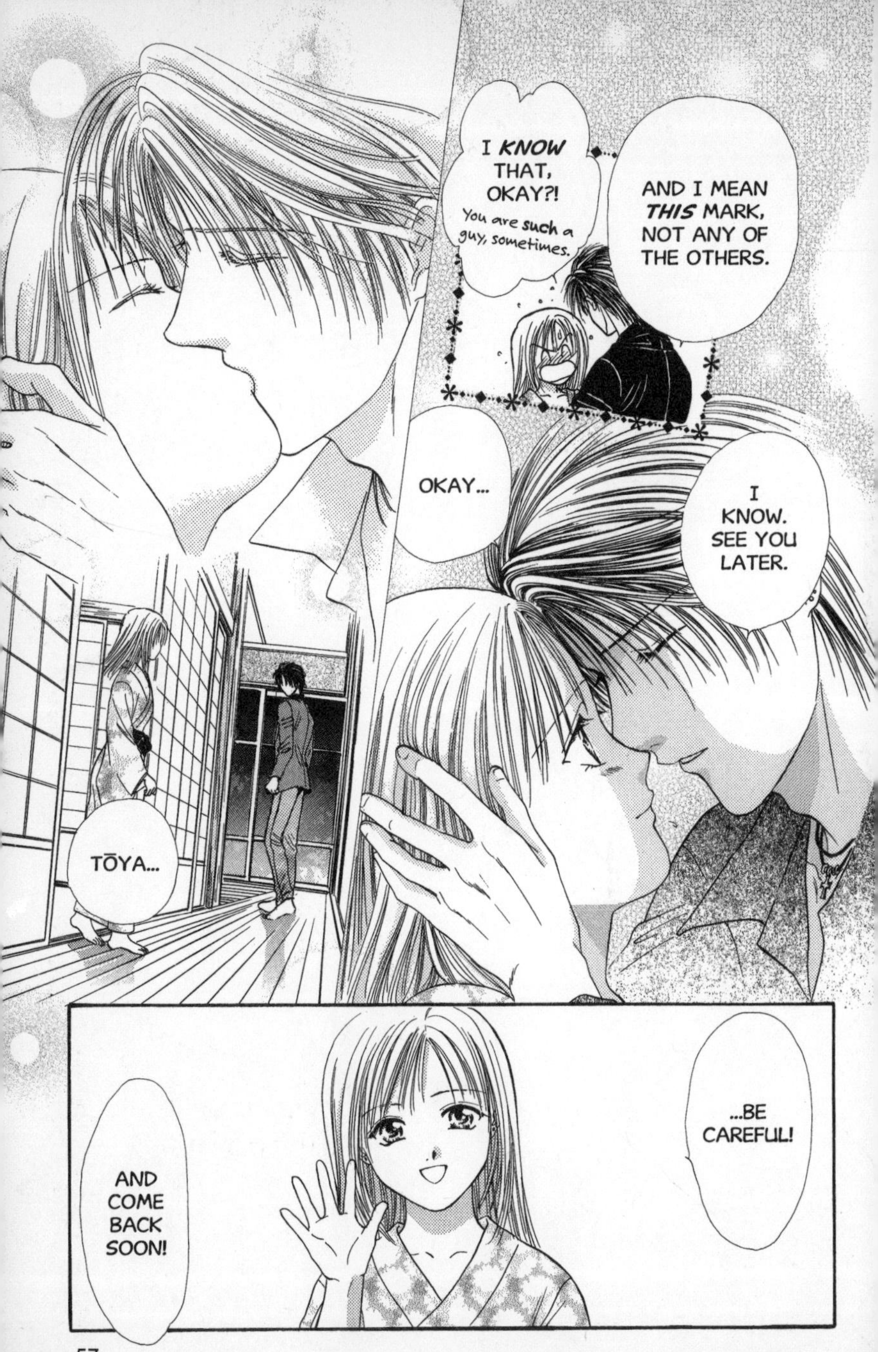
AND I MEAN *THIS* MARK, NOT ANY OF THE OTHERS.
I *KNOW* THAT, OKAY?! You are such a guy, sometimes.
I KNOW. SEE YOU LATER.
OKAY...
TŌYA...
...BE CAREFUL!
AND COME BACK SOON!

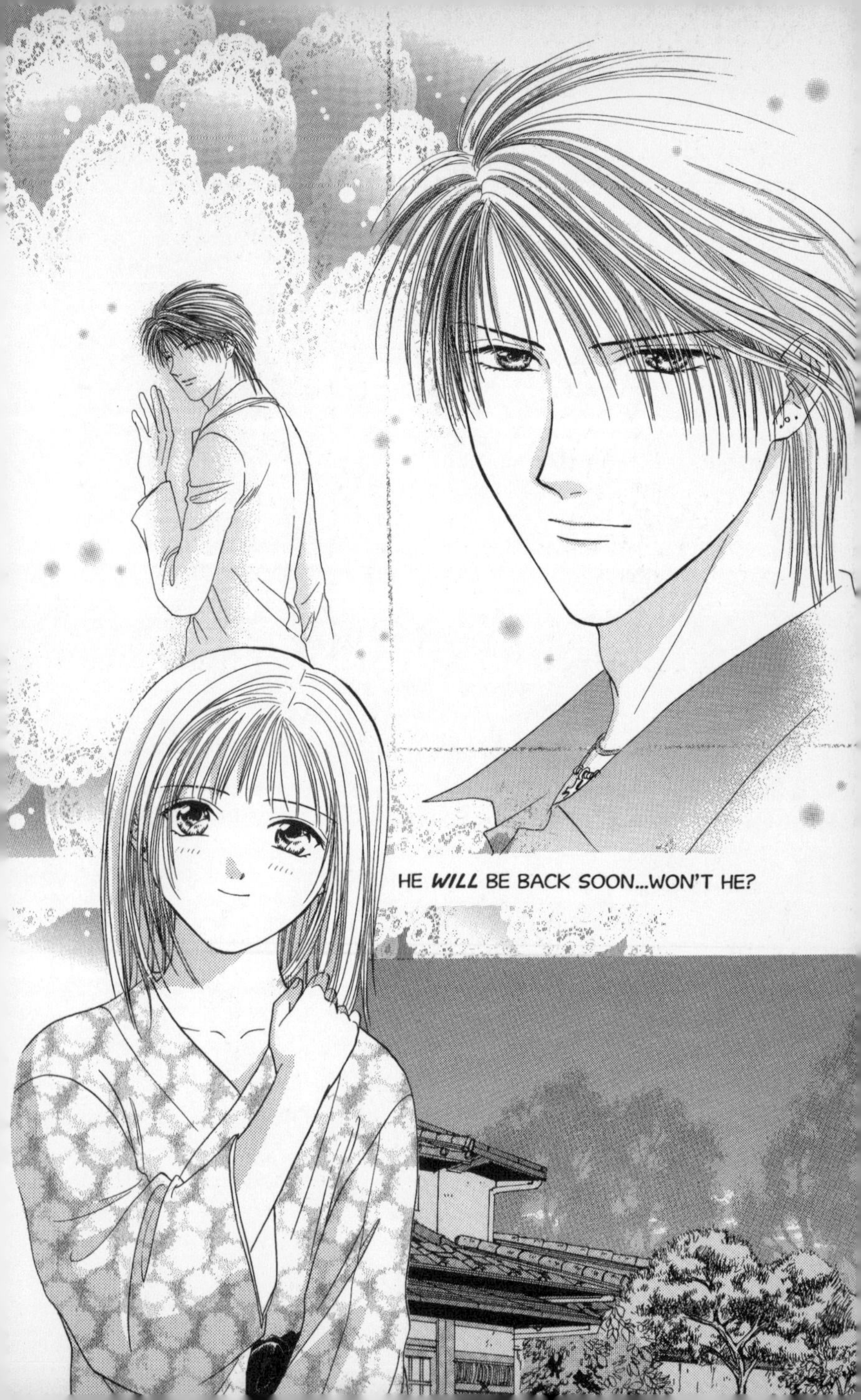
HE *WILL* BE BACK SOON...WON'T HE?

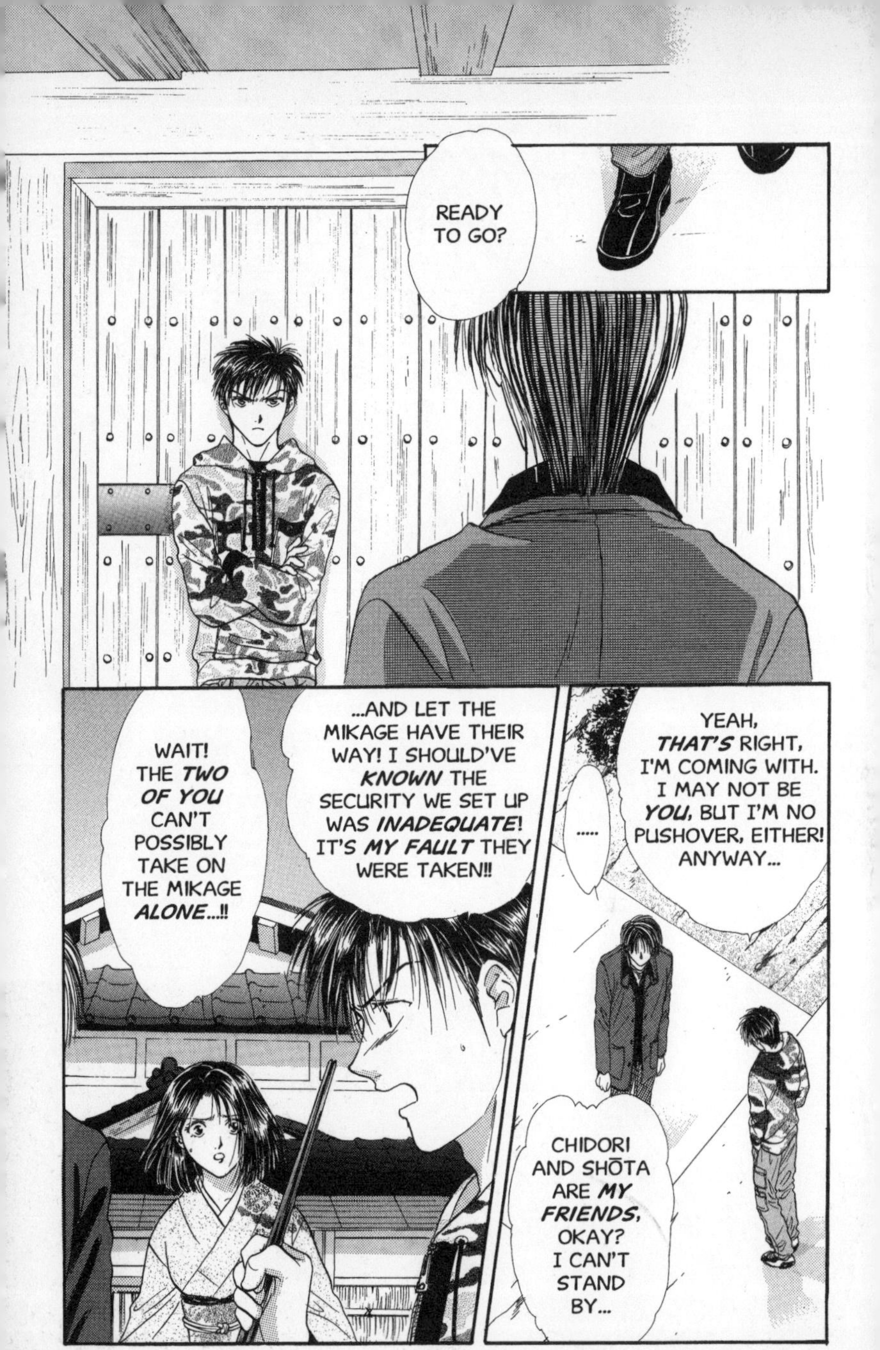
READY TO GO?
YEAH, THAT'S RIGHT, I'M COMING WITH. I MAY NOT BE YOU, BUT I'M NO PUSHOVER, EITHER! ANYWAY...
.....
CHIDORI AND SHŌTA ARE MY FRIENDS, OKAY? I CAN'T STAND BY...
...AND LET THE MIKAGE HAVE THEIR WAY! I SHOULD'VE KNOWN THE SECURITY WE SET UP WAS INADEQUATE! IT'S MY FAULT THEY WERE TAKEN!!
WAIT! THE TWO OF YOU CAN'T POSSIBLY TAKE ON THE MIKAGE ALONE...!!

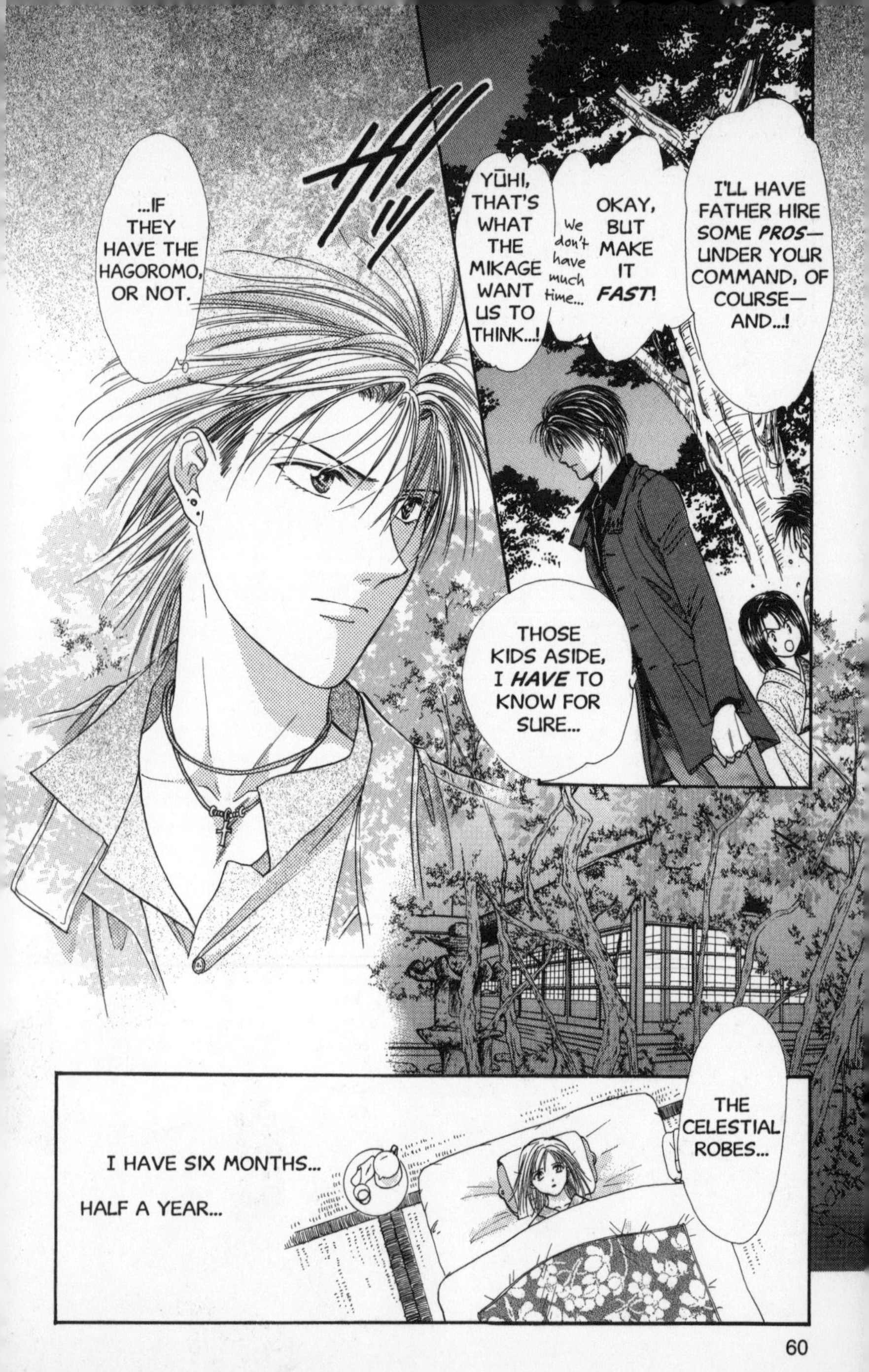
I'LL HAVE FATHER HIRE SOME *PROS*—UNDER YOUR COMMAND, OF COURSE—AND...!
OKAY, BUT MAKE IT *FAST*!
We don't have much time...
YŪHI, THAT'S WHAT THE MIKAGE WANT US TO THINK...!
THOSE KIDS ASIDE, I *HAVE* TO KNOW FOR SURE...
...IF THEY HAVE THE HAGOROMO, OR NOT.
THE CELESTIAL ROBES...
I HAVE SIX MONTHS...
HALF A YEAR...

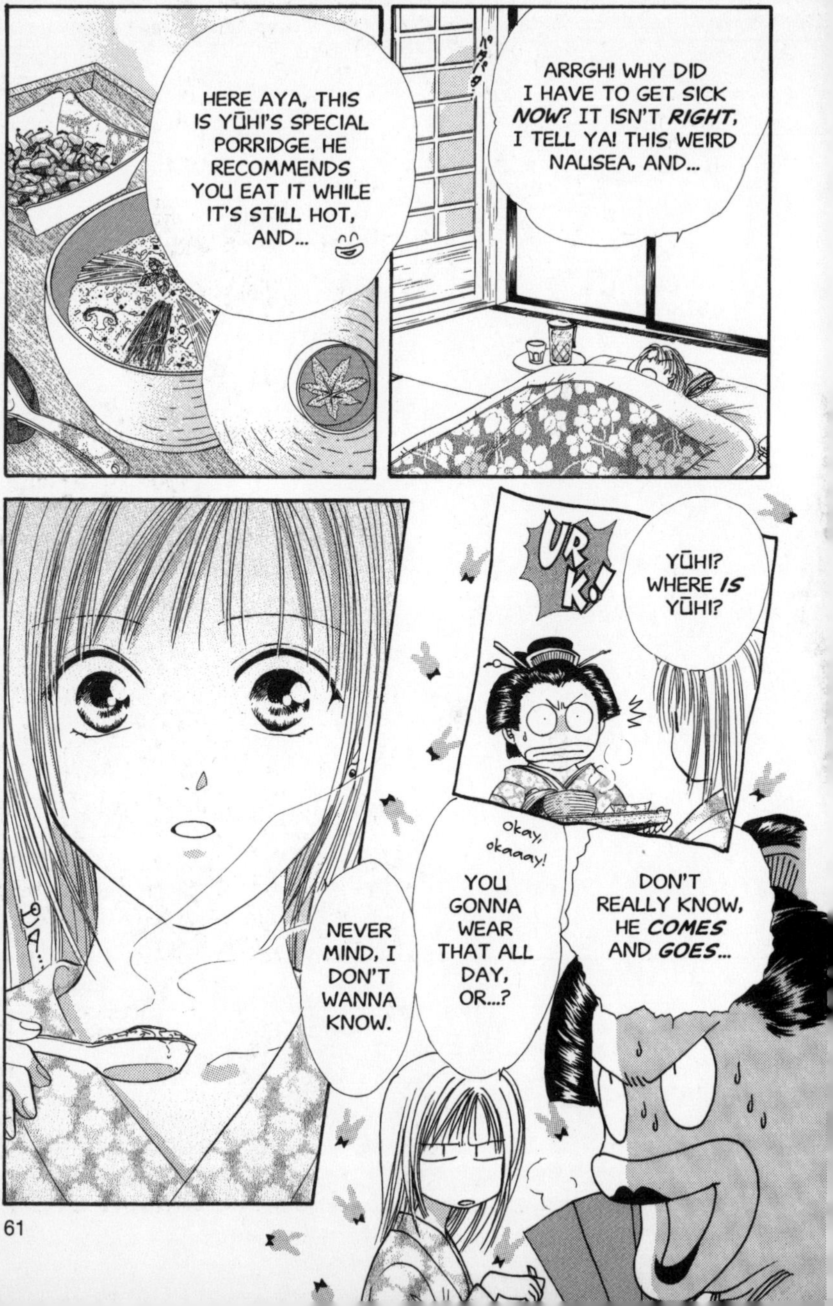
ARRGH! WHY DID I HAVE TO GET SICK *NOW*? IT ISN'T *RIGHT*, I TELL YA! THIS WEIRD NAUSEA, AND...
HERE AYA, THIS IS YŪHI'S SPECIAL PORRIDGE. HE RECOMMENDS YOU EAT IT WHILE IT'S STILL HOT, AND...
URK!
YŪHI? WHERE *IS* YŪHI?
DON'T REALLY KNOW, HE *COMES* AND *GOES*...
okay, okaaay!
YOU GONNA WEAR THAT ALL DAY, OR...?
NEVER MIND, I DON'T WANNA KNOW.

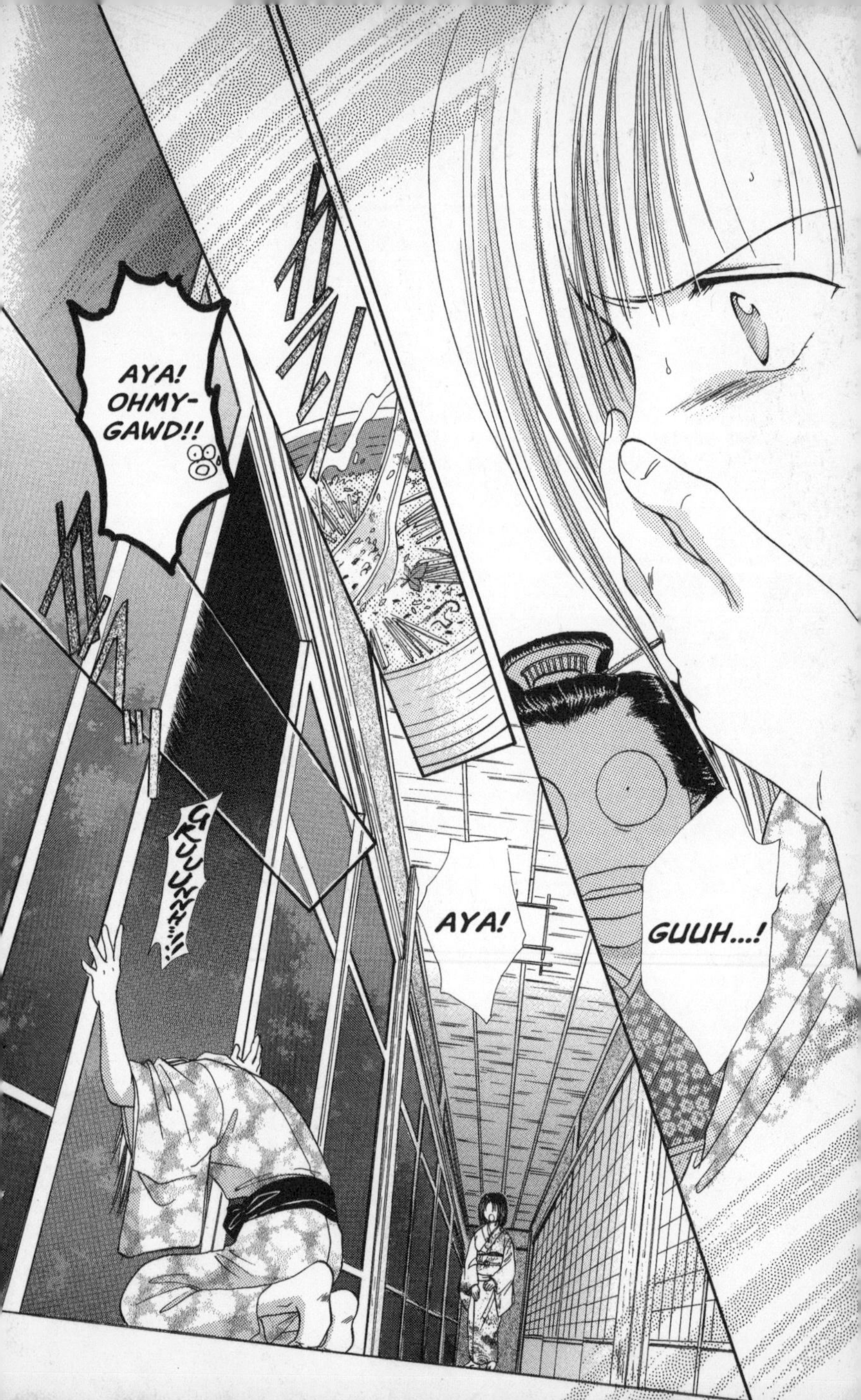
GUUH...!
AYA!
AYA! OHMY-GAWD!!
GKUUUNNH...!!

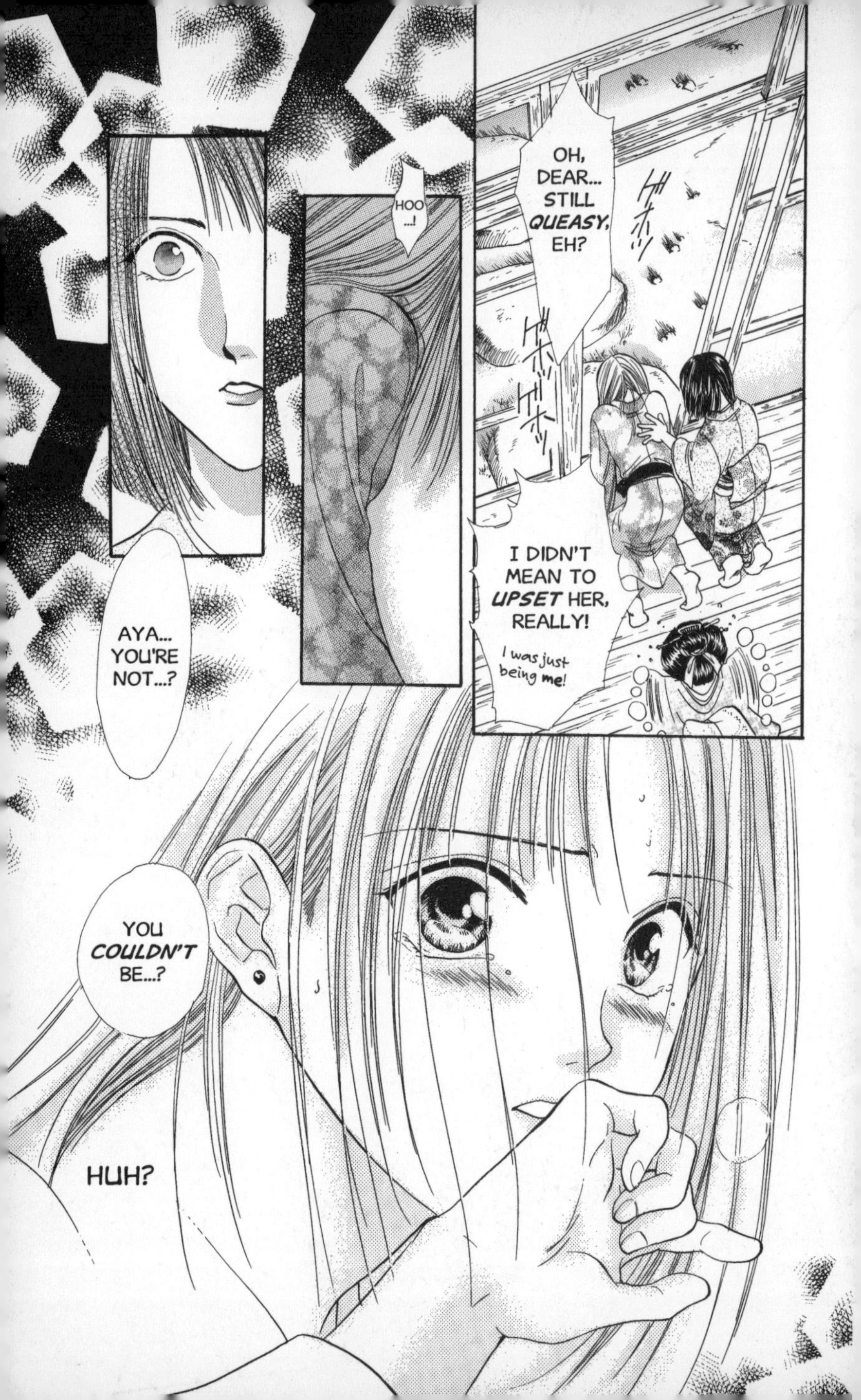
OH, DEAR... STILL QUEASY, EH?
I DIDN'T MEAN TO UPSET HER, REALLY!
I was just being me!
HOO ...!
AYA... YOU'RE NOT...?
YOU COULDN'T BE...?
HUH?

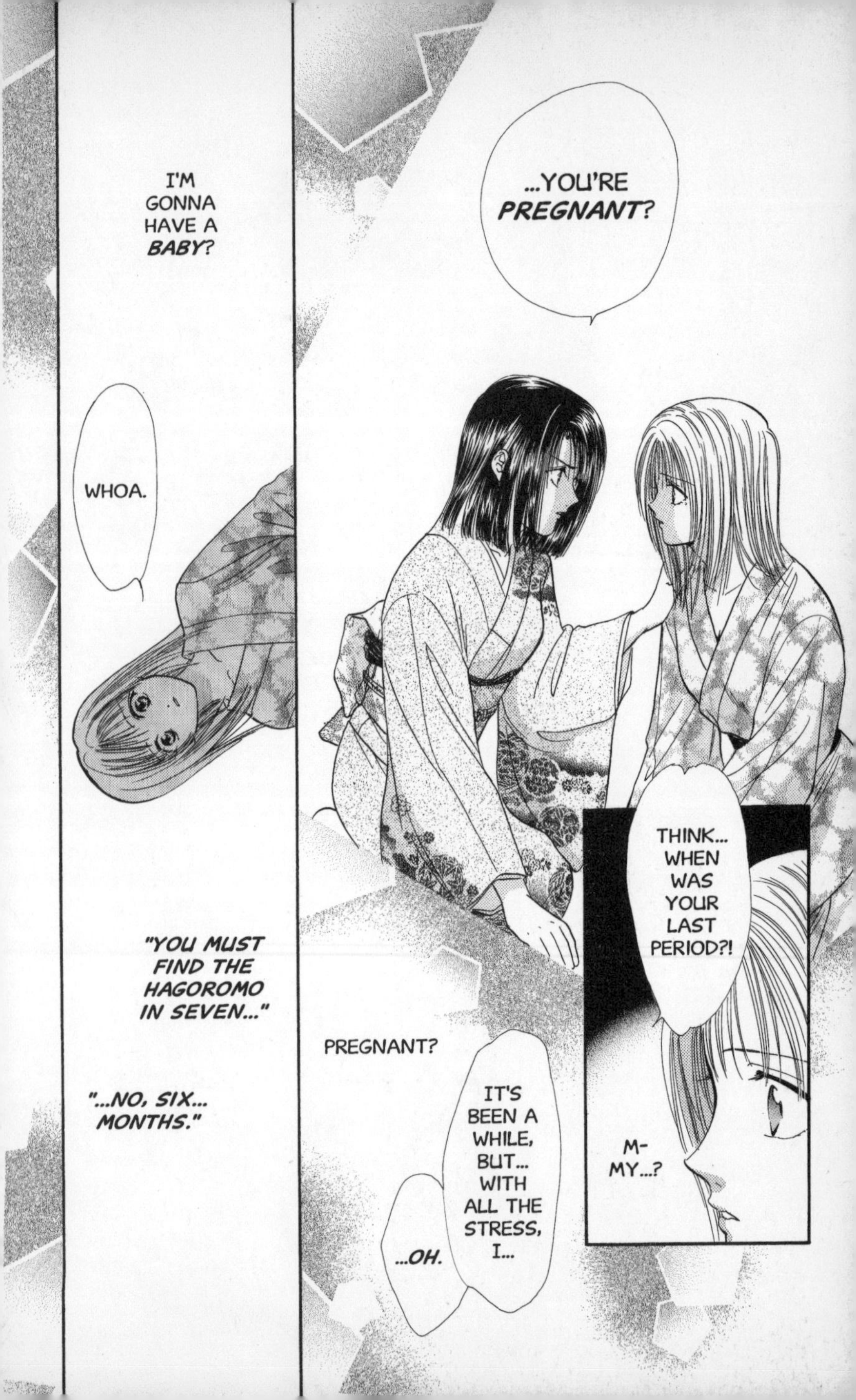
...YOU'RE *PREGNANT*?
THINK... WHEN WAS YOUR LAST PERIOD?!
M- MY...?
PREGNANT?
IT'S BEEN A WHILE, BUT... WITH ALL THE STRESS, I...
...OH.
I'M GONNA HAVE A *BABY*?
WHOA.
"YOU MUST FIND THE HAGOROMO IN SEVEN..."
"...NO, SIX... MONTHS."

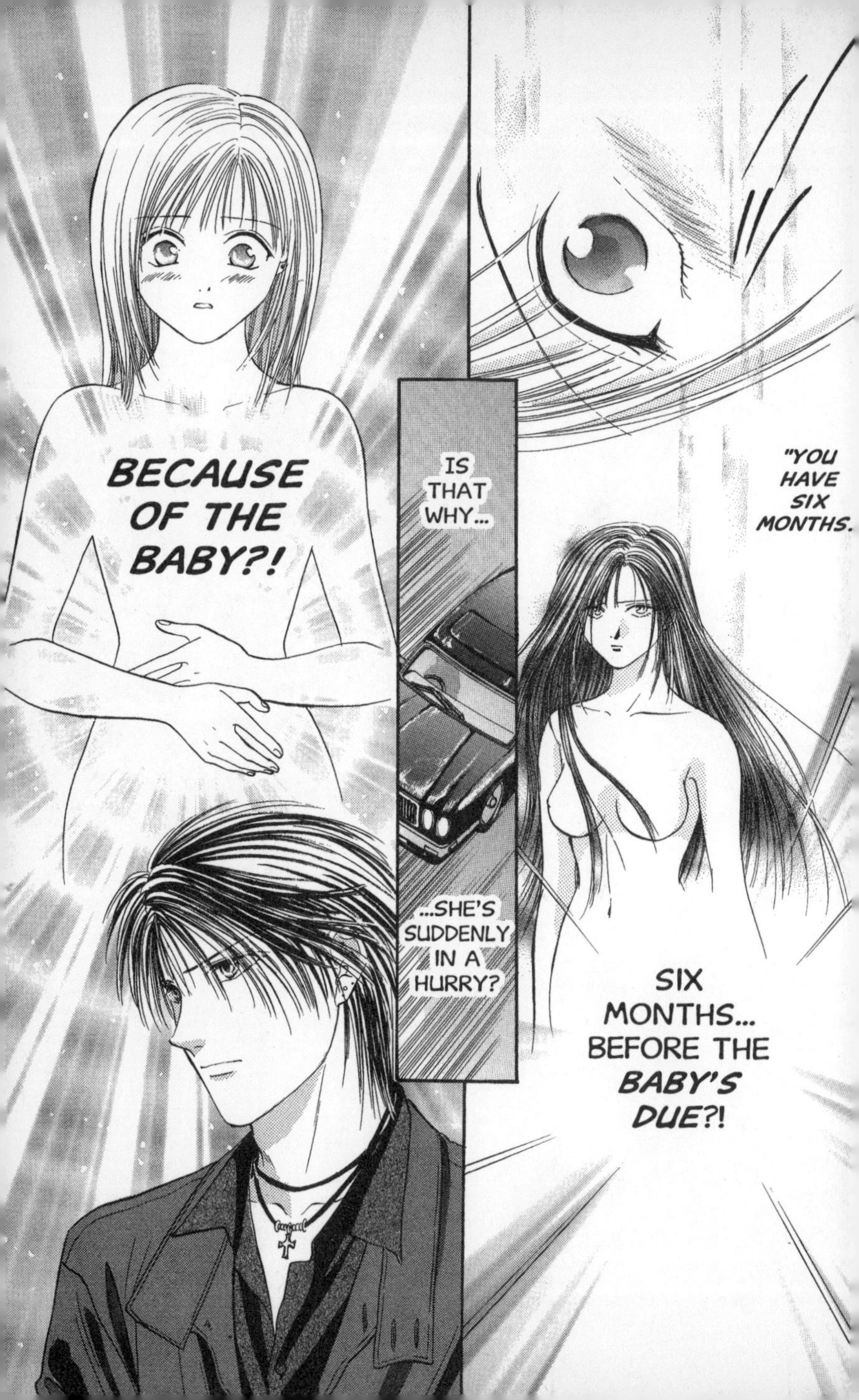
"YOU HAVE SIX MONTHS.
SIX MONTHS... BEFORE THE BABY'S DUE?!
IS THAT WHY...
...SHE'S SUDDENLY IN A HURRY?
BECAUSE OF THE BABY?!

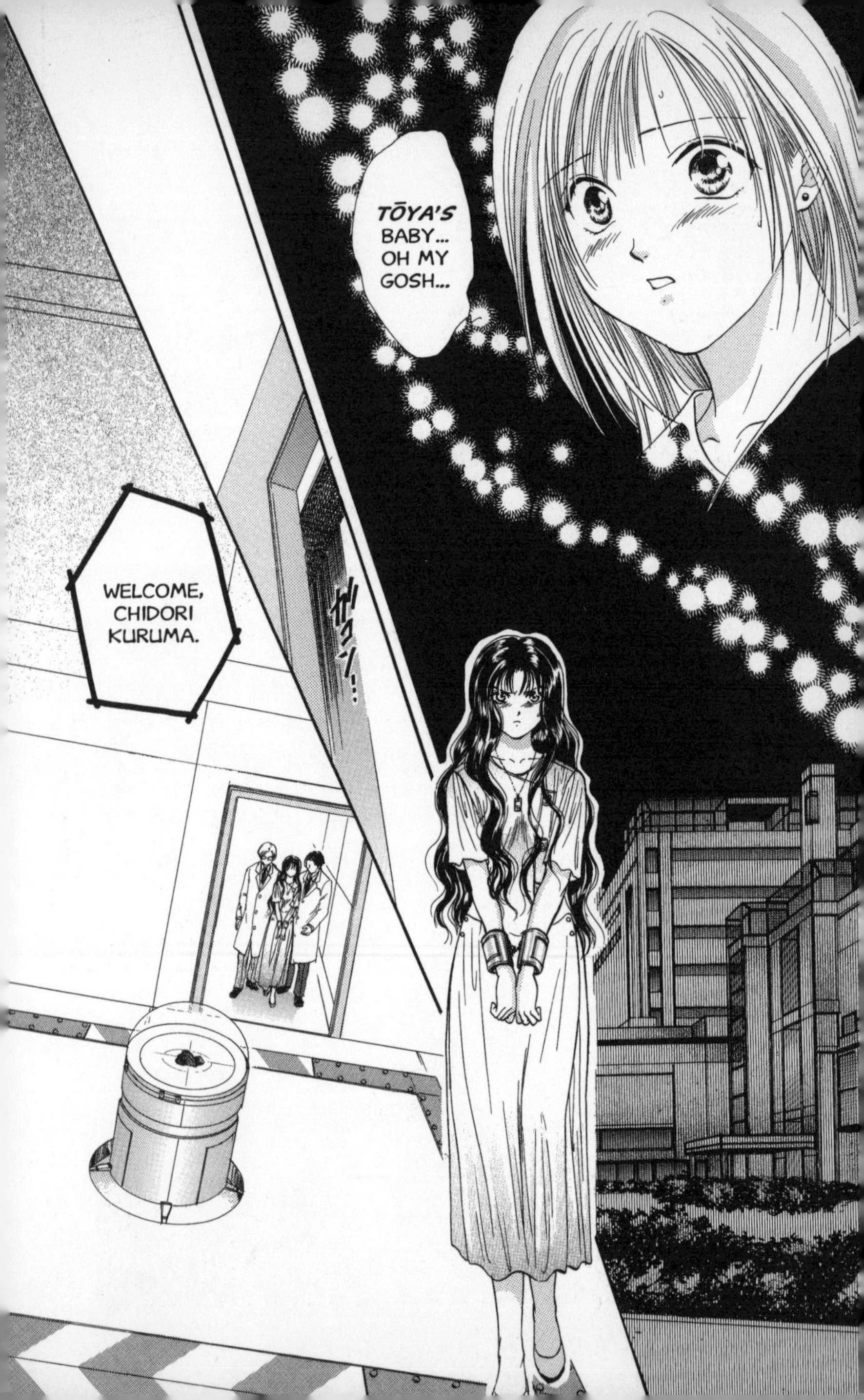
TŌYA'S BABY... OH MY GOSH...
WELCOME, CHIDORI KURUMA.

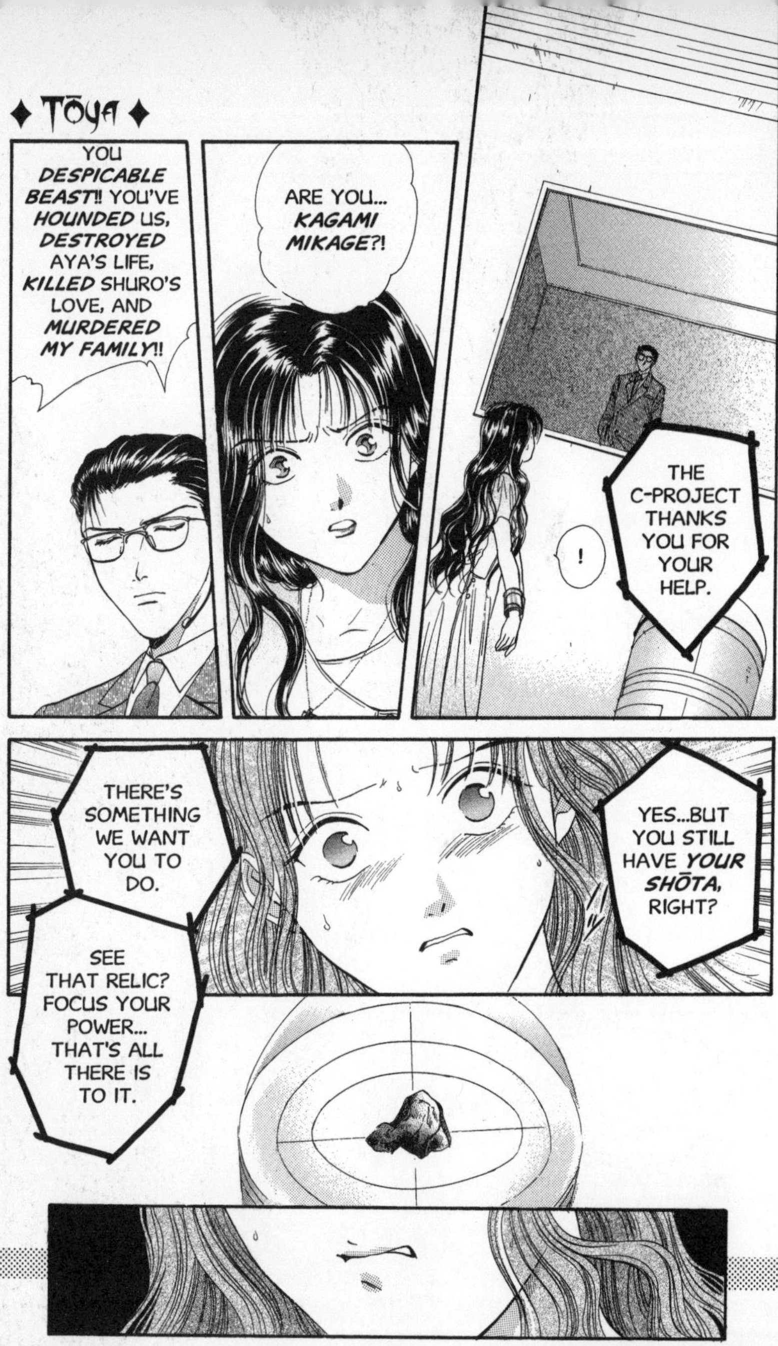
THE C-PROJECT THANKS YOU FOR YOUR HELP.
!
ARE YOU... *KAGAMI MIKAGE*?!
YOU *DESPICABLE BEAST*!! YOU'VE *HOUNDED* US, *DESTROYED* AYA'S LIFE, *KILLED* SHURO'S LOVE, AND *MURDERED MY FAMILY*!!
YES...BUT YOU STILL HAVE *YOUR SHŌTA*, RIGHT?
THERE'S SOMETHING WE WANT YOU TO DO.
SEE THAT RELIC? FOCUS YOUR POWER... THAT'S ALL THERE IS TO IT.

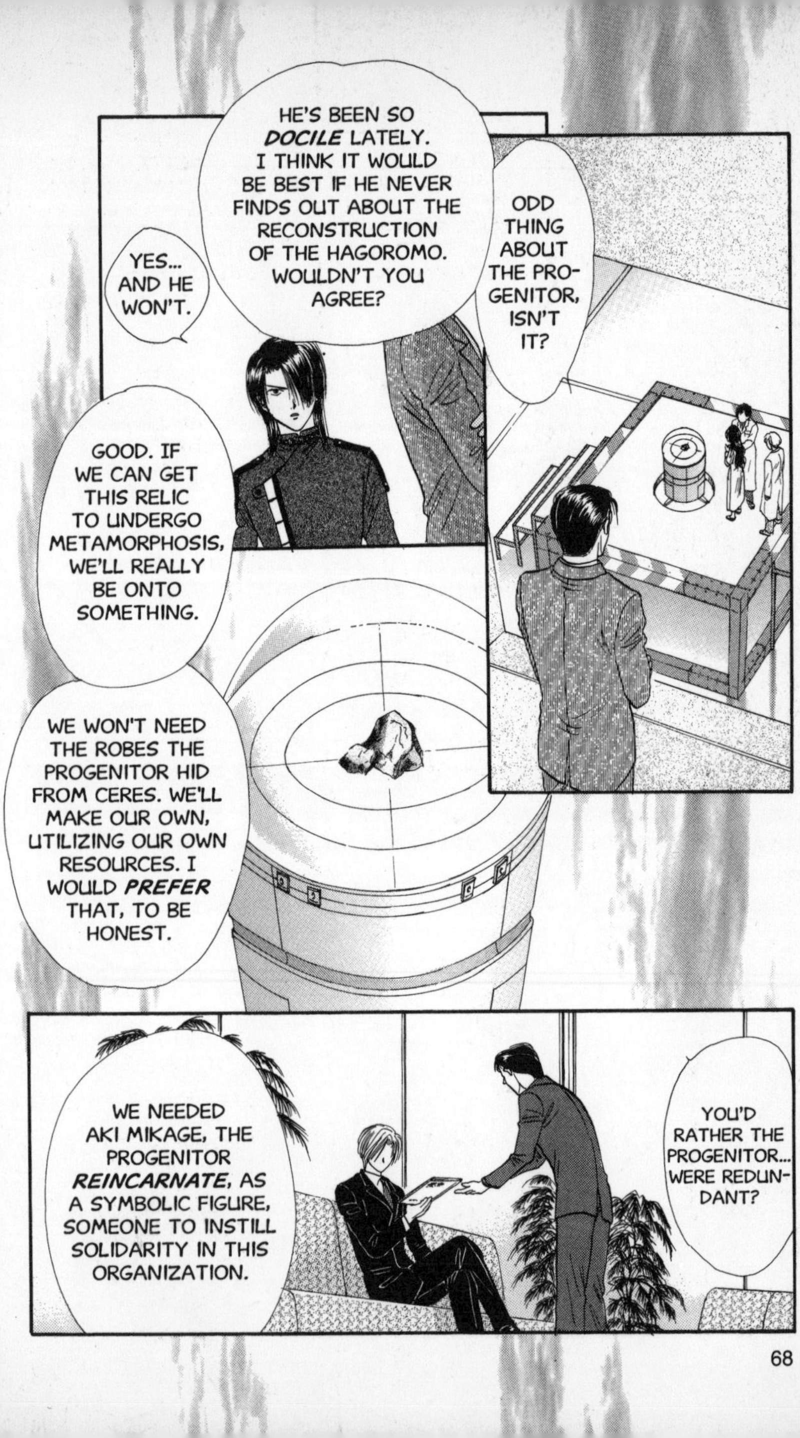
ODD THING ABOUT THE PRO-GENITOR, ISN'T IT?
HE'S BEEN SO *DOCILE* LATELY. I THINK IT WOULD BE BEST IF HE NEVER FINDS OUT ABOUT THE RECONSTRUCTION OF THE HAGOROMO. WOULDN'T YOU AGREE?
YES... AND HE WON'T.
GOOD. IF WE CAN GET THIS RELIC TO UNDERGO METAMORPHOSIS, WE'LL REALLY BE ONTO SOMETHING.
WE WON'T NEED THE ROBES THE PROGENITOR HID FROM CERES. WE'LL MAKE OUR OWN, UTILIZING OUR OWN RESOURCES. I WOULD *PREFER* THAT, TO BE HONEST.
YOU'D RATHER THE PROGENITOR... WERE REDUN-DANT?
WE NEEDED AKI MIKAGE, THE PROGENITOR *REINCARNATE*, AS A SYMBOLIC FIGURE, SOMEONE TO INSTILL SOLIDARITY IN THIS ORGANIZATION.

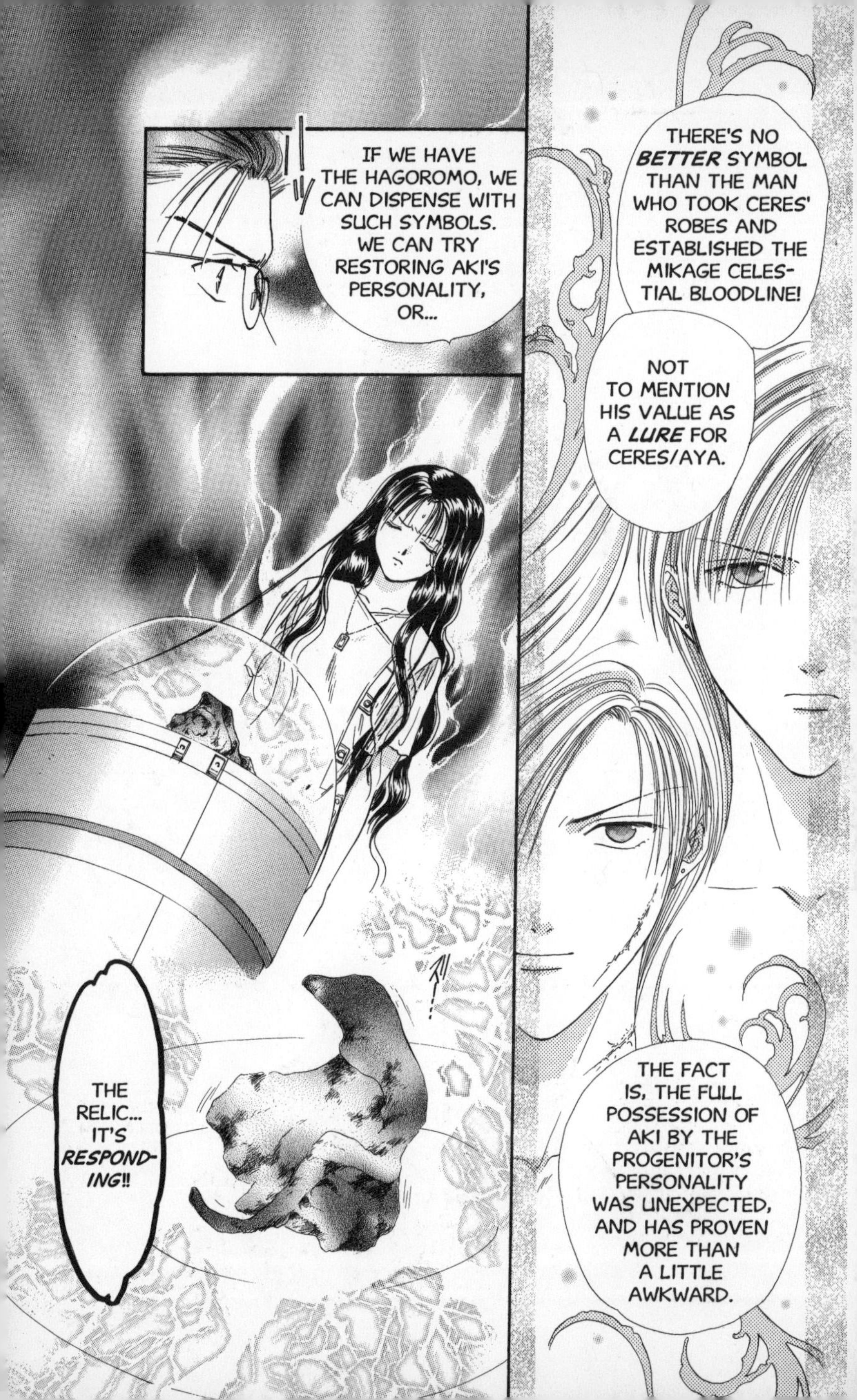
THERE'S NO BETTER SYMBOL THAN THE MAN WHO TOOK CERES' ROBES AND ESTABLISHED THE MIKAGE CELES-TIAL BLOODLINE!
NOT TO MENTION HIS VALUE AS A LURE FOR CERES/AYA.
THE FACT IS, THE FULL POSSESSION OF AKI BY THE PROGENITOR'S PERSONALITY WAS UNEXPECTED, AND HAS PROVEN MORE THAN A LITTLE AWKWARD.
IF WE HAVE THE HAGOROMO, WE CAN DISPENSE WITH SUCH SYMBOLS. WE CAN TRY RESTORING AKI'S PERSONALITY, OR...
THE RELIC... IT'S RESPONDING!!

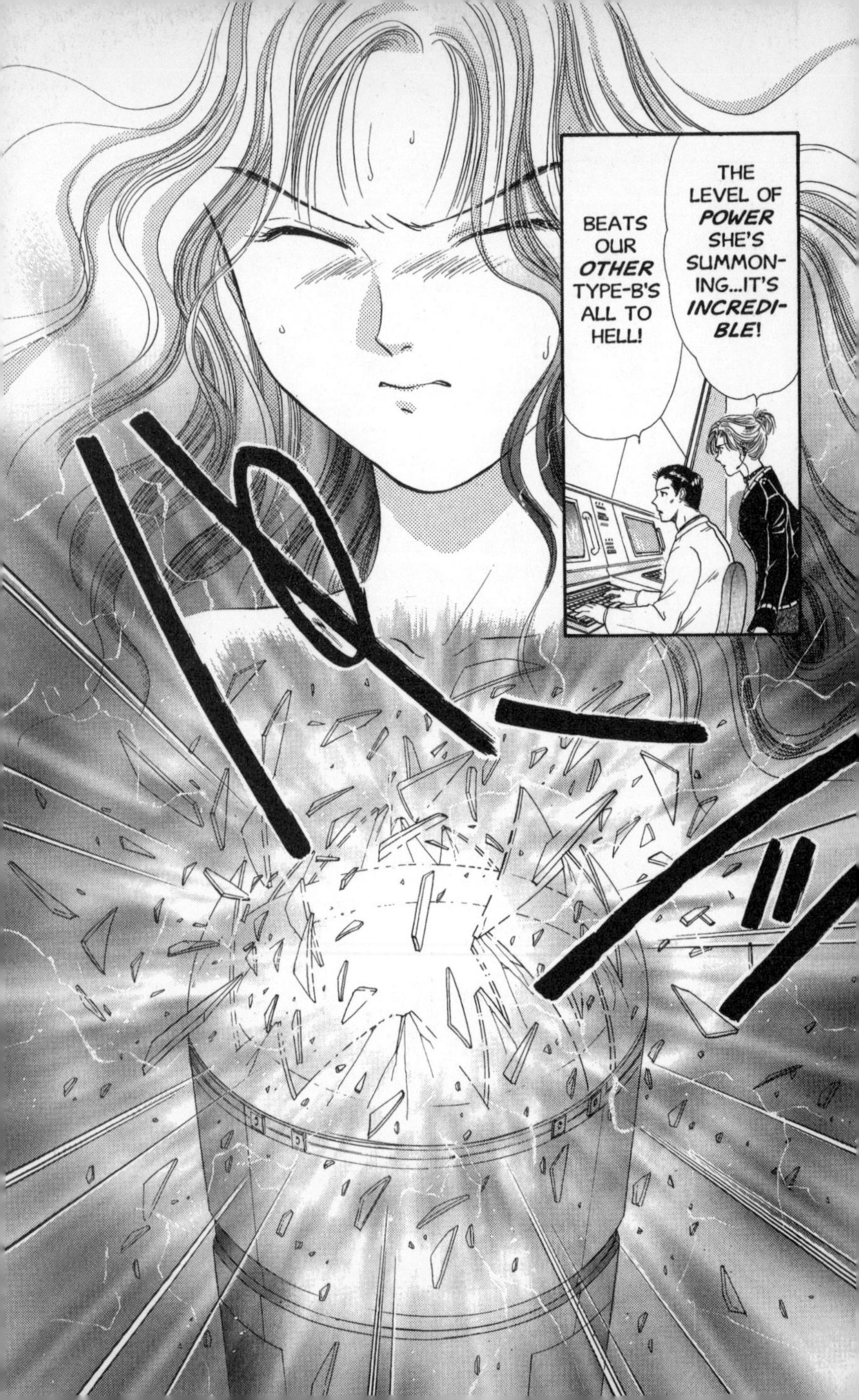
THE LEVEL OF POWER SHE'S SUMMONING...IT'S INCREDIBLE!
BEATS OUR OTHER TYPE-B'S ALL TO HELL!

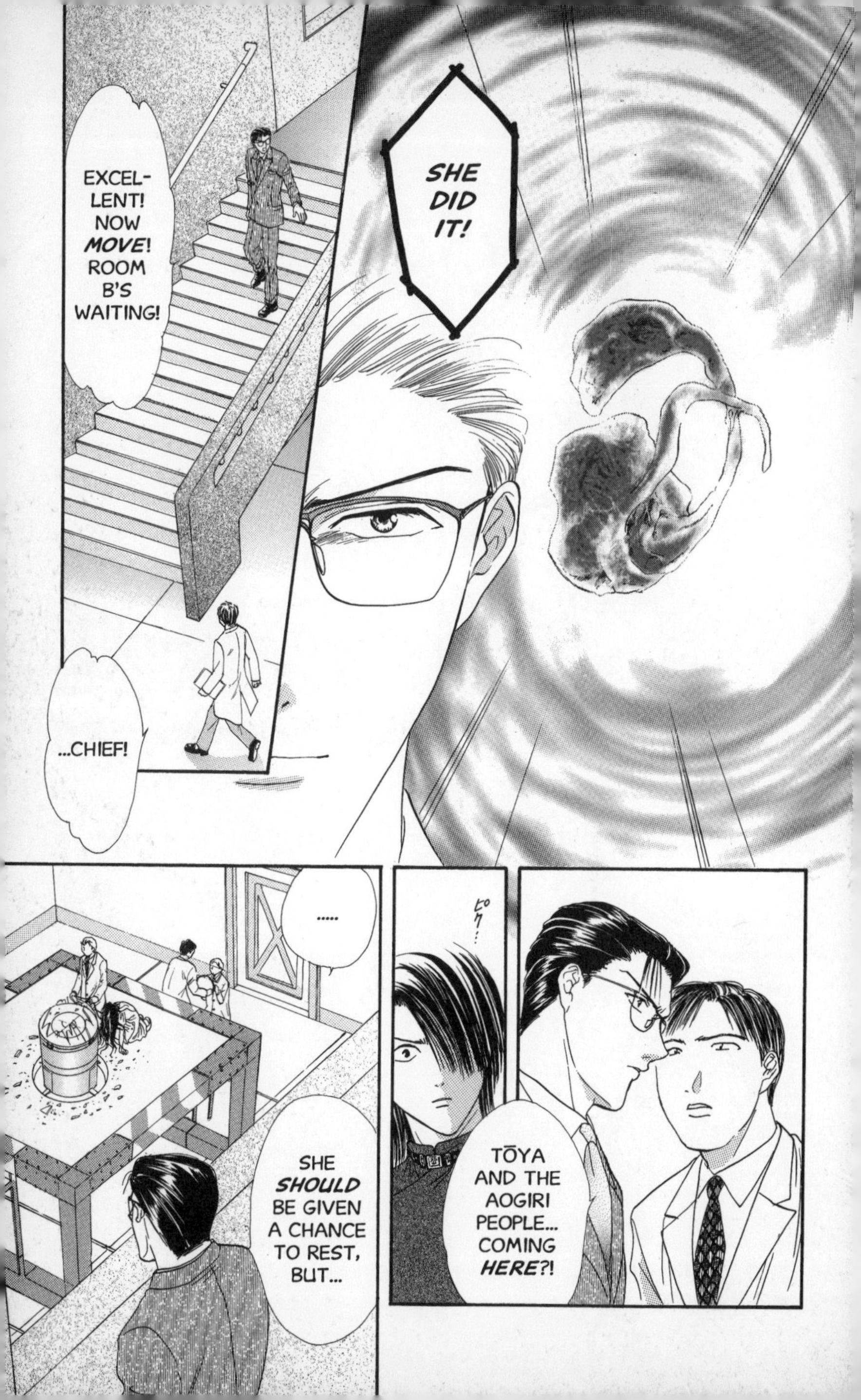

SHE DID IT!
EXCEL-LENT! NOW MOVE! ROOM B'S WAITING!
...CHIEF!
TŌYA AND THE AOGIRI PEOPLE... COMING HERE?!
ピク…
.....
SHE SHOULD BE GIVEN A CHANCE TO REST, BUT...

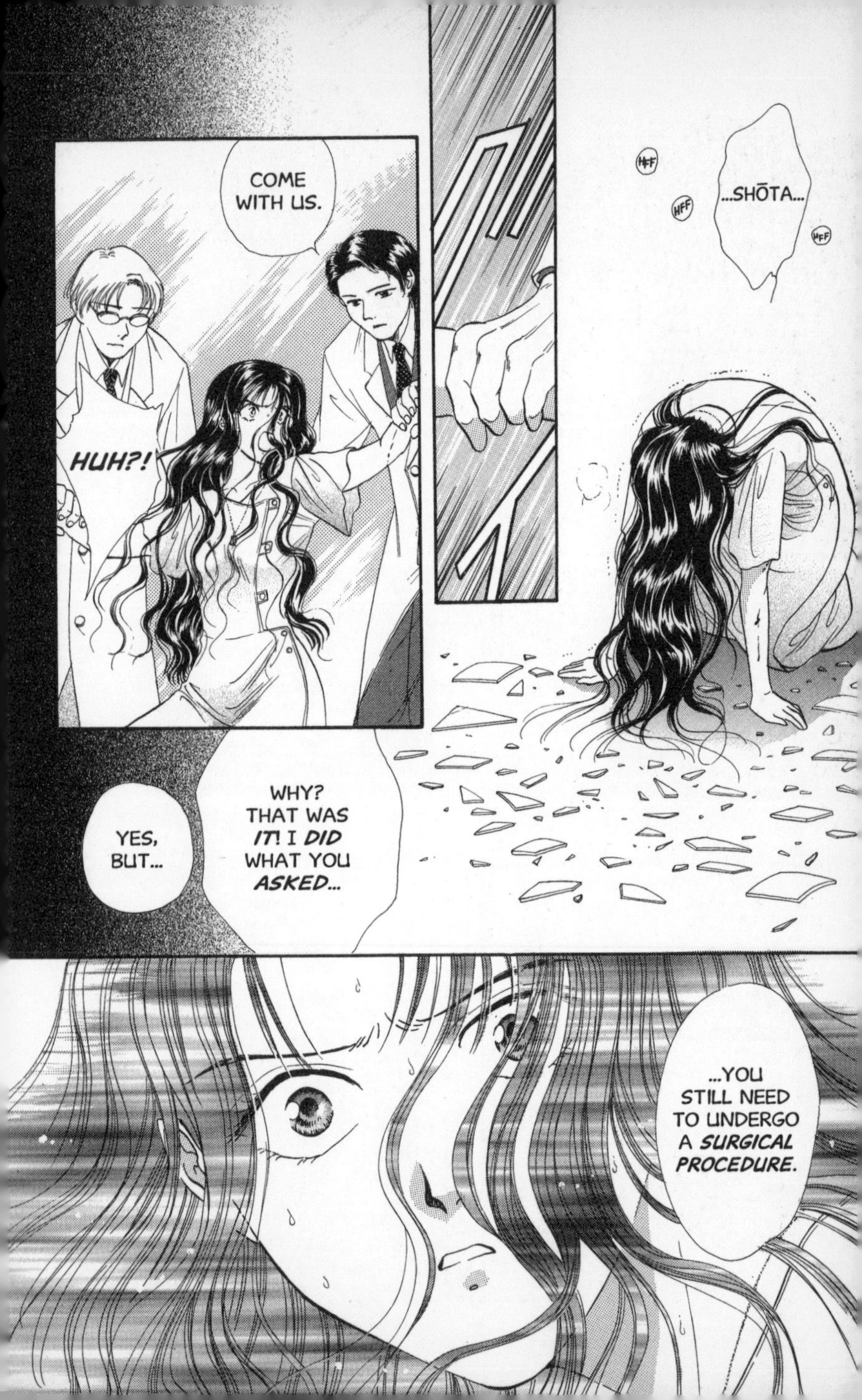
...SHŌTA...
HFF
HFF
HFF
COME WITH US.
HUH?!
WHY? THAT WAS IT! I DID WHAT YOU ASKED...
YES, BUT...
...YOU STILL NEED TO UNDERGO A SURGICAL PROCEDURE.

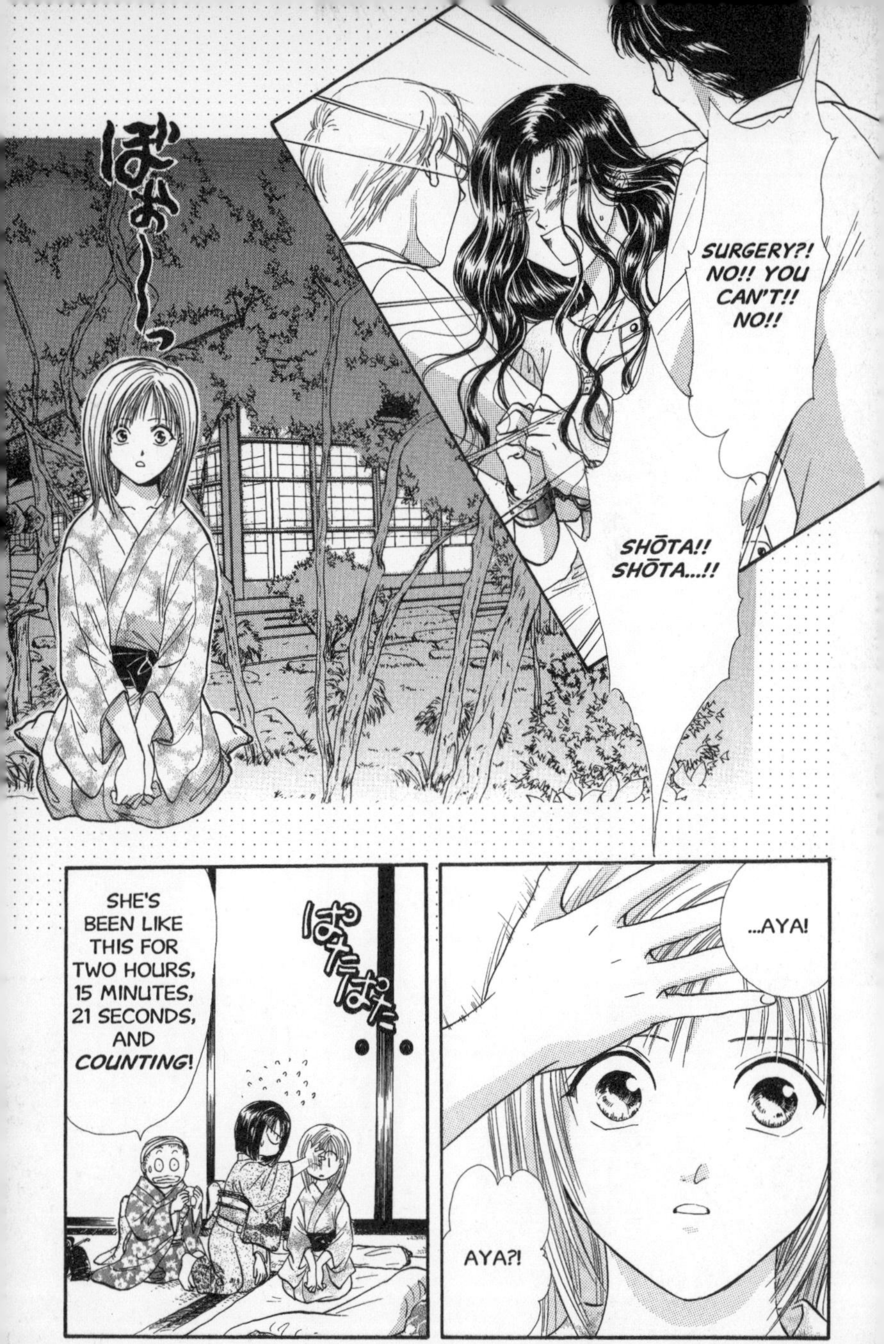
SURGERY?! NO!! YOU CAN'T!! NO!!
SHŌTA!! SHŌTA...!!
ぼぉ〜っ
...AYA!
AYA?!
SHE'S BEEN LIKE THIS FOR TWO HOURS, 15 MINUTES, 21 SECONDS, AND *COUNTING*!
ぱたぱた

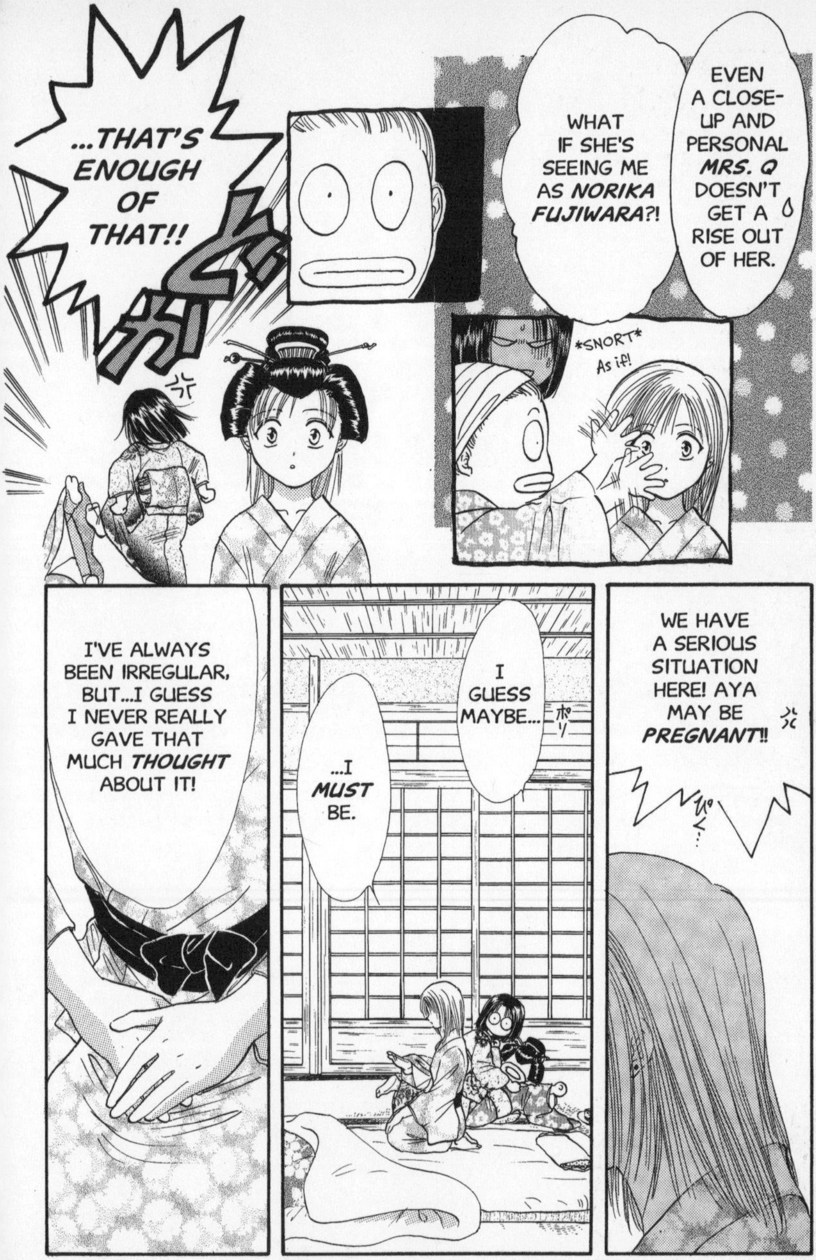
EVEN A CLOSE-UP AND PERSONAL MRS. Q DOESN'T GET A RISE OUT OF HER.
WHAT IF SHE'S SEEING ME AS NORIKA FUJIWARA?!
SNORT As if!
...THAT'S ENOUGH OF THAT!!
WE HAVE A SERIOUS SITUATION HERE! AYA MAY BE PREGNANT!!
I GUESS MAYBE...
...I MUST BE.
I'VE ALWAYS BEEN IRREGULAR, BUT...I GUESS I NEVER REALLY GAVE THAT MUCH THOUGHT ABOUT IT!

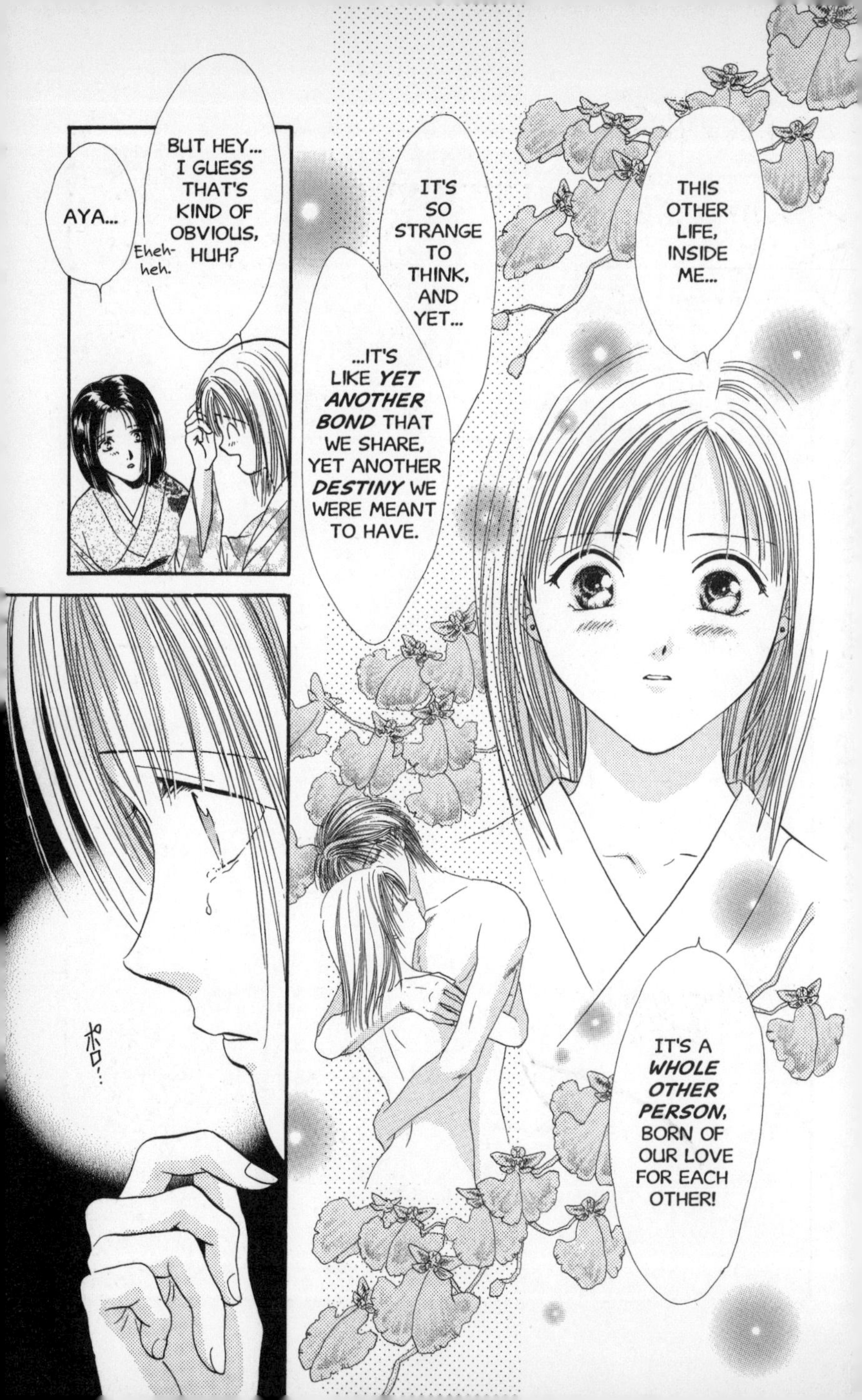
THIS OTHER LIFE, INSIDE ME...
IT'S A *WHOLE OTHER PERSON*, BORN OF OUR LOVE FOR EACH OTHER!
IT'S SO STRANGE TO THINK, AND YET...
...IT'S LIKE *YET ANOTHER BOND* THAT WE SHARE, YET ANOTHER *DESTINY* WE WERE MEANT TO HAVE.
BUT HEY... I GUESS THAT'S KIND OF OBVIOUS, HUH?
Eheh-heh.
AYA...
ポロ...

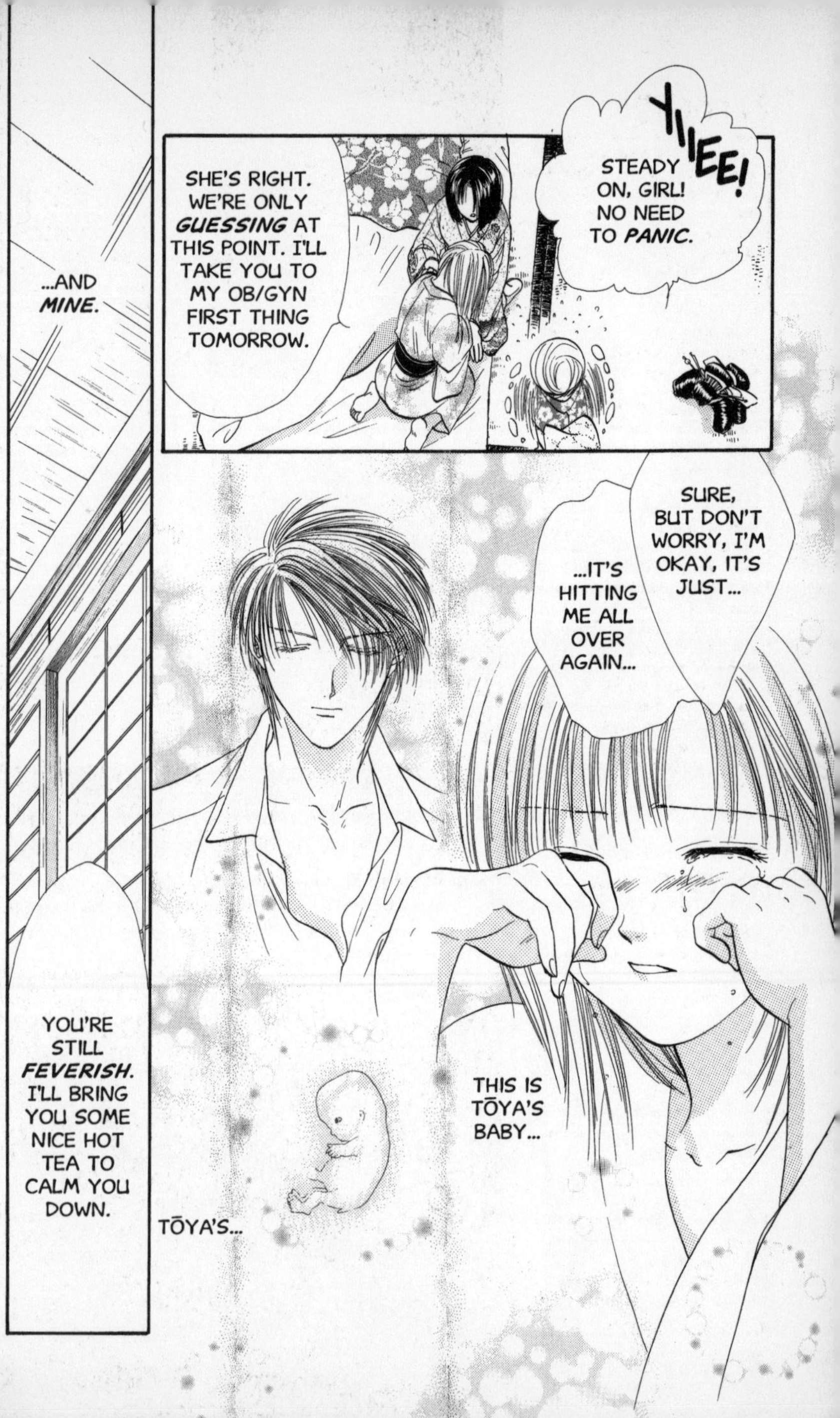
YIIEE!
STEADY ON, GIRL! NO NEED TO PANIC.
SHE'S RIGHT. WE'RE ONLY GUESSING AT THIS POINT. I'LL TAKE YOU TO MY OB/GYN FIRST THING TOMORROW.
SURE, BUT DON'T WORRY, I'M OKAY, IT'S JUST...
...IT'S HITTING ME ALL OVER AGAIN...
THIS IS TŌYA'S BABY...
TŌYA'S...
...AND MINE.
YOU'RE STILL FEVERISH. I'LL BRING YOU SOME NICE HOT TEA TO CALM YOU DOWN.

Ceres: 12

It was around then that I realized, this was **my first time ever** in the ocean!! I hadn't even been to a **pool** in the past 18 years. Of **course**, I'd be nervous! But, I did it. Deeper...bit by bit...my tensed-up muscles slowly loosened, and I could actually pay attention to something other than fear for my own survival, and actually watch some **fish** toward the end. Visibility wasn't very good, because of the bad weather, but it really is a whole different world down there. Since air pockets were inevitable in the "drysuit," I kept drifting upside-down. Even that became fun, once I got used to it. Breathing underwater, though, isn't like breathing above water, so if you get too fascinated by the sights, you forget to breathe. ◡̈ There's also the ear-popping you have to do whenever the pressure builds (which is whenever you go deeper). And **then**, if you can keep all that straight, **then** you can look at the fish...! All of it, every little thing, seemed so intense. ◡̈ We dived to an eventual depth of 10m, and called it a day.

You know, I probably **would** have gotten good at it if I could do it every day for a week. It was almost sad to have to go back up to the surface. I'd love to dive again, in Okinawa or thereabouts, if I could. I hear there's lots of dolphins over by Mikura Island, but if any of them did a swim-over, I'm sure I'd panic. ◡̈ I'd better get more used to diving, first. I love dolphins, by the way. I so want one as a friend. Looking at dolphin pictures, now **that** makes me happy. ◡̈

It really is too bad how human beings can't go anywhere in the air or under the water without heavy, cumbersome apparatus. I like the ocean, but what I really wish is that I could fly. I envy Ceres....

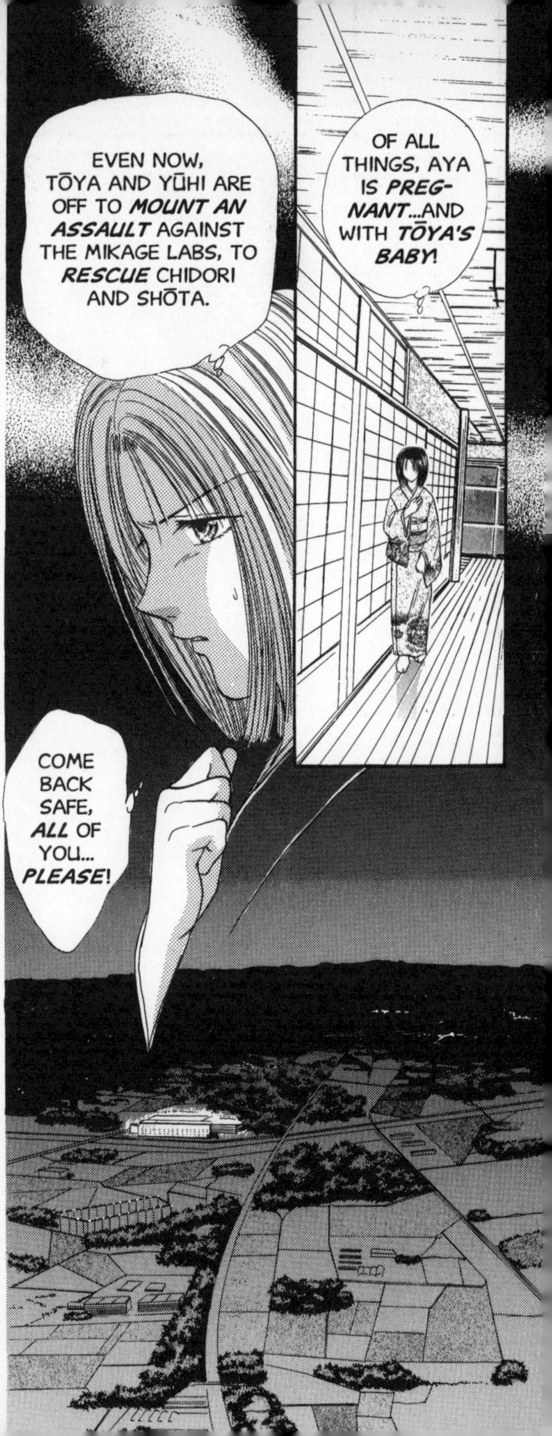
OF ALL THINGS, AYA IS PREGNANT...AND WITH TŌYA'S BABY!
EVEN NOW, TŌYA AND YŪHI ARE OFF TO MOUNT AN ASSAULT AGAINST THE MIKAGE LABS, TO RESCUE CHIDORI AND SHŌTA.
COME BACK SAFE, ALL OF YOU... PLEASE!

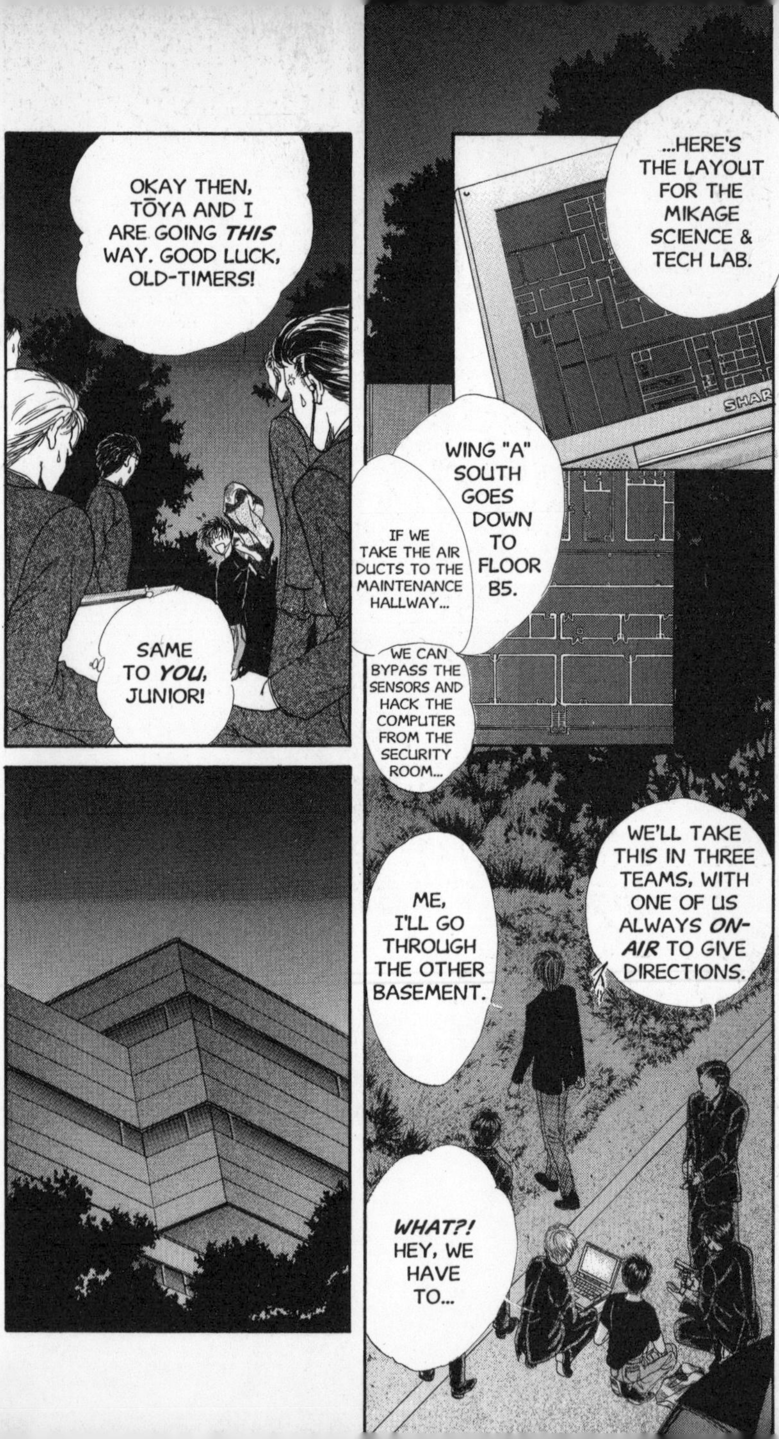
...HERE'S THE LAYOUT FOR THE MIKAGE SCIENCE & TECH LAB.
WING "A" SOUTH GOES DOWN TO FLOOR B5.
IF WE TAKE THE AIR DUCTS TO THE MAINTENANCE HALLWAY...
WE CAN BYPASS THE SENSORS AND HACK THE COMPUTER FROM THE SECURITY ROOM...
WE'LL TAKE THIS IN THREE TEAMS, WITH ONE OF US ALWAYS *ON-AIR* TO GIVE DIRECTIONS.
ME, I'LL GO THROUGH THE OTHER BASEMENT.
WHAT?! HEY, WE HAVE TO...
OKAY THEN, TŌYA AND I ARE GOING *THIS* WAY. GOOD LUCK, OLD-TIMERS!
SAME TO *YOU*, JUNIOR!

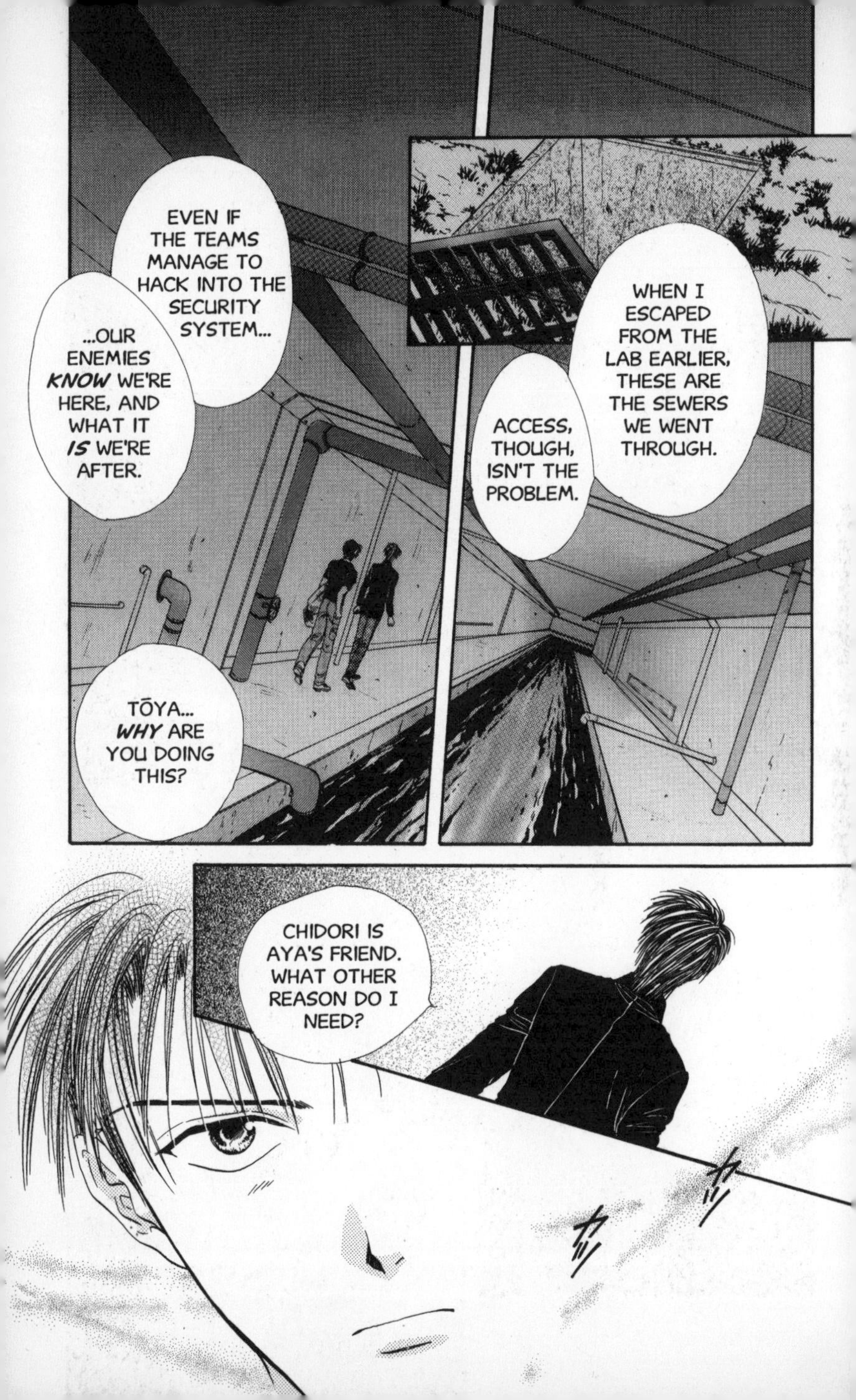
WHEN I ESCAPED FROM THE LAB EARLIER, THESE ARE THE SEWERS WE WENT THROUGH.
ACCESS, THOUGH, ISN'T THE PROBLEM.
EVEN IF THE TEAMS MANAGE TO HACK INTO THE SECURITY SYSTEM...
...OUR ENEMIES *KNOW* WE'RE HERE, AND WHAT IT *IS* WE'RE AFTER.
TŌYA... *WHY* ARE YOU DOING THIS?
CHIDORI IS AYA'S FRIEND. WHAT OTHER REASON DO I NEED?

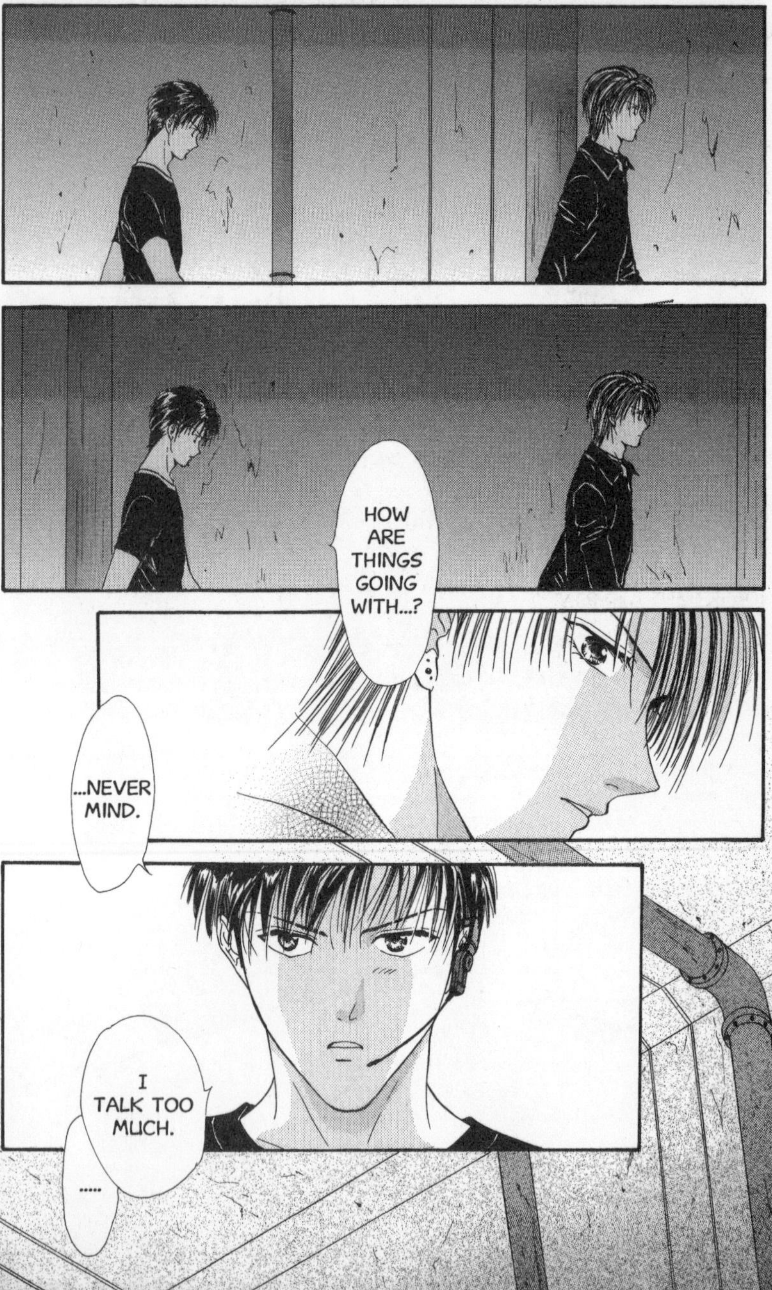
HOW ARE THINGS GOING WITH...?
...NEVER MIND.
I TALK TOO MUCH.
.....

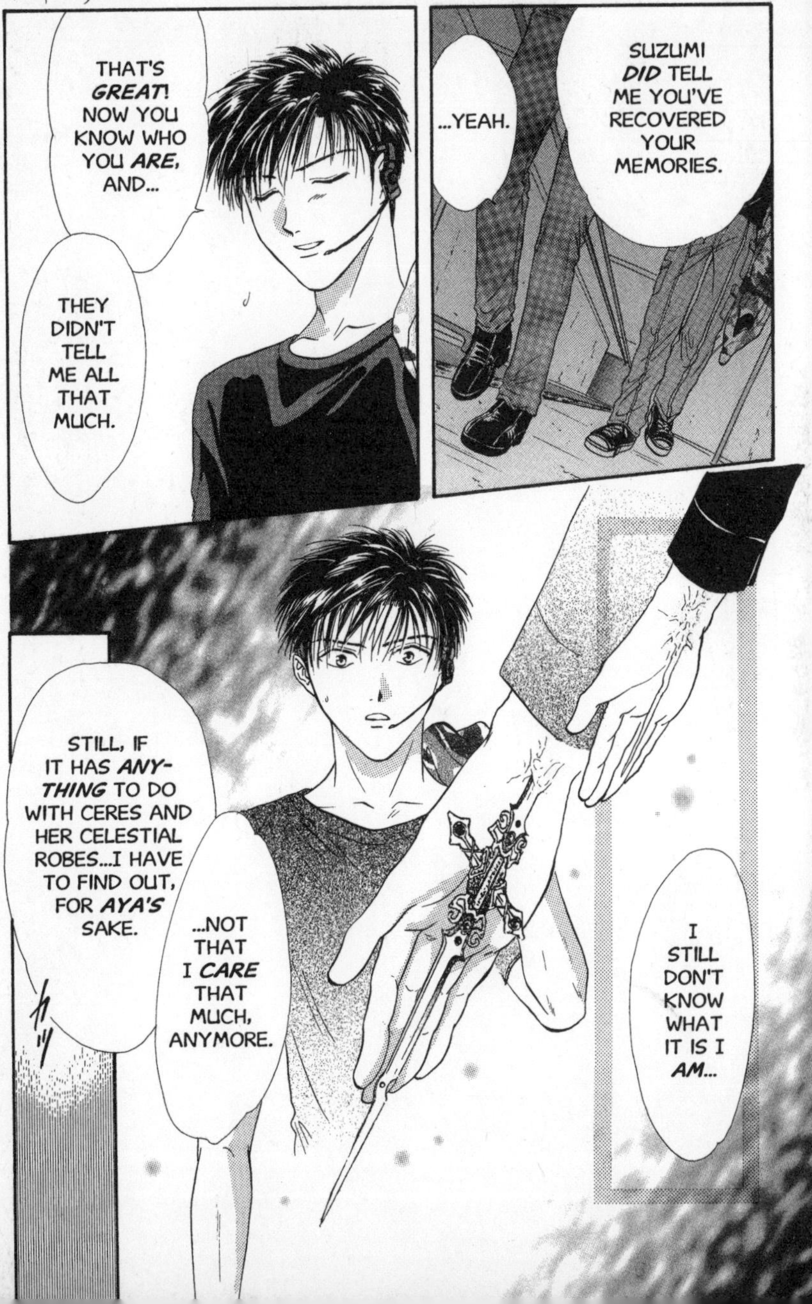
SUZUMI *DID* TELL ME YOU'VE RECOVERED YOUR MEMORIES.
...YEAH.
THAT'S *GREAT*! NOW YOU KNOW WHO YOU *ARE*, AND...
THEY DIDN'T TELL ME ALL THAT MUCH.
STILL, IF IT HAS *ANYTHING* TO DO WITH CERES AND HER CELESTIAL ROBES...I HAVE TO FIND OUT, FOR *AYA'S* SAKE.
...NOT THAT I *CARE* THAT MUCH, ANYMORE.
I STILL DON'T KNOW WHAT IT IS I *AM*...
カッ

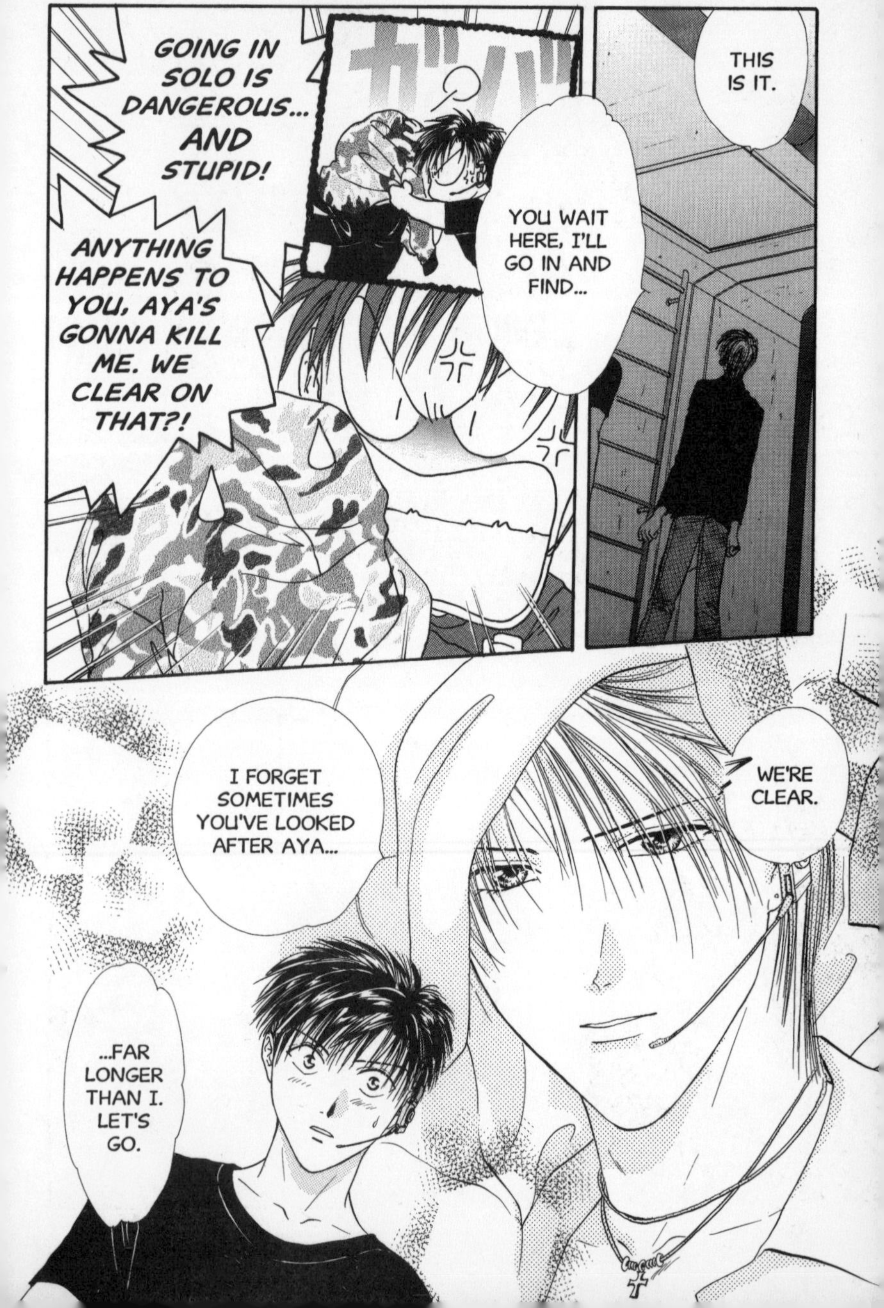
THIS IS IT.
YOU WAIT HERE, I'LL GO IN AND FIND...
GOING IN SOLO IS DANGEROUS... AND STUPID!
ANYTHING HAPPENS TO YOU, AYA'S GONNA KILL ME. WE CLEAR ON THAT?!
WE'RE CLEAR.
I FORGET SOMETIMES YOU'VE LOOKED AFTER AYA...
...FAR LONGER THAN I. LET'S GO.

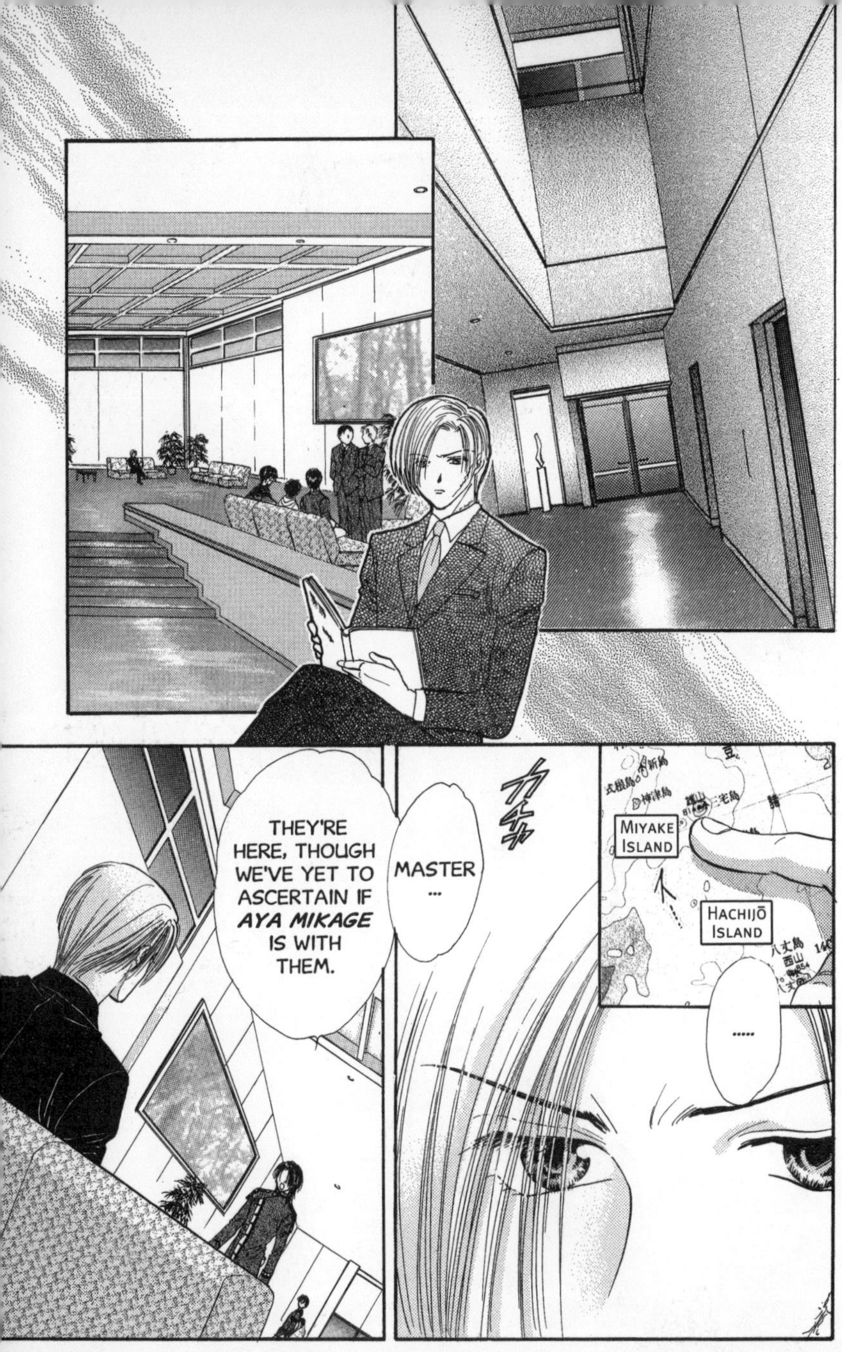

MIYAKE ISLAND
HACHIJŌ ISLAND
カチャ
MASTER ...
.....
THEY'RE HERE, THOUGH WE'VE YET TO ASCERTAIN IF ***AYA MIKAGE*** IS WITH THEM.

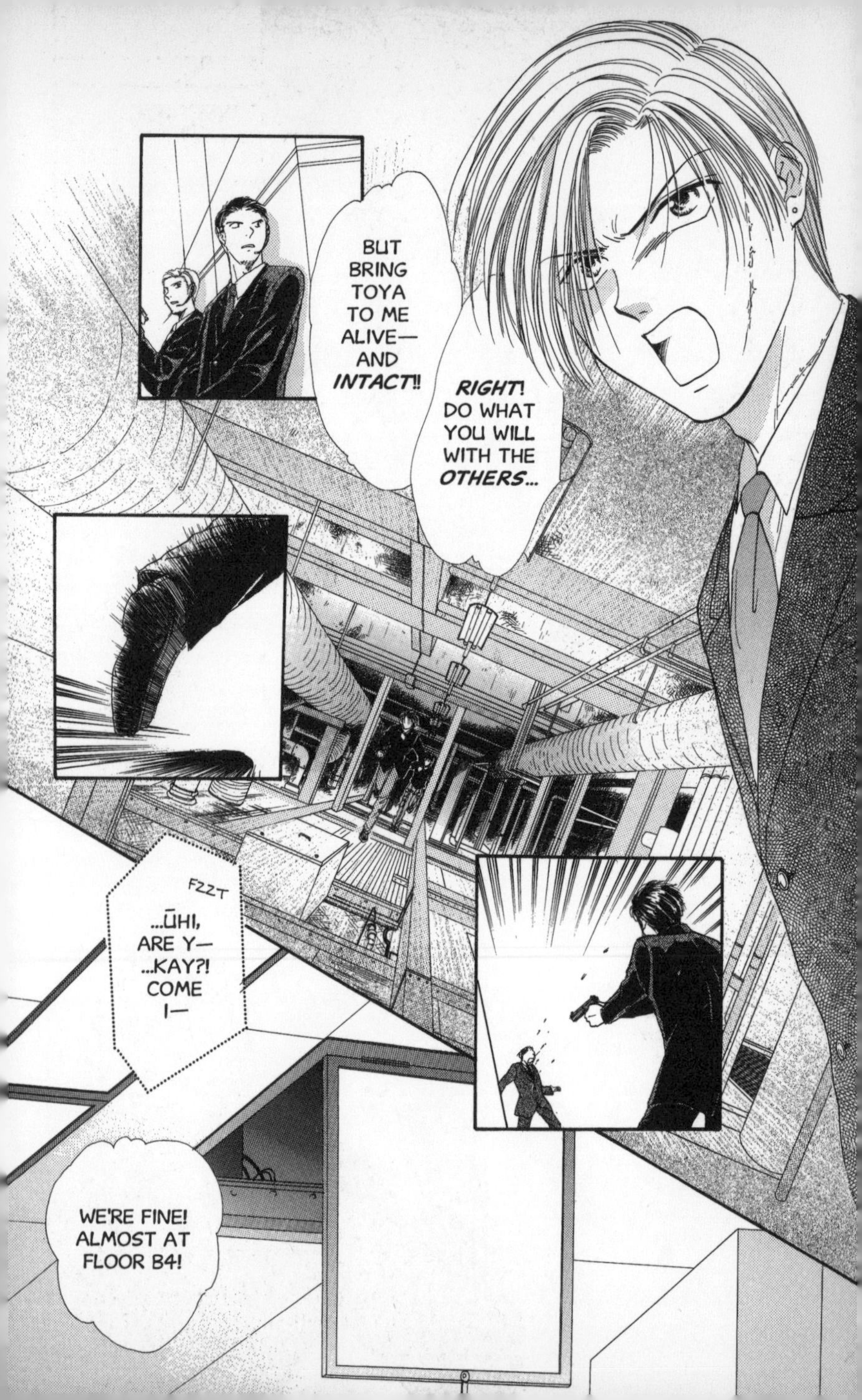
RIGHT! DO WHAT YOU WILL WITH THE OTHERS...
BUT BRING TOYA TO ME ALIVE—AND INTACT!!
FZZT
...ŪHI, ARE Y— ...KAY?! COME I—
WE'RE FINE! ALMOST AT FLOOR B4!

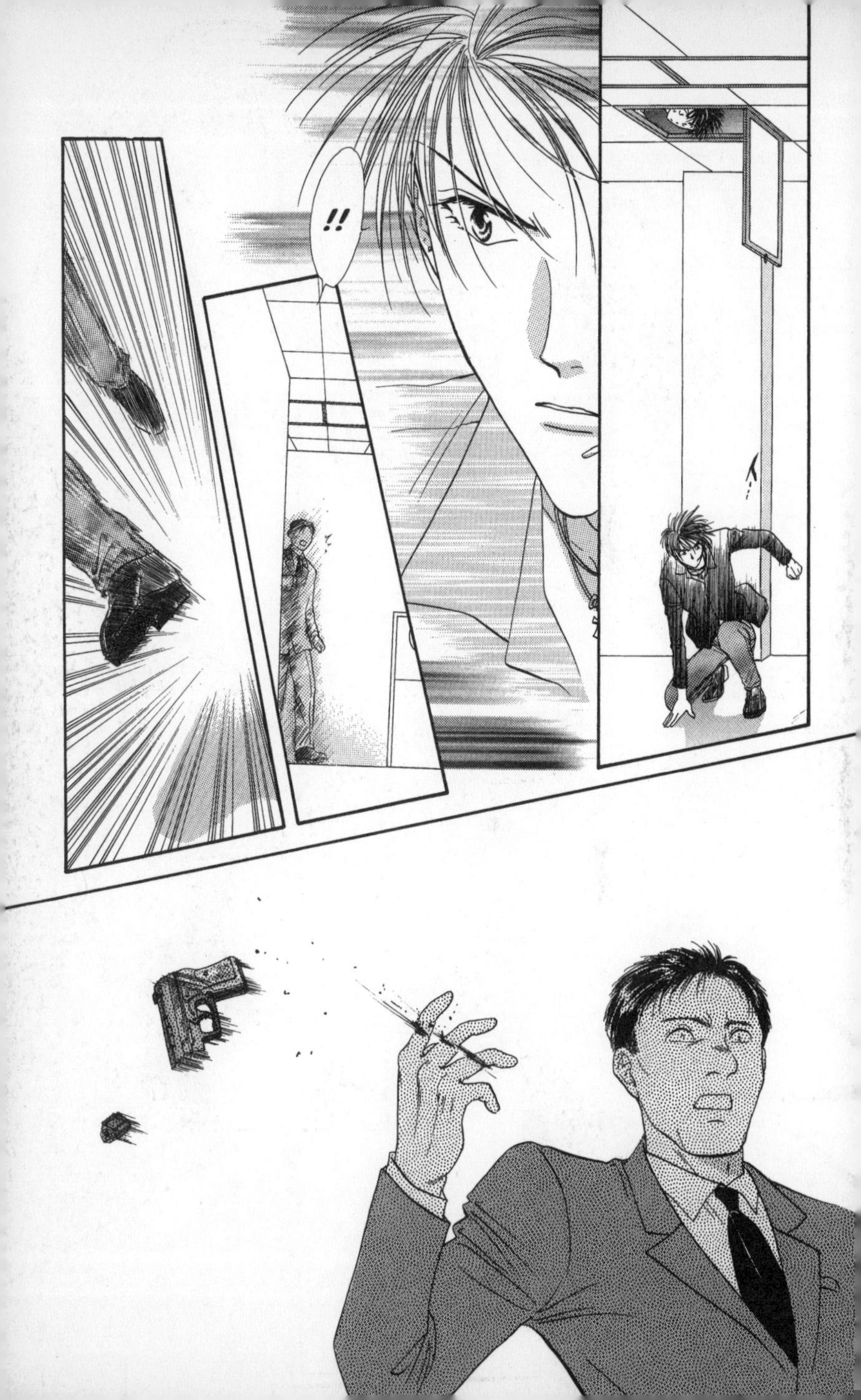
!!

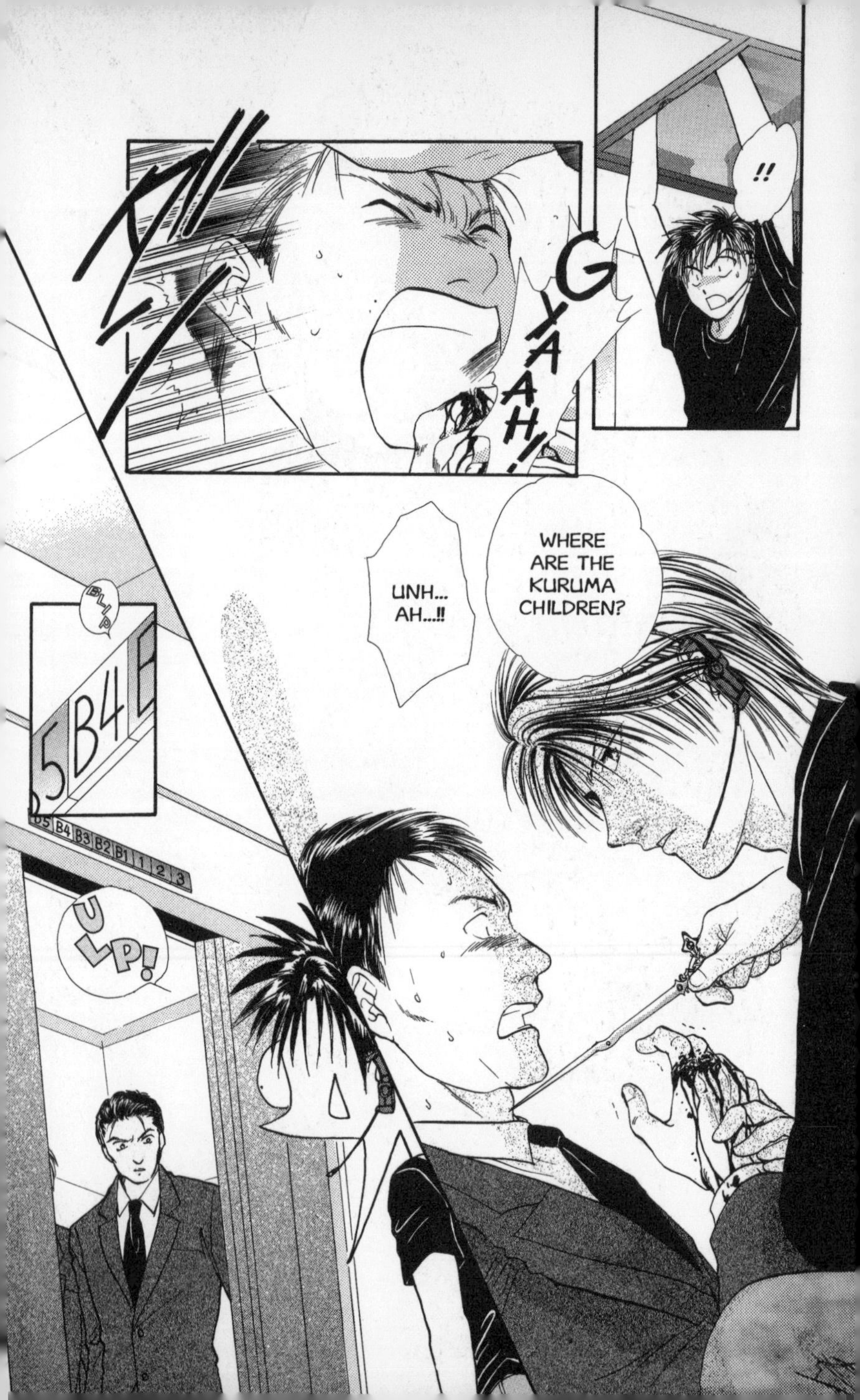
!!
GYAAAH!!
WHERE ARE THE KURUMA CHILDREN?
UNH... AH...!!
BLIP
B5 B4 B3 B2 B1 1 2 3
ULP!

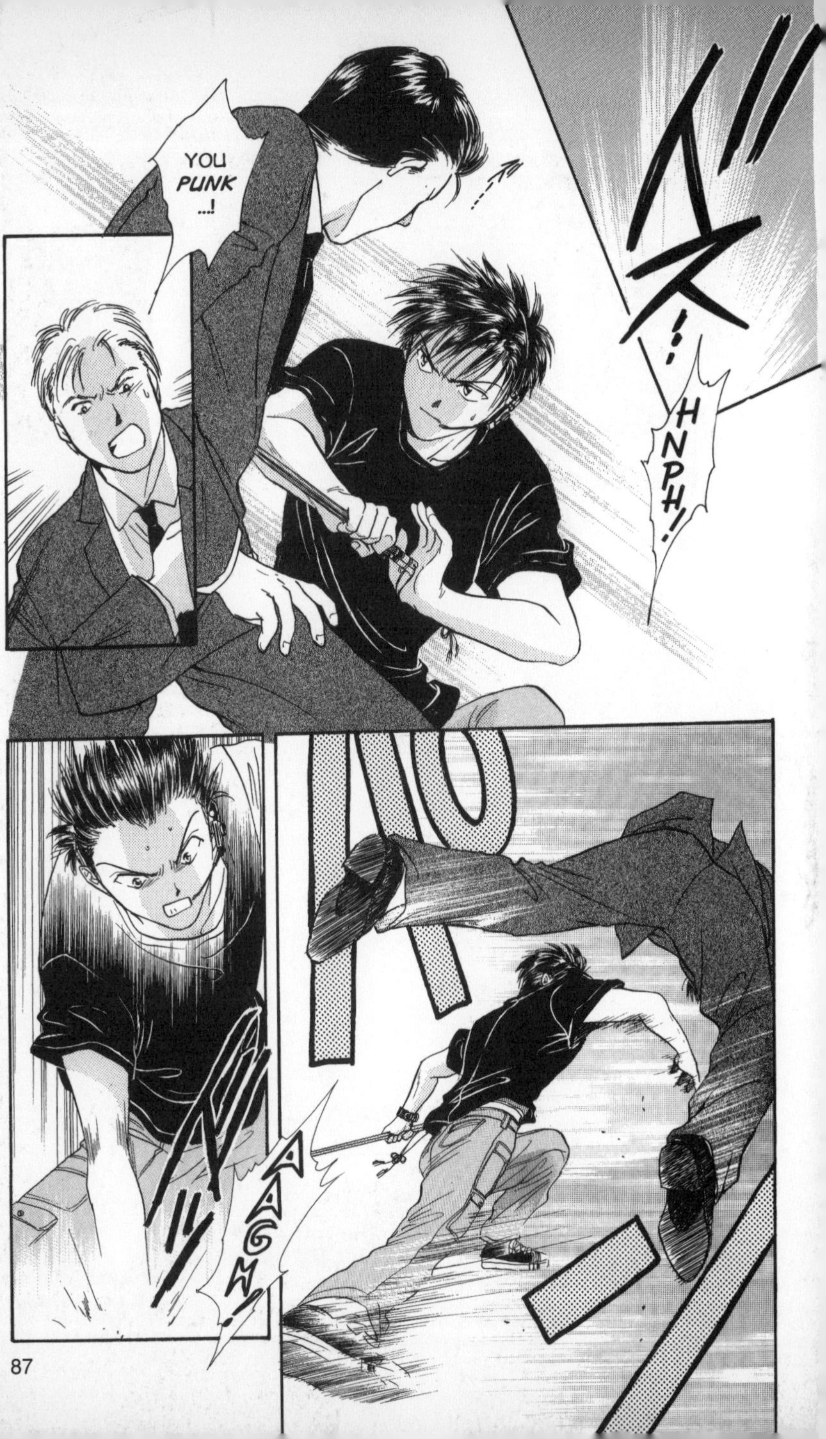
HNPH!
YOU PUNK ...!
AAGH!

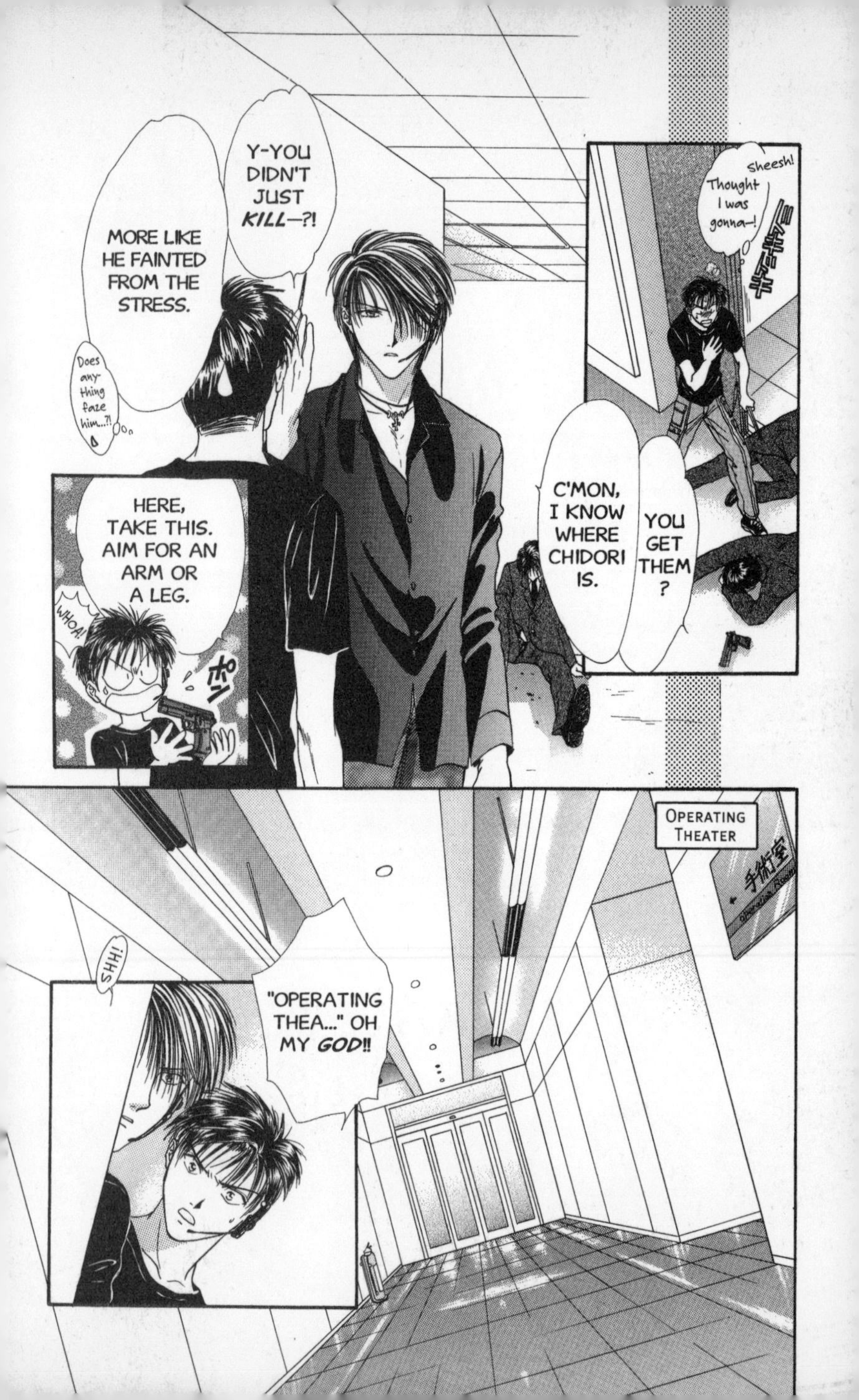
Sheesh! Thought I was gonna—!
YOU GET THEM?
C'MON, I KNOW WHERE CHIDORI IS.
Y-YOU DIDN'T JUST *KILL*—?!
MORE LIKE HE FAINTED FROM THE STRESS.
Does any-thing faze him...?!
HERE, TAKE THIS. AIM FOR AN ARM OR A LEG.
ポン
WHOA!
OPERATING THEATER
手術室
"OPERATING THEA..." OH MY *GOD*!!
SHH!

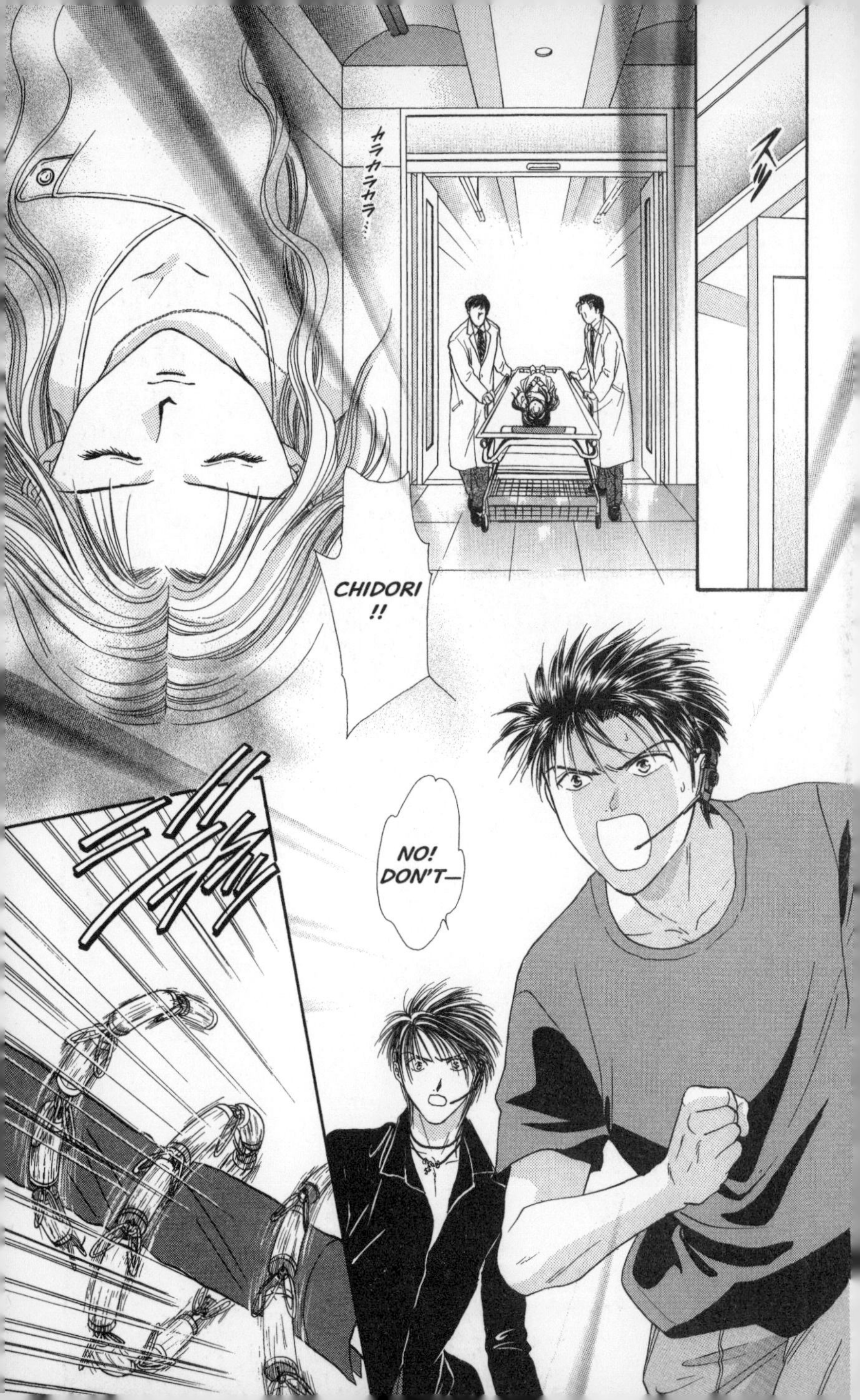
スッ
カラカラカラ…
CHIDORI !!
NO! DON'T—

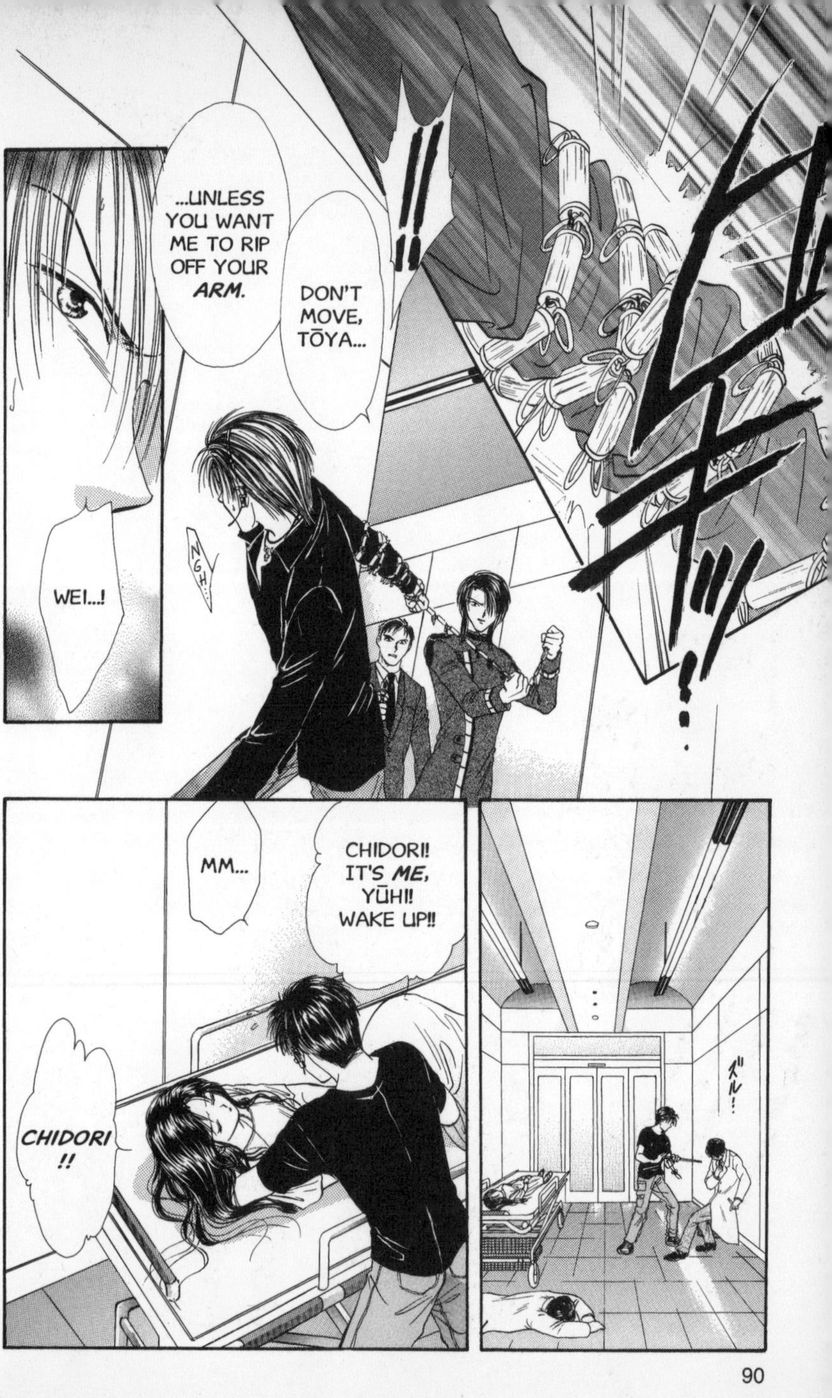
!!
DON'T MOVE, TŌYA...
...UNLESS YOU WANT ME TO RIP OFF YOUR *ARM*.
NGH...
WEI...!
...
ズル!
CHIDORI! IT'S *ME*, YŪHI! WAKE UP!!
MM...
CHIDORI !!

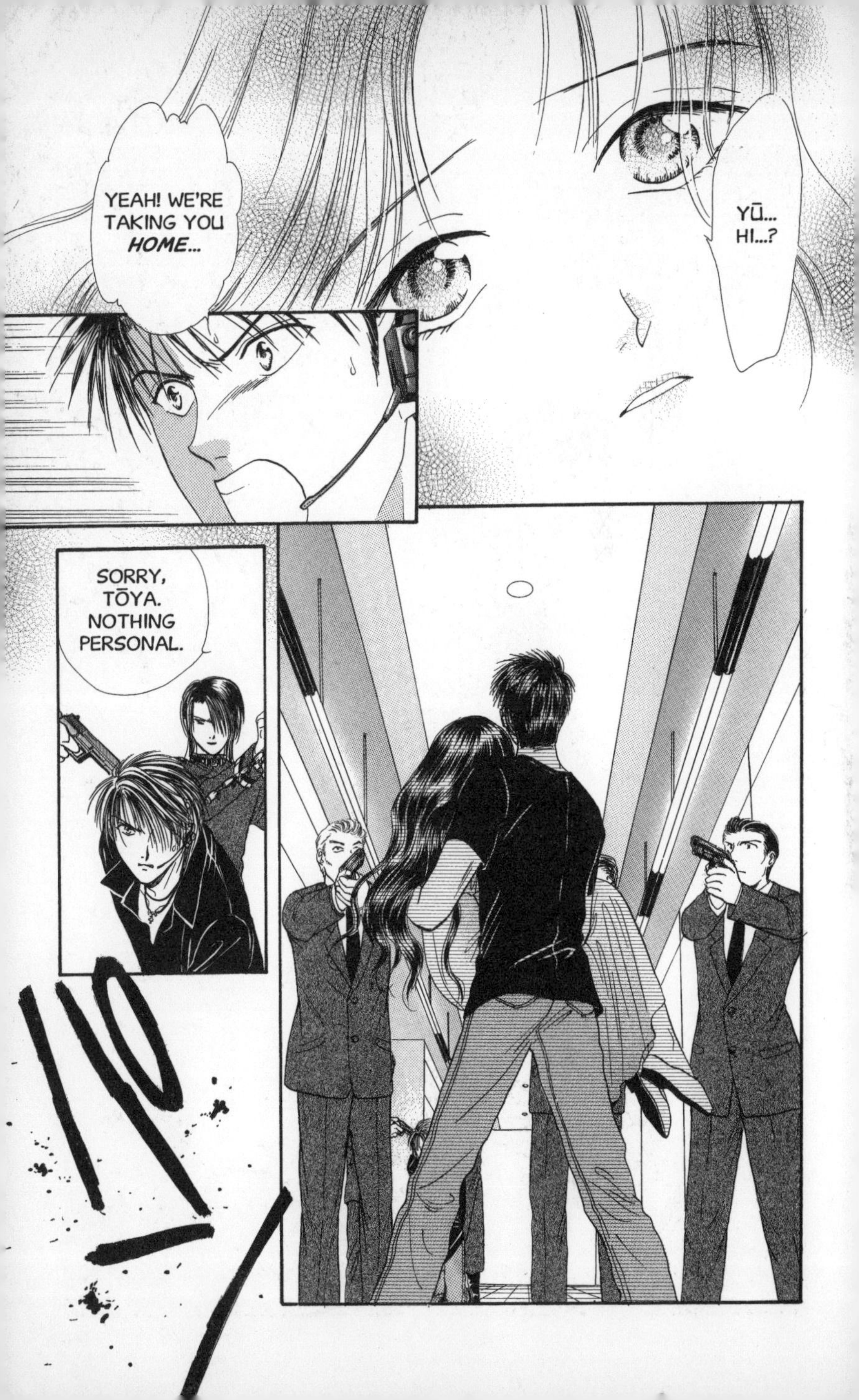
YŪ... HI...?
YEAH! WE'RE TAKING YOU *HOME*...
SORRY, TŌYA. NOTHING PERSONAL.

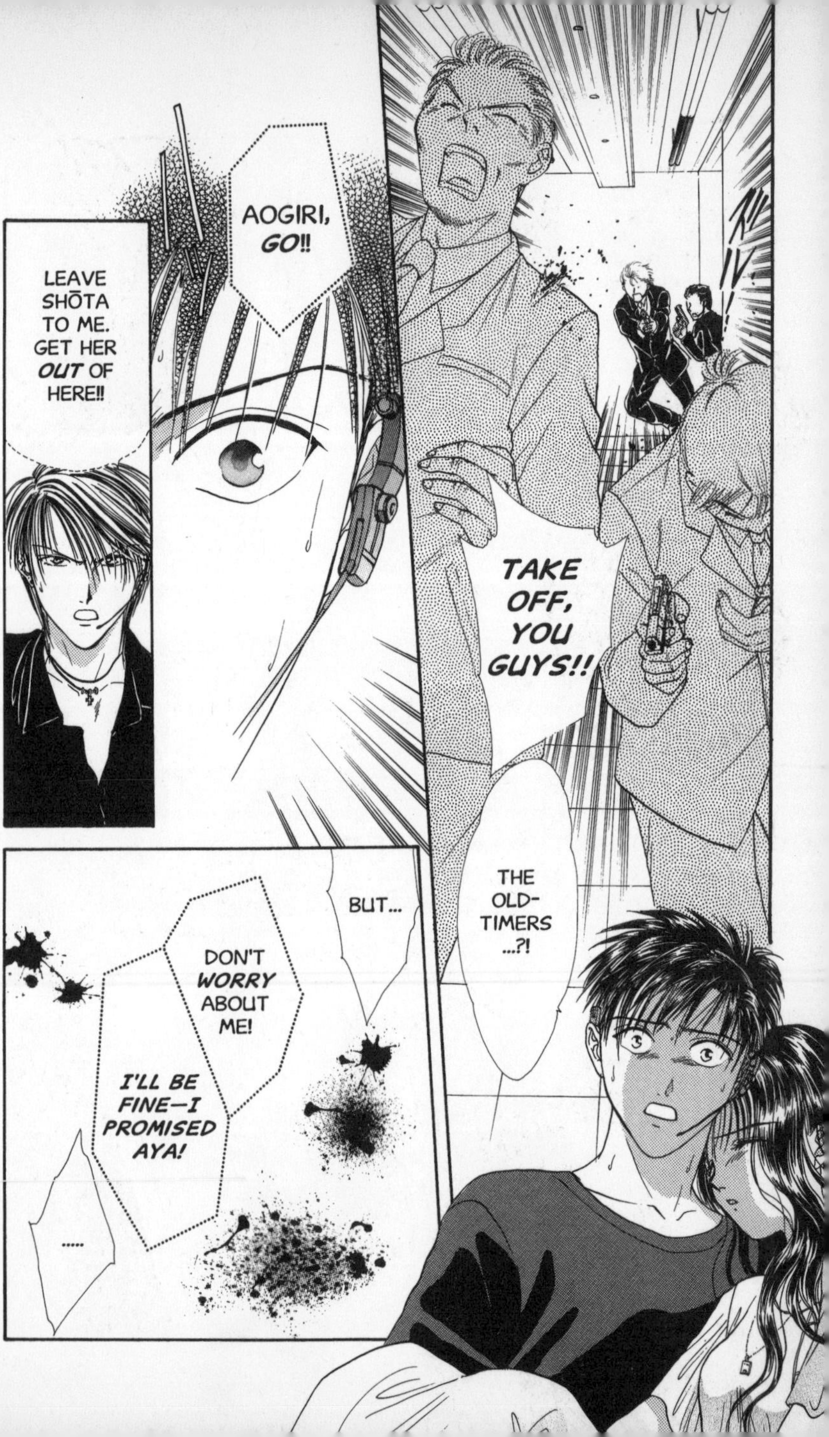
TAKE OFF, YOU GUYS!!
THE OLD-TIMERS ...?!
AOGIRI, GO!!
LEAVE SHŌTA TO ME. GET HER OUT OF HERE!!
BUT...
DON'T WORRY ABOUT ME!
I'LL BE FINE—I PROMISED AYA!
....

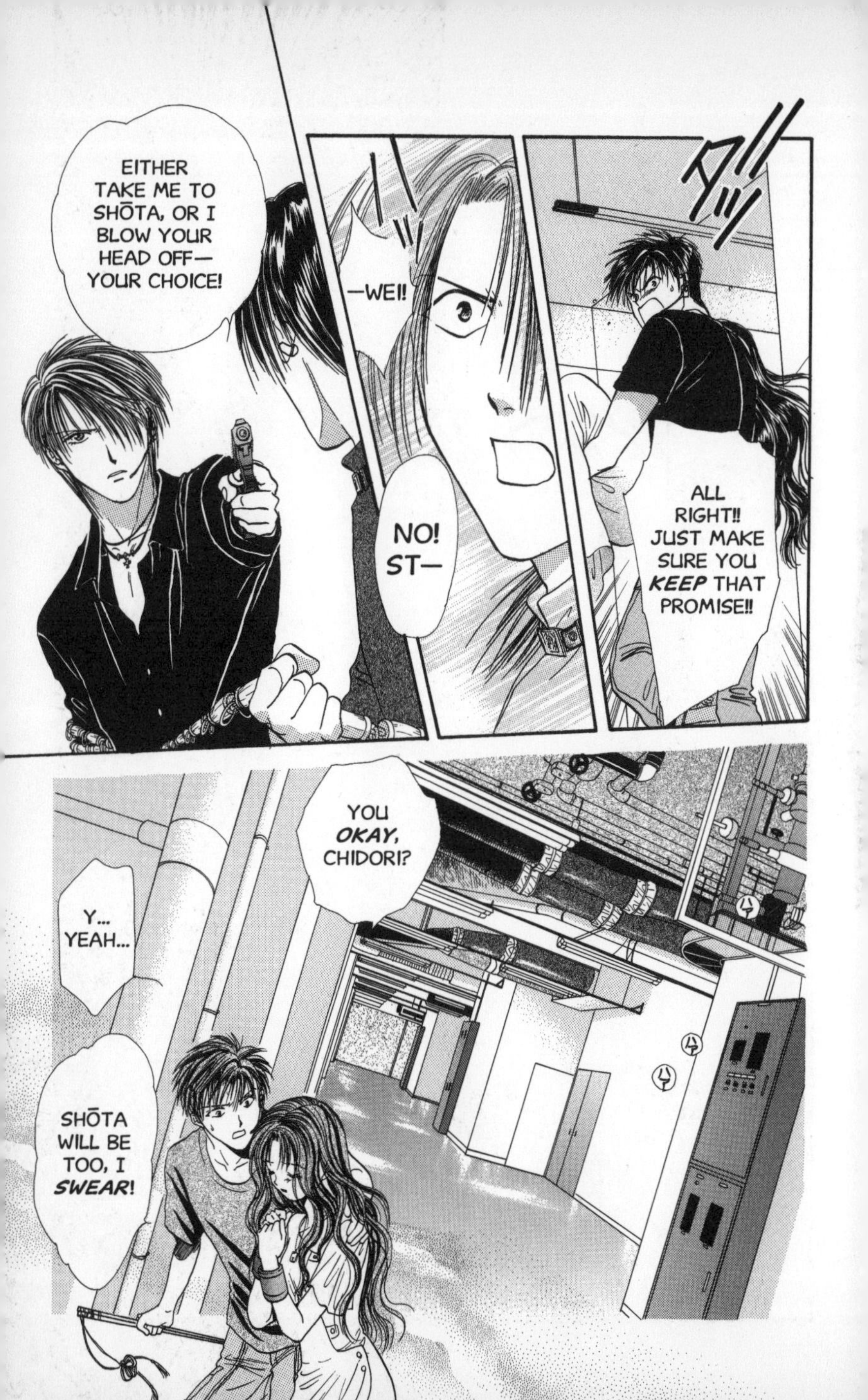
ダッ
ALL RIGHT!! JUST MAKE SURE YOU *KEEP* THAT PROMISE!!
—WEI!!
NO! ST—
EITHER TAKE ME TO SHŌTA, OR I BLOW YOUR HEAD OFF— YOUR CHOICE!
YOU *OKAY,* CHIDORI?
Y... YEAH...
SHŌTA WILL BE TOO, I *SWEAR*!

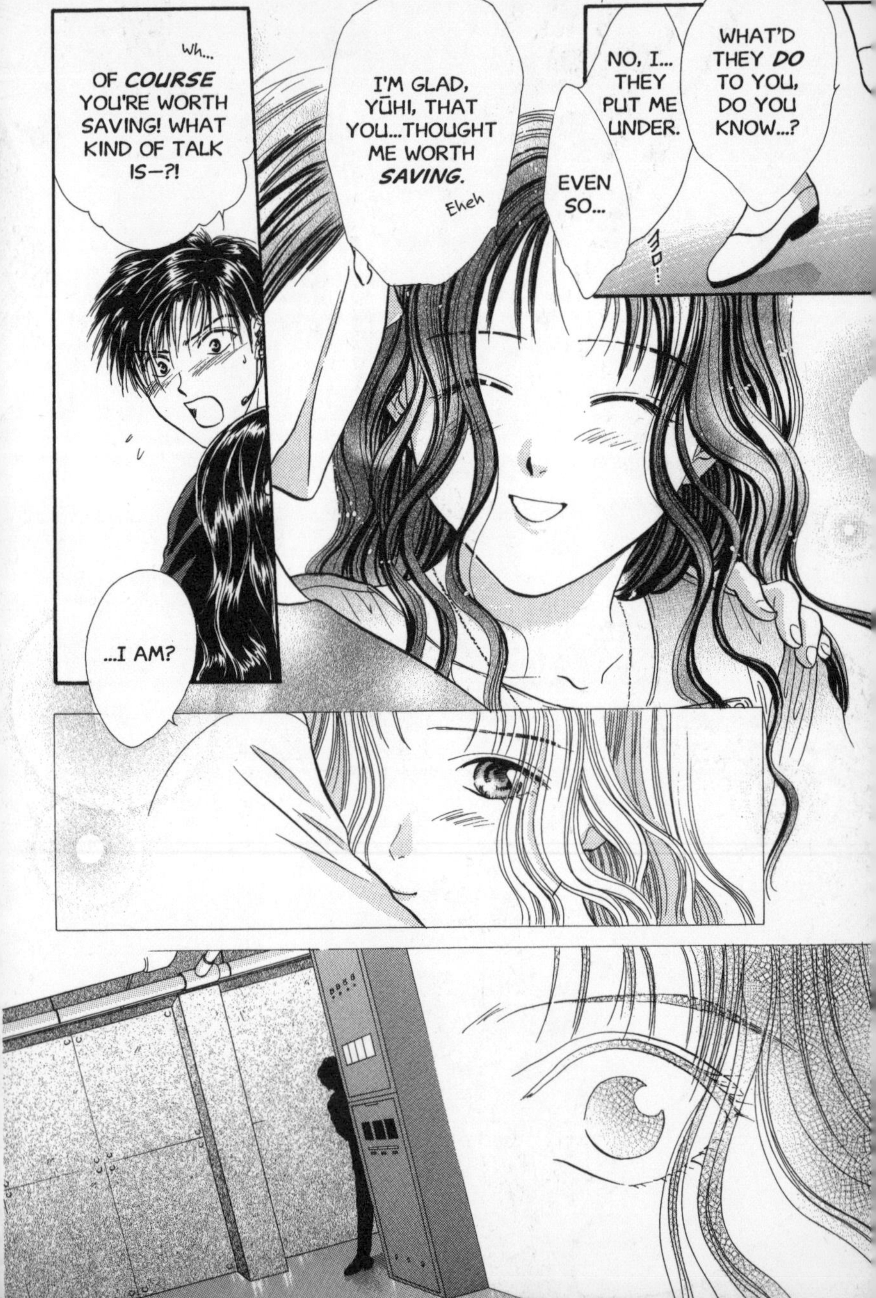

WHAT'D THEY DO TO YOU, DO YOU KNOW...?
NO, I... THEY PUT ME UNDER.
EVEN SO...
I'M GLAD, YŪHI, THAT YOU...THOUGHT ME WORTH SAVING.
Eheh
Wh...
OF COURSE YOU'RE WORTH SAVING! WHAT KIND OF TALK IS—?!
...I AM?

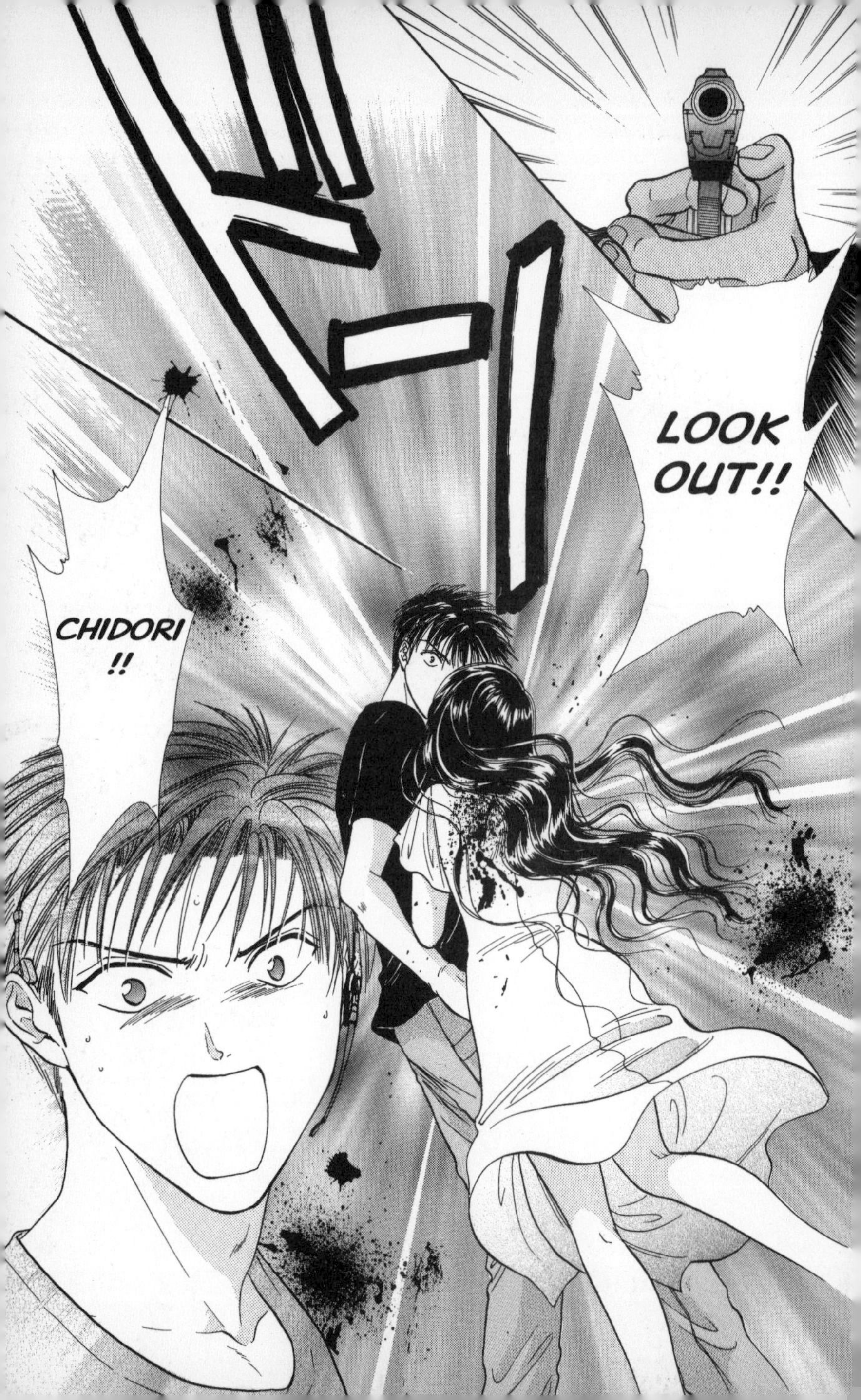
LOOK OUT!!
CHIDORI !!

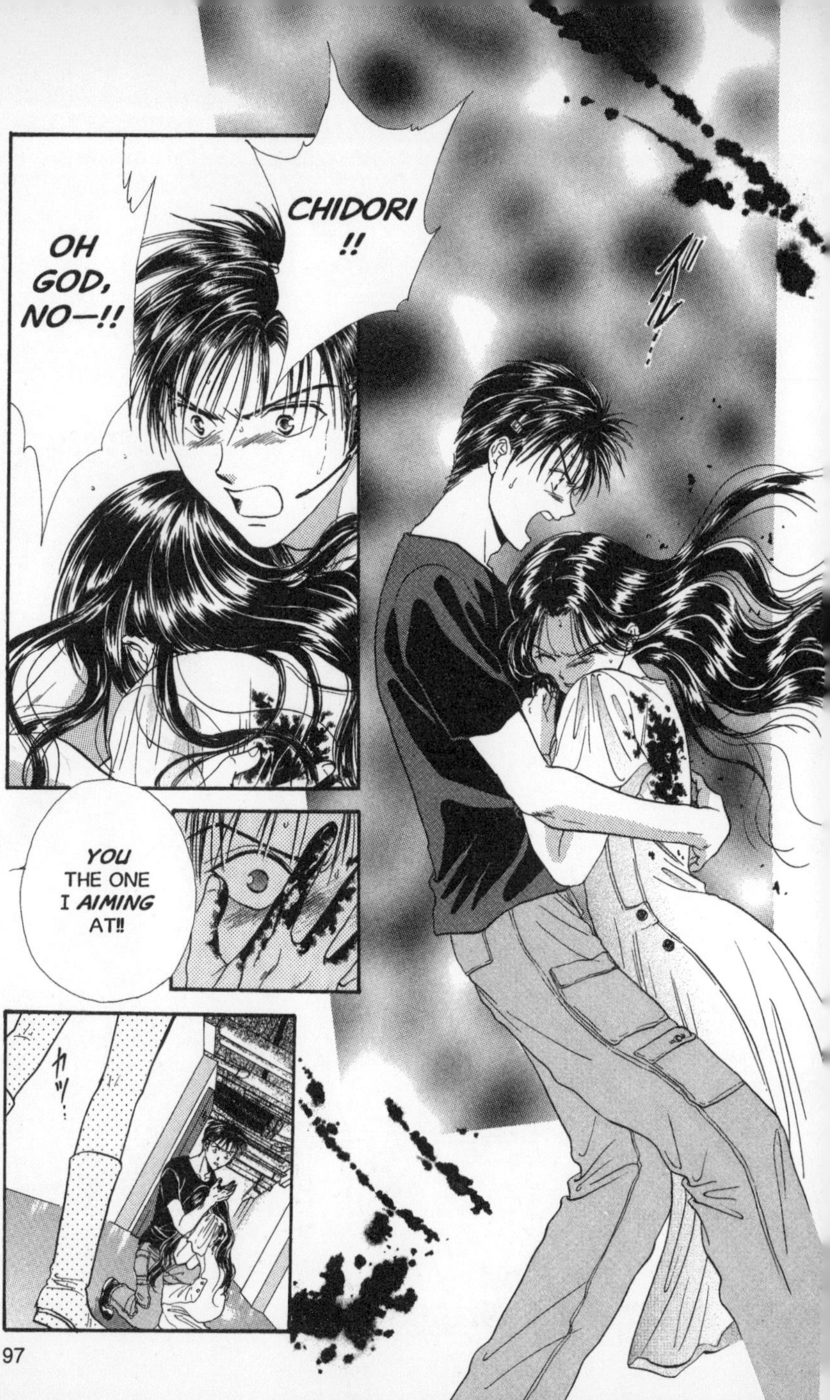

CHIDORI!!
OH GOD, NO—!!
YOU THE ONE I AIMING AT!!
カッ…

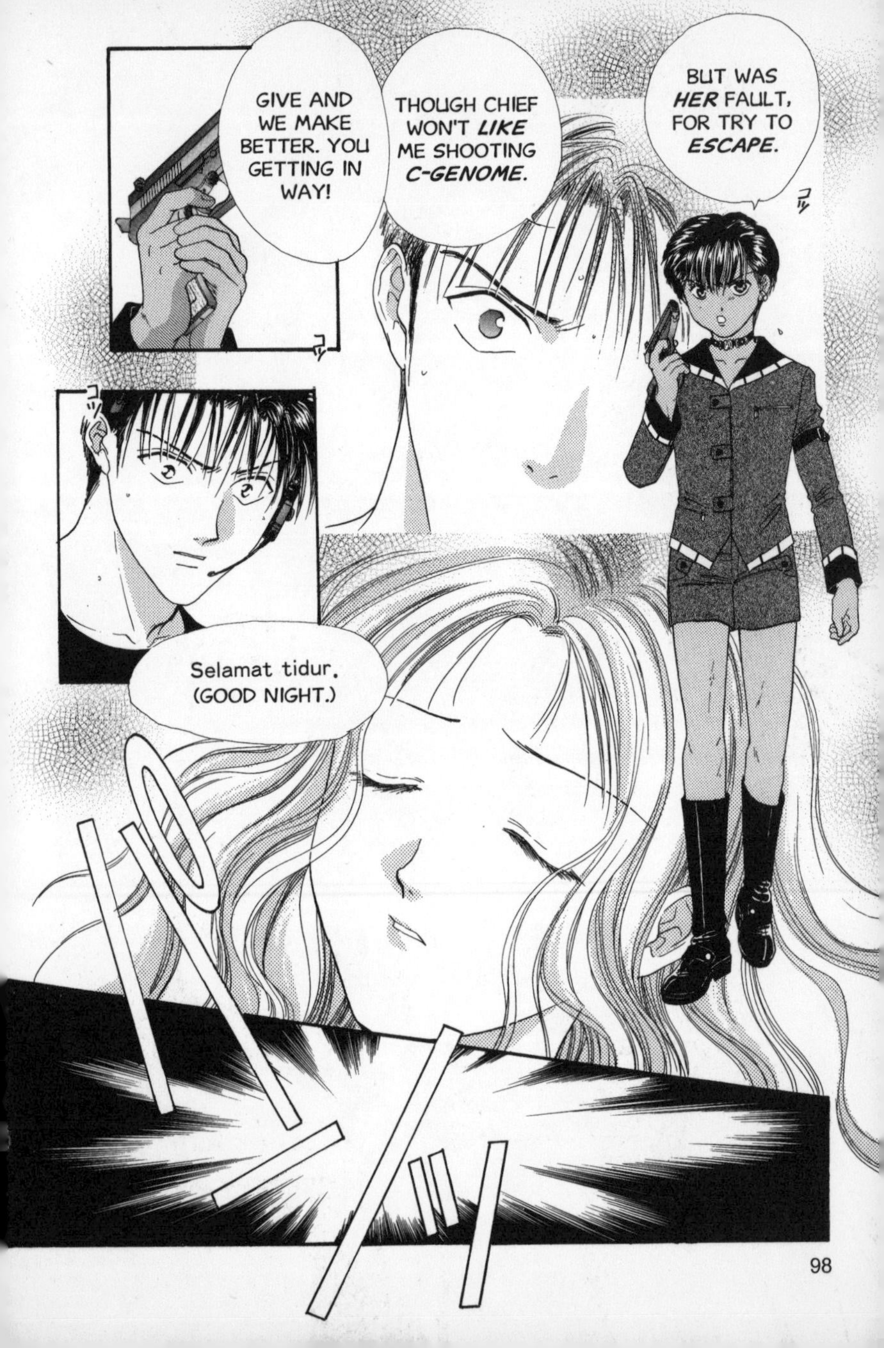
BUT WAS *HER* FAULT, FOR TRY TO *ESCAPE*.
THOUGH CHIEF WON'T *LIKE* ME SHOOTING *C-GENOME*.
GIVE AND WE MAKE BETTER. YOU GETTING IN WAY!
Selamat tidur. (GOOD NIGHT.)

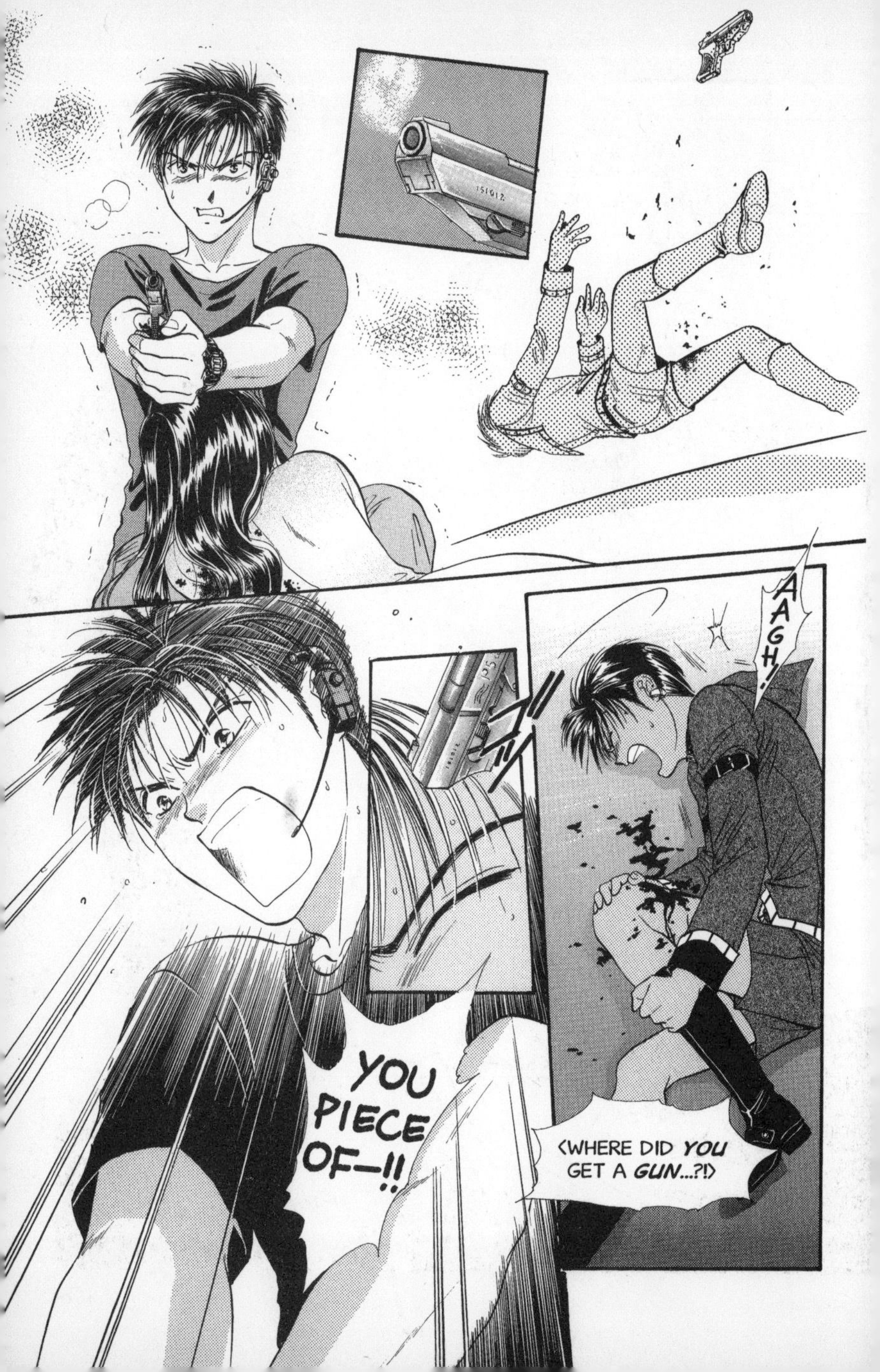
AAGH!!
<WHERE DID YOU GET A GUN...?!>
YOU PIECE OF—!!

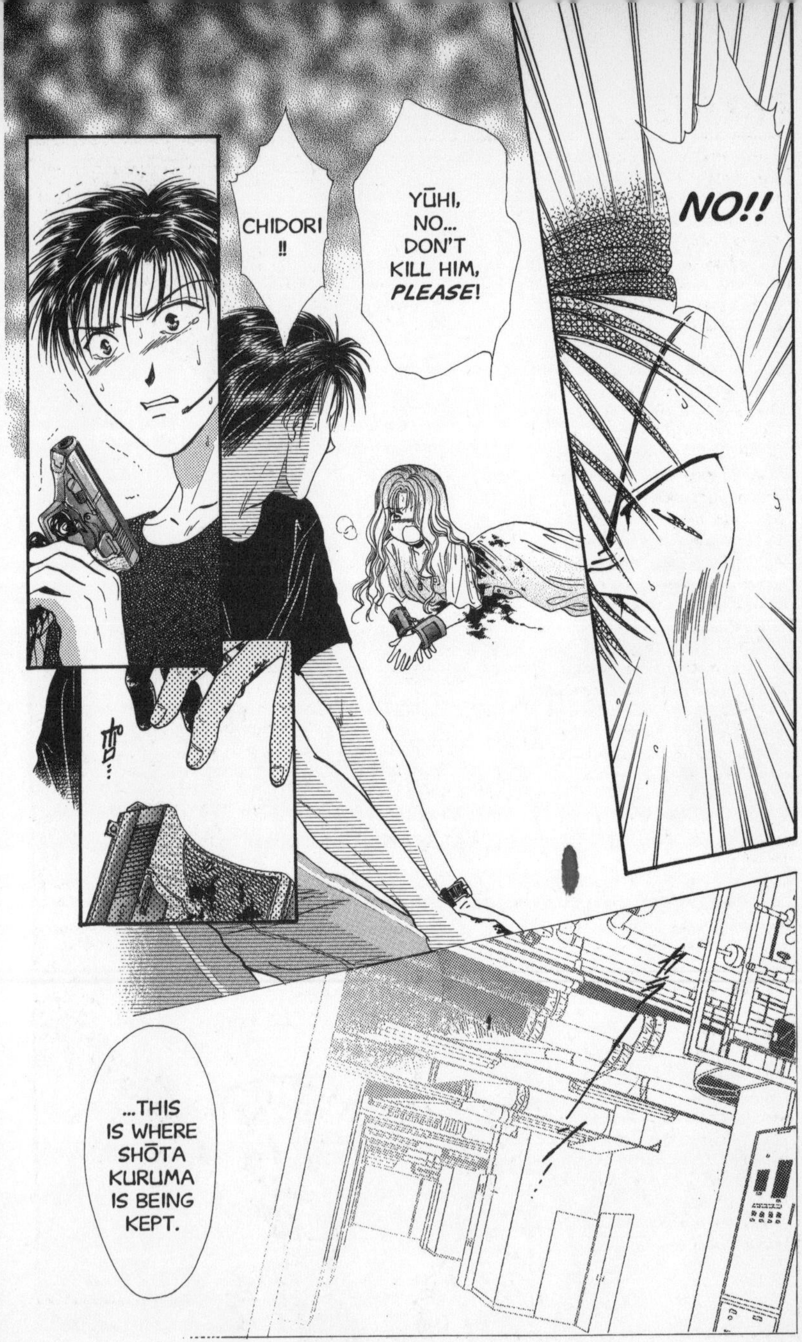
NO!!
YŪHI, NO... DON'T KILL HIM, PLEASE!
CHIDORI !!
...THIS IS WHERE SHŌTA KURUMA IS BEING KEPT.

Ceres: 12

I had another autograph session this summer of '99...back in Osaka! I hadn't had one at home in a while. Thanks for coming, everyone. You were all so **fashionable**, too! (Though this **is** Osaka we're talking about.) I kept noticing people wearing chokers—lots of them had cross-shaped charms on them, too, so while I was autographing, I asked one of the girls about it. As I'd guessed, she'd deliberately picked one similar to what Aya had given Toya. Thanks again to everyone who brought flowers, letters, and presents!

There **were** a few "stand-ins" (family and friends) of people who couldn't attend themselves, due to school activities and stuff—nice of them, huh? For those of you who couldn't make it, for whatever reason, we'll have other chances to meet. /// Not that I wasn't just as excited to meet those of you who **did** come in person!

In any event, it was **hot**. It's usually very humid in Osaka anyway, but this year, it felt **especially** hot. But then, Tokyo isn't getting any break from the heat, either. I thought I was about to give in...but I was still happy to meet everyone in Osaka. There were lots of people with cute names....

Some seemed to have been under the impression that I was a guy ∴. Sorry—I'm a woman. Maybe it's because of the pseudonym (or the series' content?). ...I'd wanted to make use of my native Osaka accent in my initial greeting, but then I got stage-fright and forgot. Darn! It was supposed to be my chance to make a connection with my fellow Osakans! Next time for sure....

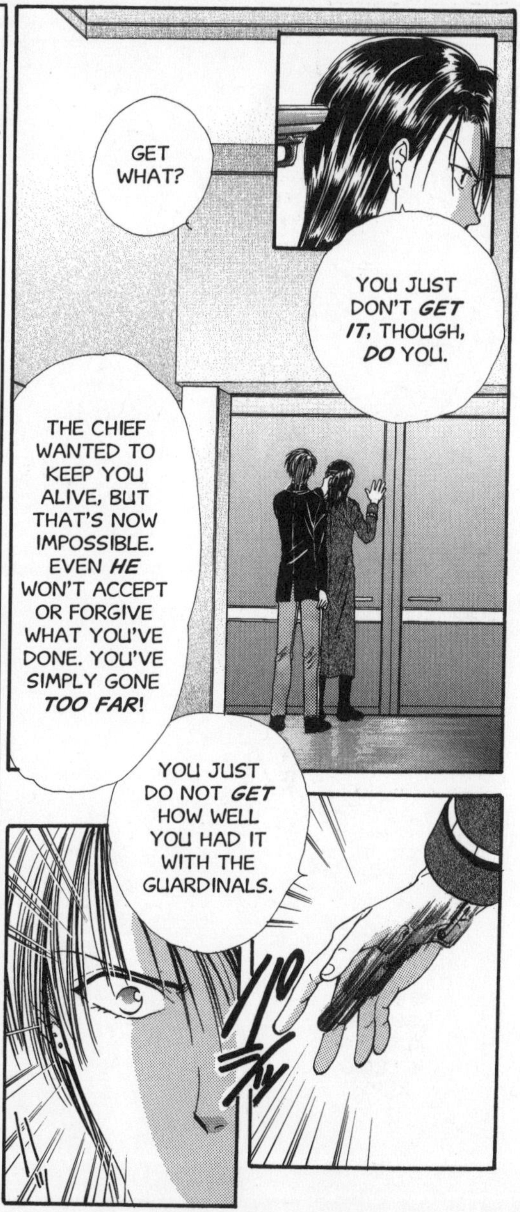
GET WHAT?
YOU JUST DON'T *GET IT*, THOUGH, *DO* YOU.
THE CHIEF WANTED TO KEEP YOU ALIVE, BUT THAT'S NOW IMPOSSIBLE. EVEN *HE* WON'T ACCEPT OR FORGIVE WHAT YOU'VE DONE. YOU'VE SIMPLY GONE *TOO FAR*!
YOU JUST DO NOT *GET* HOW WELL YOU HAD IT WITH THE GUARDINALS.

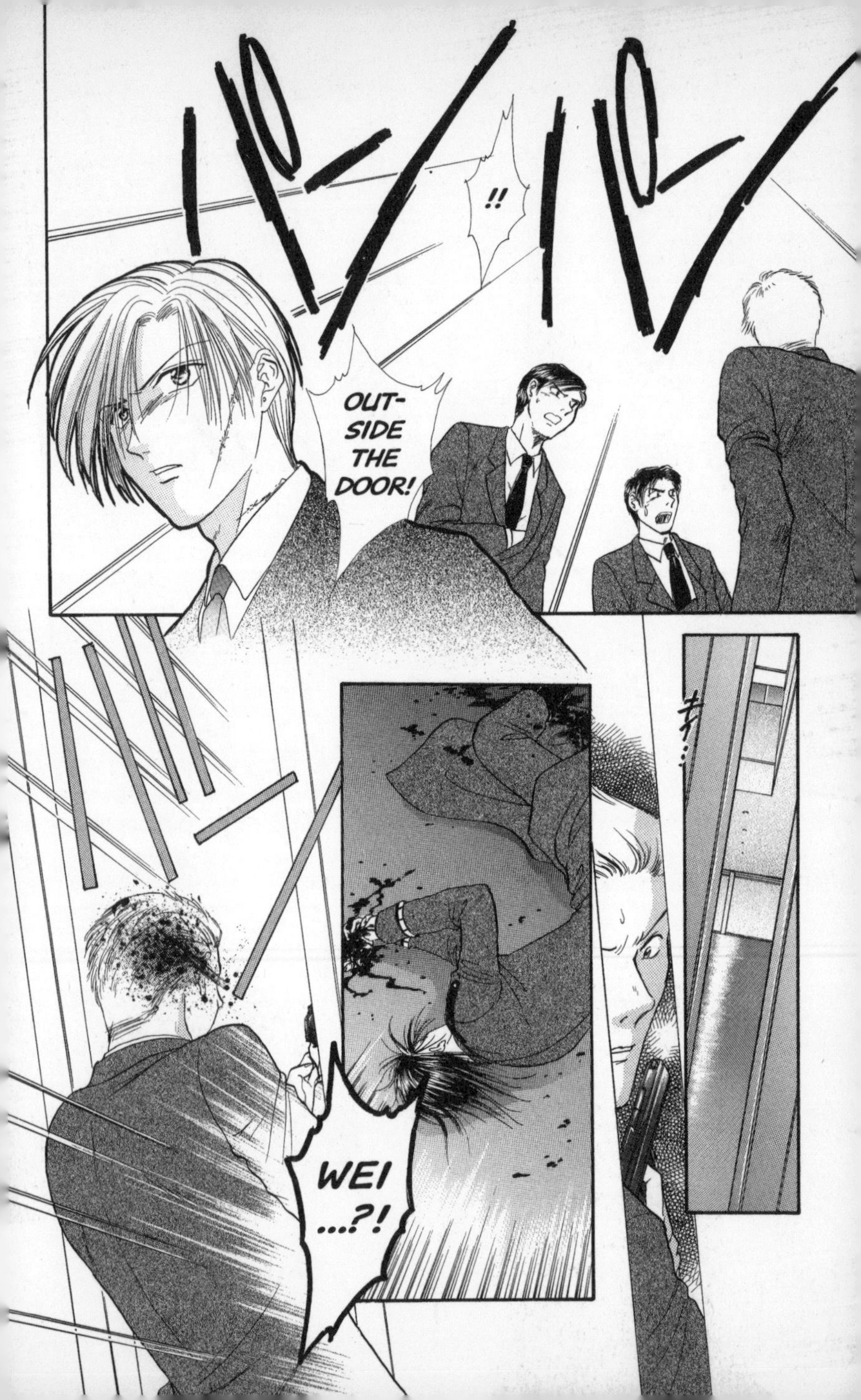
!!
OUT-SIDE THE DOOR!
WEI ...?!

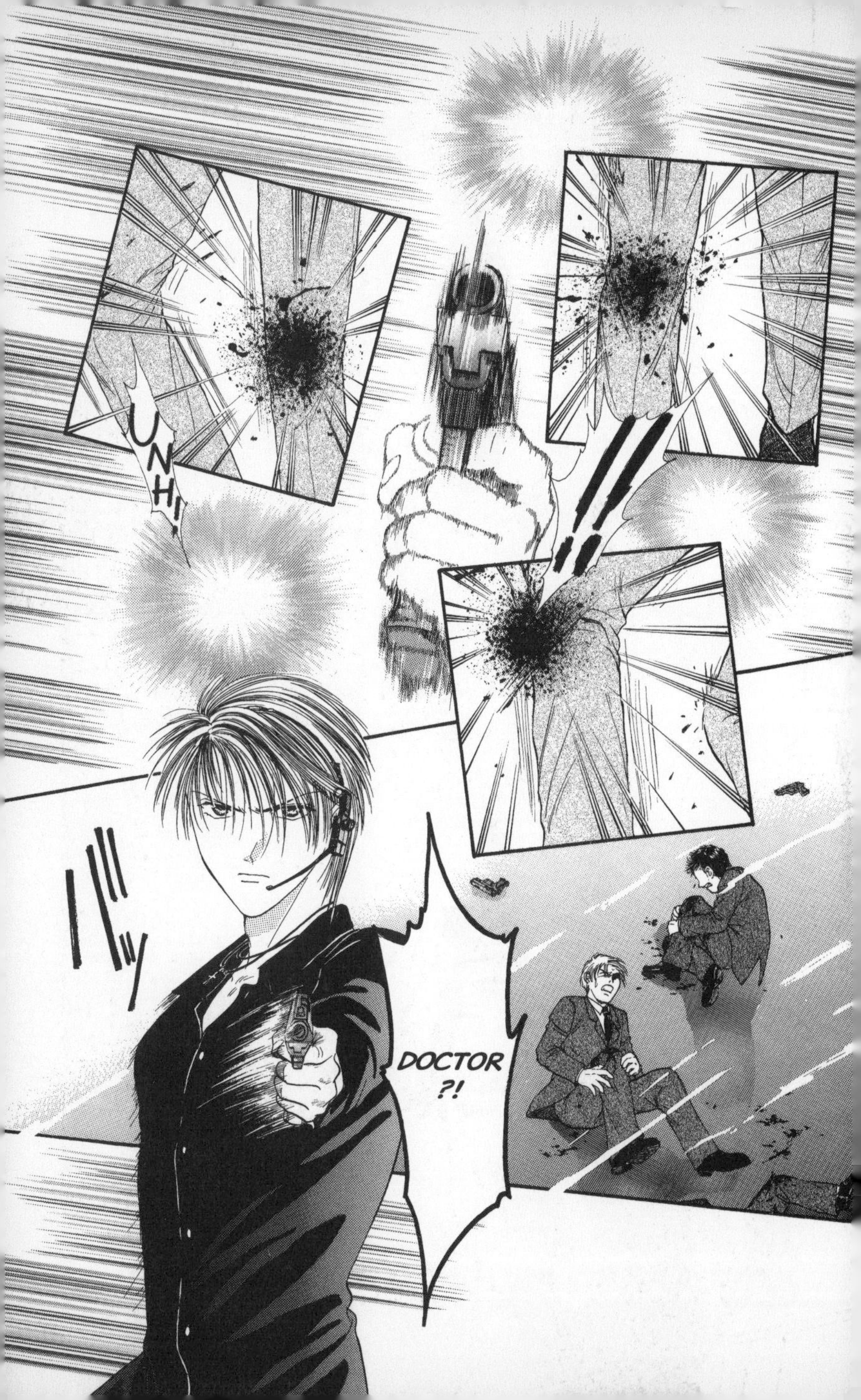
UNH!
DOCTOR ?!
バッ

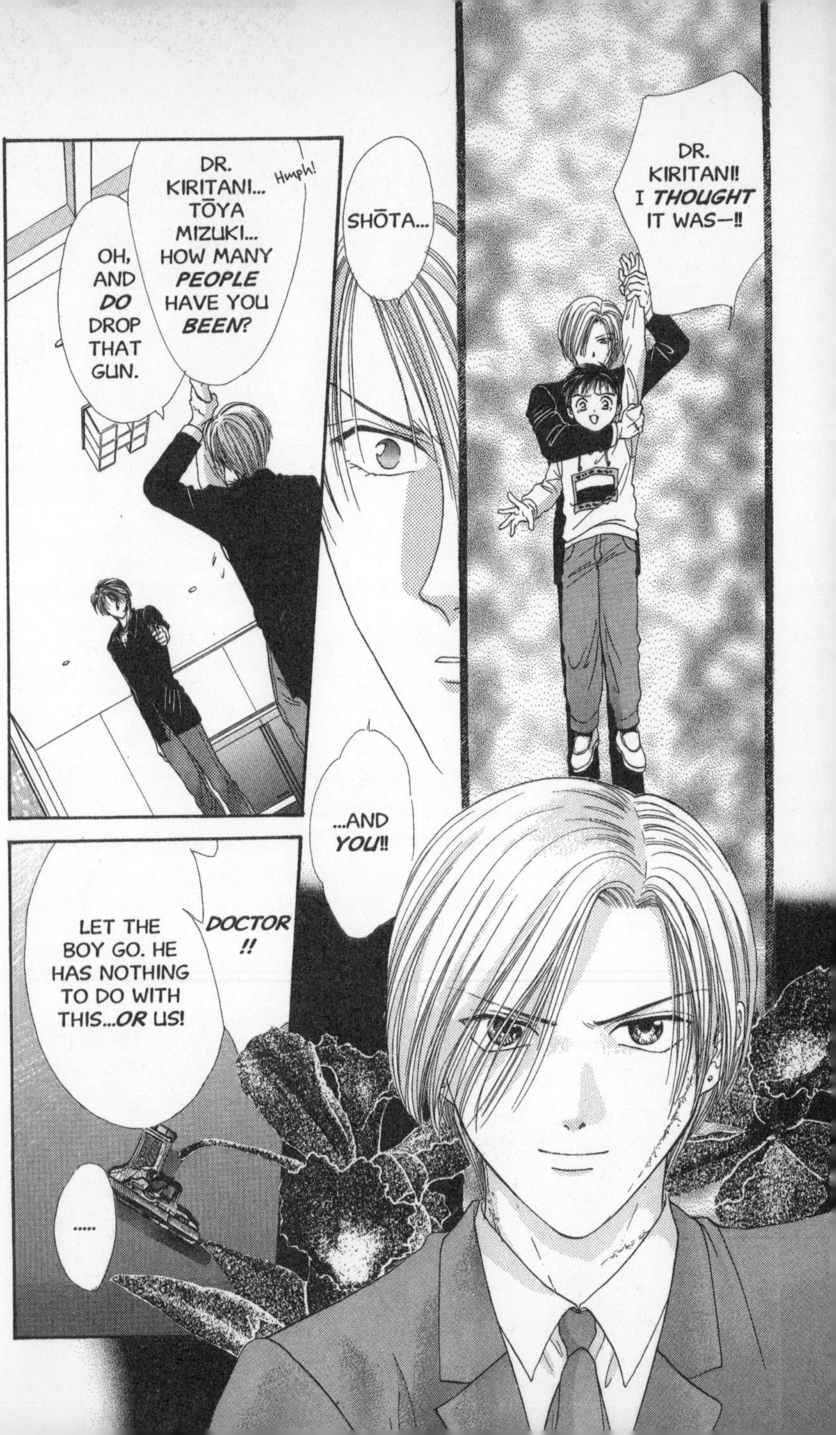
DR. KIRITANI!! I THOUGHT IT WAS—!!
SHŌTA...
...AND YOU!!
DR. KIRITANI... TŌYA MIZUKI... HOW MANY PEOPLE HAVE YOU BEEN?
Hmph!
OH, AND DO DROP THAT GUN.
DOCTOR !!
LET THE BOY GO. HE HAS NOTHING TO DO WITH THIS...OR US!
.....

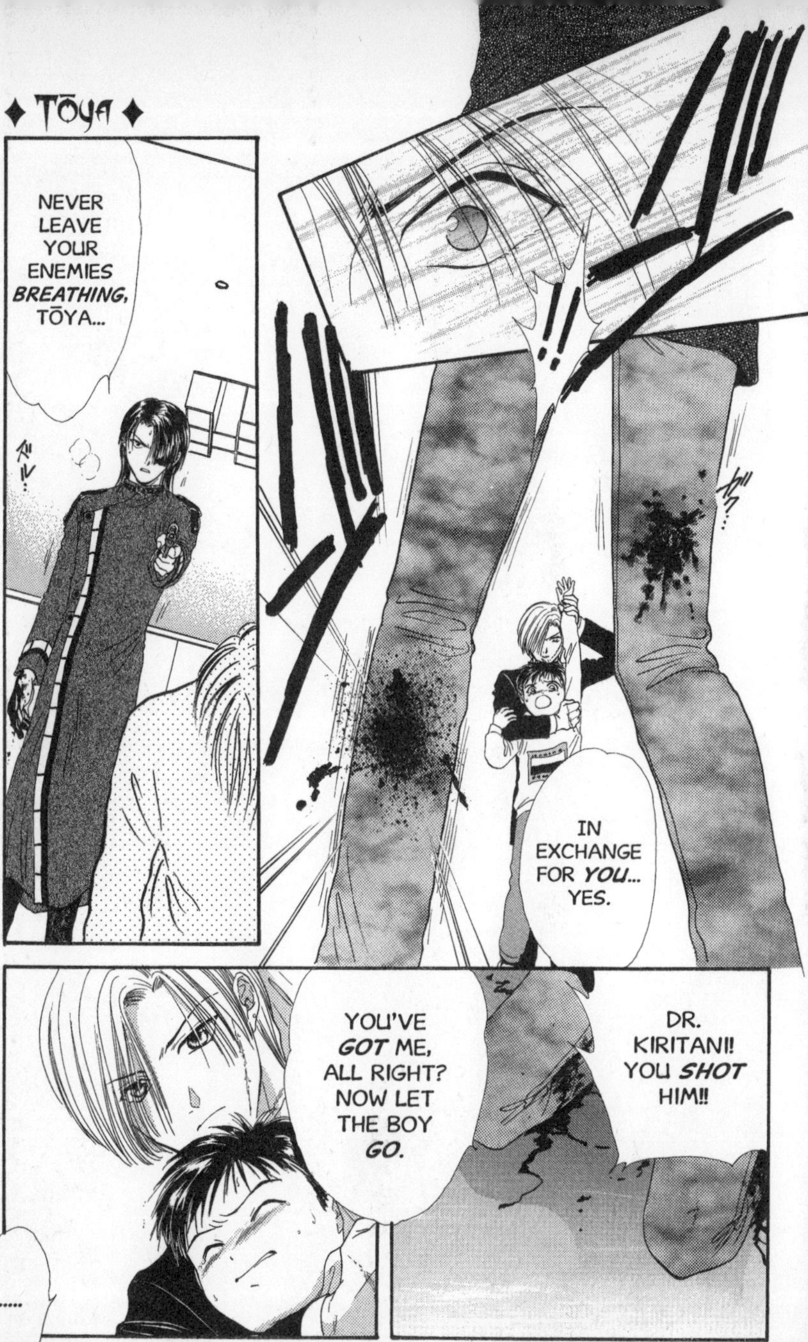
!!
IN EXCHANGE FOR *YOU*... YES.
NEVER LEAVE YOUR ENEMIES *BREATHING*, TŌYA...
DR. KIRITANI! YOU *SHOT* HIM!!
YOU'VE *GOT* ME, ALL RIGHT? NOW LET THE BOY *GO*.
......

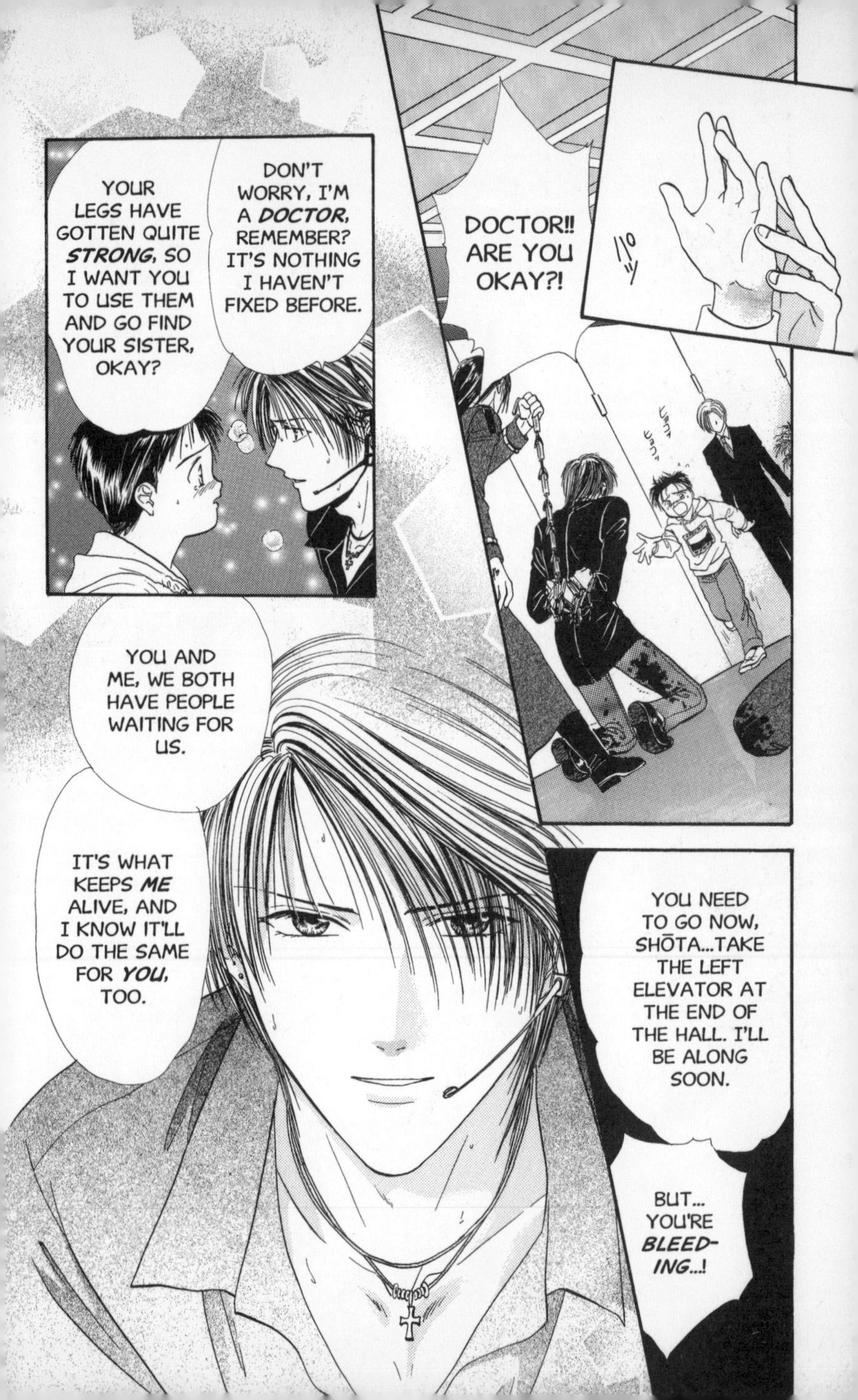
DOCTOR!! ARE YOU OKAY?!
YOU NEED TO GO NOW, SHŌTA...TAKE THE LEFT ELEVATOR AT THE END OF THE HALL. I'LL BE ALONG SOON.
BUT... YOU'RE *BLEEDING*...!
DON'T WORRY, I'M A *DOCTOR*, REMEMBER? IT'S NOTHING I HAVEN'T FIXED BEFORE.
YOUR LEGS HAVE GOTTEN QUITE *STRONG*, SO I WANT YOU TO USE THEM AND GO FIND YOUR SISTER, OKAY?
YOU AND ME, WE BOTH HAVE PEOPLE WAITING FOR US.
IT'S WHAT KEEPS *ME* ALIVE, AND I KNOW IT'LL DO THE SAME FOR *YOU*, TOO.

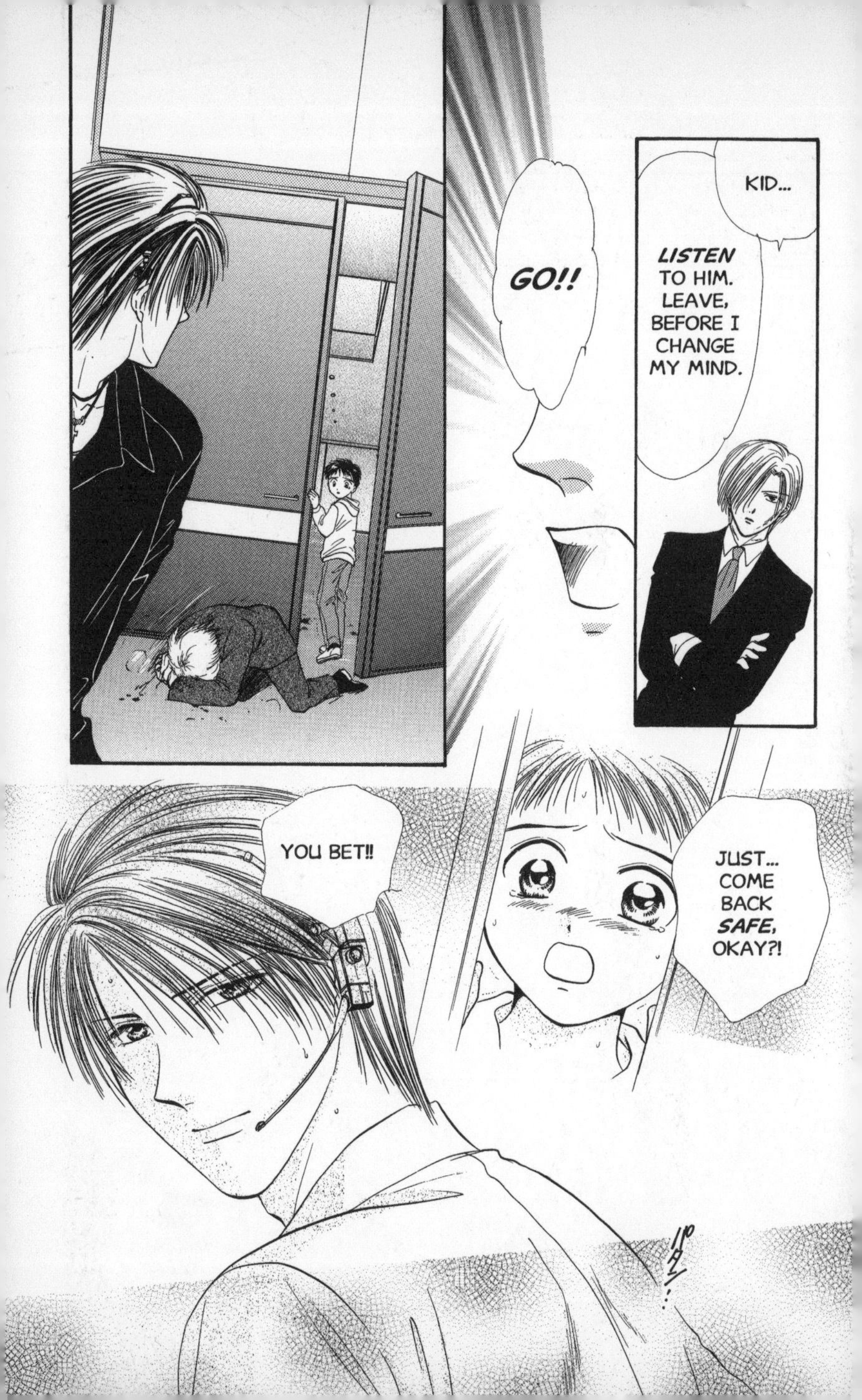
KID...
LISTEN TO HIM. LEAVE, BEFORE I CHANGE MY MIND.
GO!!
JUST... COME BACK SAFE, OKAY?!
YOU BET!!

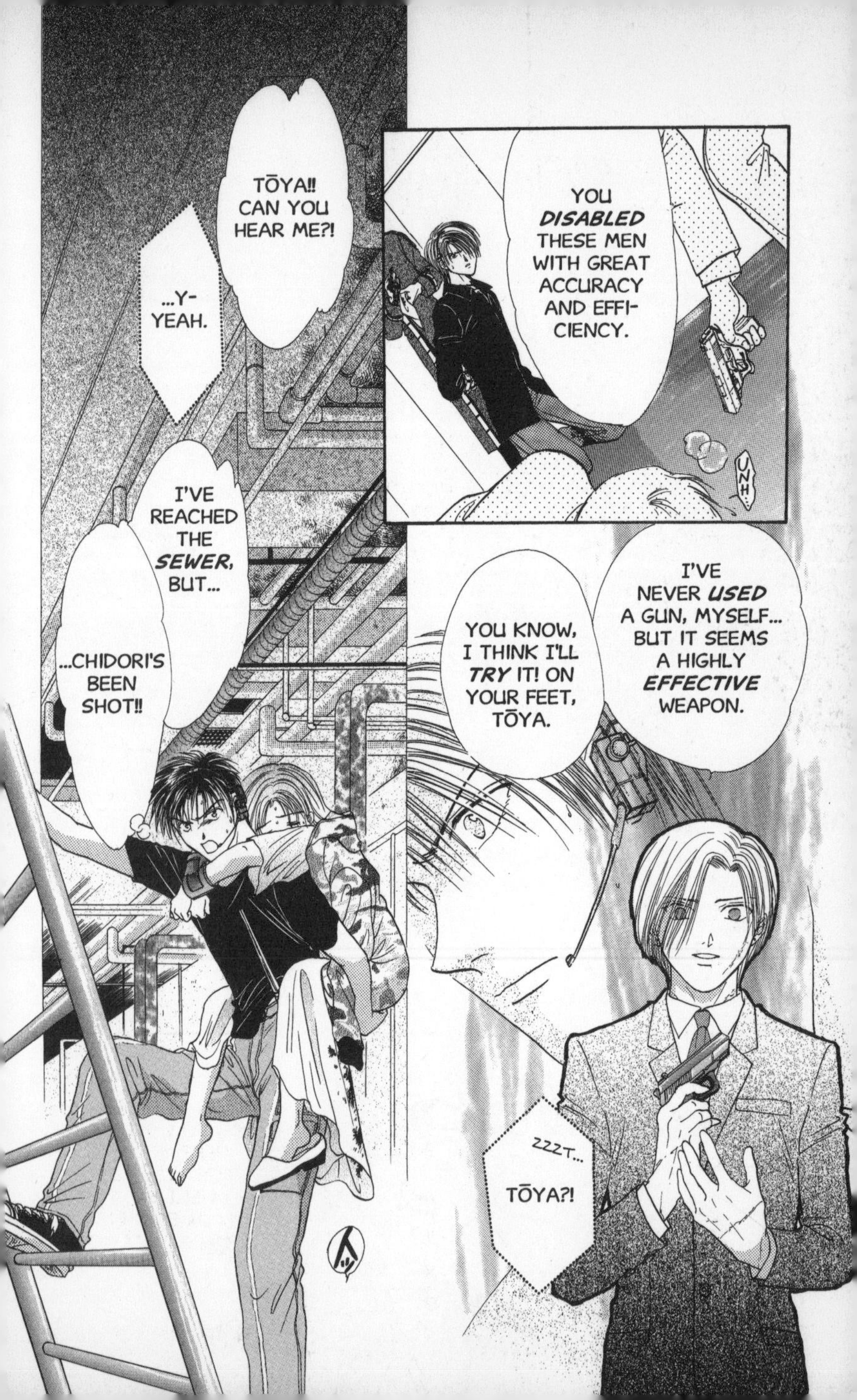
YOU *DISABLED* THESE MEN WITH GREAT ACCURACY AND EFFI-CIENCY.
UNH...
I'VE NEVER *USED* A GUN, MYSELF... BUT IT SEEMS A HIGHLY *EFFECTIVE* WEAPON.
YOU KNOW, I THINK I'LL *TRY* IT! ON YOUR FEET, TŌYA.
ZZZT...
TŌYA?!
TŌYA!! CAN YOU HEAR ME?!
...Y-YEAH.
I'VE REACHED THE *SEWER*, BUT...
...CHIDORI'S BEEN SHOT!!

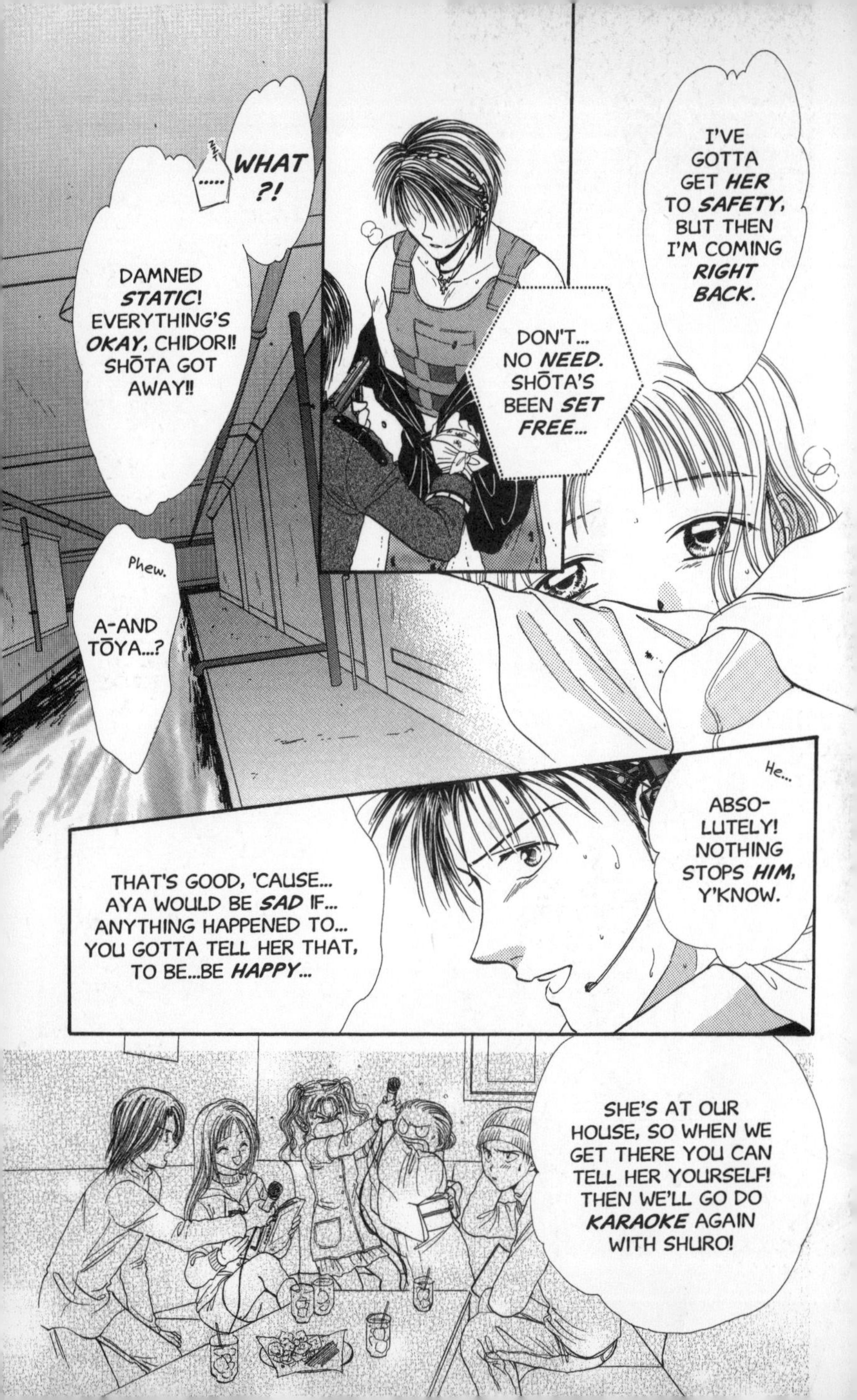
I'VE GOTTA GET *HER* TO *SAFETY*, BUT THEN I'M COMING *RIGHT BACK*.
DON'T... NO *NEED*. SHŌTA'S BEEN *SET FREE*...
......
WHAT ?!
DAMNED *STATIC*! EVERYTHING'S *OKAY*, CHIDORI! SHŌTA GOT AWAY!!
Phew.
A-AND TŌYA...?
He...
ABSO-LUTELY! NOTHING STOPS *HIM*, Y'KNOW.
THAT'S GOOD, 'CAUSE... AYA WOULD BE *SAD* IF... ANYTHING HAPPENED TO... YOU GOTTA TELL HER THAT, TO BE...BE *HAPPY*...
SHE'S AT OUR HOUSE, SO WHEN WE GET THERE YOU CAN TELL HER YOURSELF! THEN WE'LL GO DO *KARAOKE* AGAIN WITH SHURO!

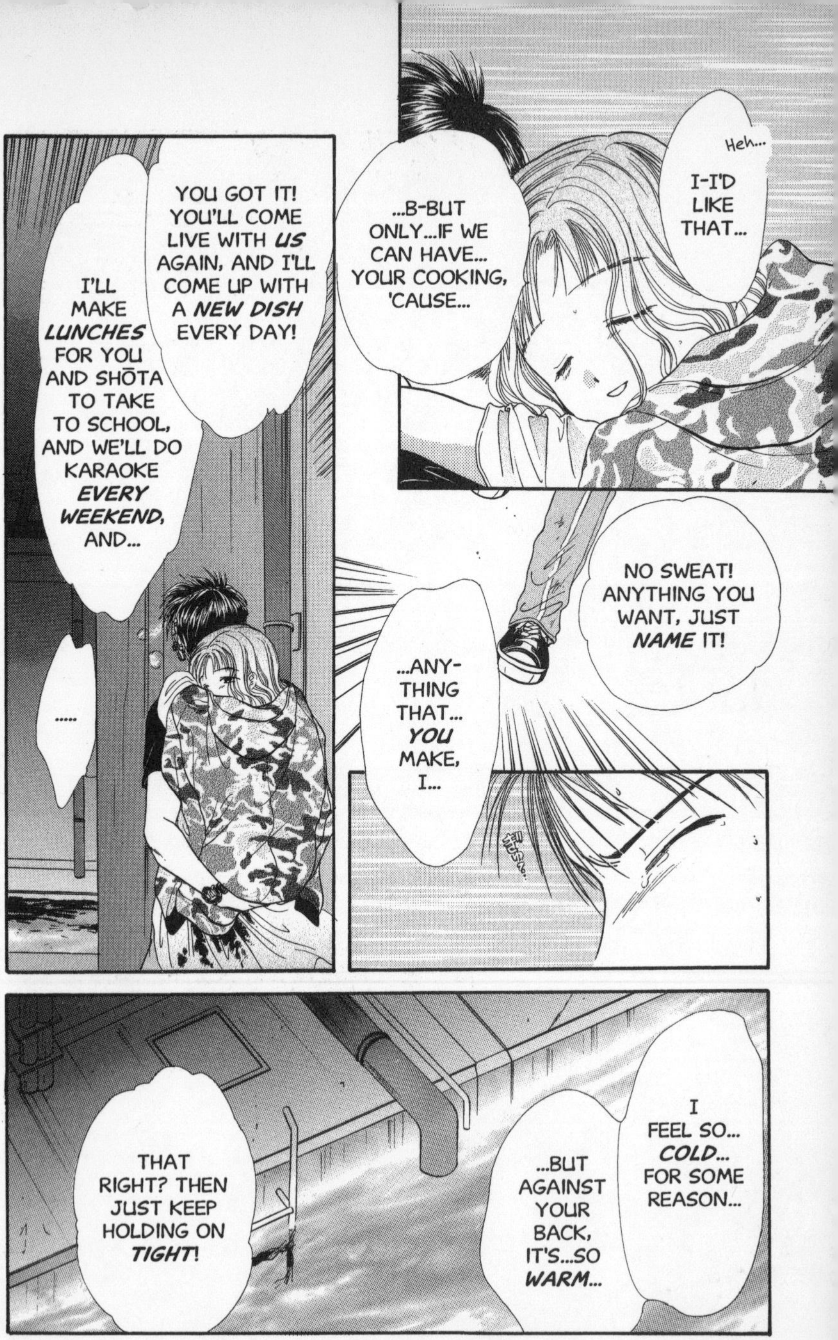
Heh...
I-I'D LIKE THAT...
...B-BUT ONLY...IF WE CAN HAVE... YOUR COOKING, 'CAUSE...
NO SWEAT! ANYTHING YOU WANT, JUST NAME IT!
...ANY-THING THAT... YOU MAKE, I...
YOU GOT IT! YOU'LL COME LIVE WITH US AGAIN, AND I'LL COME UP WITH A NEW DISH EVERY DAY!
I'LL MAKE LUNCHES FOR YOU AND SHŌTA TO TAKE TO SCHOOL, AND WE'LL DO KARAOKE EVERY WEEKEND, AND...
.....
I FEEL SO... COLD... FOR SOME REASON...
...BUT AGAINST YOUR BACK, IT'S...SO WARM...
THAT RIGHT? THEN JUST KEEP HOLDING ON TIGHT!

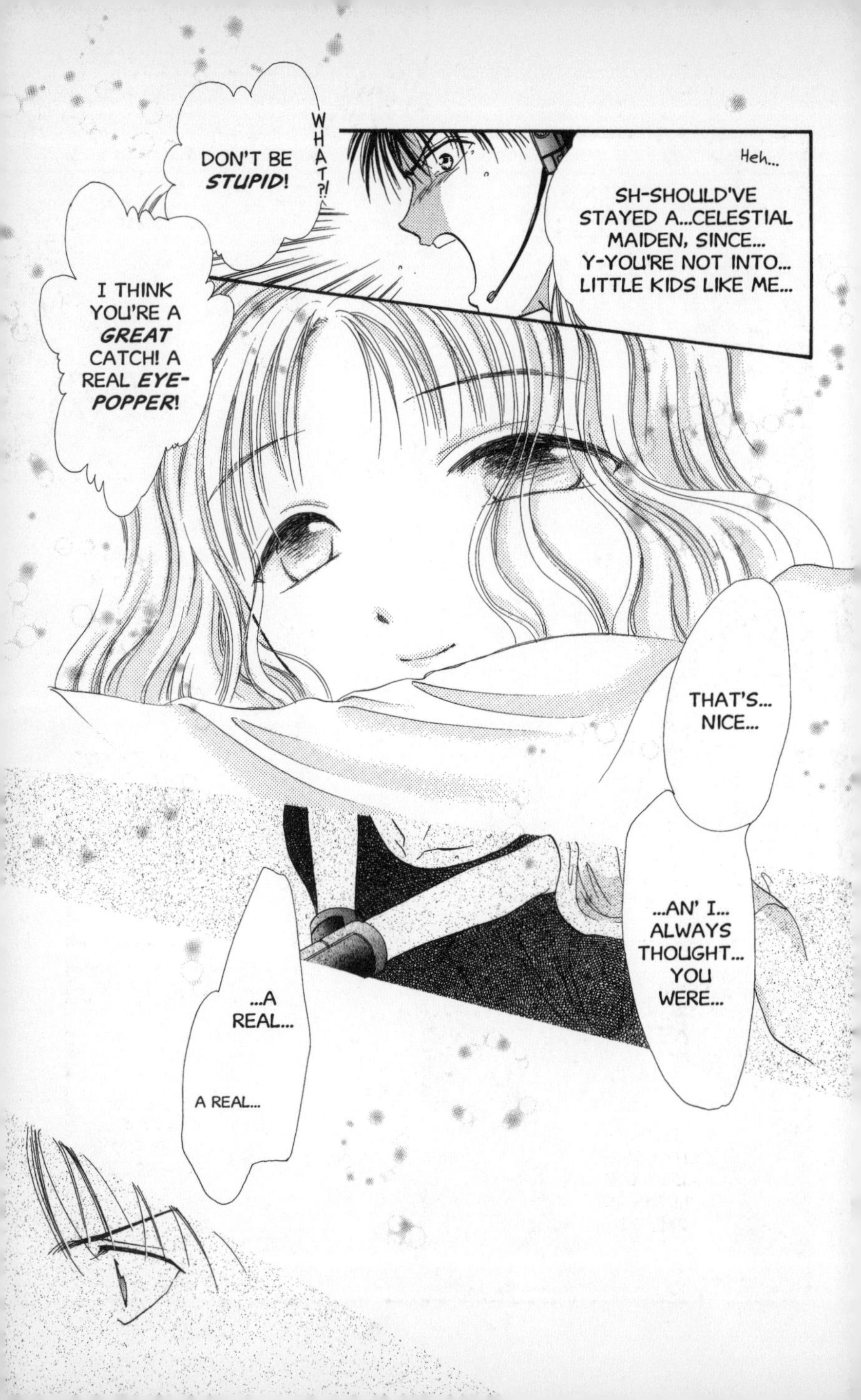
Heh...
SH-SHOULD'VE STAYED A...CELESTIAL MAIDEN, SINCE... Y-YOU'RE NOT INTO... LITTLE KIDS LIKE ME...
WHAT?!
DON'T BE STUPID!
I THINK YOU'RE A GREAT CATCH! A REAL EYE-POPPER!
THAT'S... NICE...
...AN' I... ALWAYS THOUGHT... YOU WERE...
...A REAL...
A REAL...

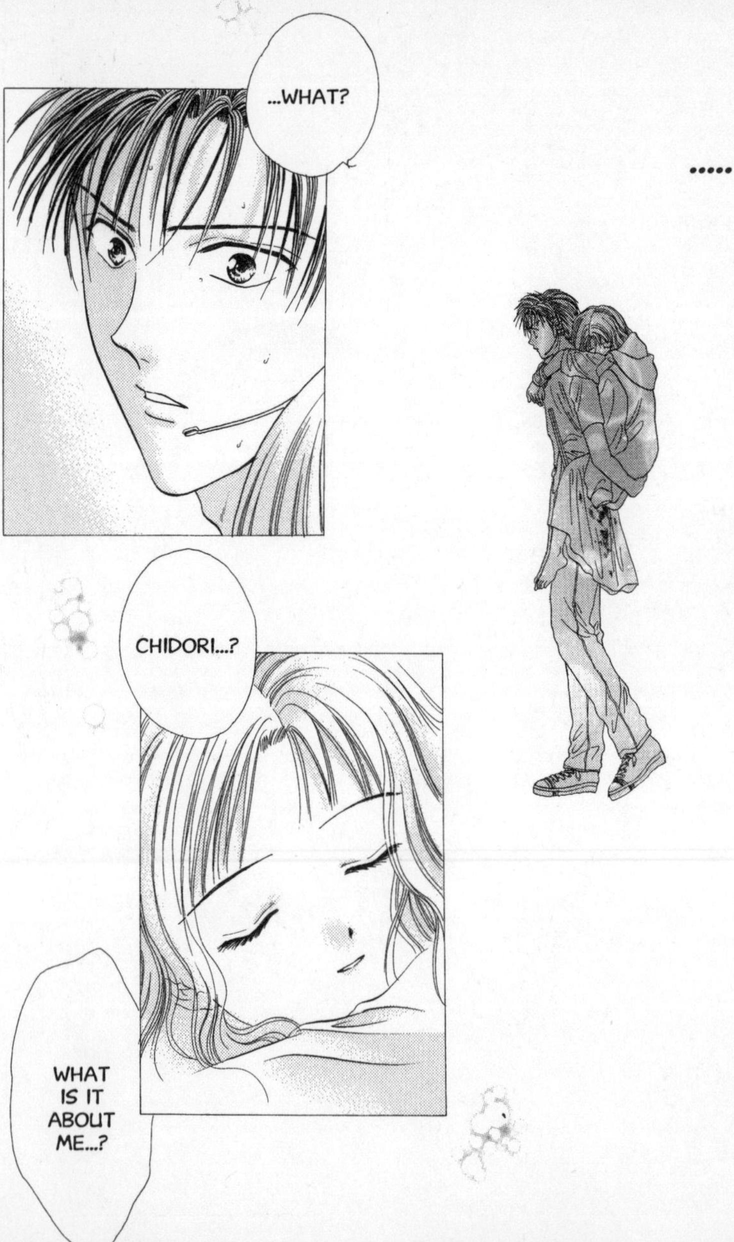
.....
...WHAT?
CHIDORI...?
WHAT IS IT ABOUT ME...?

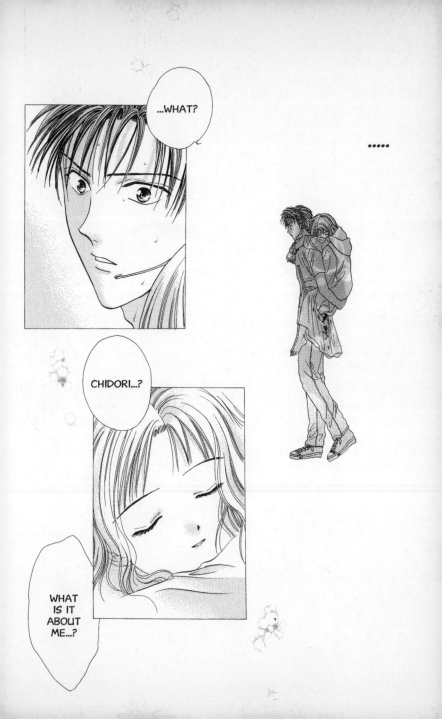

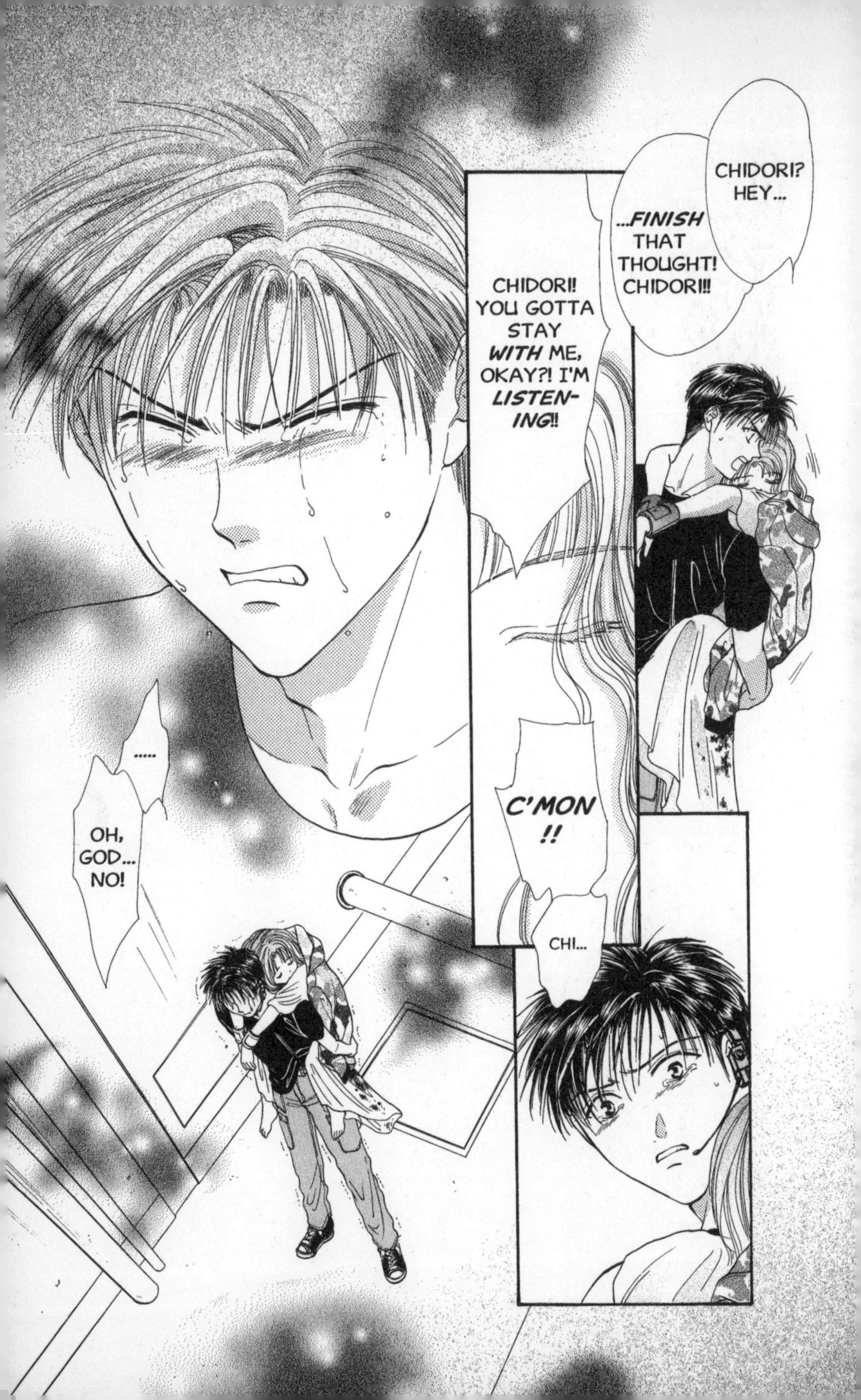
CHIDORI? HEY...
...FINISH THAT THOUGHT! CHIDORI!!
CHIDORI! YOU GOTTA STAY WITH ME, OKAY?! I'M LISTENING!!
C'MON !!
CHI...
......
OH, GOD... NO!

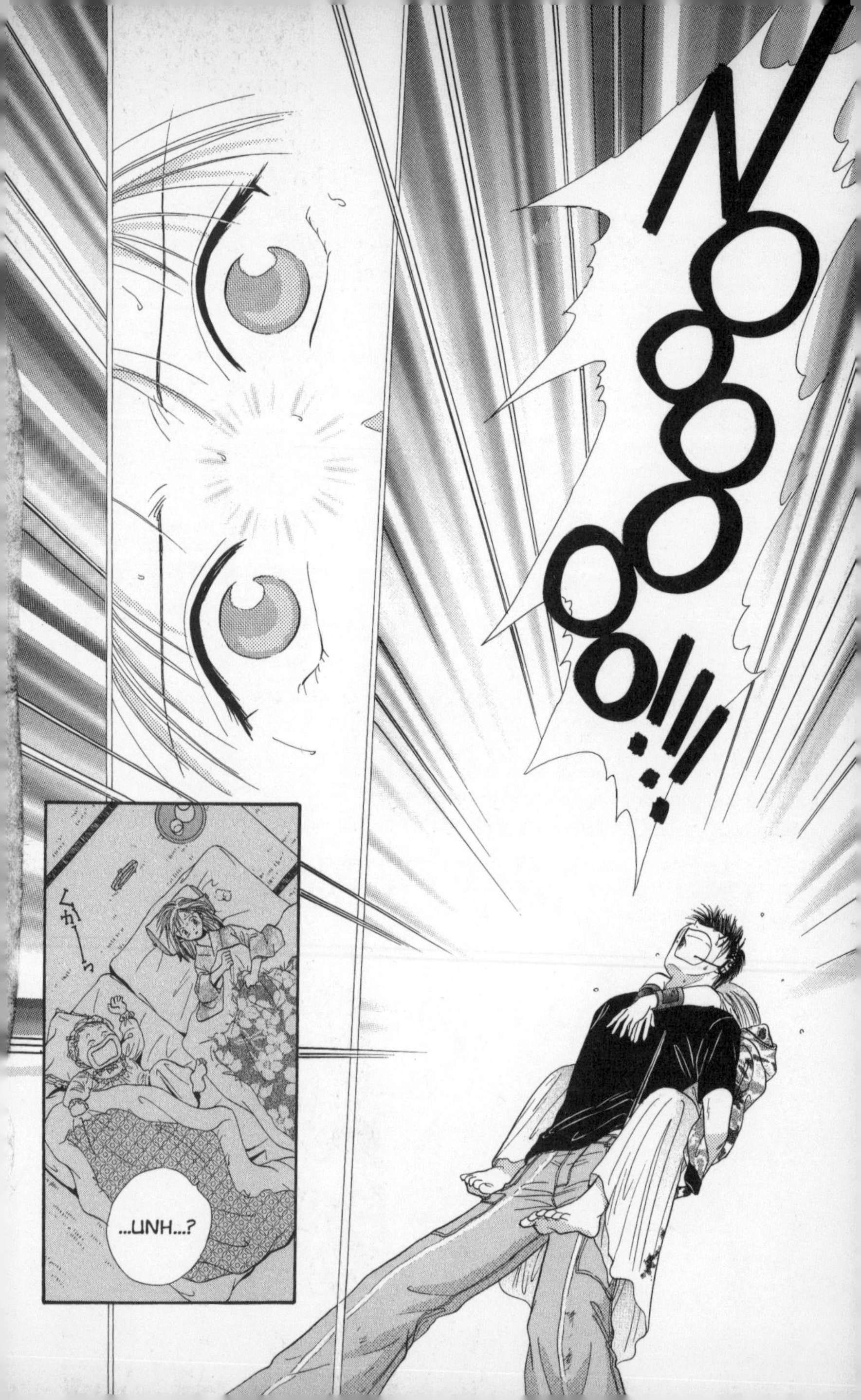
NOOOOOO!!!
くかー
...UNH...?

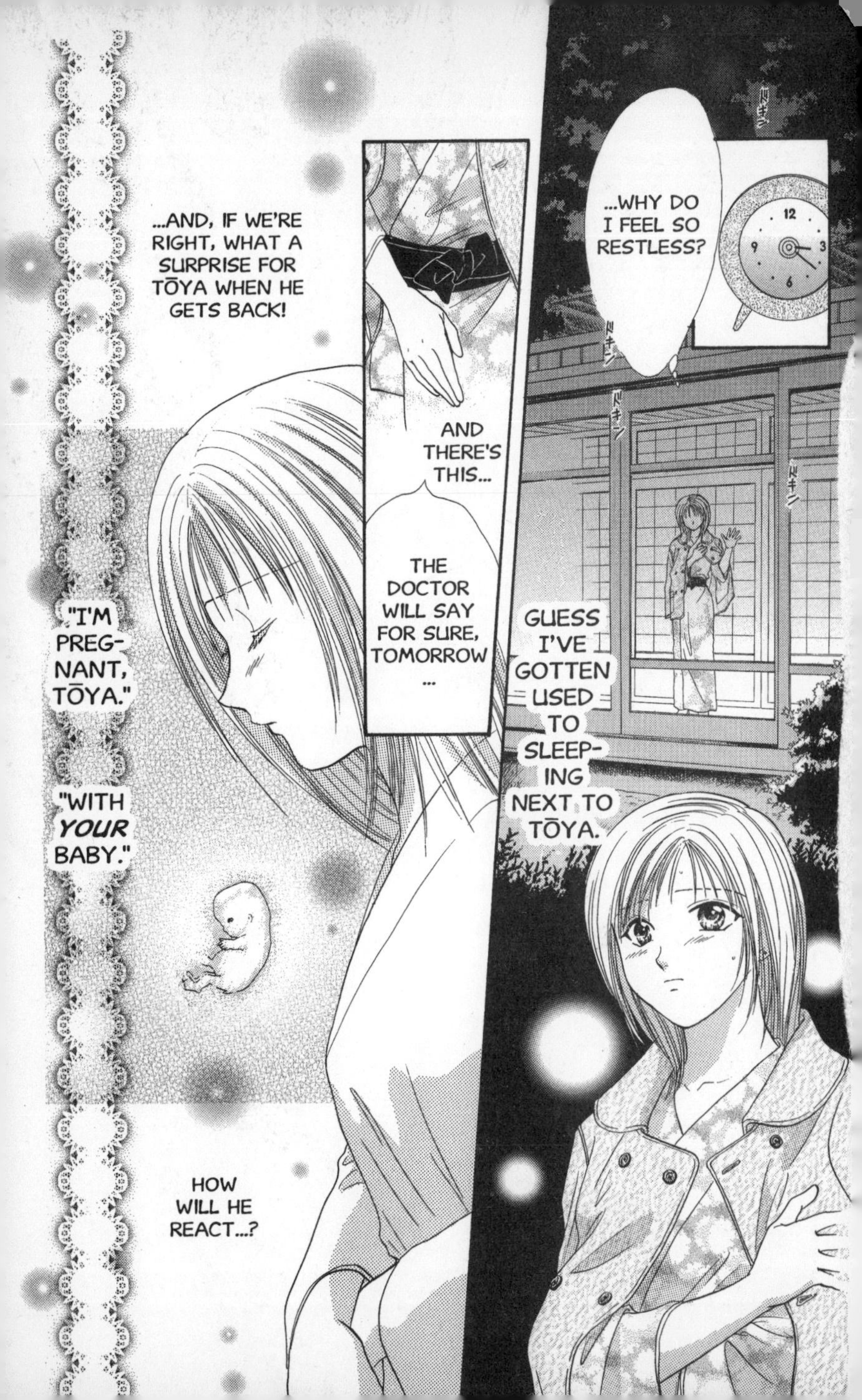

...WHY DO I FEEL SO RESTLESS?
GUESS I'VE GOTTEN USED TO SLEEPING NEXT TO TŌYA.
AND THERE'S THIS...
THE DOCTOR WILL SAY FOR SURE, TOMORROW...
...AND, IF WE'RE RIGHT, WHAT A SURPRISE FOR TŌYA WHEN HE GETS BACK!
"I'M PREGNANT, TŌYA."
"WITH *YOUR* BABY."
HOW WILL HE REACT...?

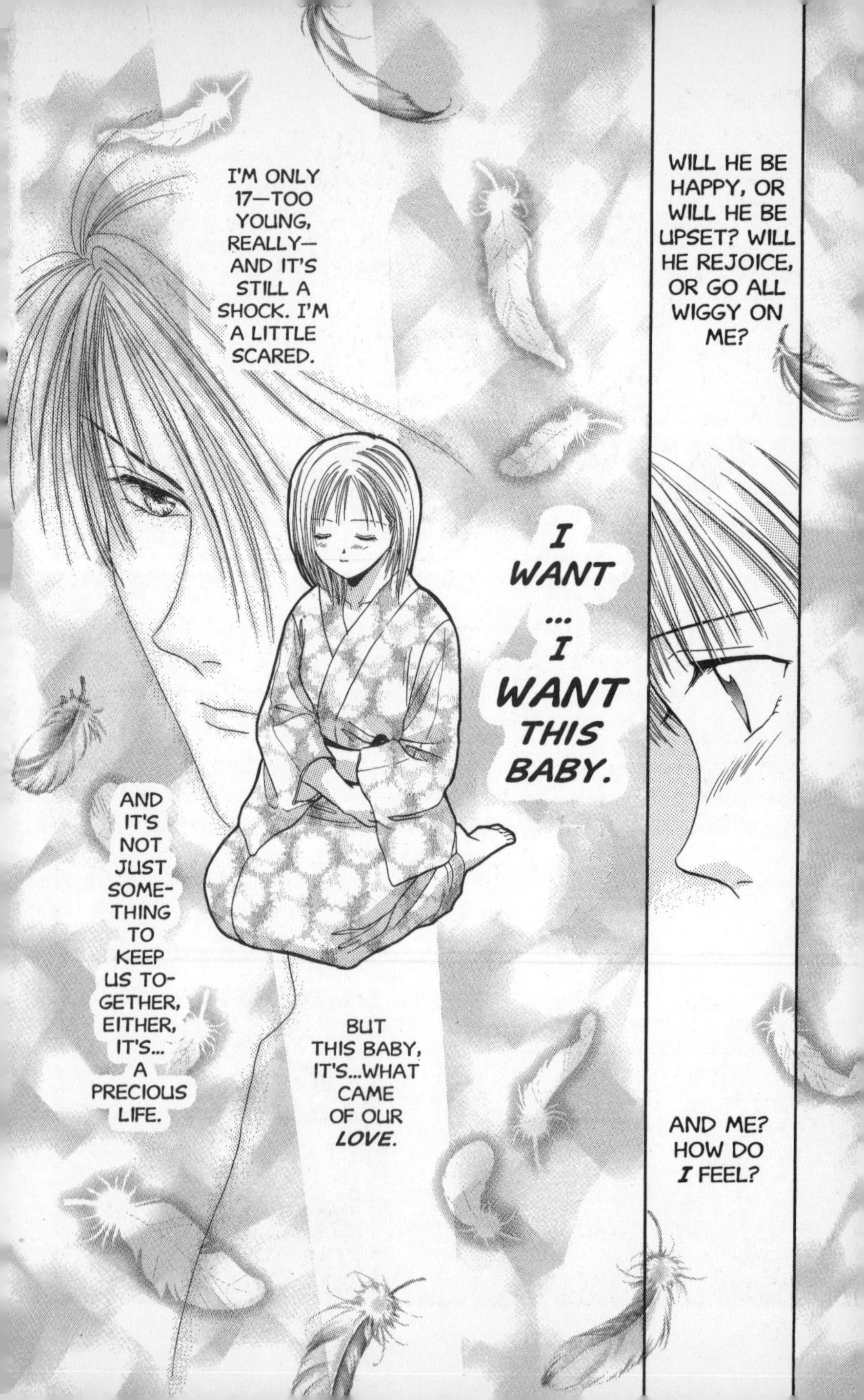

WILL HE BE HAPPY, OR WILL HE BE UPSET? WILL HE REJOICE, OR GO ALL WIGGY ON ME?
AND ME? HOW DO *I* FEEL?
I'M ONLY 17—TOO YOUNG, REALLY—AND IT'S STILL A SHOCK. I'M A LITTLE SCARED.
AND IT'S NOT JUST SOME-THING TO KEEP US TO-GETHER, EITHER, IT'S... A PRECIOUS LIFE.
BUT THIS BABY, IT'S...WHAT CAME OF OUR *LOVE*.
I WANT ... I WANT THIS BABY.

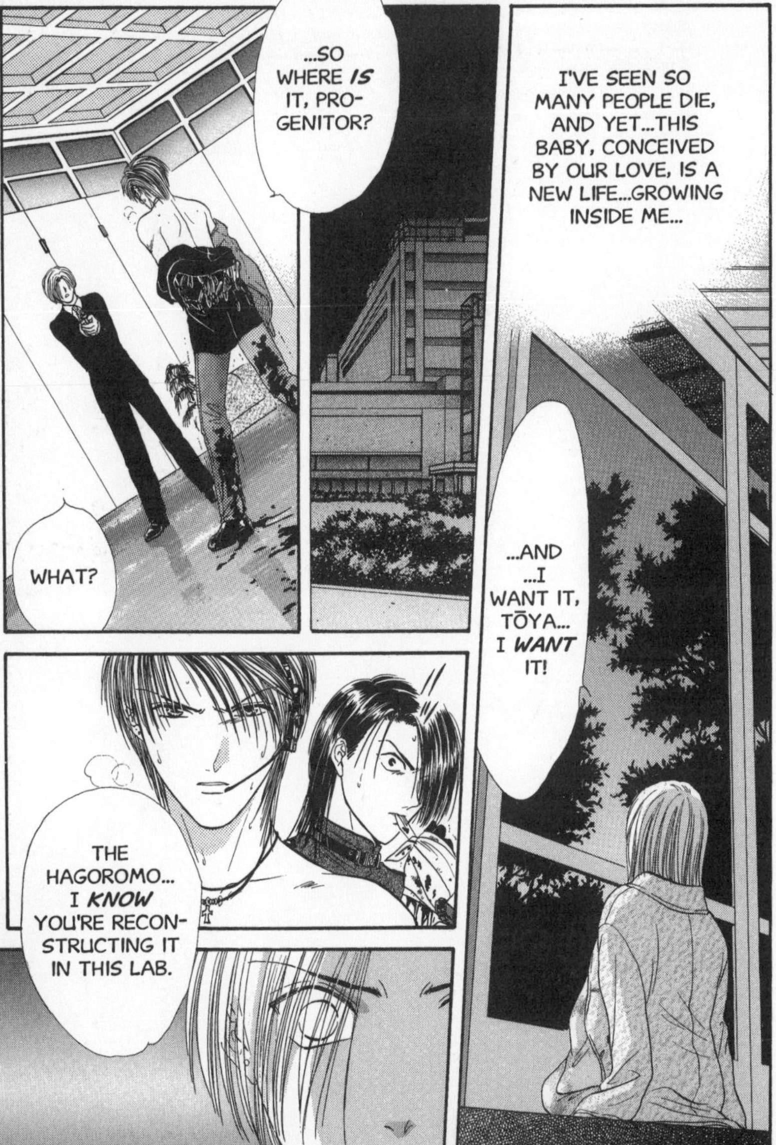
I'VE SEEN SO MANY PEOPLE DIE, AND YET...THIS BABY, CONCEIVED BY OUR LOVE, IS A NEW LIFE...GROWING INSIDE ME...
...AND ...I WANT IT, TŌYA... I *WANT* IT!
...SO WHERE *IS* IT, PRO-GENITOR?
WHAT?
THE HAGOROMO... I *KNOW* YOU'RE RECON-STRUCTING IT IN THIS LAB.

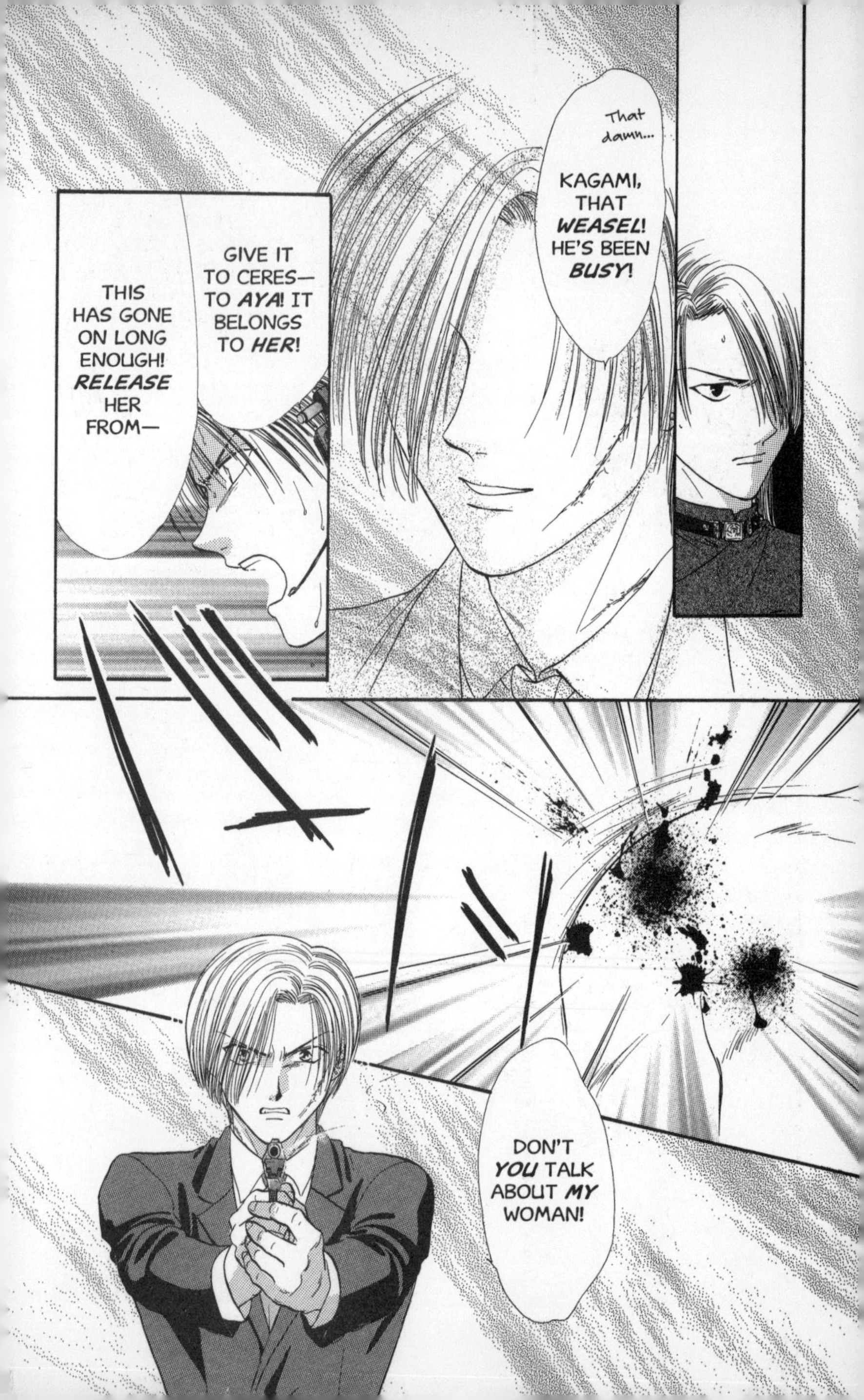
That damn...
KAGAMI, THAT WEASEL! HE'S BEEN BUSY!
GIVE IT TO CERES— TO AYA! IT BELONGS TO HER!
THIS HAS GONE ON LONG ENOUGH! RELEASE HER FROM—
DON'T YOU TALK ABOUT MY WOMAN!

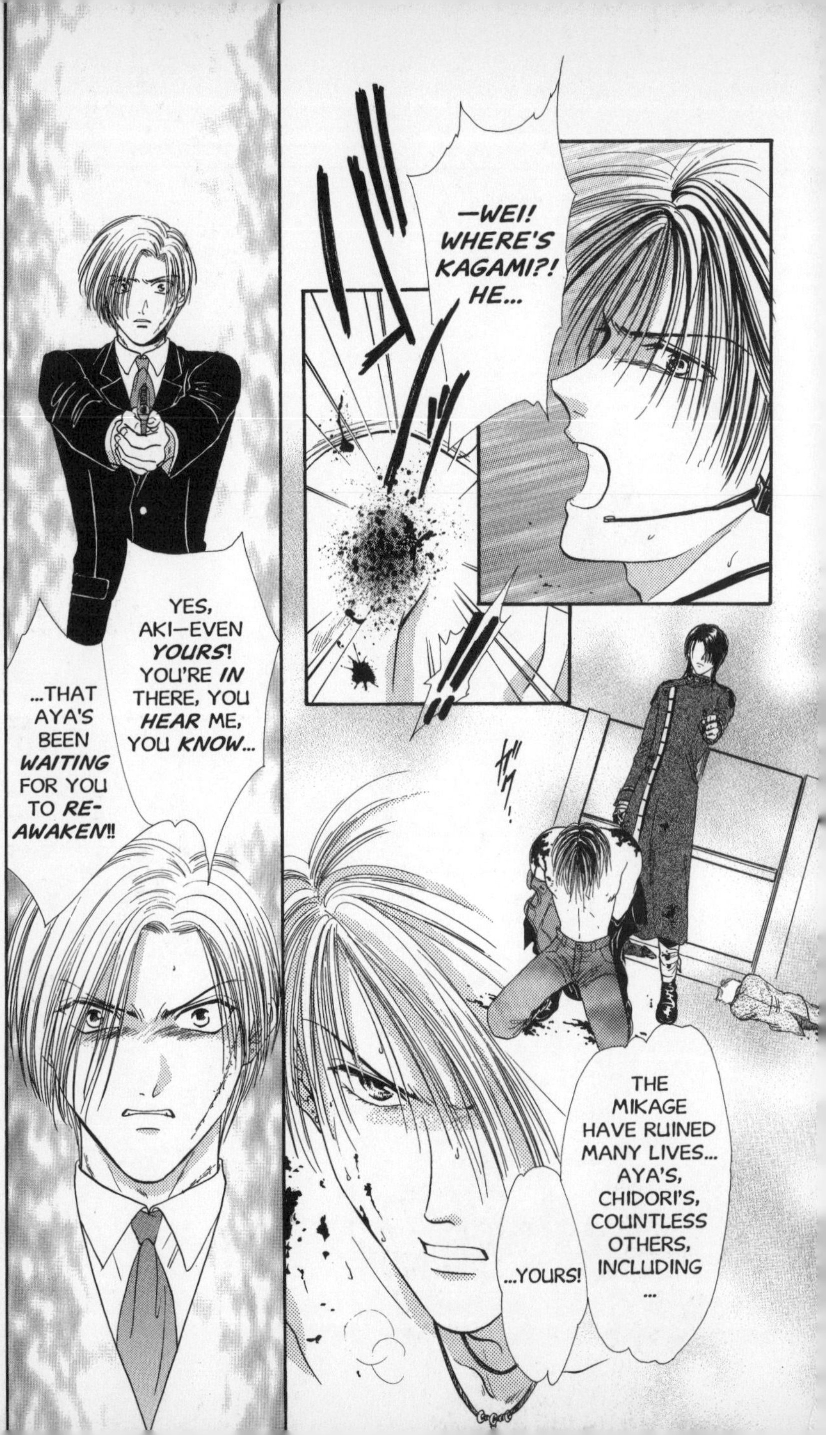
—WEI! WHERE'S KAGAMI?! HE...
THE MIKAGE HAVE RUINED MANY LIVES... AYA'S, CHIDORI'S, COUNTLESS OTHERS, INCLUDING ...
...YOURS!
YES, AKI—EVEN *YOURS*! YOU'RE *IN* THERE, YOU *HEAR* ME, YOU *KNOW*...
...THAT AYA'S BEEN *WAITING* FOR YOU TO *RE-AWAKEN*!!

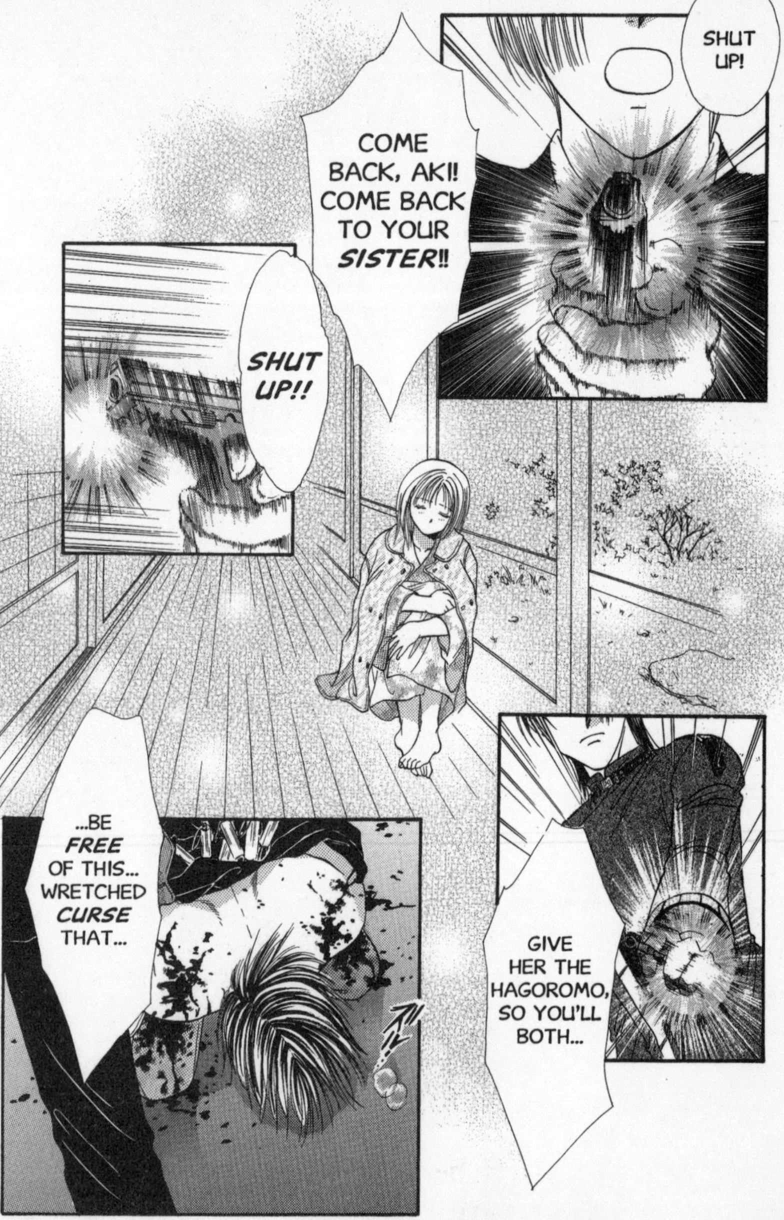
SHUT UP!
COME BACK, AKI! COME BACK TO YOUR SISTER!!
SHUT UP!!
GIVE HER THE HAGOROMO, SO YOU'LL BOTH...
...BE FREE OF THIS... WRETCHED CURSE THAT...

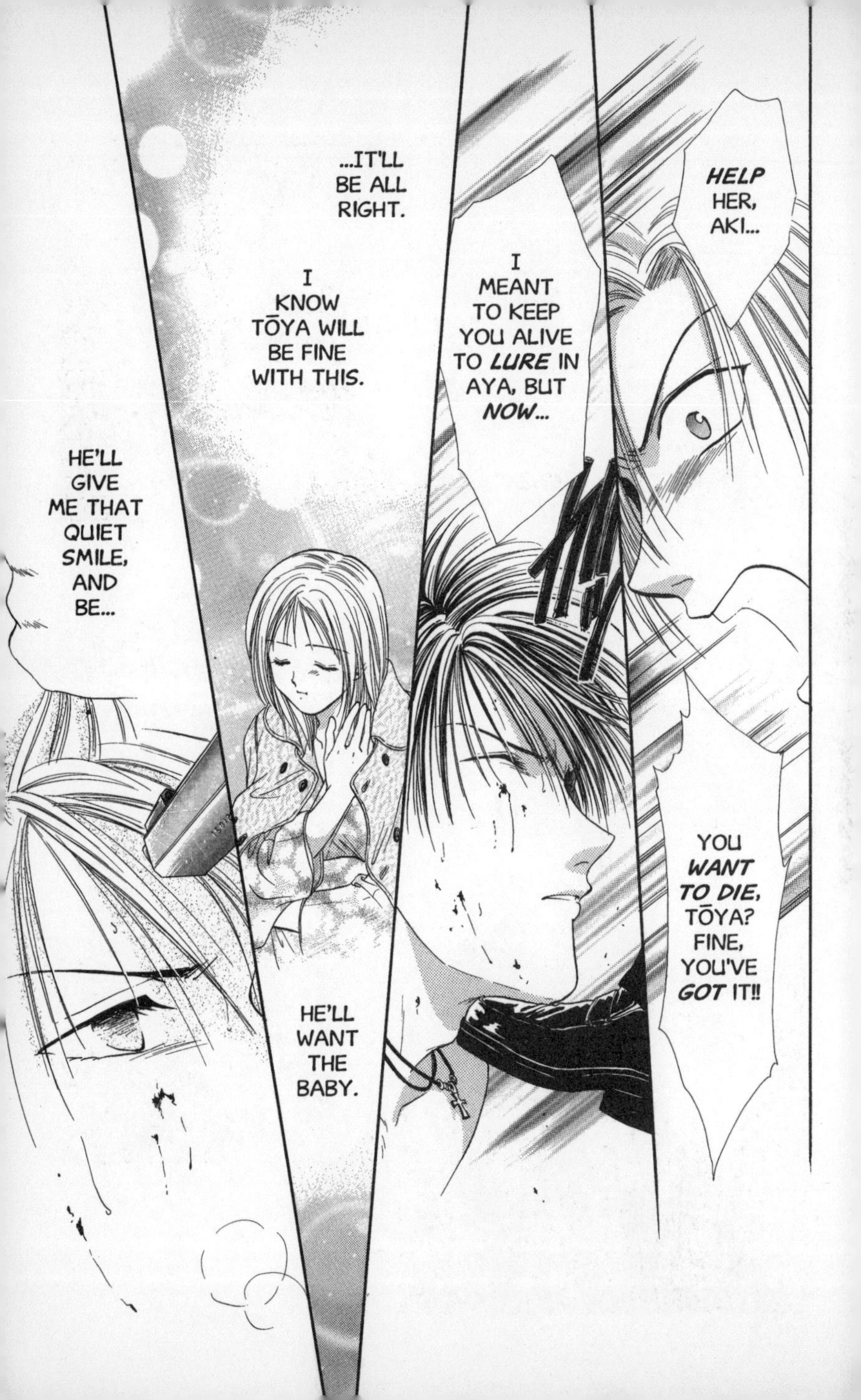
HELP HER, AKI...
YOU WANT TO DIE, TŌYA? FINE, YOU'VE GOT IT!!
I MEANT TO KEEP YOU ALIVE TO LURE IN AYA, BUT NOW...
...IT'LL BE ALL RIGHT.
I KNOW TŌYA WILL BE FINE WITH THIS.
HE'LL WANT THE BABY.
HE'LL GIVE ME THAT QUIET SMILE, AND BE...

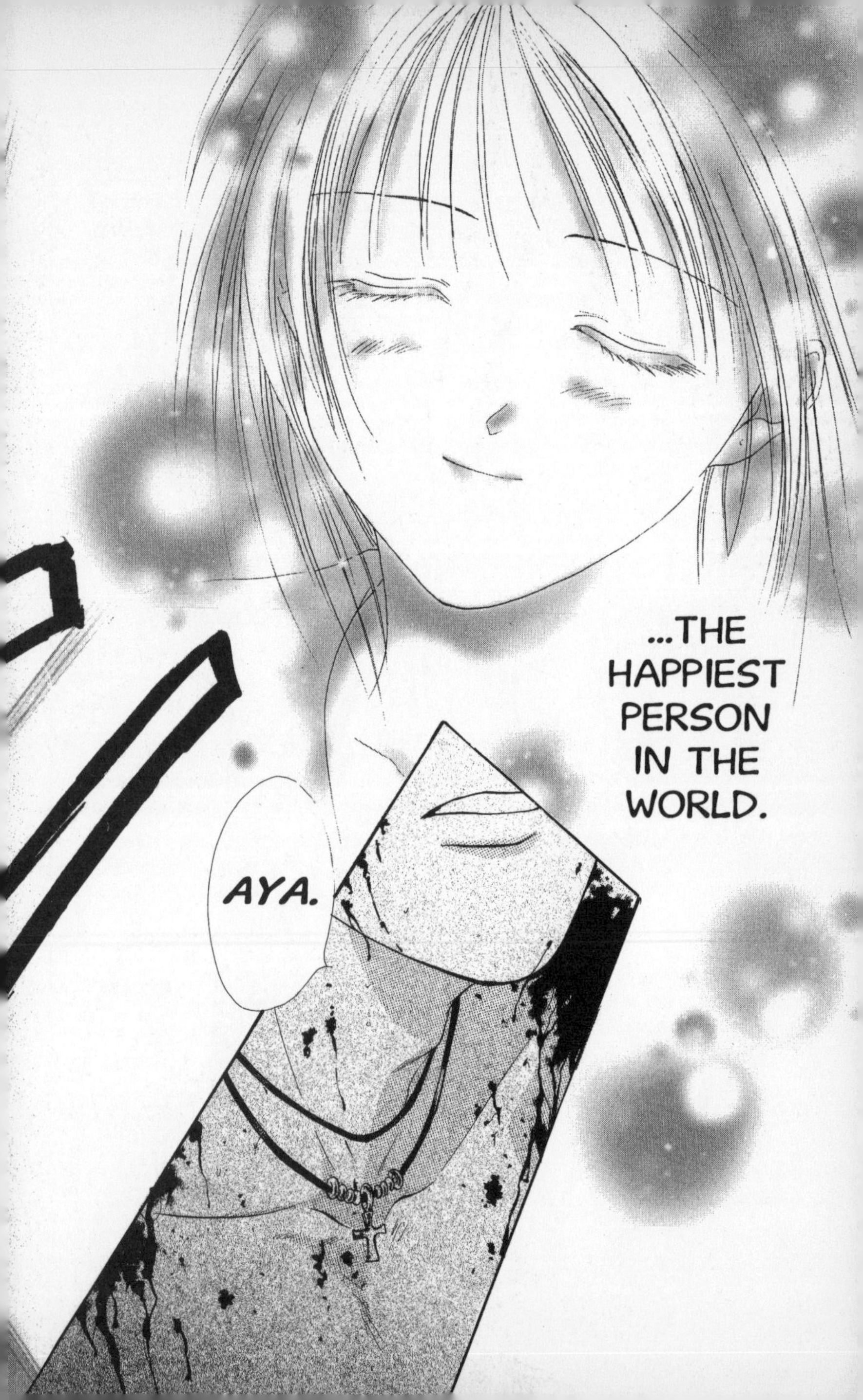
...THE HAPPIEST PERSON IN THE WORLD.
AYA.

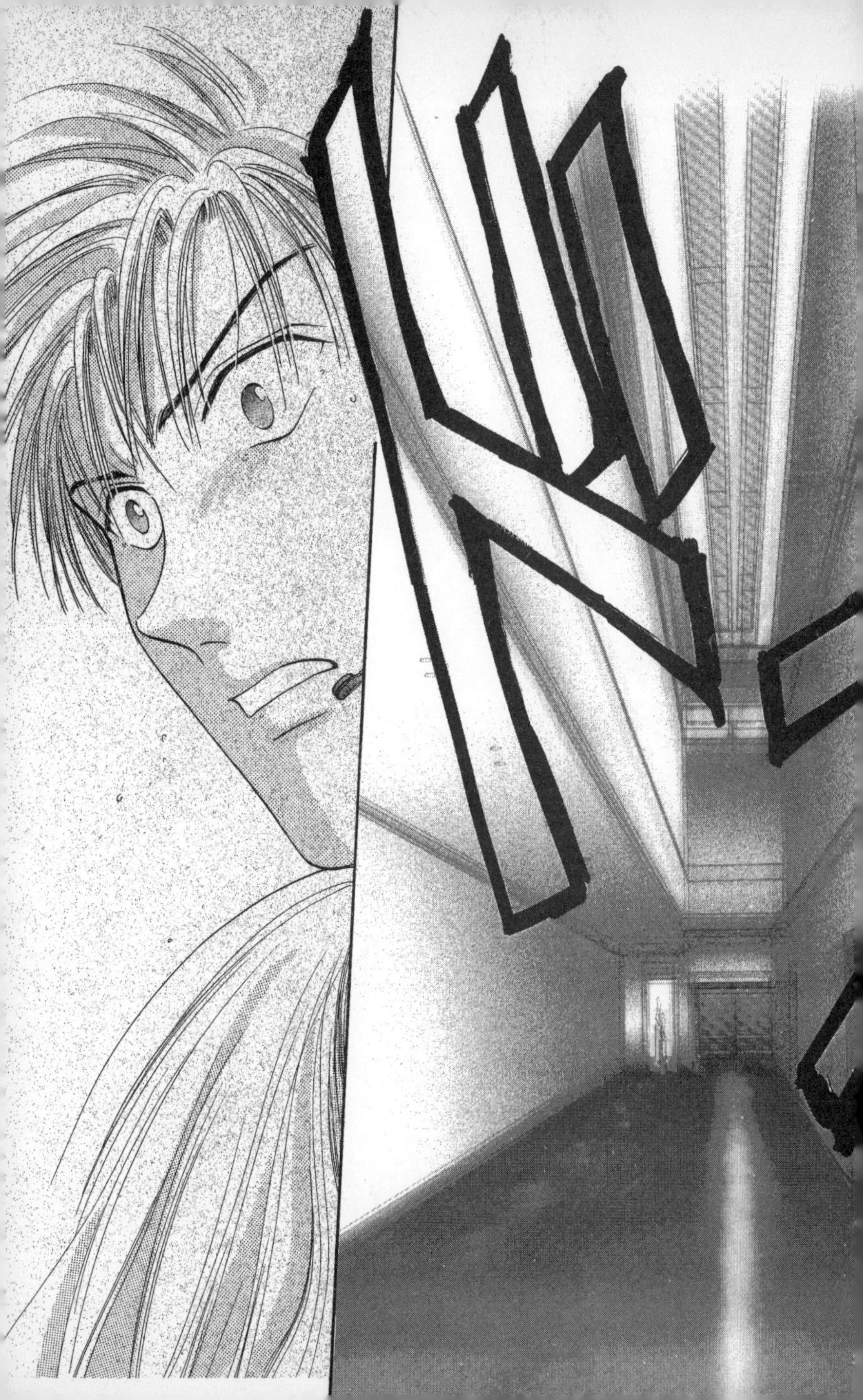

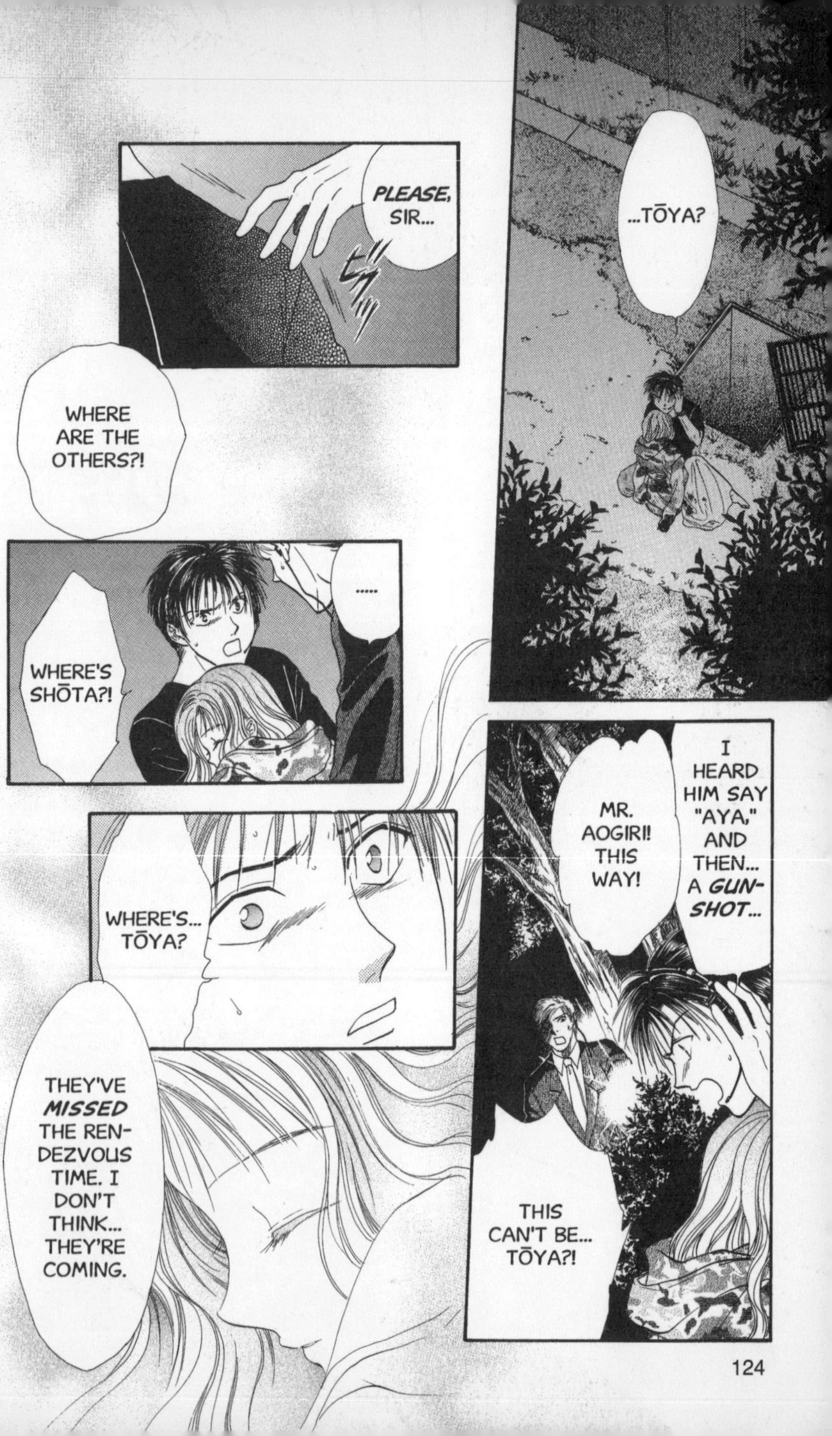
...TŌYA?
PLEASE, SIR...
WHERE ARE THE OTHERS?!
.....
WHERE'S SHŌTA?!
I HEARD HIM SAY "AYA," AND THEN... A GUN-SHOT...
MR. AOGIRI! THIS WAY!
THIS CAN'T BE... TŌYA?!
WHERE'S... TŌYA?
THEY'VE MISSED THE REN-DEZVOUS TIME. I DON'T THINK... THEY'RE COMING.

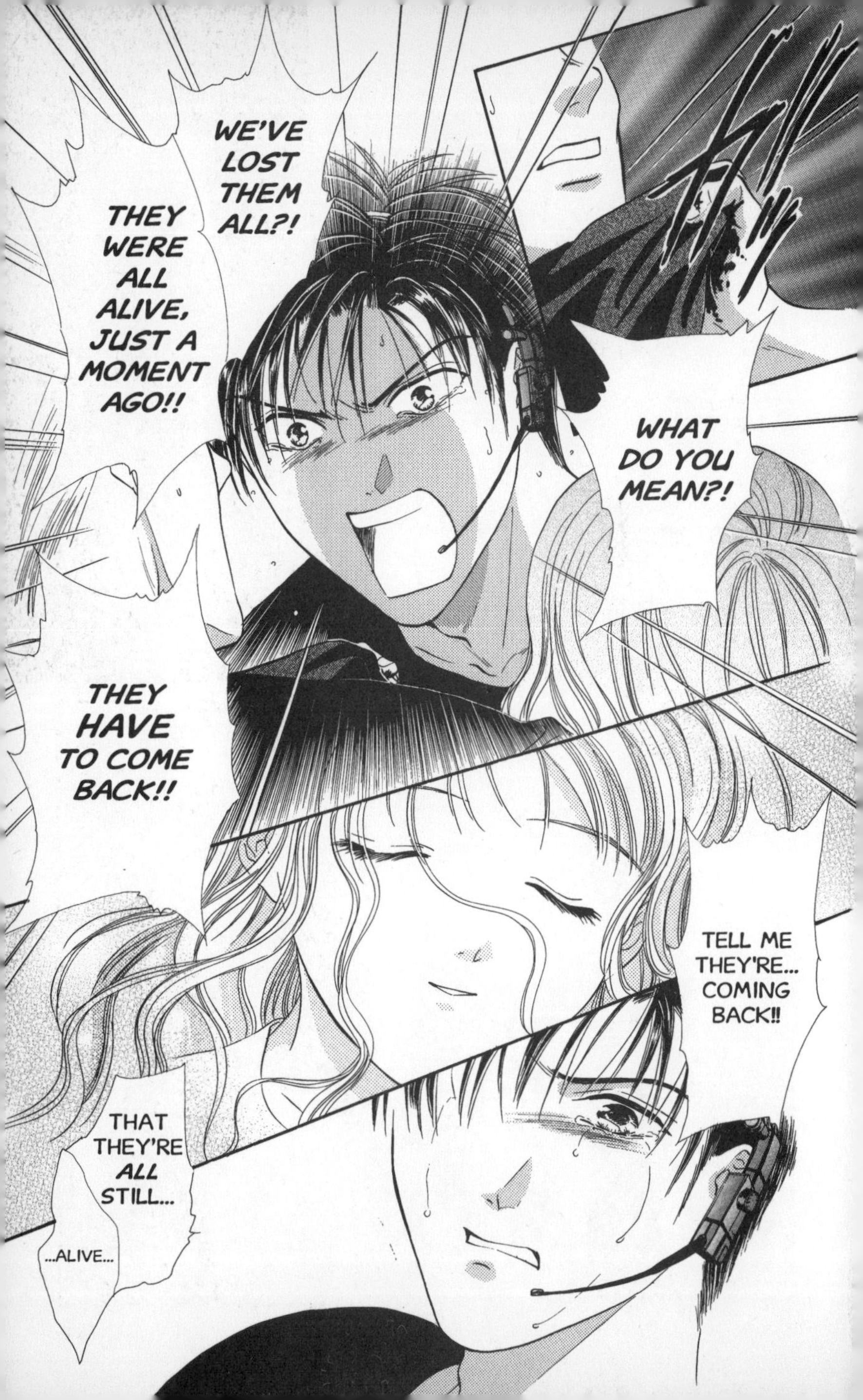
WHAT DO YOU MEAN?!
WE'VE LOST THEM ALL?!
THEY WERE ALL ALIVE, JUST A MOMENT AGO!!
THEY HAVE TO COME BACK!!
TELL ME THEY'RE... COMING BACK!!
THAT THEY'RE ALL STILL...
...ALIVE...

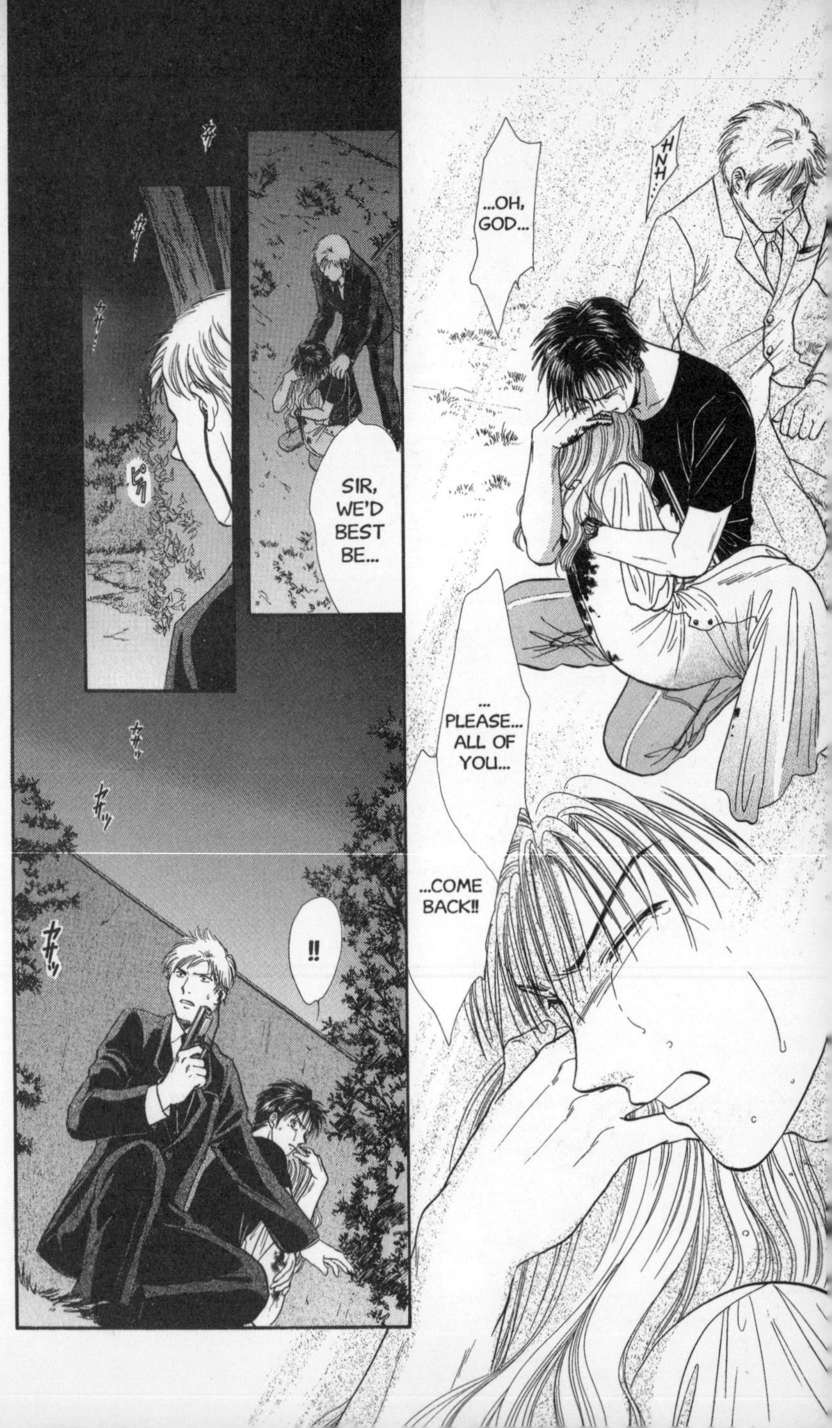
HNH...
...OH, GOD...
...PLEASE... ALL OF YOU...
...COME BACK!!
SIR, WE'D BEST BE...
!!

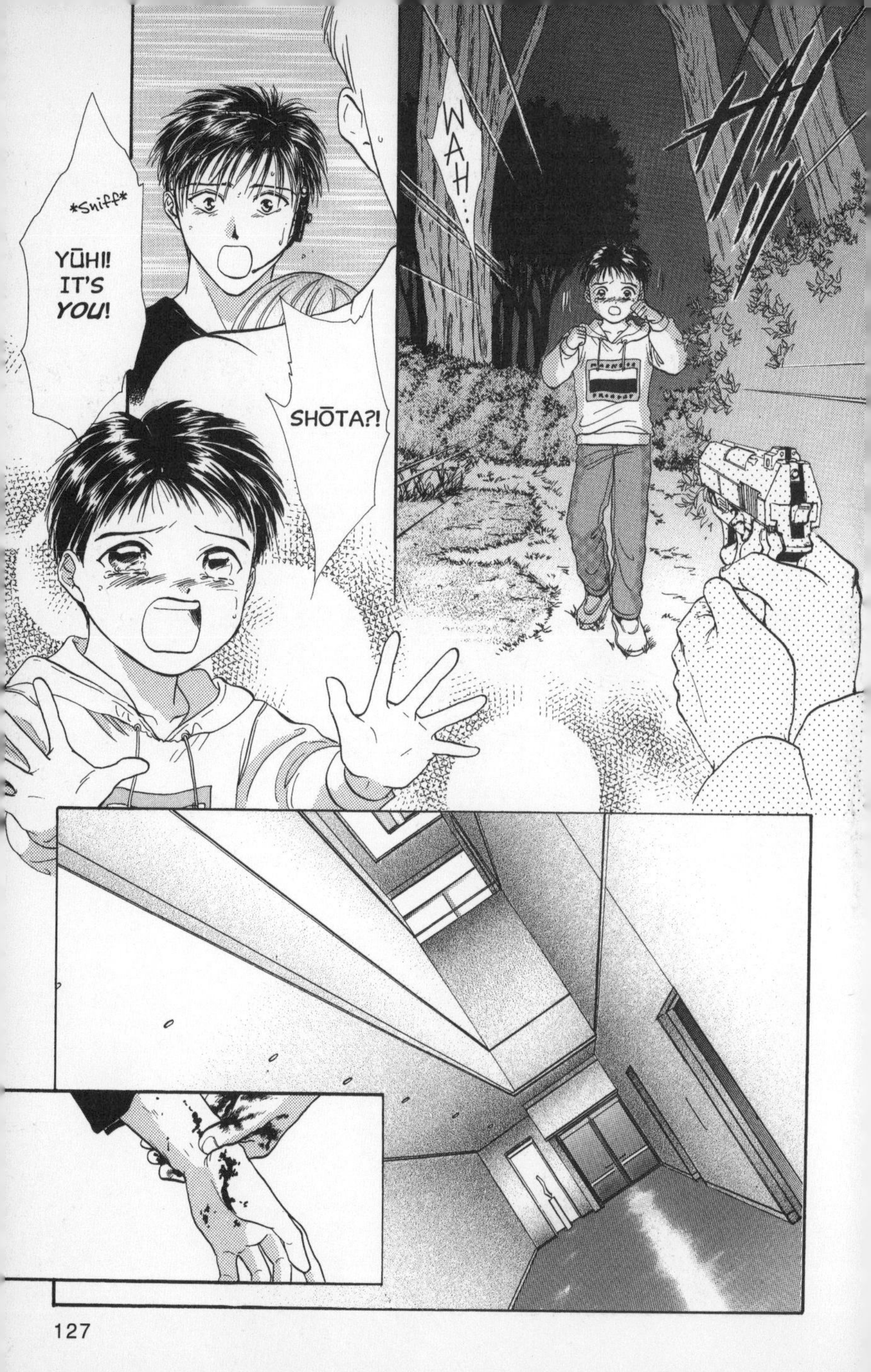
WAH...
Sniff
YŪHI! IT'S *YOU*!
SHŌTA?!

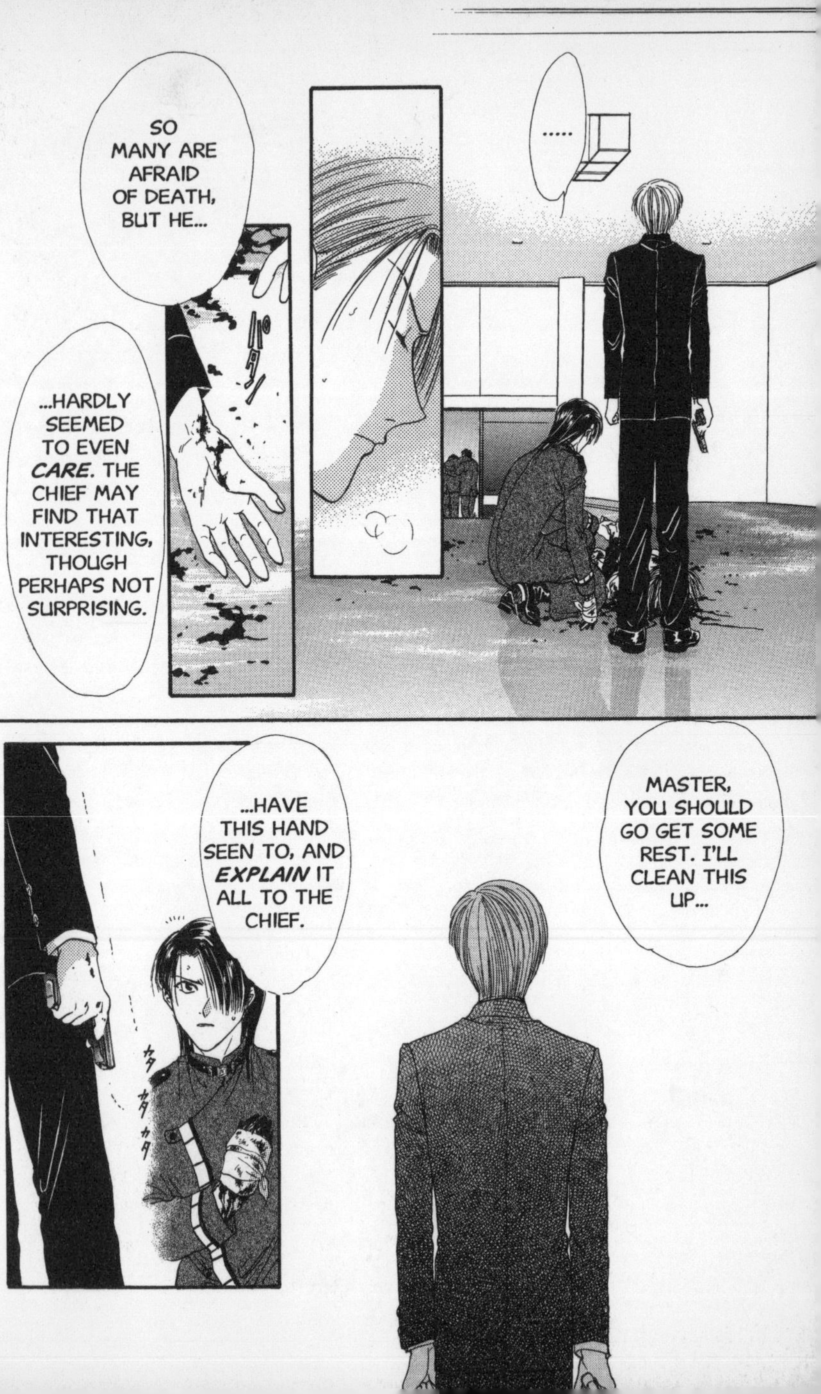
.....
SO MANY ARE AFRAID OF DEATH, BUT HE...
...HARDLY SEEMED TO EVEN CARE. THE CHIEF MAY FIND THAT INTERESTING, THOUGH PERHAPS NOT SURPRISING.
MASTER, YOU SHOULD GO GET SOME REST. I'LL CLEAN THIS UP...
...HAVE THIS HAND SEEN TO, AND EXPLAIN IT ALL TO THE CHIEF.
カタ カタ カタ

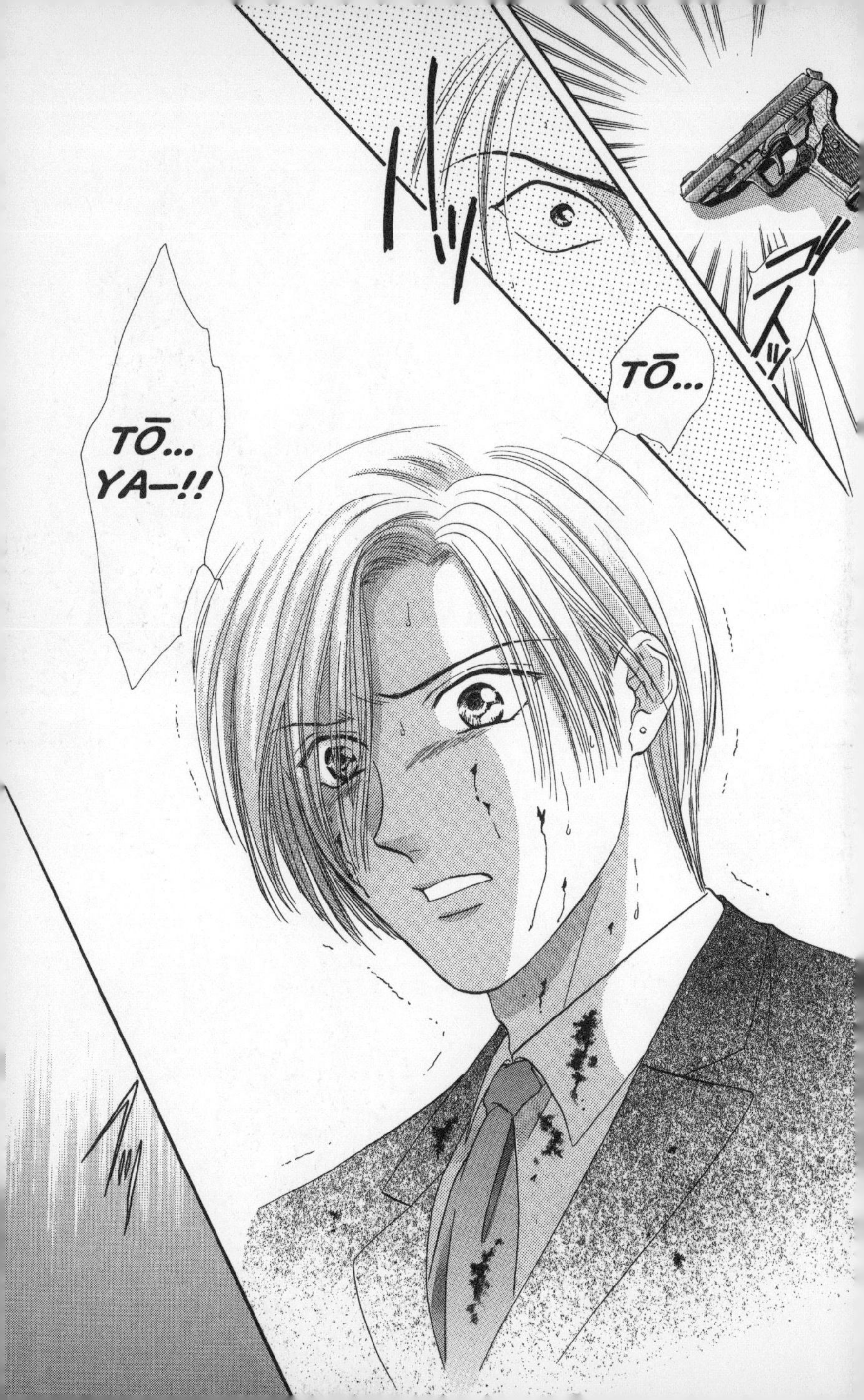

ゴトッ
ハッ
TŌ...
TŌ...
YA—!!

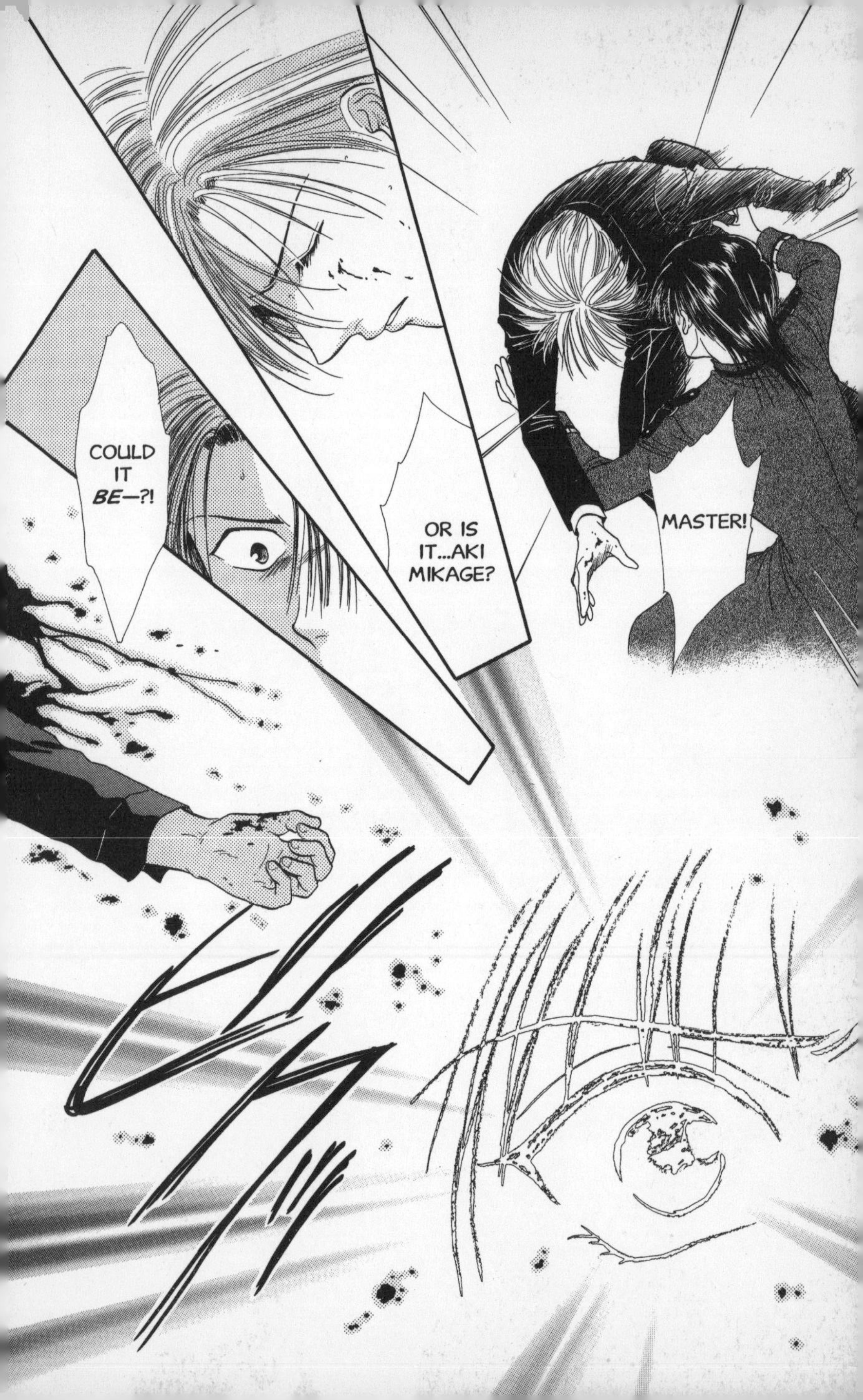
MASTER!
OR IS IT...AKI MIKAGE?
COULD IT *BE*—?!

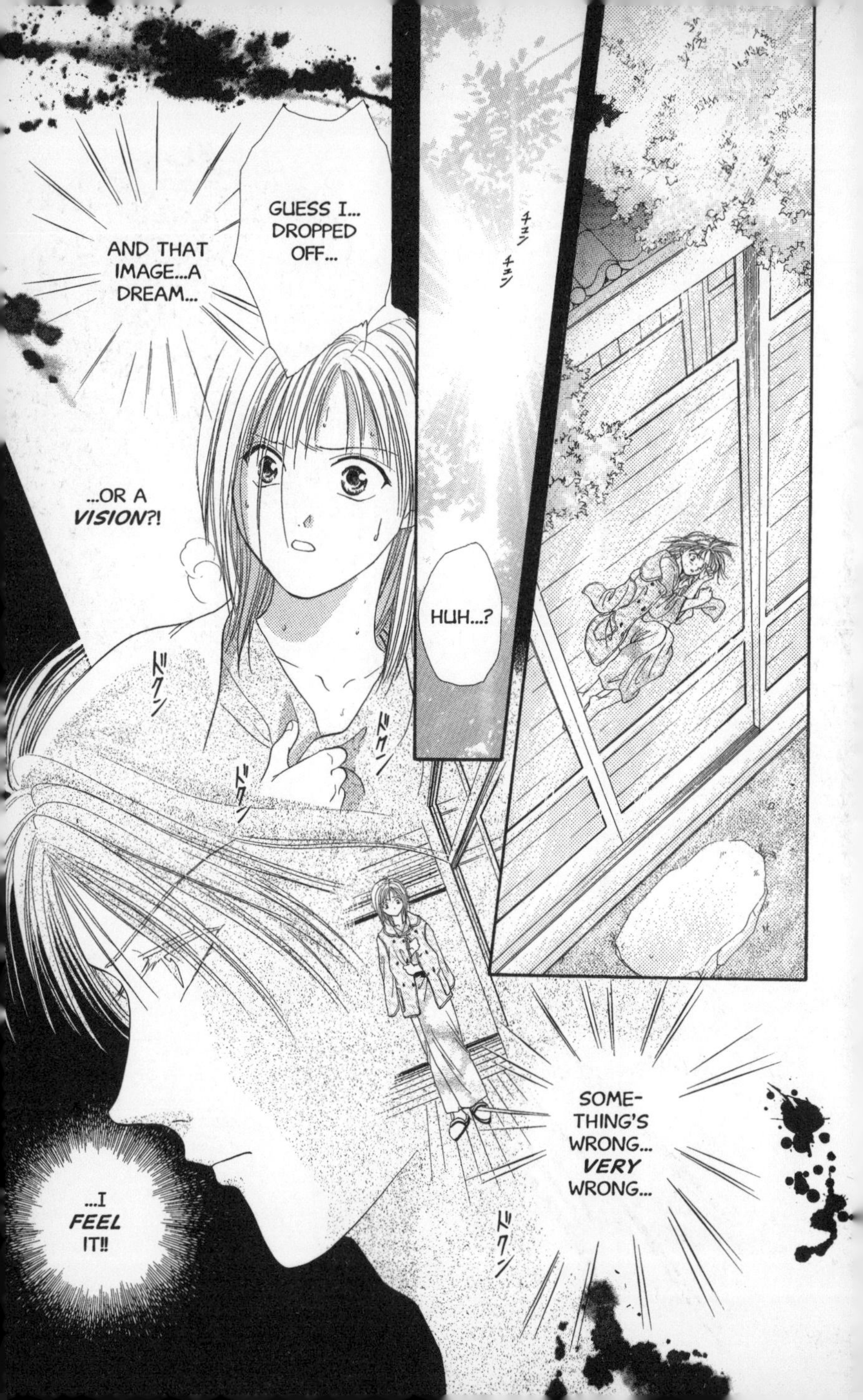
チュン チュン
HUH...?
GUESS I... DROPPED OFF...
AND THAT IMAGE...A DREAM...
...OR A *VISION*?!
ドクン
ドクン
ドクン
SOME-THING'S WRONG... *VERY* WRONG...
ドクン
...I *FEEL* IT!!

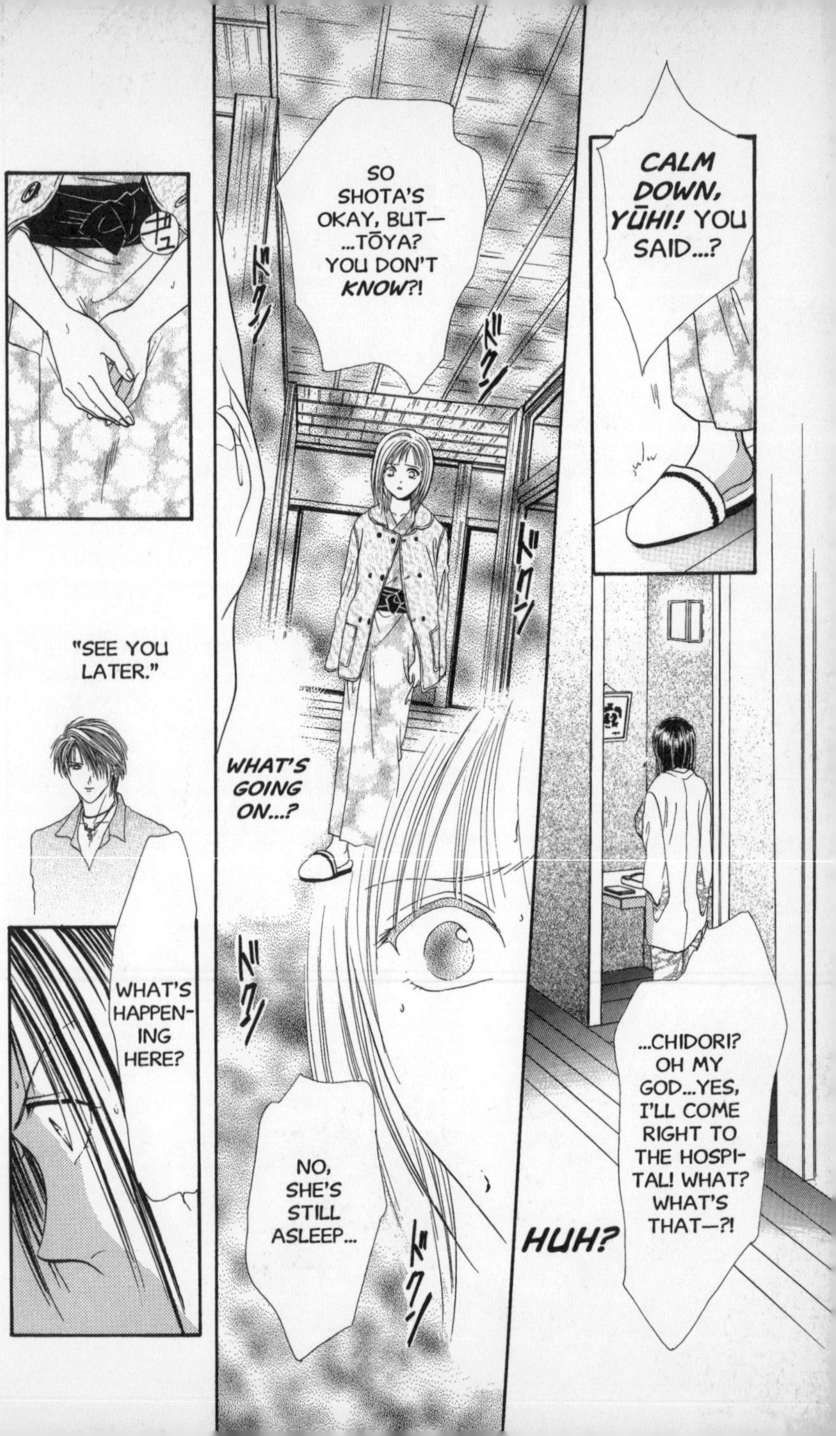

CALM DOWN, YŪHI! YOU SAID...?
...CHIDORI? OH MY GOD...YES, I'LL COME RIGHT TO THE HOSPITAL! WHAT? WHAT'S THAT—?!
HUH?
SO SHOTA'S OKAY, BUT— ...TŌYA? YOU DON'T KNOW?!
WHAT'S GOING ON...?
NO, SHE'S STILL ASLEEP...
"SEE YOU LATER."
WHAT'S HAPPENING HERE?

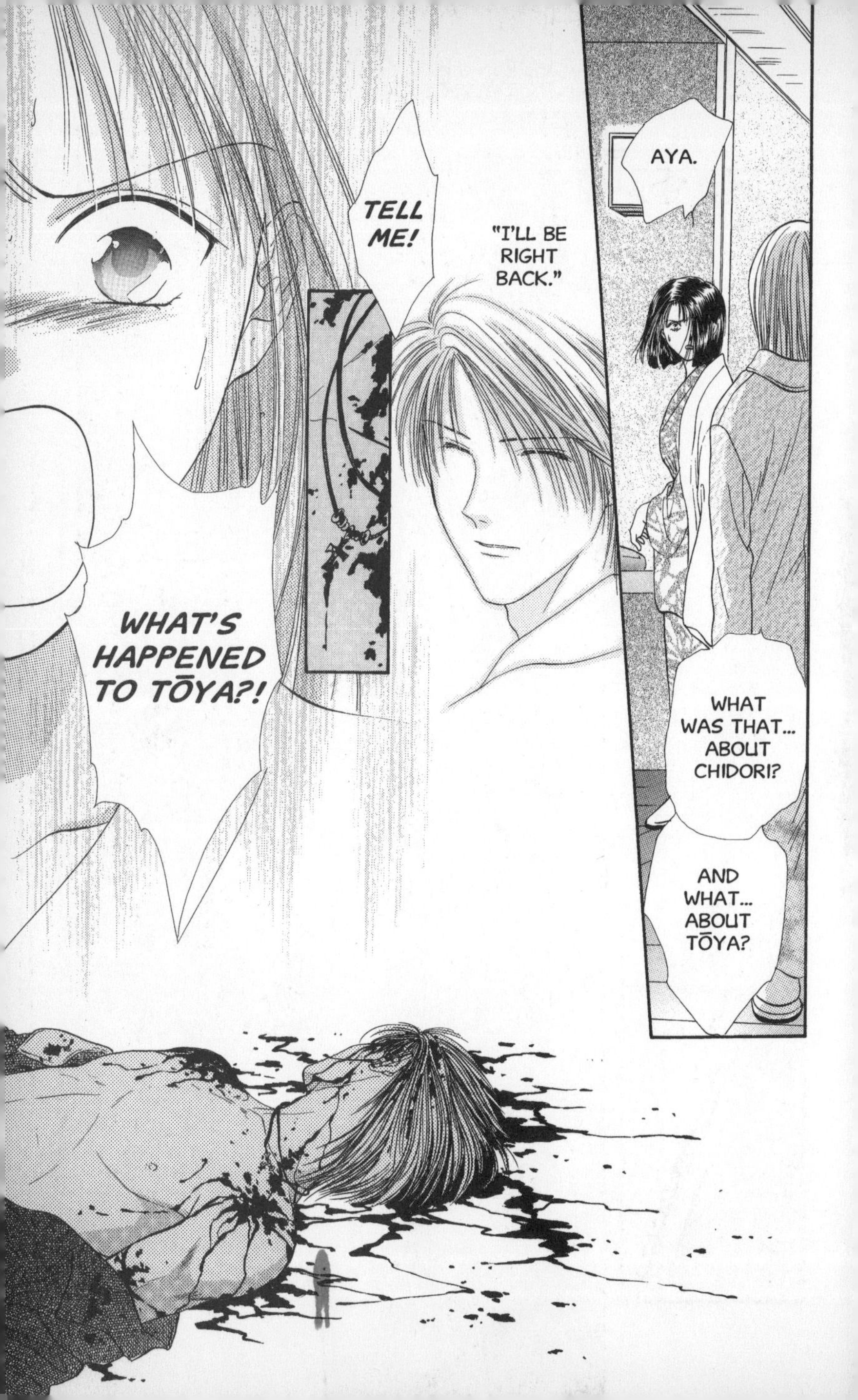
AYA.
WHAT WAS THAT... ABOUT CHIDORI?
AND WHAT... ABOUT TŌYA?
"I'LL BE RIGHT BACK."
TELL ME!
WHAT'S HAPPENED TO TŌYA?!

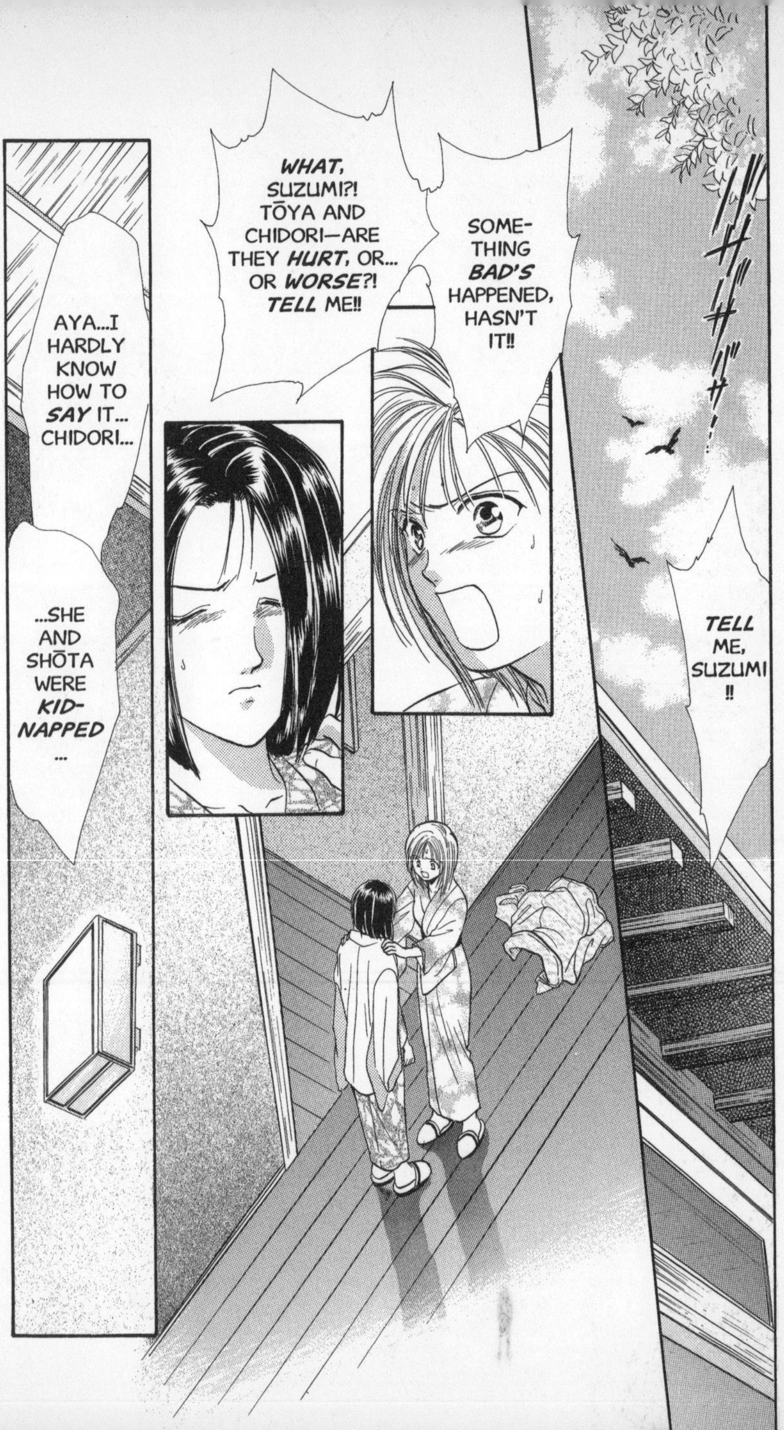
SOMETHING BAD'S HAPPENED, HASN'T IT!!
WHAT, SUZUMI?! TŌYA AND CHIDORI—ARE THEY HURT, OR... OR WORSE?! TELL ME!!
TELL ME, SUZUMI!!
AYA...I HARDLY KNOW HOW TO SAY IT... CHIDORI...
...SHE AND SHŌTA WERE KIDNAPPED...

...AND TŌYA AND YŪHI WENT OFF TO *SAVE* THEM! I AGREED NOT TO SAY ANYTHING TO YOU.

TŌYA ALSO WANTED TO *CONFIRM* THAT THE MIKAGE WERE *RECONSTRUCTING* THE HAGOROMO...

NO!

"I FOUND SOME CLUES IN KANAGAWA..."

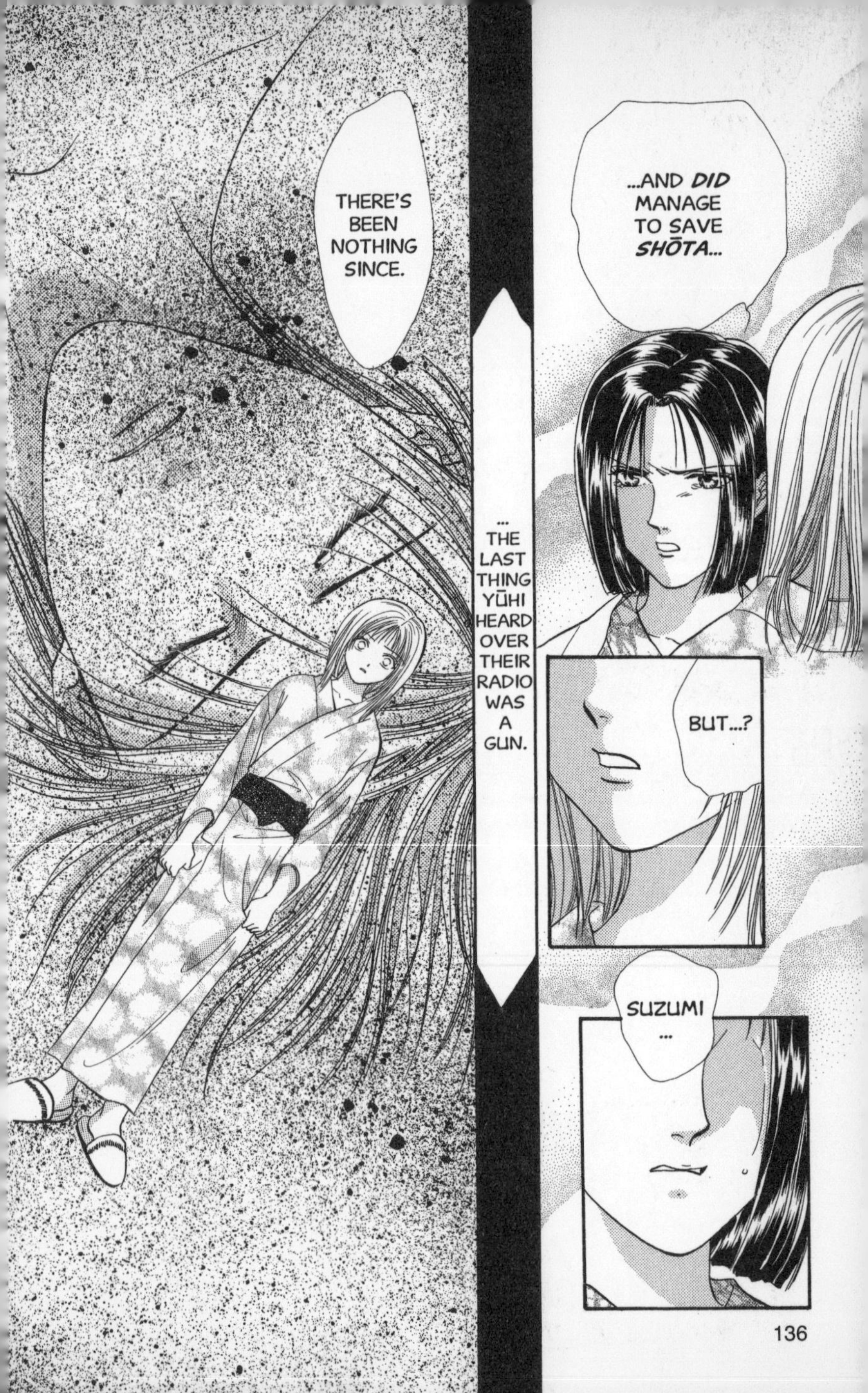
...AND *DID* MANAGE TO SAVE *SHŌTA*...
BUT...?
SUZUMI ...
... THE LAST THING YŪHI HEARD OVER THEIR RADIO WAS A GUN.
THERE'S BEEN NOTHING SINCE.

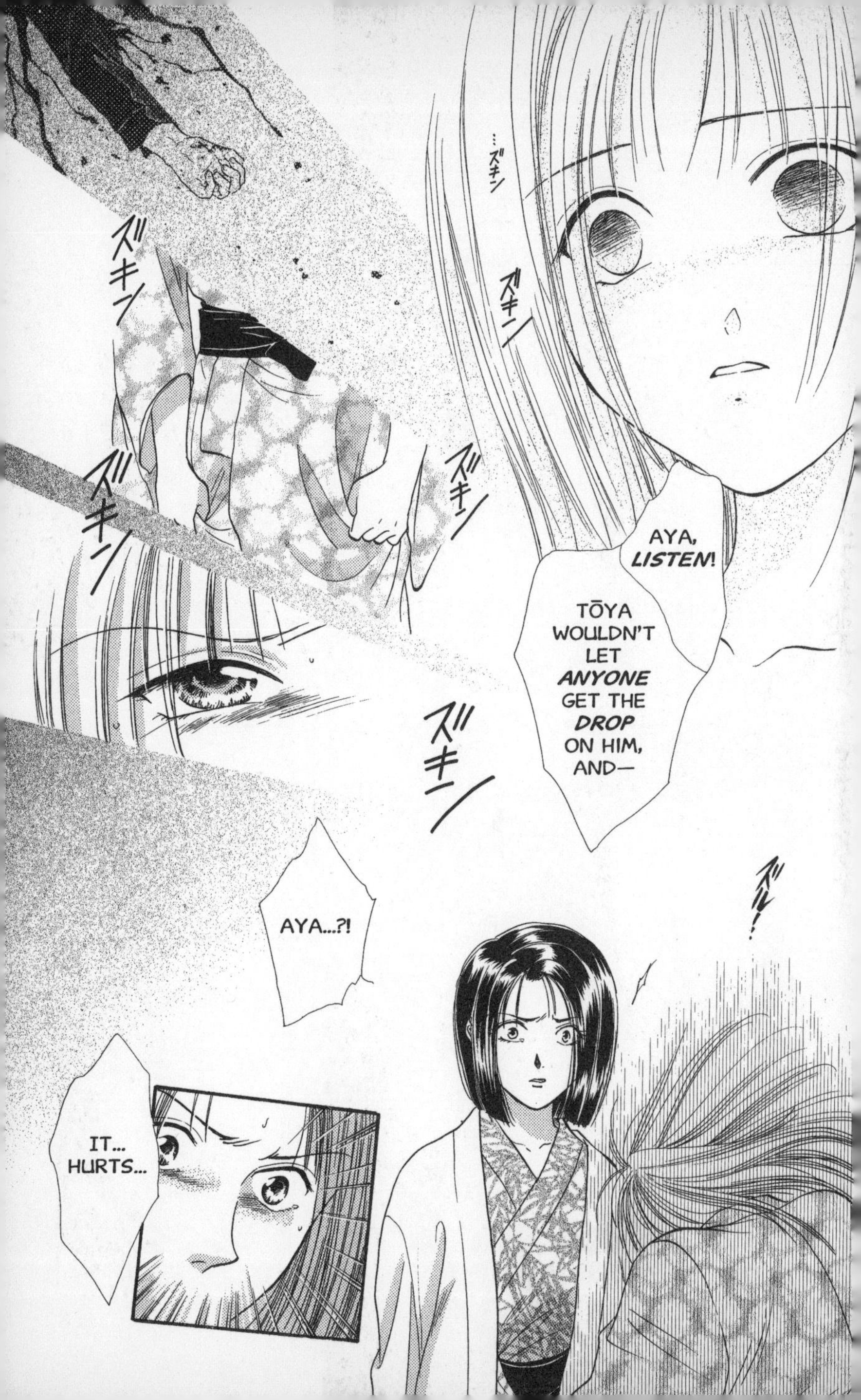
…ズキン
ズキン
AYA, LISTEN!
TŌYA WOULDN'T LET ANYONE GET THE DROP ON HIM, AND—
ズキン
ズキン
ズキン
ズキン
ズキン
AYA…?!
IT… HURTS…

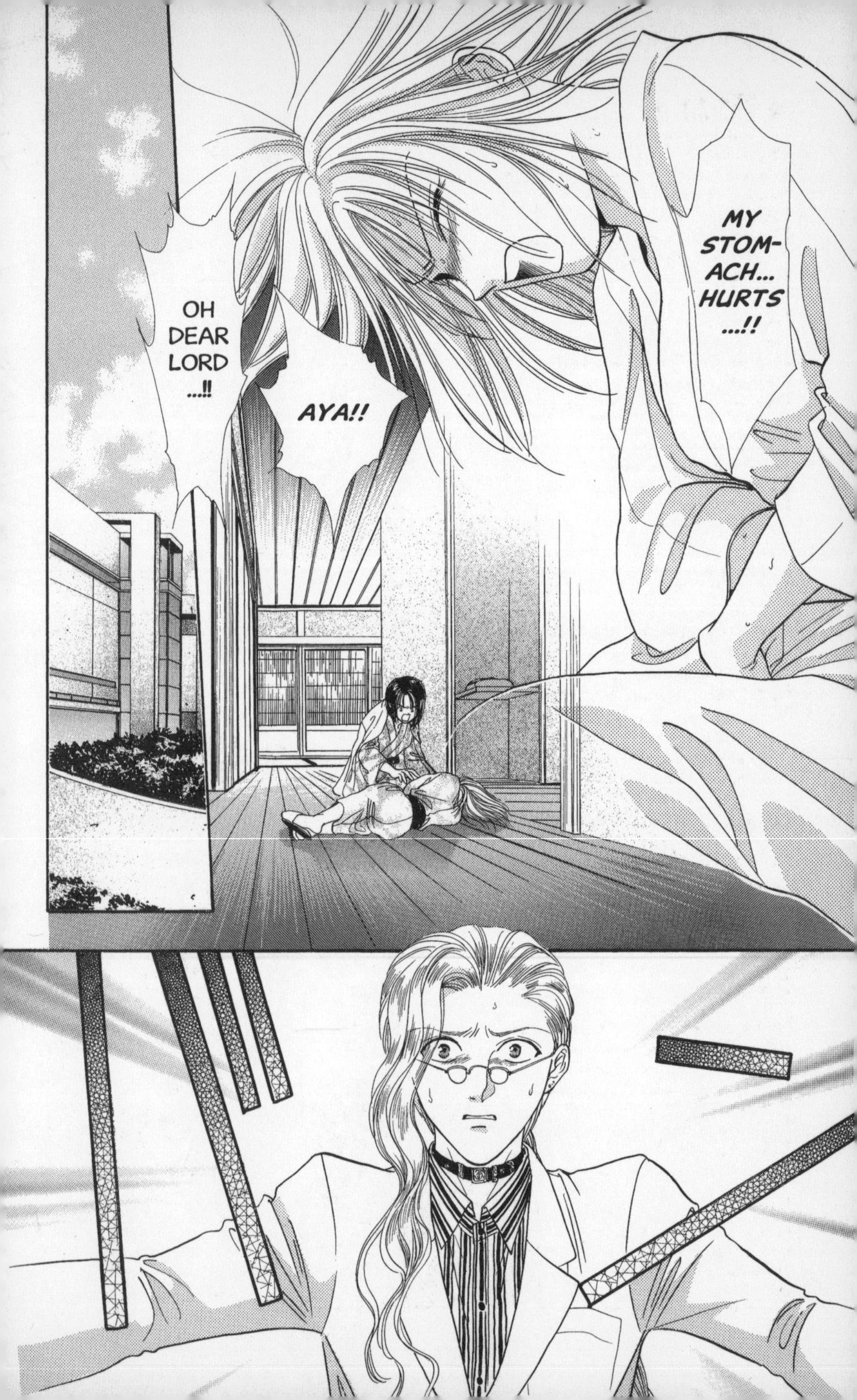
MY STOM-ACH... HURTS ...!!
AYA!!
OH DEAR LORD ...!!

✦ TŌYA ✦

So, I thought Osaka would be the last, but I recently got news of another autograph session, this time in Fukuoka. It's still the beginning of August, now, so not too many details. But I've also just received a postcard from someone there who said that Osaka was too far for her to make the trek, so.... A bookstore in Okayama also wants to host an autograph session, in October, so I guess I'll be going to that, too. That's all I have for details as of now, and who knows—the schedule may change. Keep an eye out for news in "Shōjo Comics"!

...Well, here we are, approaching the climax, in this 12th volume of "Ceres." I'm sure people who buy only the graphic novels (and not read it in serialization) are totally freaking out at the moment about Tōya and Chidori (who wouldn't!). So many have expressed sadness over Chidori, but the response to **Tōya** was something else—it was **beyond** sadness, more like—an angry uproar. ◡̈ (What do you mean, this is no place for a smiley? Sorry.) Tōya has far and away been the most popular male character, so I've been a bit worried how this might go over. I assumed it would have been okay...but, boy, was **that** a gross miscalculation. Gee, y' think?!

Someone even went so far as to write, "I'll have no further need to keep buying 'Shōjo Comics,' now." Oops. Guess that means I have to worry about reactions from the readers of the graphic novels too, now—from the second wave. There, there. Shh, shh... It's okay...

(As I slo-o-owly step away....)

What's done is done, right? (As I make my escape.)

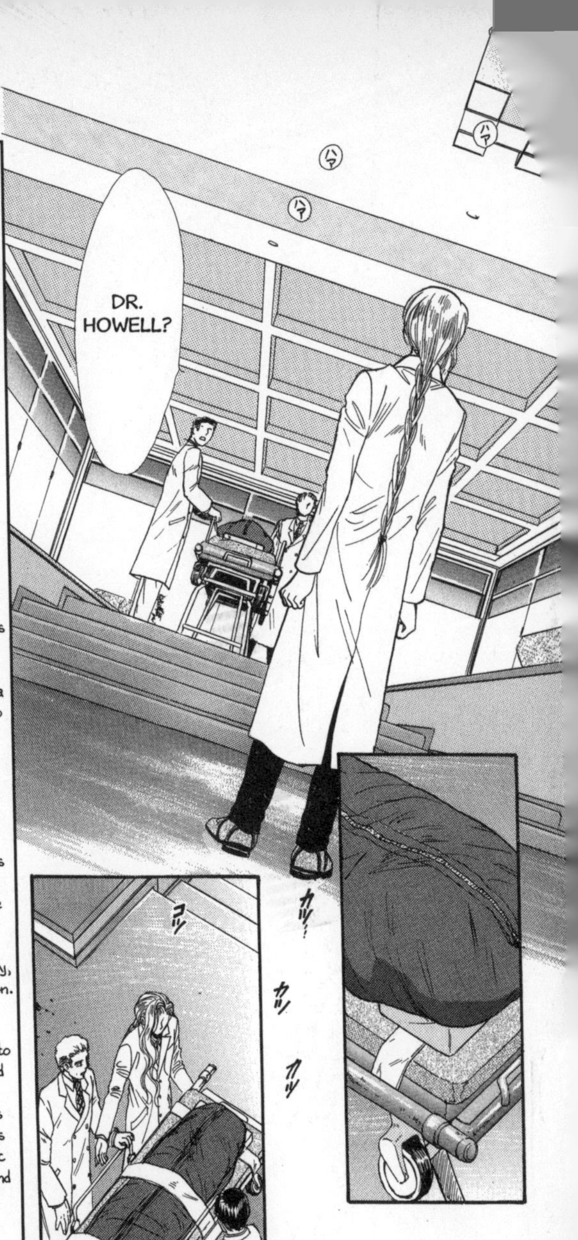
ハァ
ハァ
ハァ
DR. HOWELL?
カッ
コッ
カッ
カッ

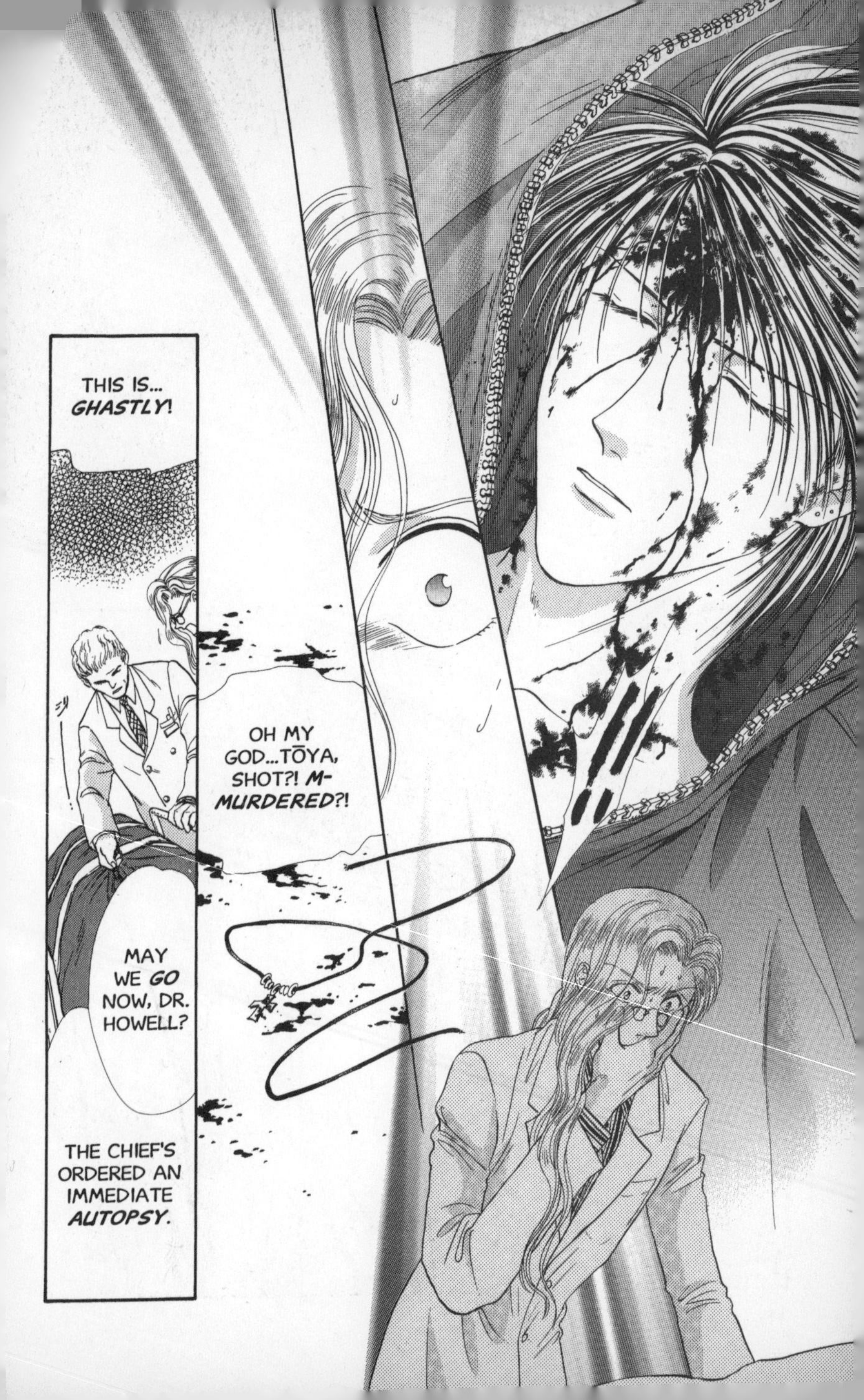
OH MY GOD...TŌYA, SHOT?! M-MURDERED?!
THIS IS... GHASTLY!
MAY WE GO NOW, DR. HOWELL?
THE CHIEF'S ORDERED AN IMMEDIATE AUTOPSY.

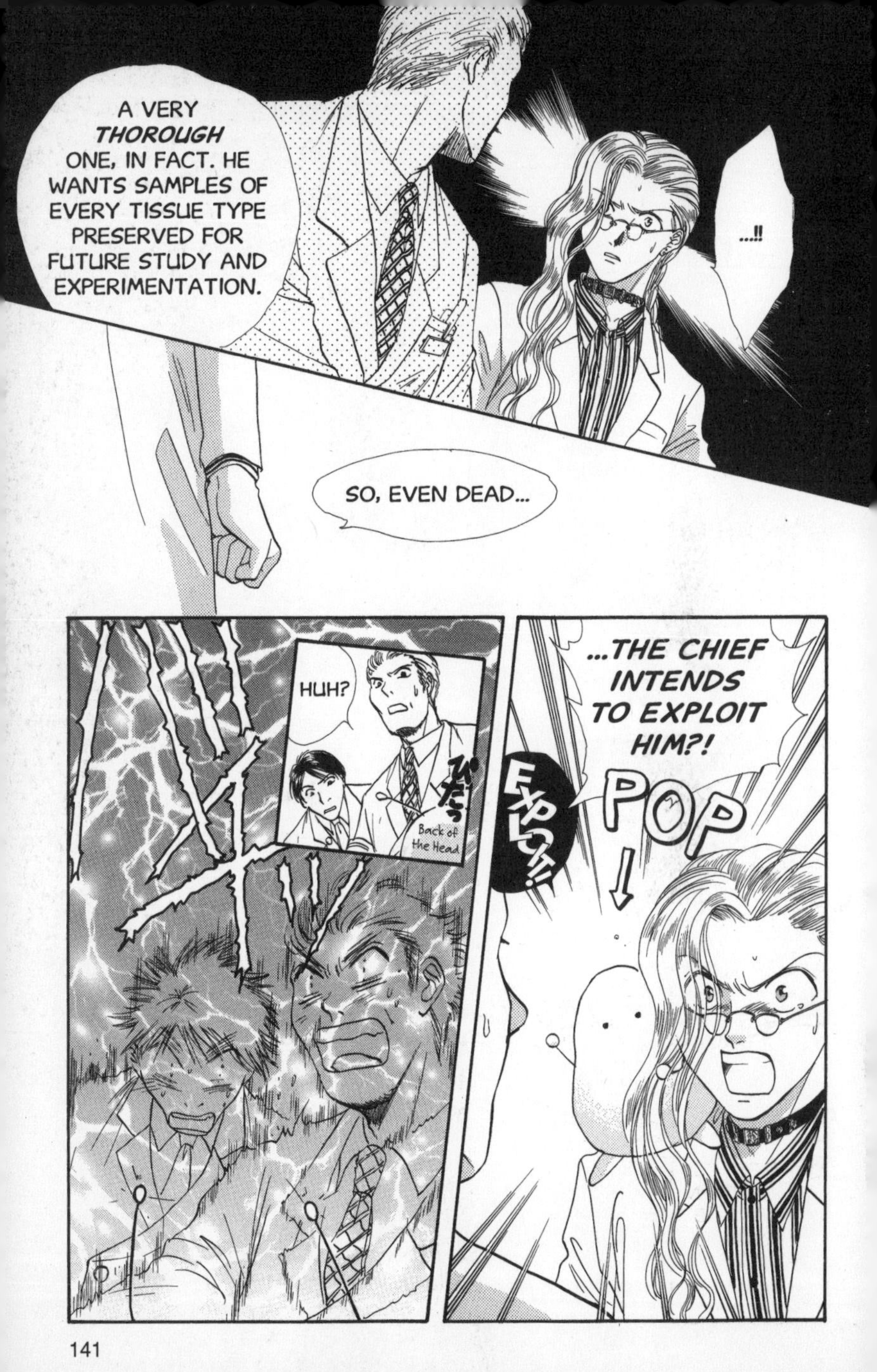
A VERY *THOROUGH* ONE, IN FACT. HE WANTS SAMPLES OF EVERY TISSUE TYPE PRESERVED FOR FUTURE STUDY AND EXPERIMENTATION.
...!!
SO, EVEN DEAD...
...THE CHIEF INTENDS TO EXPLOIT HIM?!
EXPLOIT!!
POP
HUH?
ぴたっ
Back of the Head

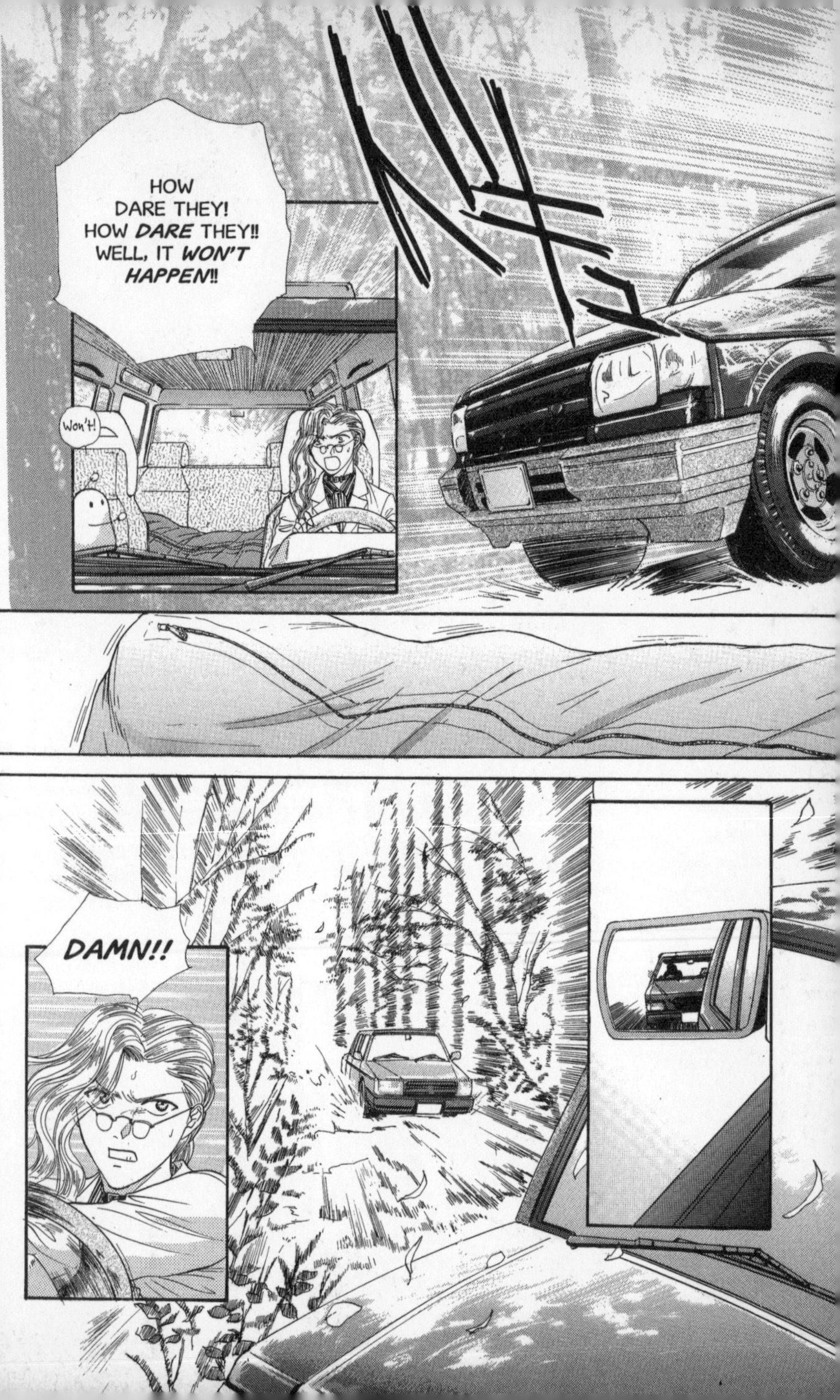
HOW DARE THEY! HOW DARE THEY!! WELL, IT WON'T HAPPEN!!
Won't!
DAMN!!

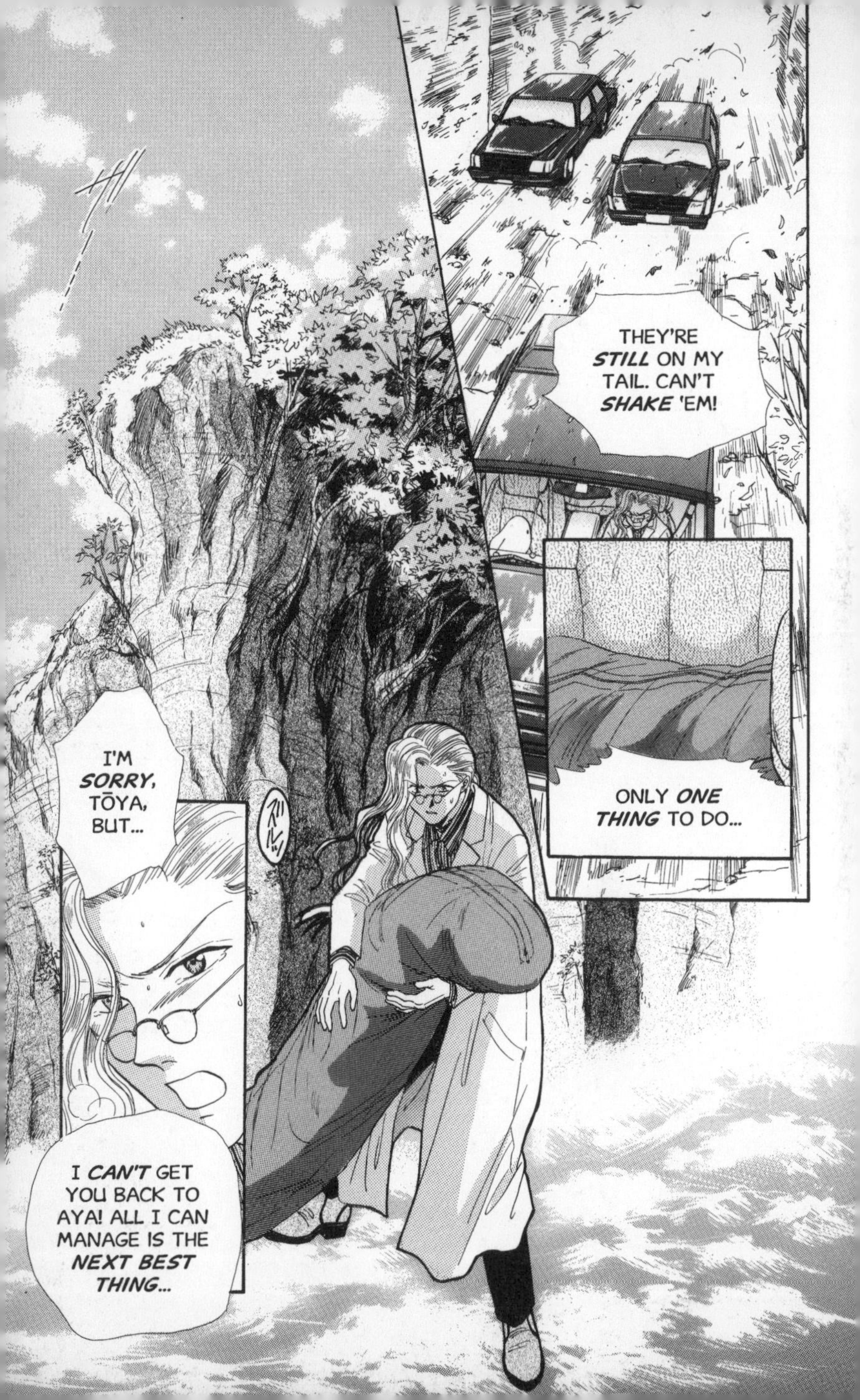
THEY'RE *STILL* ON MY TAIL. CAN'T *SHAKE* 'EM!
ONLY *ONE THING* TO DO...
I'M *SORRY,* TŌYA, BUT...
I *CAN'T* GET YOU BACK TO AYA! ALL I CAN MANAGE IS THE *NEXT BEST THING*...

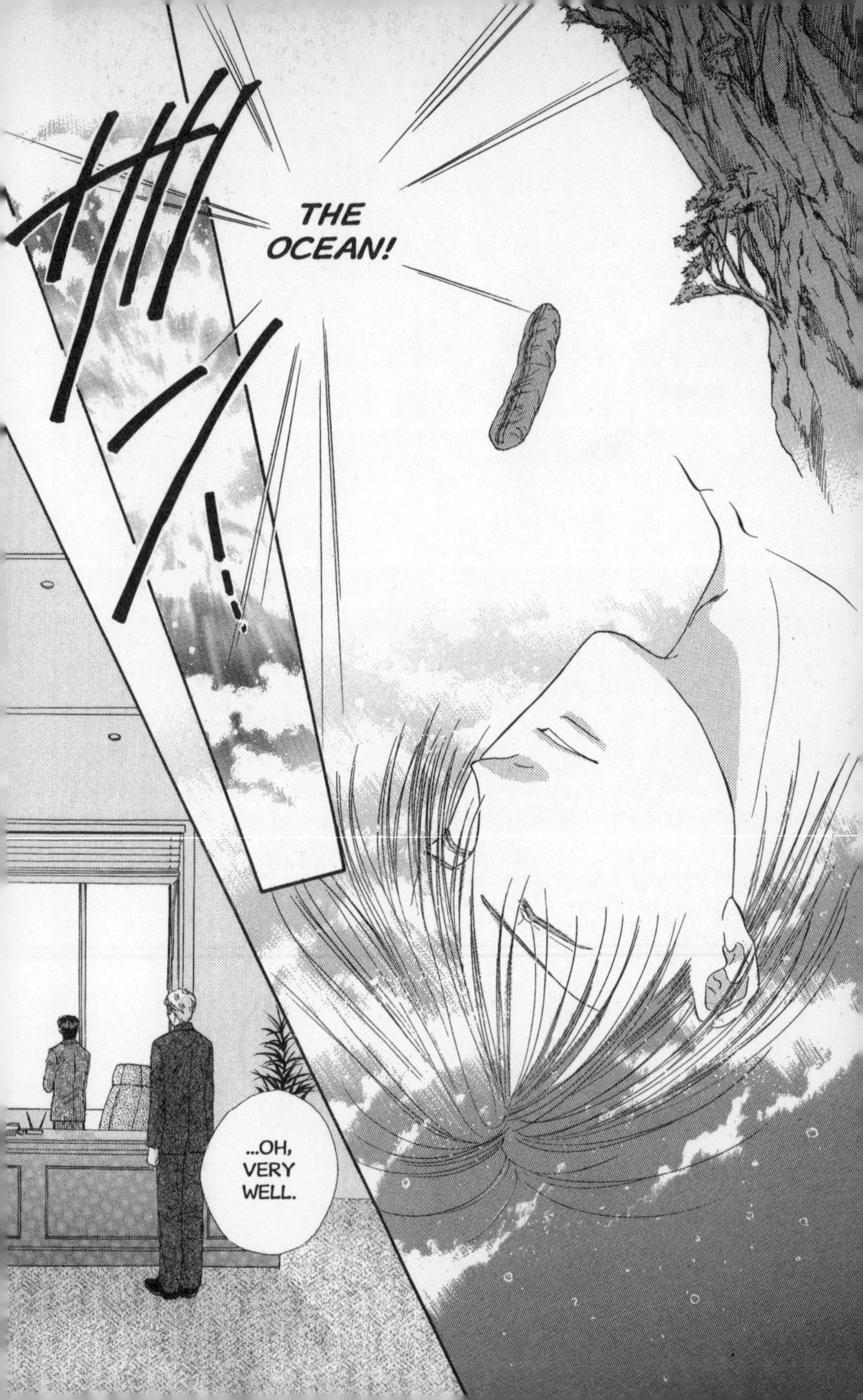
THE OCEAN!
...OH, VERY WELL.

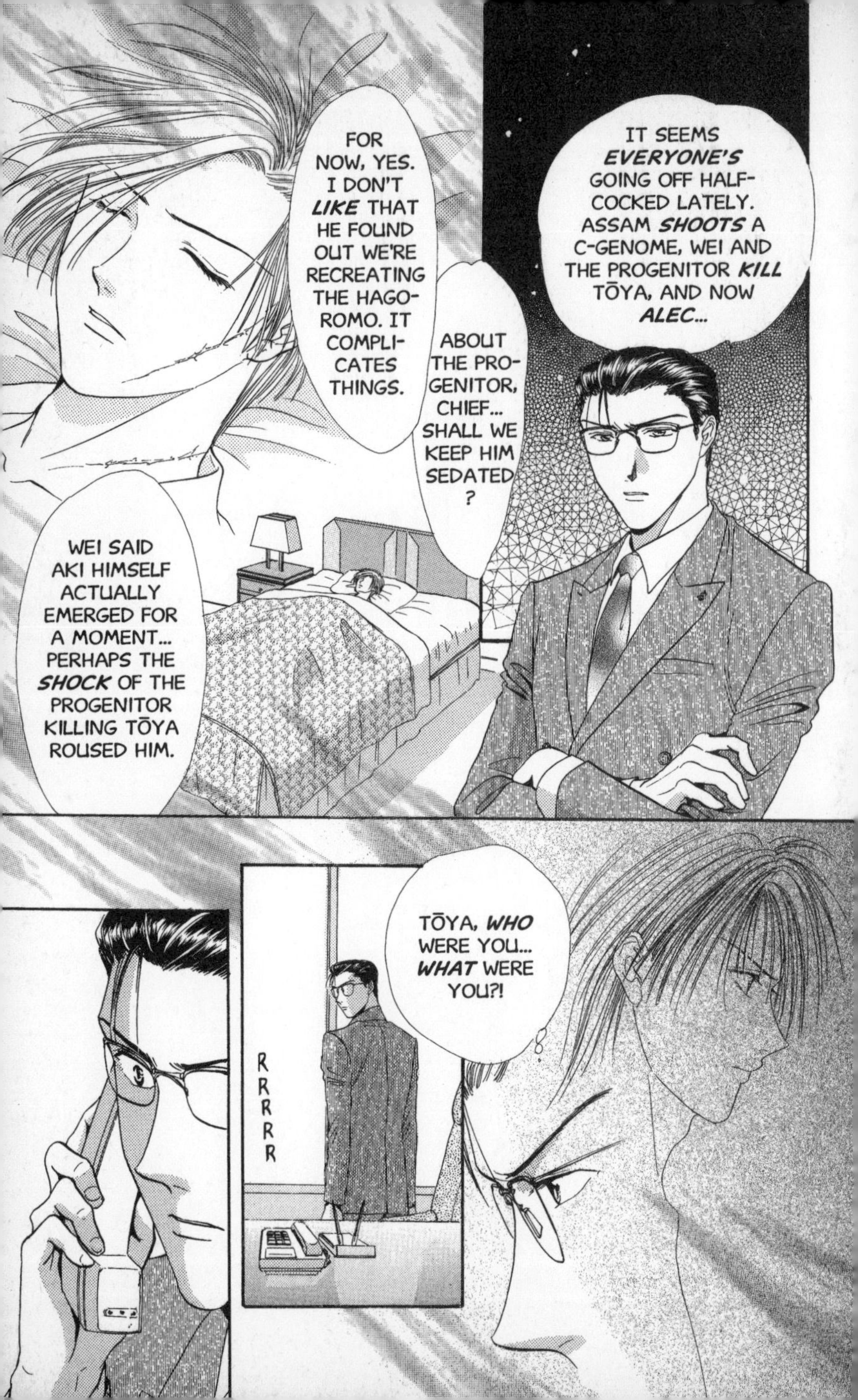
IT SEEMS EVERYONE'S GOING OFF HALF-COCKED LATELY. ASSAM SHOOTS A C-GENOME, WEI AND THE PROGENITOR KILL TŌYA, AND NOW ALEC...
ABOUT THE PROGENITOR, CHIEF... SHALL WE KEEP HIM SEDATED?
FOR NOW, YES. I DON'T LIKE THAT HE FOUND OUT WE'RE RECREATING THE HAGO-ROMO. IT COMPLI-CATES THINGS.
WEI SAID AKI HIMSELF ACTUALLY EMERGED FOR A MOMENT... PERHAPS THE SHOCK OF THE PROGENITOR KILLING TŌYA ROUSED HIM.
TŌYA, WHO WERE YOU... WHAT WERE YOU?!
RRRRRR

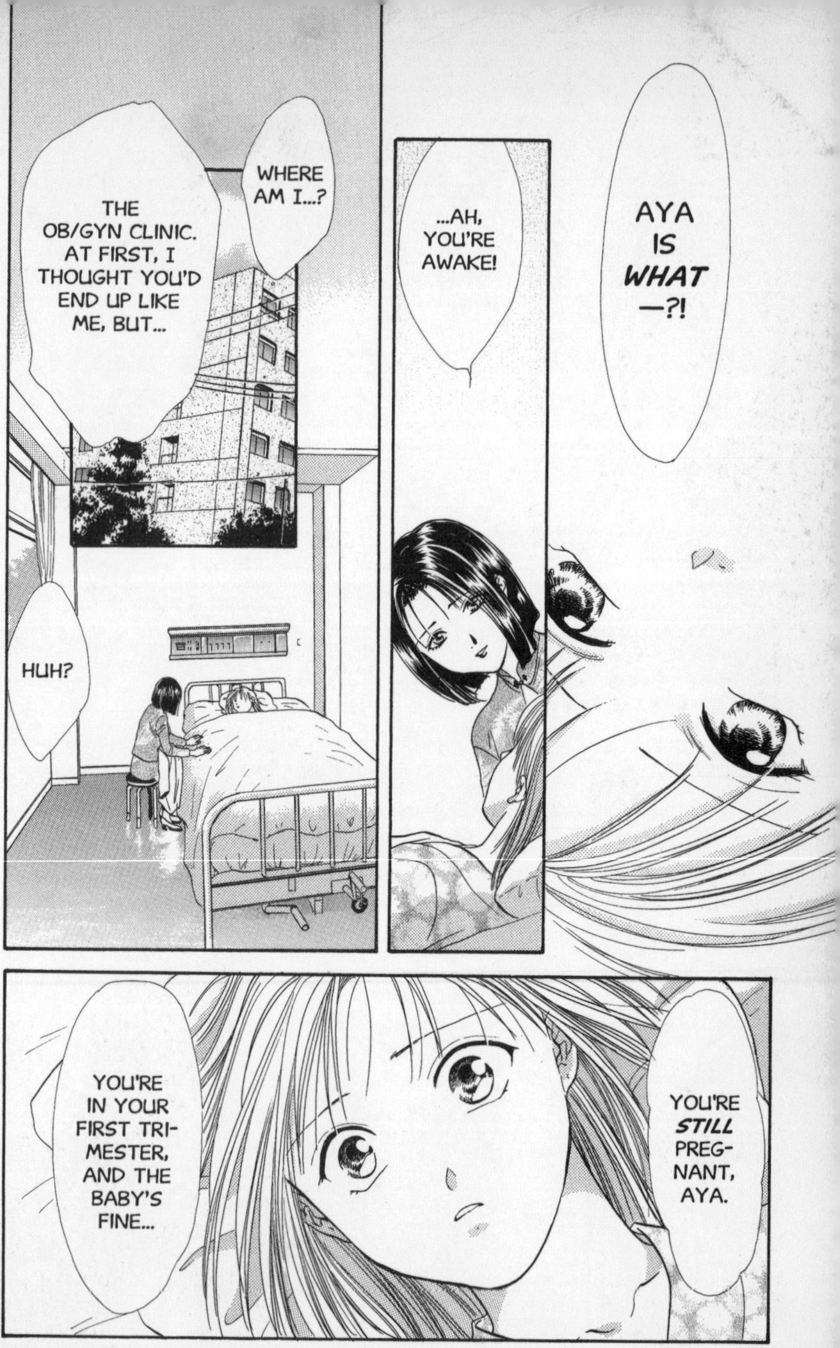
AYA IS WHAT—?!
...AH, YOU'RE AWAKE!
WHERE AM I...?
THE OB/GYN CLINIC. AT FIRST, I THOUGHT YOU'D END UP LIKE ME, BUT...
HUH?
YOU'RE STILL PREGNANT, AYA.
YOU'RE IN YOUR FIRST TRI-MESTER, AND THE BABY'S FINE...

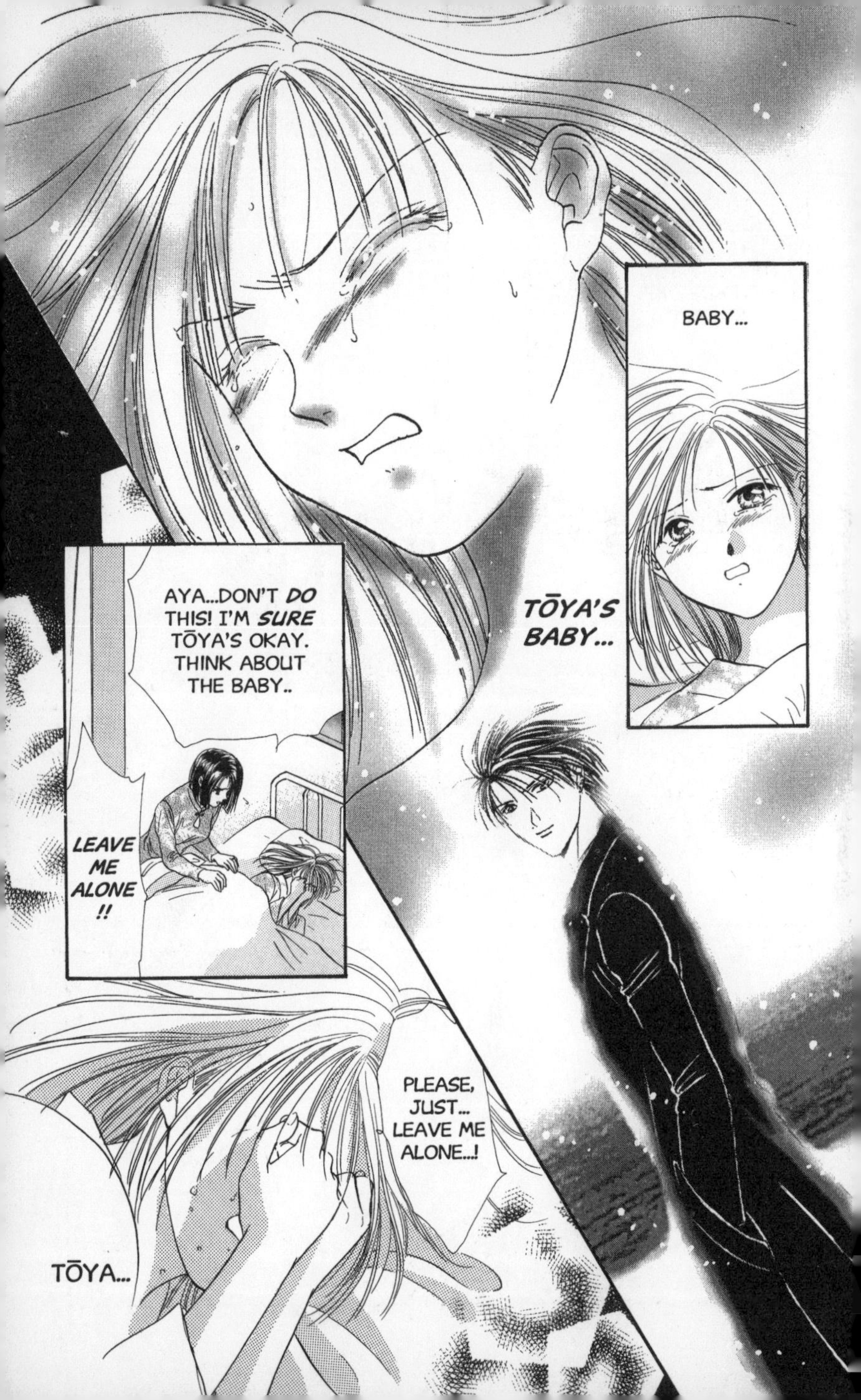
BABY...
TŌYA'S BABY...
AYA...DON'T *DO* THIS! I'M *SURE* TŌYA'S OKAY. THINK ABOUT THE BABY..
LEAVE ME ALONE !!
PLEASE, JUST... LEAVE ME ALONE...!
TŌYA...

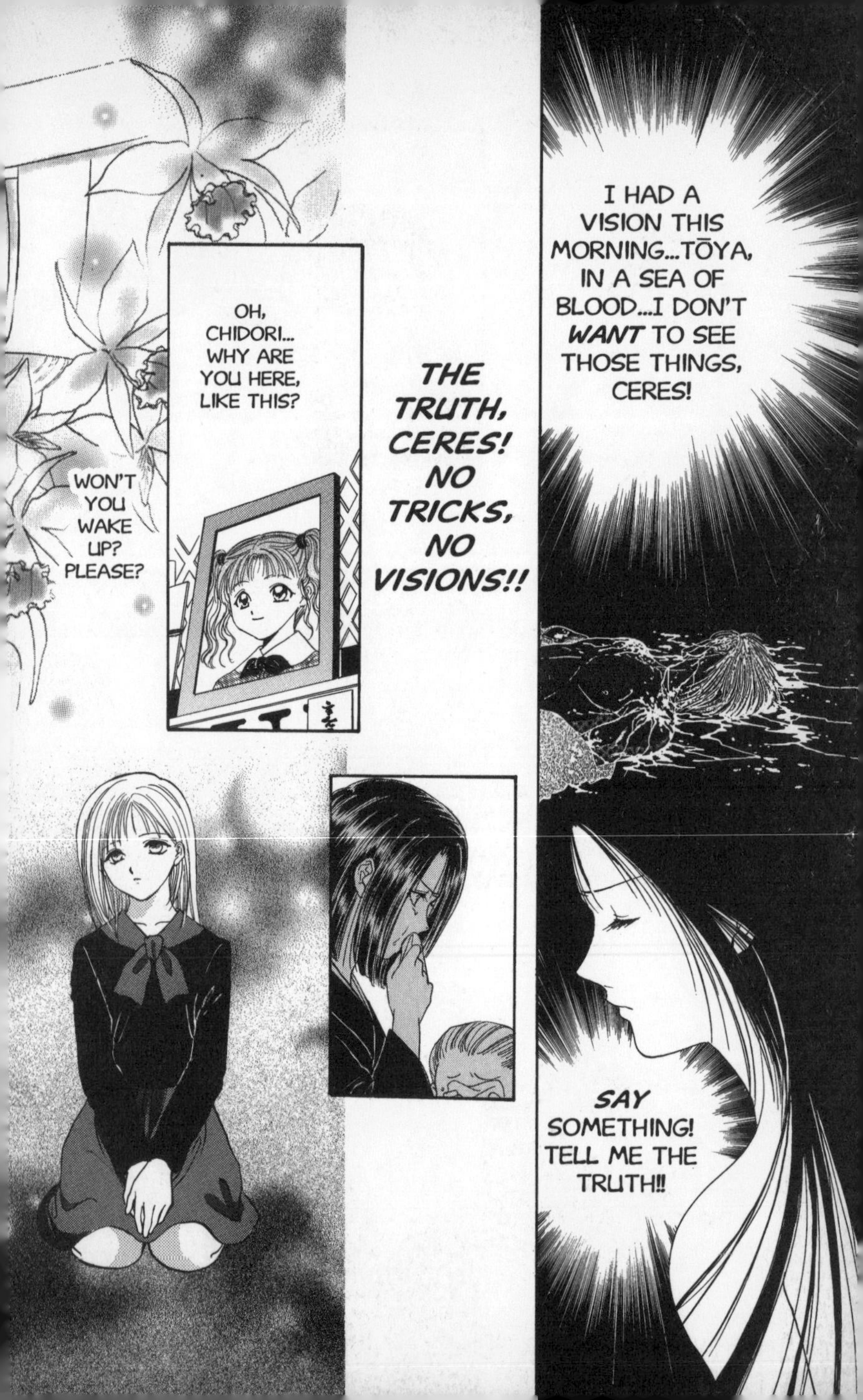
I HAD A VISION THIS MORNING...TŌYA, IN A SEA OF BLOOD...I DON'T *WANT* TO SEE THOSE THINGS, CERES!
SAY SOMETHING! TELL ME THE TRUTH!!
THE TRUTH, CERES! NO TRICKS, NO VISIONS!!
OH, CHIDORI... WHY ARE YOU HERE, LIKE THIS?
WON'T YOU WAKE UP? PLEASE?

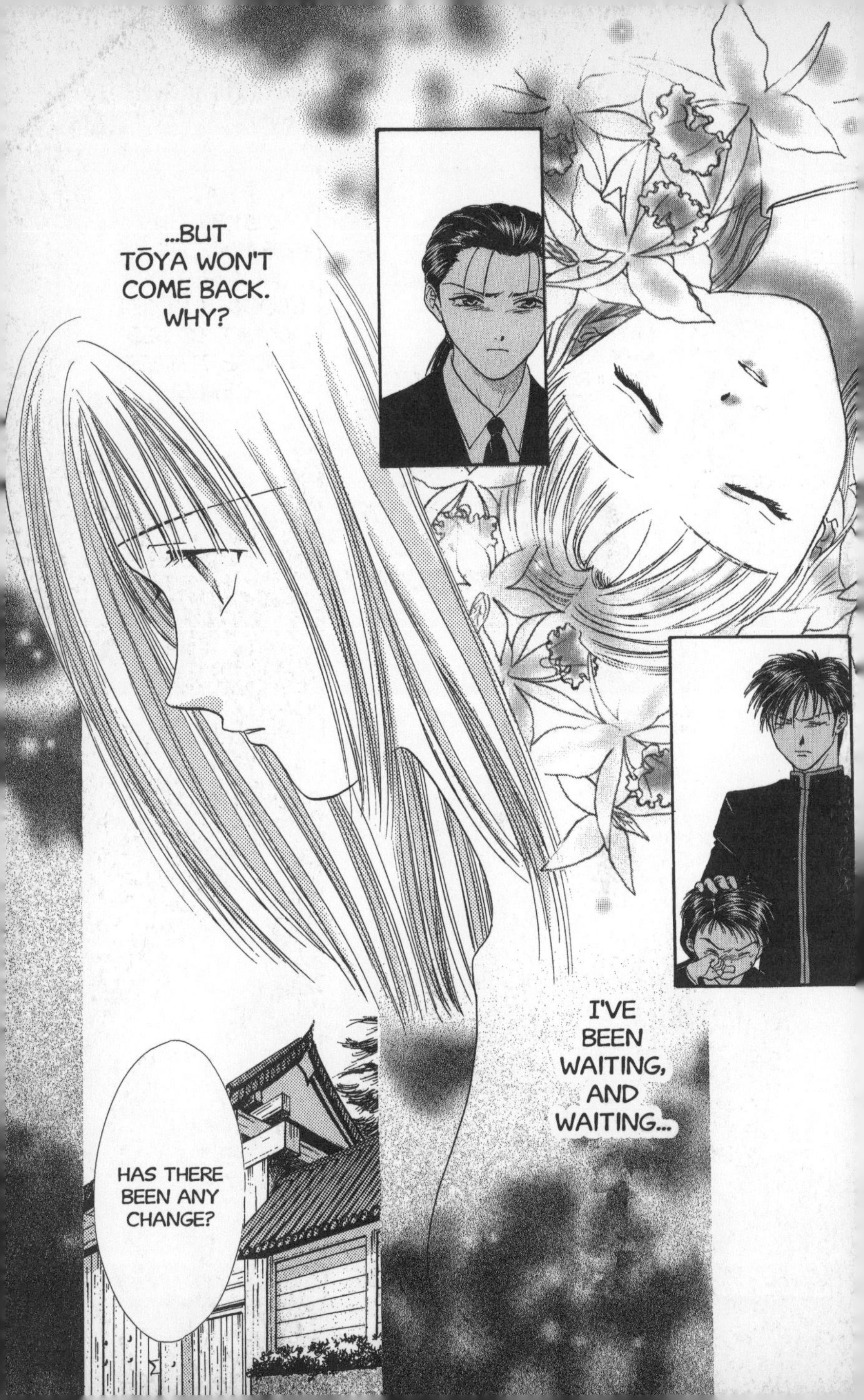
...BUT TŌYA WON'T COME BACK. WHY?
I'VE BEEN WAITING, AND WAITING...
HAS THERE BEEN ANY CHANGE?

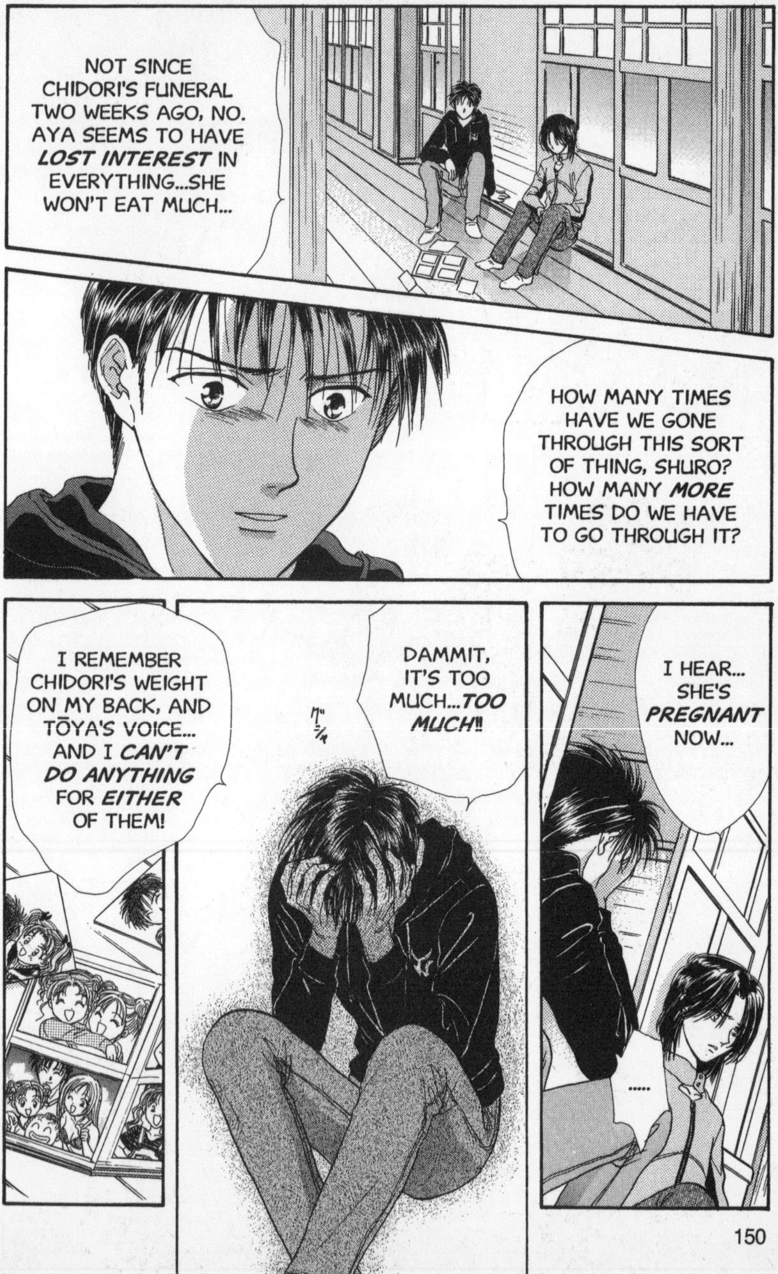
NOT SINCE CHIDORI'S FUNERAL TWO WEEKS AGO, NO. AYA SEEMS TO HAVE *LOST INTEREST* IN EVERYTHING...SHE WON'T EAT MUCH...
HOW MANY TIMES HAVE WE GONE THROUGH THIS SORT OF THING, SHURO? HOW MANY *MORE* TIMES DO WE HAVE TO GO THROUGH IT?
I HEAR... SHE'S *PREGNANT* NOW...
.....
DAMMIT, IT'S TOO MUCH...*TOO MUCH*!!
I REMEMBER CHIDORI'S WEIGHT ON MY BACK, AND TŌYA'S VOICE... AND I *CAN'T DO ANYTHING* FOR *EITHER* OF THEM!

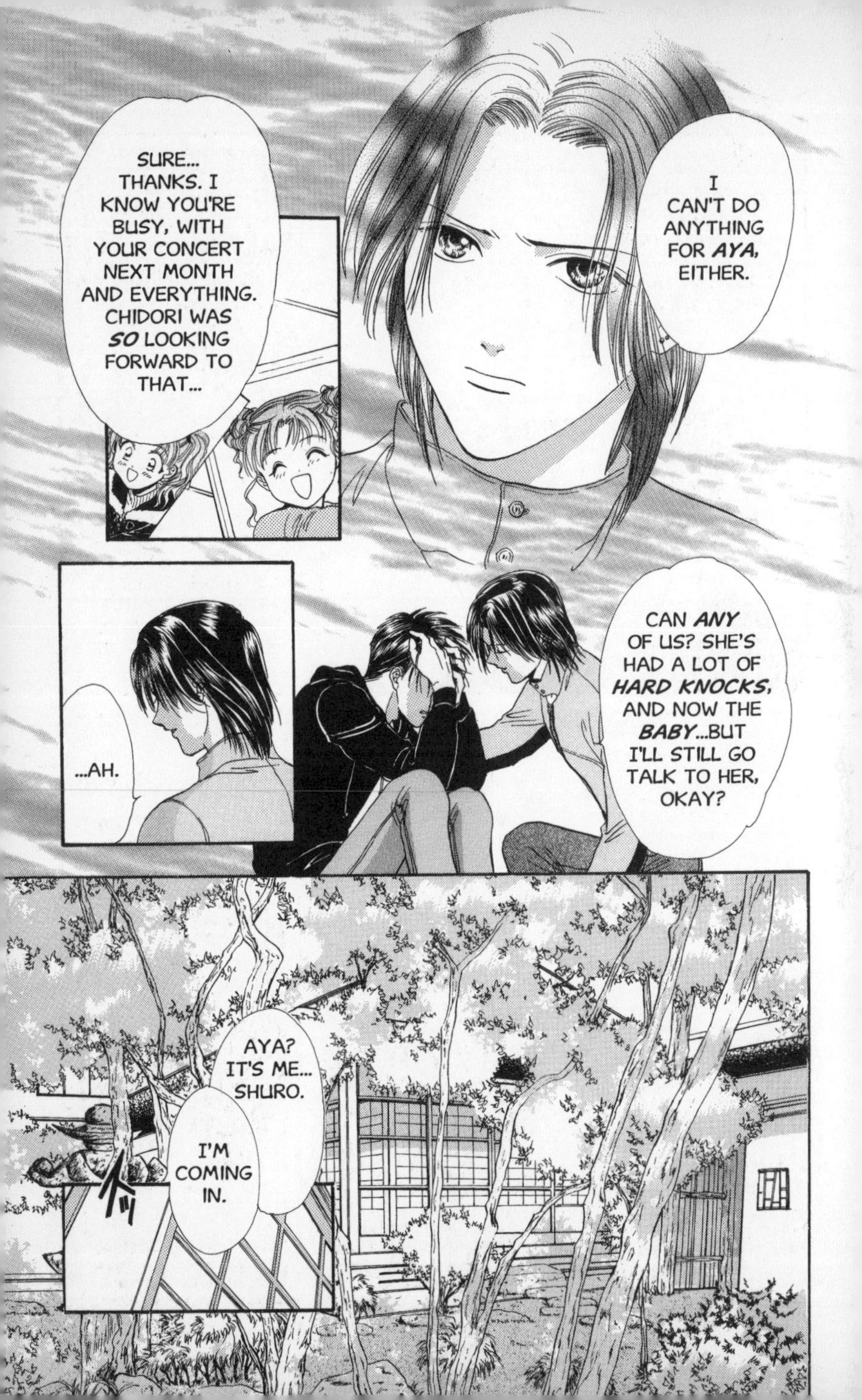
I CAN'T DO ANYTHING FOR AYA, EITHER.
SURE... THANKS. I KNOW YOU'RE BUSY, WITH YOUR CONCERT NEXT MONTH AND EVERYTHING. CHIDORI WAS SO LOOKING FORWARD TO THAT...
CAN ANY OF US? SHE'S HAD A LOT OF HARD KNOCKS, AND NOW THE BABY...BUT I'LL STILL GO TALK TO HER, OKAY?
...AH.
AYA? IT'S ME... SHURO.
I'M COMING IN.

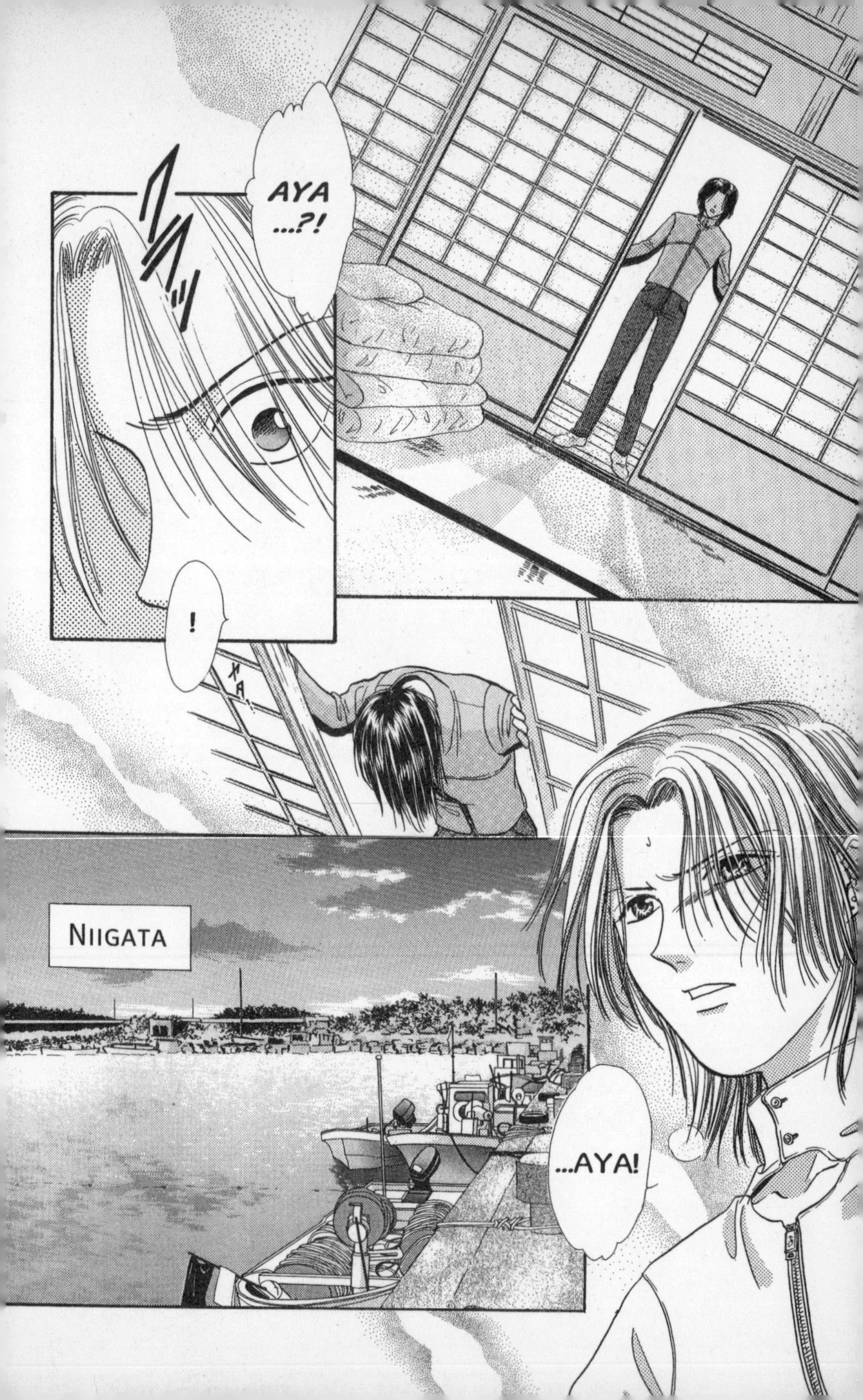
AYA ...?!
!
...AYA!
NIIGATA

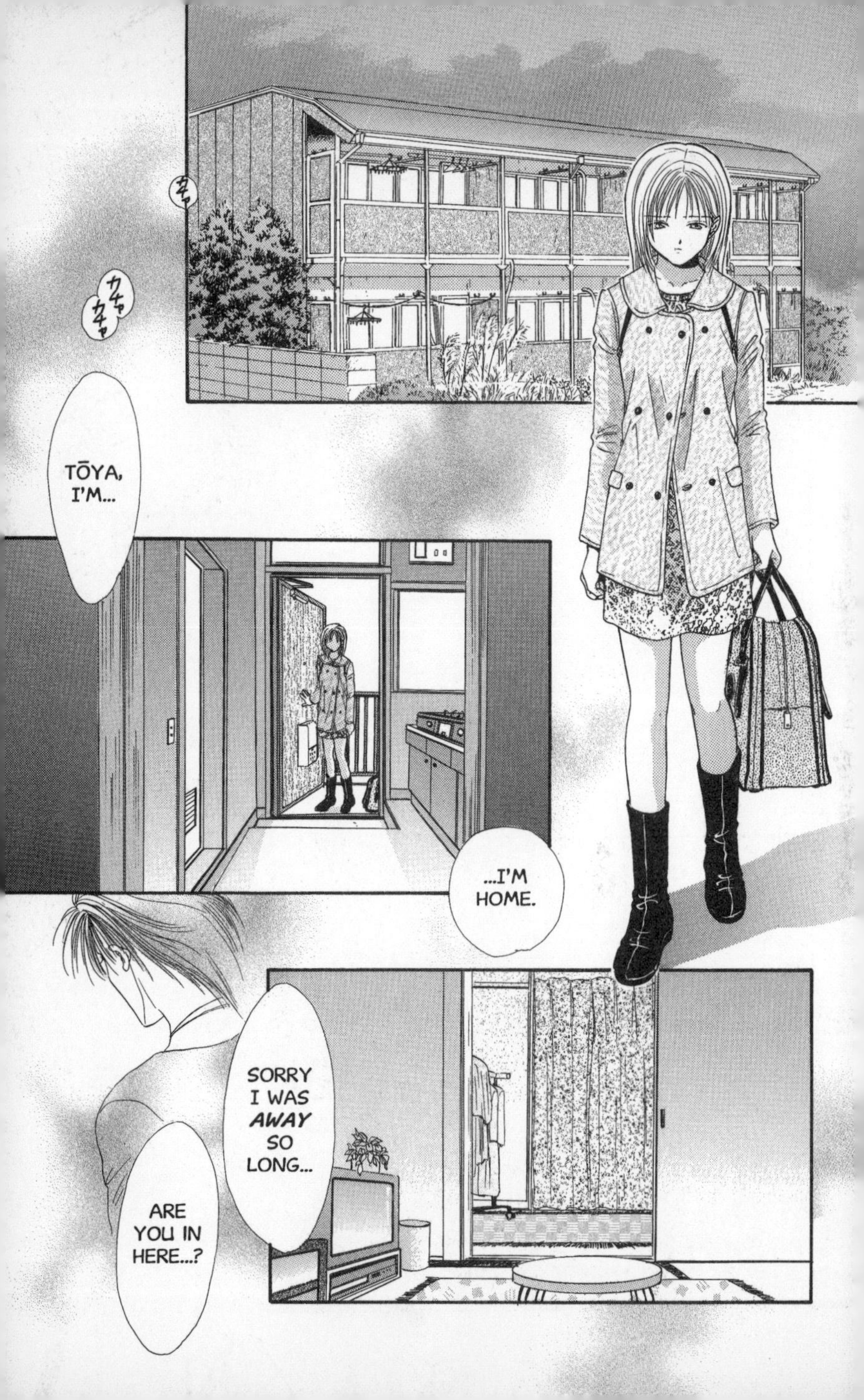
カチャ カチャ
TŌYA, I'M...
...I'M HOME.
SORRY I WAS *AWAY* SO LONG...
ARE YOU IN HERE...?

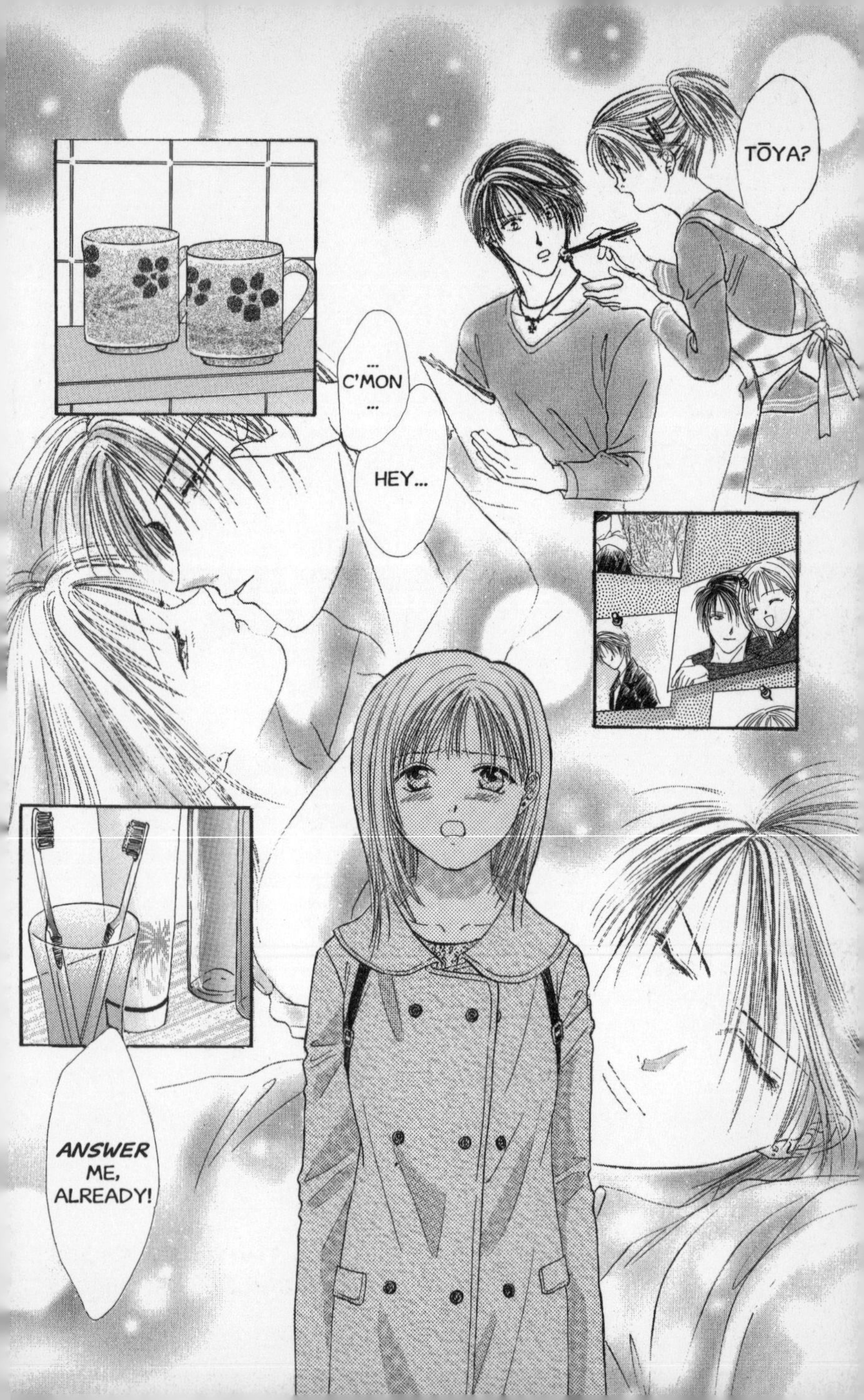
TŌYA?
... C'MON ...
HEY...
ANSWER ME, ALREADY!

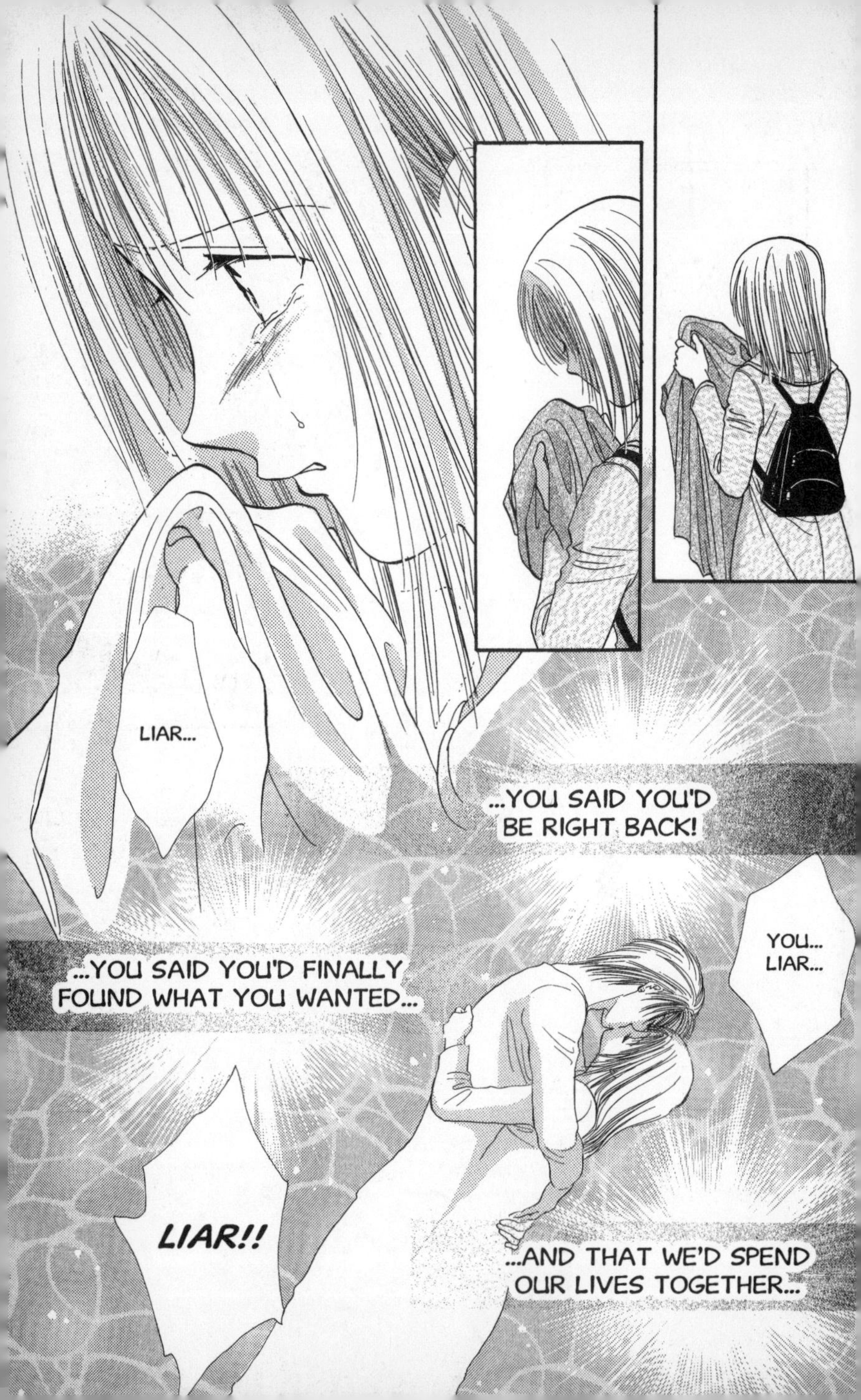
LIAR...
...YOU SAID YOU'D BE RIGHT BACK!
YOU... LIAR...
...YOU SAID YOU'D FINALLY FOUND WHAT YOU WANTED...
...AND THAT WE'D SPEND OUR LIVES TOGETHER...
LIAR!!

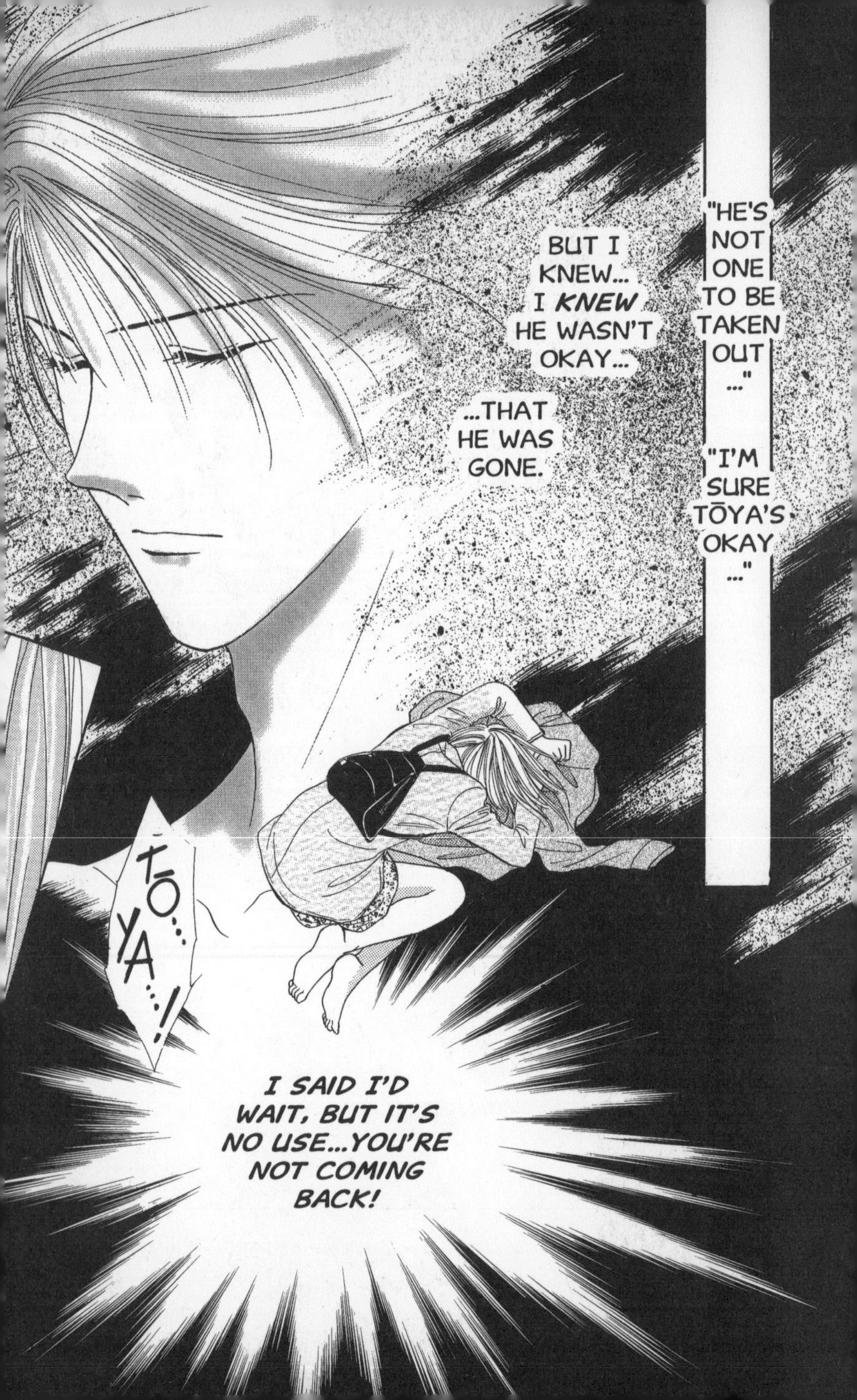
"HE'S NOT ONE TO BE TAKEN OUT ..."
"I'M SURE TŌYA'S OKAY ..."
BUT I KNEW... I *KNEW* HE WASN'T OKAY...
...THAT HE WAS GONE.
TŌ... YA...!
I SAID I'D WAIT, BUT IT'S NO USE...YOU'RE NOT COMING BACK!

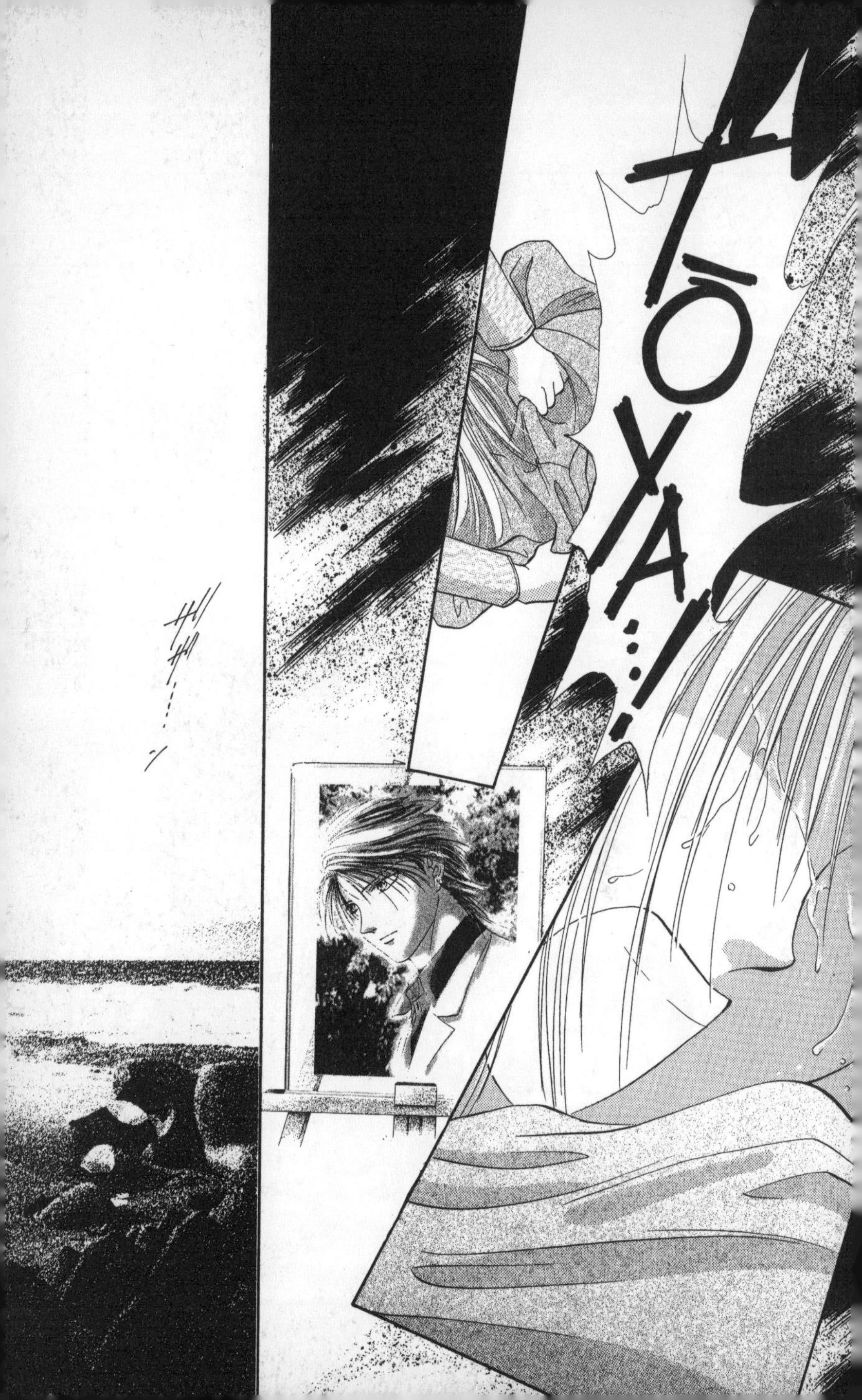
TŌYA...!!
ザザ…ン

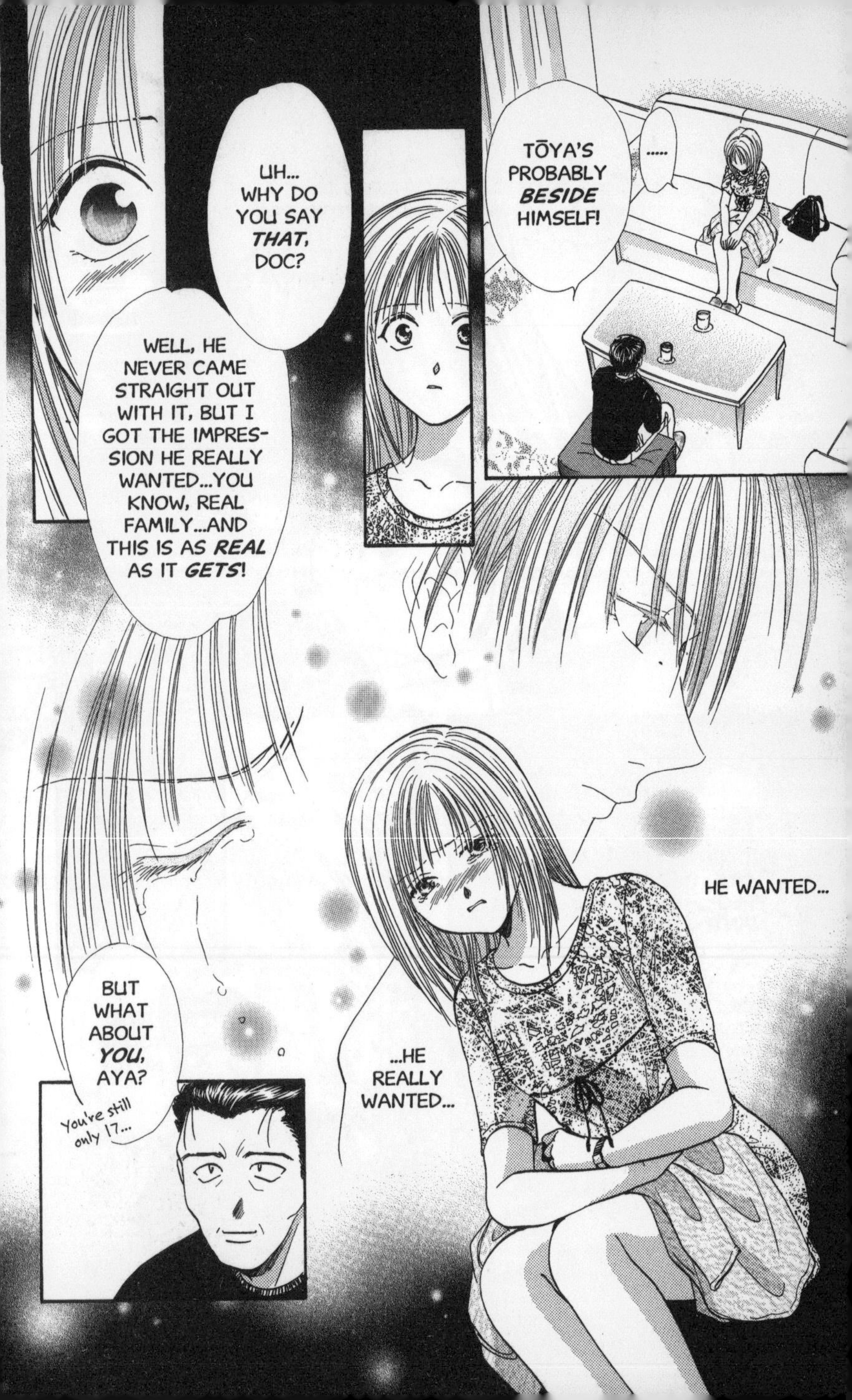
TŌYA'S PROBABLY *BESIDE* HIMSELF!
.....
UH... WHY DO YOU SAY *THAT*, DOC?
WELL, HE NEVER CAME STRAIGHT OUT WITH IT, BUT I GOT THE IMPRESSION HE REALLY WANTED...YOU KNOW, REAL FAMILY...AND THIS IS AS *REAL* AS IT *GETS*!
HE WANTED...
...HE REALLY WANTED...
BUT WHAT ABOUT *YOU*, AYA?
You're still only 17...

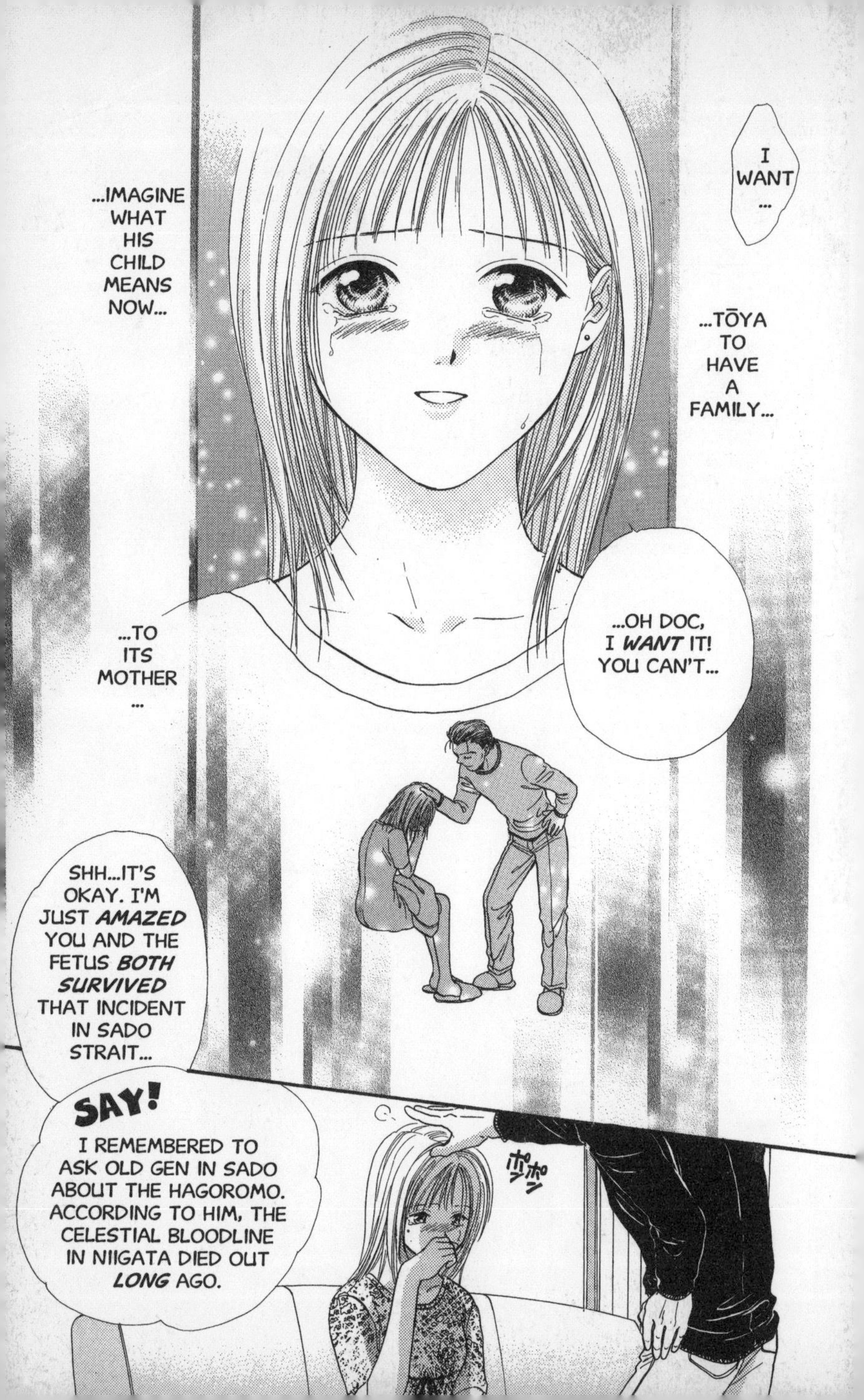
I WANT ...
...TŌYA TO HAVE A FAMILY...
...IMAGINE WHAT HIS CHILD MEANS NOW...
...TO ITS MOTHER ...
...OH DOC, I *WANT* IT! YOU CAN'T...
SHH...IT'S OKAY. I'M JUST *AMAZED* YOU AND THE FETUS *BOTH SURVIVED* THAT INCIDENT IN SADO STRAIT...
SAY! I REMEMBERED TO ASK OLD GEN IN SADO ABOUT THE HAGOROMO. ACCORDING TO HIM, THE CELESTIAL BLOODLINE IN NIIGATA DIED OUT *LONG* AGO.
ポンポン

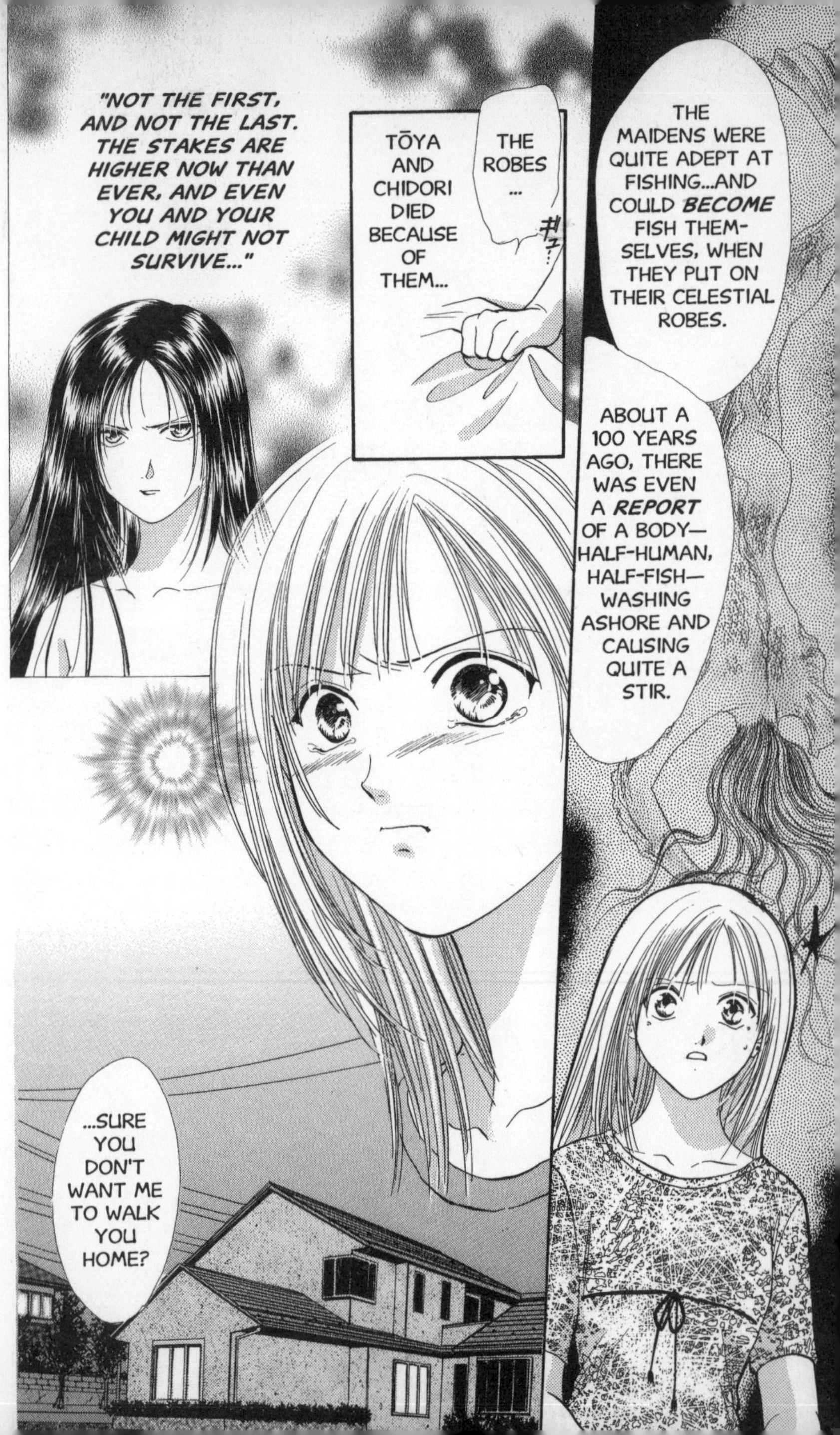
THE MAIDENS WERE QUITE ADEPT AT FISHING...AND COULD *BECOME* FISH THEMSELVES, WHEN THEY PUT ON THEIR CELESTIAL ROBES.
ABOUT A 100 YEARS AGO, THERE WAS EVEN A *REPORT* OF A BODY—HALF-HUMAN, HALF-FISH—WASHING ASHORE AND CAUSING QUITE A STIR.
THE ROBES ...
TŌYA AND CHIDORI DIED BECAUSE OF THEM...
"NOT THE FIRST, AND NOT THE LAST. THE STAKES ARE HIGHER NOW THAN EVER, AND EVEN YOU AND YOUR CHILD MIGHT NOT SURVIVE..."
...SURE YOU DON'T WANT ME TO WALK YOU HOME?

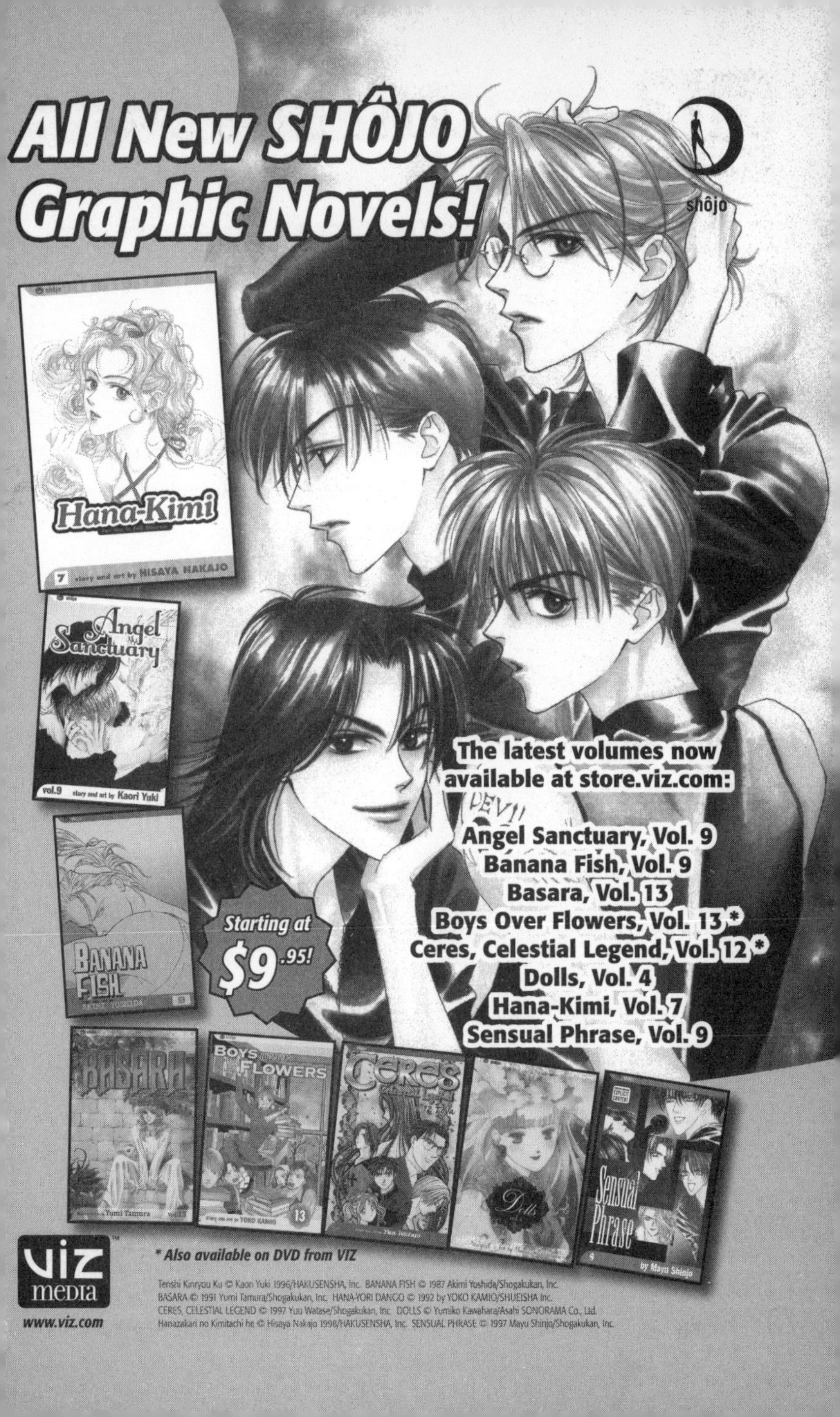
All New SHÔJO Graphic Novels!
shôjo
Hana-Kimi
7 story and art by HISAYA NAKAJO
Angel Sanctuary
vol.9 story and art by Kaori Yuki
BANANA FISH
Starting at $9.95!
The latest volumes now available at store.viz.com:
Angel Sanctuary, Vol. 9
Banana Fish, Vol. 9
Basara, Vol. 13
Boys Over Flowers, Vol. 13 *
Ceres, Celestial Legend, Vol. 12 *
Dolls, Vol. 4
Hana-Kimi, Vol. 7
Sensual Phrase, Vol. 9
BASARA
Yumi Tamura
BOYS OVER FLOWERS
YOKO KAMIO
13
Ceres
Yuu Watase
Dolls
Sensual Phrase
by Mayu Shinjo
viz media
www.viz.com
* Also available on DVD from VIZ
Tenshi Kinryou Ku © Kaori Yuki 1996/HAKUSENSHA, Inc. BANANA FISH © 1987 Akimi Yoshida/Shogakukan, Inc.
BASARA © 1991 Yumi Tamura/Shogakukan, Inc. HANA-YORI DANGO © 1992 by YOKO KAMIO/SHUEISHA Inc.
CERES, CELESTIAL LEGEND © 1997 Yuu Watase/Shogakukan, Inc. DOLLS © Yumiko Kawahara/Asahi SONORAMA Co., Ltd.
Hanazakari no Kimitachi he © Hisaya Nakajo 1996/HAKUSENSHA, Inc. SENSUAL PHRASE © 1997 Mayu Shinjo/Shogakukan, Inc.

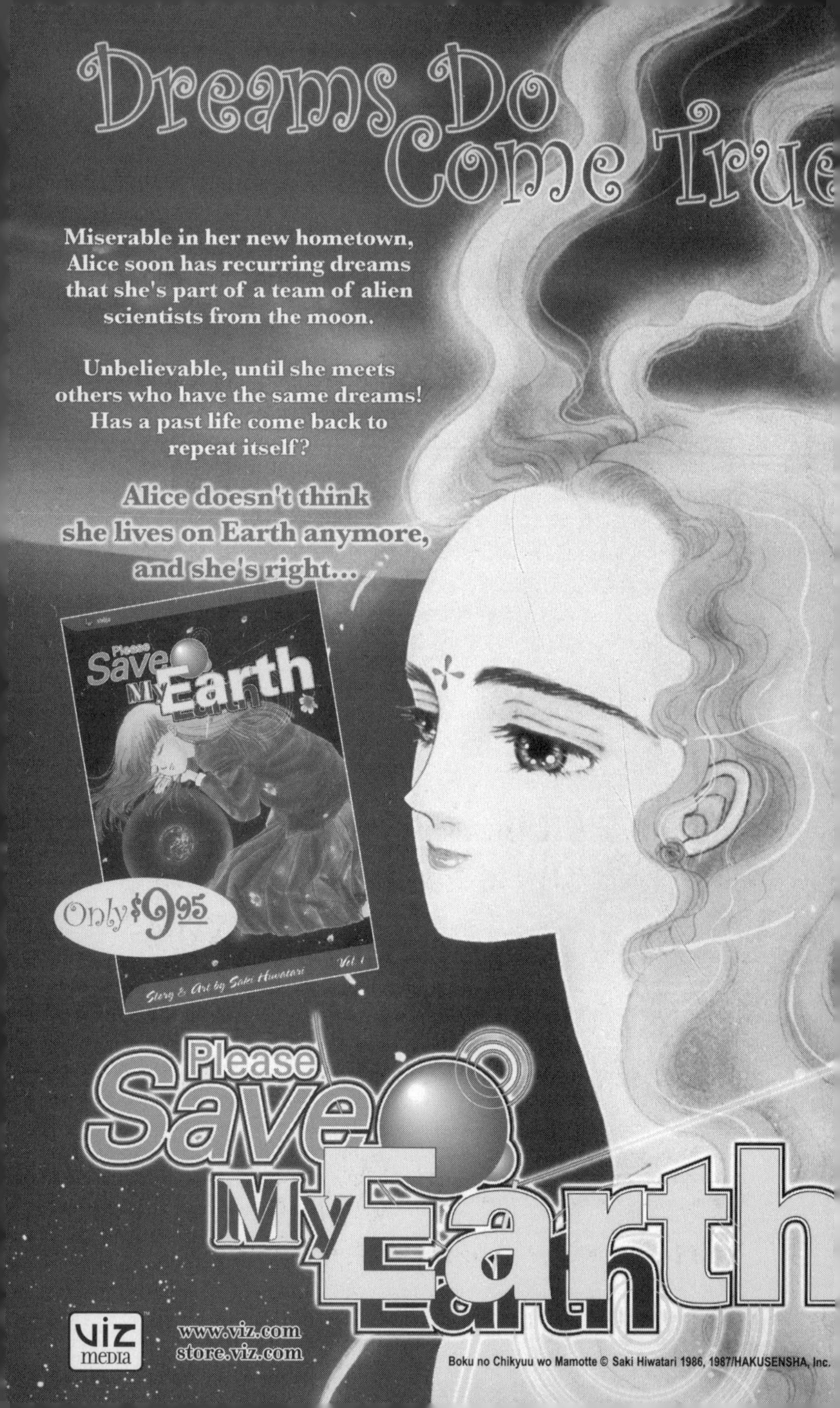
Dreams Do Come True
Miserable in her new hometown, Alice soon has recurring dreams that she's part of a team of alien scientists from the moon.
Unbelievable, until she meets others who have the same dreams! Has a past life come back to repeat itself?
Alice doesn't think she lives on Earth anymore, and she's right...
Please Save My Earth
Only $9.95
Story & Art by Saki Hiwatari
Vol. 1
Please Save My Earth
viz media
www.viz.com
store.viz.com
Boku no Chikyuu wo Mamotte © Saki Hiwatari 1986, 1987/HAKUSENSHA, Inc.

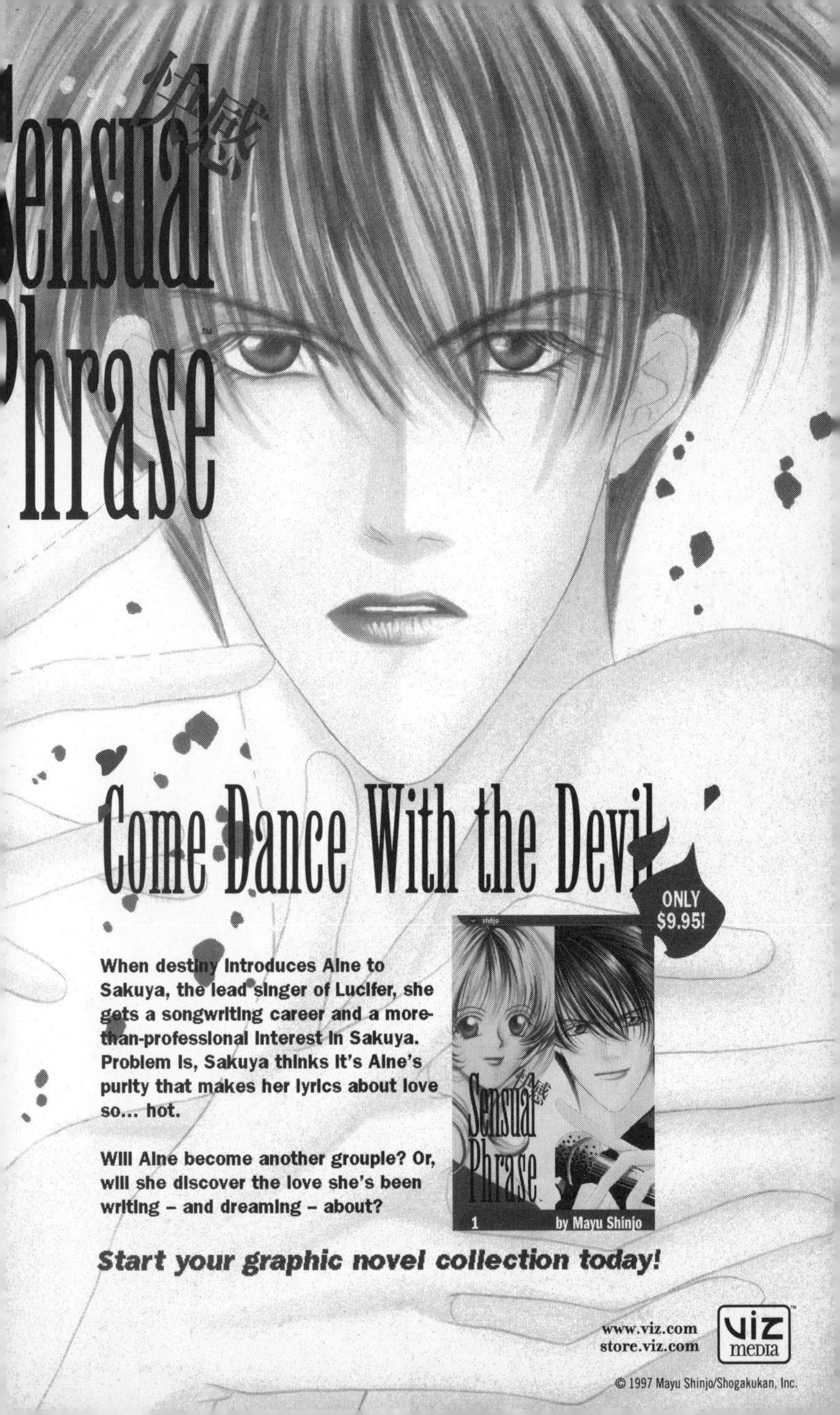

Sensual Phrase™
Come Dance With the Devil
ONLY $9.95!
When destiny introduces Aine to Sakuya, the lead singer of Lucifer, she gets a songwriting career and a more-than-professional interest in Sakuya. Problem is, Sakuya thinks it's Aine's purity that makes her lyrics about love so... hot.
Will Aine become another groupie? Or, will she discover the love she's been writing – and dreaming – about?
shōjo
Sensual Phrase
1
by Mayu Shinjo
Start your graphic novel collection today!
www.viz.com
store.viz.com
viz media
© 1997 Mayu Shinjo/Shogakukan, Inc.

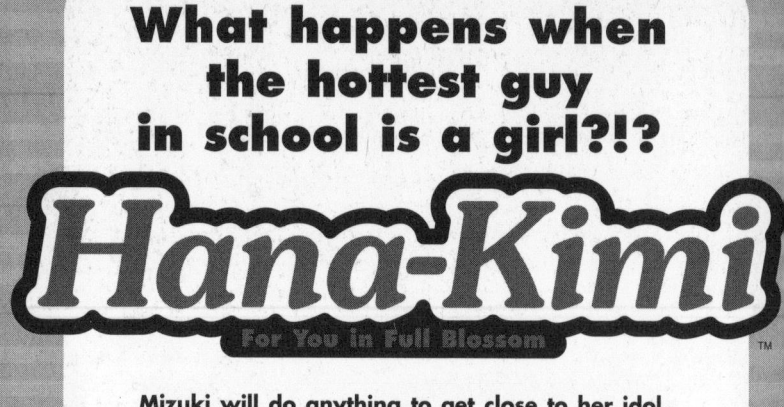

The Power of a Kiss

Soon after her first kiss, Yuri is pulled into a puddle and transported to an ancient Middle Eastern village. Surrounded by strange people speaking a language she can't understand, Yuri has no idea how to get back home and is soon embroiled in the politics and romance of the ancient Middle East. If a kiss helped get Yuri into this mess, can a kiss get her out?

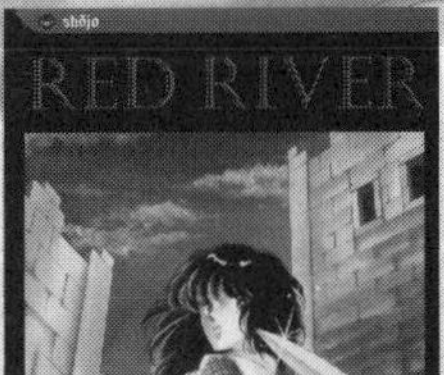

Hot Gimmick
hot gimmick
MIKI AIHARA
1

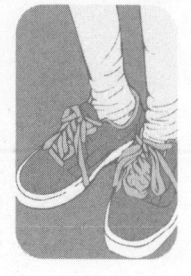

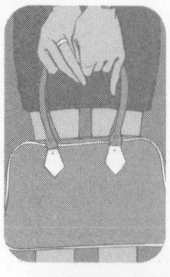

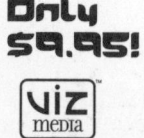

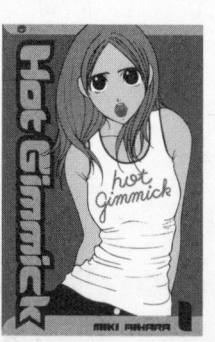

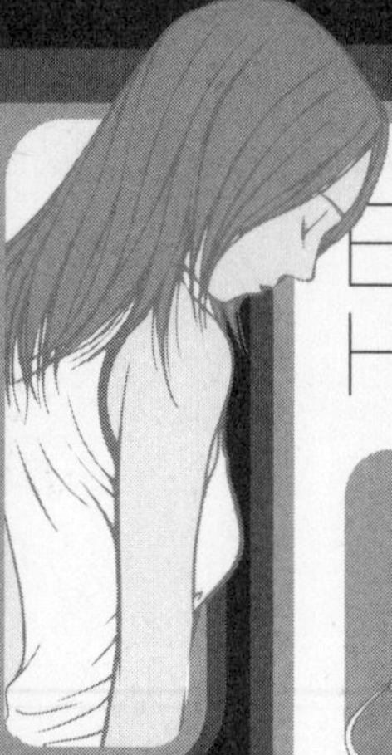

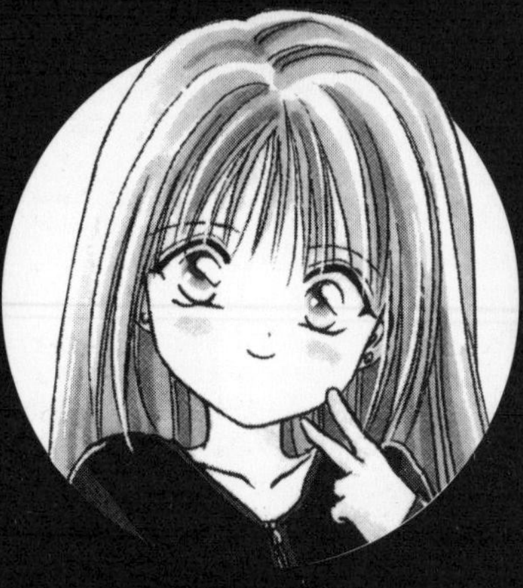

Yuu Watase was born on March 5 in a town near Osaka, Japan, and she was raised there before moving to Tokyo to follow her dream of creating manga. In the decade since her debut short story, *Pajama De Ojama* ("An Intrusion in Pajamas"), she has produced more than 50 compiled volumes of short stories and continuing series. Her latest work, *Zettai Kareshi* ("Absolute Boyfriend"), has recently completed its run in Japan in the anthology magazine *Shôjo Comic*. Watase's other beloved series *Ceres: Celestial Legend, Fushigi Yûgi, Imadoki!* (Nowadays), and *Alice 19th* are now available in North America in English editions published by VIZ.

137.3 FX: Zukin Zukin (pained throbbing)
137.4 FX: Zukin Zukin (pained throbbing)
137.5 FX: Zuru (involuntary slump)
138.3 FX: Ban (throwing open of doors)
139.1 FX: Ha— Ha— Ha— (labored, heaving breathing)
139.2 FX: Katsu Katsu Katsu (purposeful footsteps)
139.3 FX: Kotsu (purposeful footstep variant)
140.4 FX: Ji— (zipper of bodybag)
141.3 FX: Nyu (sudden emergence)
141.4 FX: Pita (light touching)
141.5 FX: Bachi ("zap" of electricity)
142.1 FX: Dokyu ("vroom" of car)
143.3 FX: Za ("sloosh" of waves)
143.3 FX: Zuru (slump of Tôya's lifeless body)
144.2 FX: Zan (heavy "break" of waves)
150.4 FX: Gusha (hands in hair)
151.5 FX: Su (light, caress-like movement)
152.2 FX: Kura ("swooning" sensation)
152.3 FX: Kata (Shuro's weight against "shoji" door)
153.1 FX: Kacha ("click" of an opened-door latch)
153.1 FX: Kacha Kacha (repeated "clicks" of opened-door latches)
157.4 FX: Zaza—n (heavy crash of waves)
159.2 FX: Zukin (pained throb)
159.4 FX: Ha ("gasp!")
161.2 FX: Pon Pon (playful "pats" atop head)
162.2 FX: Gyu (clenching, or tightening)
163.3 FX: Kyu ("wipe" of tears)
166.5 FX: Beshi (stinging hit, or "whap")
167.3 FX: Zuru (involuntary slump)
171.3 FX: Piku (pointed startlement, or twitch)
171.5 FX: Kacha ("click" of opened-door latch)
175.1 FX: Pita (sudden pause or stopping in place)
176.5 FX: Za ("fwish" of shower)
177.5 FX: Pi (pressed button of remote-control)
177.5 FX: Pi (pressed button of remote-control)
177.6 FX: Pi (pressed button of remote-control)
178.1 FX: Dokun (heavy heartbeat)
178.2 FX: Dokun Dokun Dokun (heavy heartbeats)
180.2 FX: Gacha (ominous opening of door)
180.3 FX: Ha ("gasp!")
180.4 FX: Ka (footstep)
181.2 FX: Goku ("gulp" reaction)
181.4 FX: Dokin (skipped heartbeat)
184.1 FX: Buru Buru Buru (violent shaking of head in negation)
186.2 FX: Yoro (involuntary stagger)
186.3 FX: Patan (softened "thud" of a door, closing)
186.5 FX: Geho Geho ("coughing up")
187.1 FX: Pan (slap)
192.1 FX: Dokun (heavy heartbeat)
192.2 FX: Dokun Dokun Dokun (heavy heartbeats)
192.3 FX: Do Do Do (slow, heavy heartbeats)

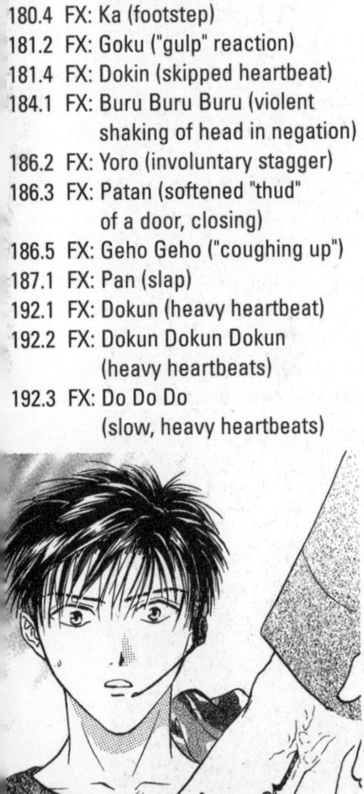

093.2 FX: Ha ("gasp!")
093.4 FX: Ha— Ha— Ha— (labored, heavy breathing)
094.1 FX: Yoro (involuntary stagger)
095.2 FX: Don (heavy report of gun)
097.1 FX: Zuru (involuntary slump)
097.4 FX: Ka (footstep)
098.1 FX: Kotsu (footstep variant)
098.2 FX: Kotsu (footstep variant)
098.3 FX: Kotsu (footstep variant)
098.5 FX: Pan ("blam" of gunshot)
099.4 FX: Go (muzzle against forehead)
100.4 FX: Poro (light release of pistol)
100.5 FX: Kara—an ("clatter" of gun, echoing down hall)
101.3 FX: Pashi (the light, sharp sound of Wei's weapon coming into play)
101.4 FX: Ha ("gasp!")
102.1 FX: Pan Pan ("blam" of gunshots)
102.2 FX: Kii ("cre-e-eak")
102.5 FX: Ban ("blam" of gunshot, heavier than "pan," above)
103.5 FX: Ba (a "bursting forward," "up," or "out")
105.1 FX: Ban ("blam" of gunshot)
105.2 FX: Gaku (stumble, or buckling of knees)
105.2 FX: Ban ("blam" of gunshot)
105.3 FX: Zuru (involuntary slump)
106.1 FX: Pa (sudden opening, as of hands)

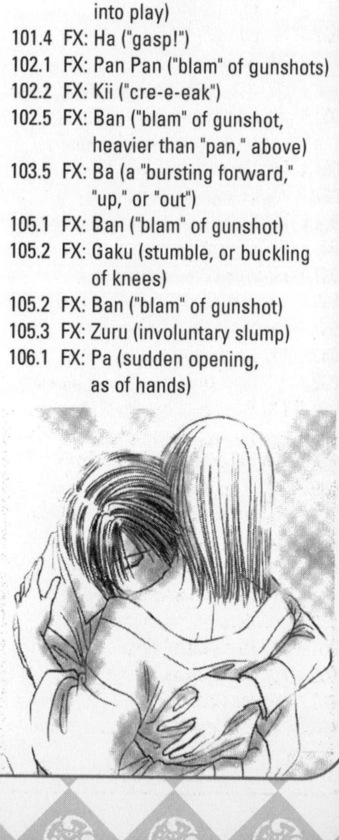

106.2 FX: Hyoko Hyoko (limping progress forward)
107.4 FX: Patan (softened "thud" of a door, closing)
108.3 FX: To (light landing)
108.3 FX: Za (burst of static)
110.3 FX: Gyu (clenching, or tightening)
114.3 FX: Kuka— (heavy "schnorr" of Mrs. Q)
115.2 FX: Dokin Dokin Dokin (rapid, sequential heartbeats)
117.4 FX: Ha ("gasp!")
118.4 FX: Ban ("blam" of gunshot)
119.2 FX: Ban ("blam" of gunshot)
119.3 FX: Gaku (stumble, or buckling)
120.5 FX: Zuru (involuntary slump)
121.2 FX: Ga (heavy, violent kick)
122.3 FX: Don (heavy report of gun)
124.3 FX: Biku (startlement, a twitch)
125.1 FX: Ga (sudden grabbing up)
126.3 FX: Kasa Kasa Kasa (rustling as of foliage)
126.3 FX: Piku (pointed startlement)
126.4 FX: Kasa Kasa Kasa (rustling)
127.1 FX: Za (quick lift of gun barrel)
128.3 FX: Patan (softened "thud," in this case, of Tôya's lifeless hand)
128.5 FX: Kata Kata Kata (uncontrollable trembling)
129.1 FX: Goto (the dull drop of the gun)
129.2 FX: Ha ("gasp!")
129.4 FX: Fu (a "faintness")
130.4 FX: Biku (startlement, a twitch)
131.2 FX: Chun Chun ("chirp, chirp" of birds)
131.3 FX: Dokun Dokun Dokun (heavy heartbeats)
132.3 FX: Dokun Dokun Dokun (heavy heartbeats)
132.4 FX: Gyu (clenching, or tightening)
134.1 FX: Basa Basa Basa (wings of birds taking flight)
137.1 FX: Zukin Zukin (pained throbbing)

043.3 FX: Pita (sudden pause or stopping in place)
044.1 FX: Su— (light breathing of peaceful sleep)
045.5 FX: Pata Pata Pata (slippered footsteps)
046.4 FX: Kacha (DVD tray closing into place)
047.1 FX: Pa (sudden burst into life, more pointed than "ba")
047.3 FX: Su— (light breathing of peaceful sleep)
048.4 FX: Bashi (stinging slap, as in across face)
050.1 FX: Ha ("gasp!")
052.1 FX: Su (light, caress-like movement)
052.2 FX: Ha ("gasp!")
053.3 FX: Ha ("gasp!")
054.2 FX: Doki Doki Doki (rapid heartbeats)
054.5 FX: Gaba (sudden rearing or popping up)
060.2 FX: Za (rustling as of foliage)
061.1 FX: Pata Pata (slippered footsteps)
061.3 FX: Giku (a heavy, unpleasant startlement)
061.5 FX: Pita (sudden pause or stopping in place)
062.2 FX: Karan (a noisy dropping, but less heavy than "garan")
062.4 FX: Kara (rattle, as of a sliding shoji door)
063.1 FX: Geho Geho Geho ("coughing up")
065.1 FX: Ha ("gasp!")
066.2 FX: Gakon (a "clunk," as in the heavy close of doors)
067.4 FX: Ha ("gasp!")
069.2 FX: Ha ("gasp!")
069.3 FX: Zu (a "twitch")
070.2 FX: Pan (smashing "pop" of the glass)
071.4 FX: Piku (pointed startlement)
072.1 FX: Ha— Ha— Ha— (labored, heavy breathing)
072.2 FX: Gui (sudden "tug")
073.2 FX: Bo— (vacuous absence of thought or emotion)
073.4 FX: Pata Pata (wave of hand before Aya's eyes)
074.4 FX: Doka (violent "booting")
074.5 FX: Piku (pointed startlement)
074.6 FX: Poso (light mumbling)
075.4 FX: Poro ("plip" of tears)
078.3 FX: Su (light, caress-like movement)
079.5 FX: Ka Ka (footsteps)
081.5 FX: Ka (footstep)
082.2 FX: Gaba (a sudden "covering," as in a hockey jersey over the head)
082.4 FX: Fu (soft laugh)
083.3 FX: Su (light, caress-like movement)
083.4 FX: Kacha ("click" of an opened-door latch)
084.5 FX: Za (burst of static)
085.1 FX: To (light landing)
086.2 FX: Dan (sudden "slam")
086.4 FX: Pa (sudden burst into life)
087.1 FX: Dosu (heavy impact)
087.2 FX: Zu ("slump" movement)
087.4 FX: Pan (violent throw)
087.5 FX: Do (impact, as of a fist)
088.1 FX: Doki Doki (rapid heartbeats)
088.3 FX: Pon (careless toss)
089.1 FX: Su (light, caress-like movement)
089.2 FX: Kara Kara Kara (rattling of gurney's wheels)
089.3 FX: Ja (jangle of heavy chain)
090.1 FX: Biki (snapping/constriction of chain into place)
090.4 FX: Zuru (involuntary slump)
091.5 FX: Pan ("blam" of gunshot)
092.1 FX: Zuru (involuntary slump)
092.2 FX: Ha ("gasp!")
093.1 FX: Da ("dash"-type movement)

The CERES Guide to Sound Effects

We've left most of the sound effects in CERES as Yuu Watase originally created them—in Japanese. VIZ has created this glossary to help you decipher, page-by-page and panel-by-panel, what all those foreign words and background noises mean. Use this guide to impress your friends with your new Japanese vocabulary. The glossary lists the page number then panel. For example, 3.1 indicates page 3, panel 1.

006.2 FX: Kachi Kachi Kachi (chattering of teeth)
007.1 FX: Ba (a "bursting forward," "up," or "out")
008.1 FX: Garan (a noisy dropping)
008.1 FX: Ha— Ha— (labored, heavy breathing)
008.2 FX: Su (light, caress-like movement, as in a rush of air)
010.1 FX: Gachan (handcuffs being closed, with finality)
010.4 FX: Batan (close of car door)
011.2 FX: Za ("sloosh" of waves)
012.3 FX: Ha ("gasp!")
014.1 FX: Ha Ha (laughter)
015.6 FX: Dokun Dokun Dokun (heavy heartbeat)
016.2 FX: Gaku Gaku (violent shake or rattling)
016.4 FX: Hogya Hogya (wails of a newborn infant)
016.5 FX: Hogya Hogya (wails of a newborn infant)
016.6 FX: Zaza (choppy sound of waves)
017.1 FX: Hogya Hogya (wails of a newborn infant)
018.2 FX: Nuru (tactile sensation of "slime")
021.4 FX: Za ("sloosh" of waves)
021.5 FX: Biku (startlement, a twitch)
022.3 FX: Dokun (heavy heartbeat)
024.4 FX: Gako (heavy "thud" of piled-up stones)

025.3 FX: Dokin (skipped heartbeat)
025.4 FX: Pacha (a light splash, or "splish")
028.3 FX: Kokun (nod)
028.5 FX: Gyu (clenching, or tightening)
034.1 FX: Zuki (pained throb)
034.3 FX: Ba (a "bursting forward," "up," or "out")
036.1 FX: Za ("sloosh" of waves)
037.1 FX: Ha ("gasp!")
040.3 FX: Pinpo—n ("ding don-n-ng" of doorbell)
040.5 FX: Gii ("cre-e-eak," less high-pitched than "kii," below)
041.1 FX: Gya— (horrified scream or cry)
041.4 FX: Beshi (stinging hit, or "whap")
042.2 FX: Kuru (sudden whirling away, or "vwip")
042.3 FX: Piku (startlement, more pointed than "biku," above)
042.4 FX: Nihera (creepy laugh)
042.5 FX: Aha Ha Ha (laughter)

A NOTE FROM THE AUTHOR

In response to criticism she received regarding the storyline about Aya's pregnancy, Yuu Watase posted this message to an online fan forum:

The themes of *Ceres* may have been complex and difficult to grasp, but I think my fans were able to understand most of my points most of the time. However, I can't avoid the fact that people may have opinions and viewpoints different from my own. To be honest, manga are only comic books. They depict made-up worlds, but even those made-up worlds have their own sets of rules.

For example, *Ceres* was written on the premise that the love between Aya and Tôya is sacred and inviolable, as a necessary foil to Kagami's ideals. If anyone were to question that, the entire composition would fall apart.

At the same time, Aya's unintended pregnancy has been controversial. I think the issue here was more about how she dealt with life's problems, especially when things did not go as planned. That is one theme I wanted to present in *Ceres*, anyway. If the same situation were to arise in a different title, I know I would handle it differently.

When Tôya and Aya started living together, they were ready to be committed to each other for life—even if they could never get married [since Tôya does not officially exist as a person]. I remember that Miaka's decision to drop out of high school in *Fushigi Yûgi* was also criticized by many people. I chose that action to reflect Miaka's determination to fight alongside Taka, even if she had to abandon the only way of life she'd ever known. I always try to push my characters to the utmost of their abilities in their respective situations—even, at times, making them summon the courage to risk their lives.

If any of this *had* happened in "real life", I, too, would have been critical about these issues. I considered having Aya mention that she had been careful to use birth control. However, my editor persuaded me not to include the line. This was a fictional world—it was nonsense to address every real-world detail, and to do so would have subtly spoiled the flow of the story. I still think it was the correct decision, if only to stick to my themes....

In the end, manga are just manga. Still, my characters do their best to live their lives responsibly within the confines of their worlds. I have never let them be reckless in their behavior or allowed them to tackle a problem half-heartedly. They may seem immature or incompetent from the reader's perspective, but I think that's okay. After all, we've all been immature at one time or another, and we're just as far from being perfect. That's what being human is all about. I only hope that we can learn to be just as positive and constructive as my characters attempt to be....

—Yuu Watase, from the Web site "Warau Choro no Seikatsu"

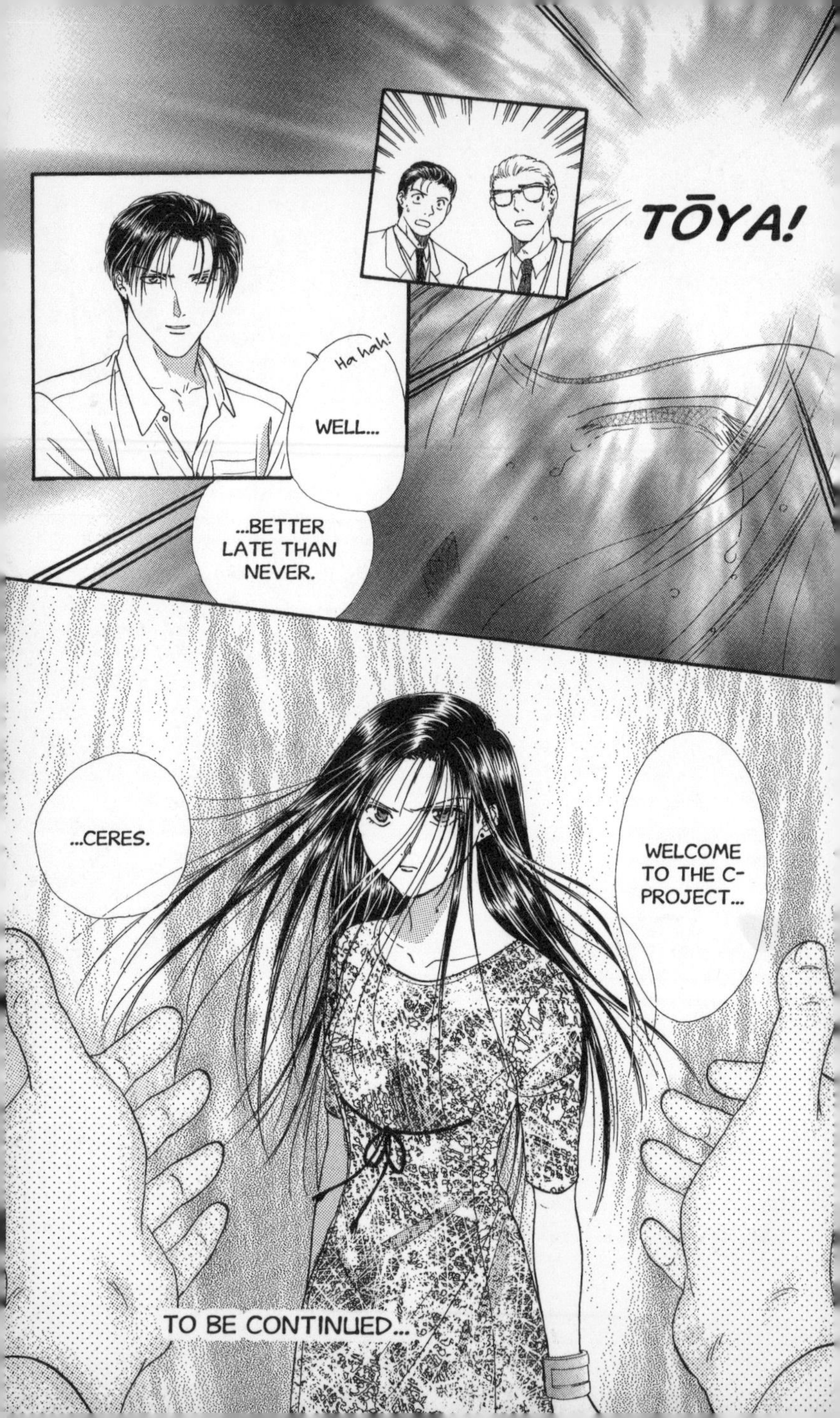
TŌYA!
Ha hah!
WELL...
...BETTER LATE THAN NEVER.
WELCOME TO THE C-PROJECT...
...CERES.
TO BE CONTINUED...

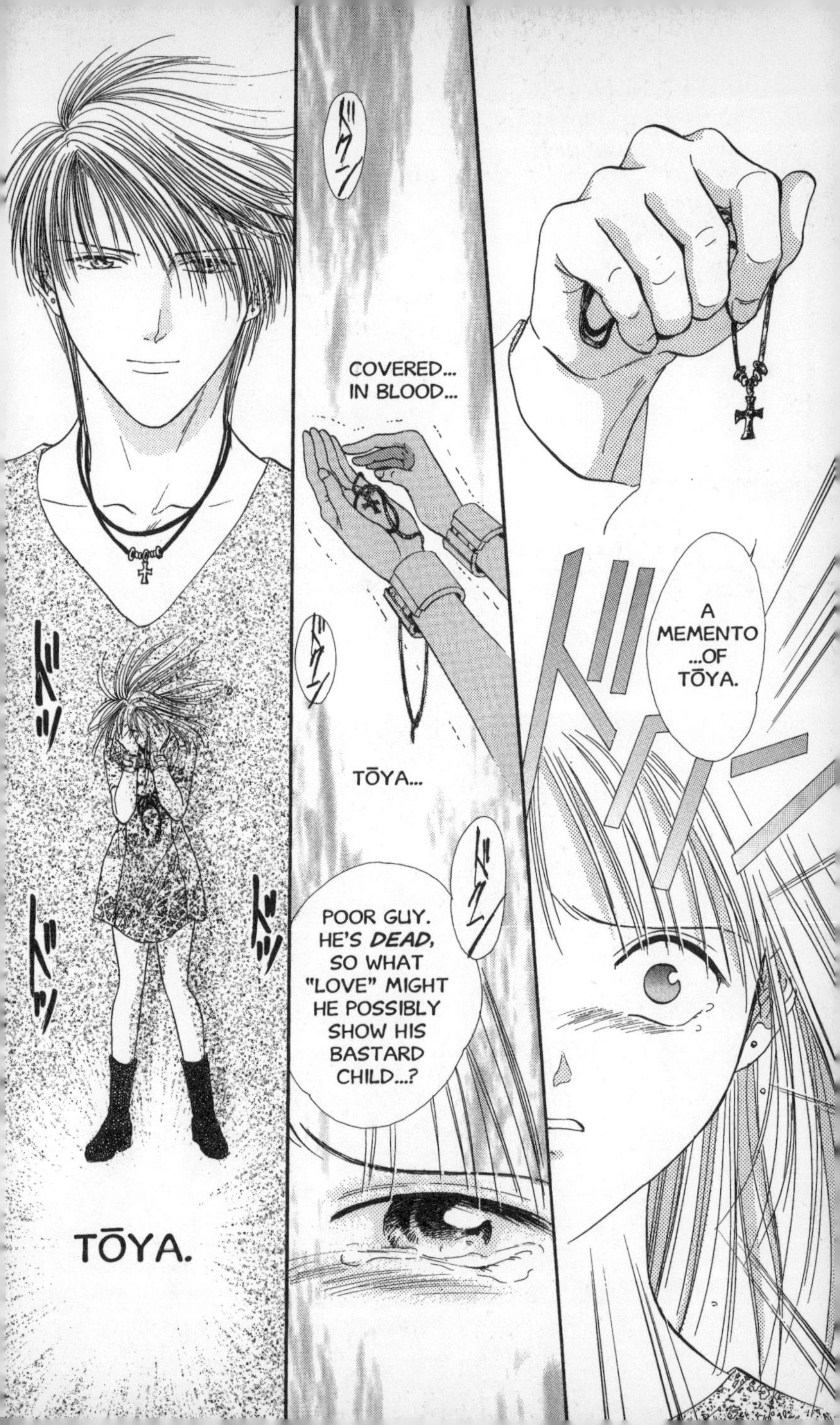
A MEMENTO ...OF TŌYA.
COVERED... IN BLOOD...
TŌYA...
POOR GUY. HE'S *DEAD*, SO WHAT "LOVE" MIGHT HE POSSIBLY SHOW HIS BASTARD CHILD...?
TŌYA.

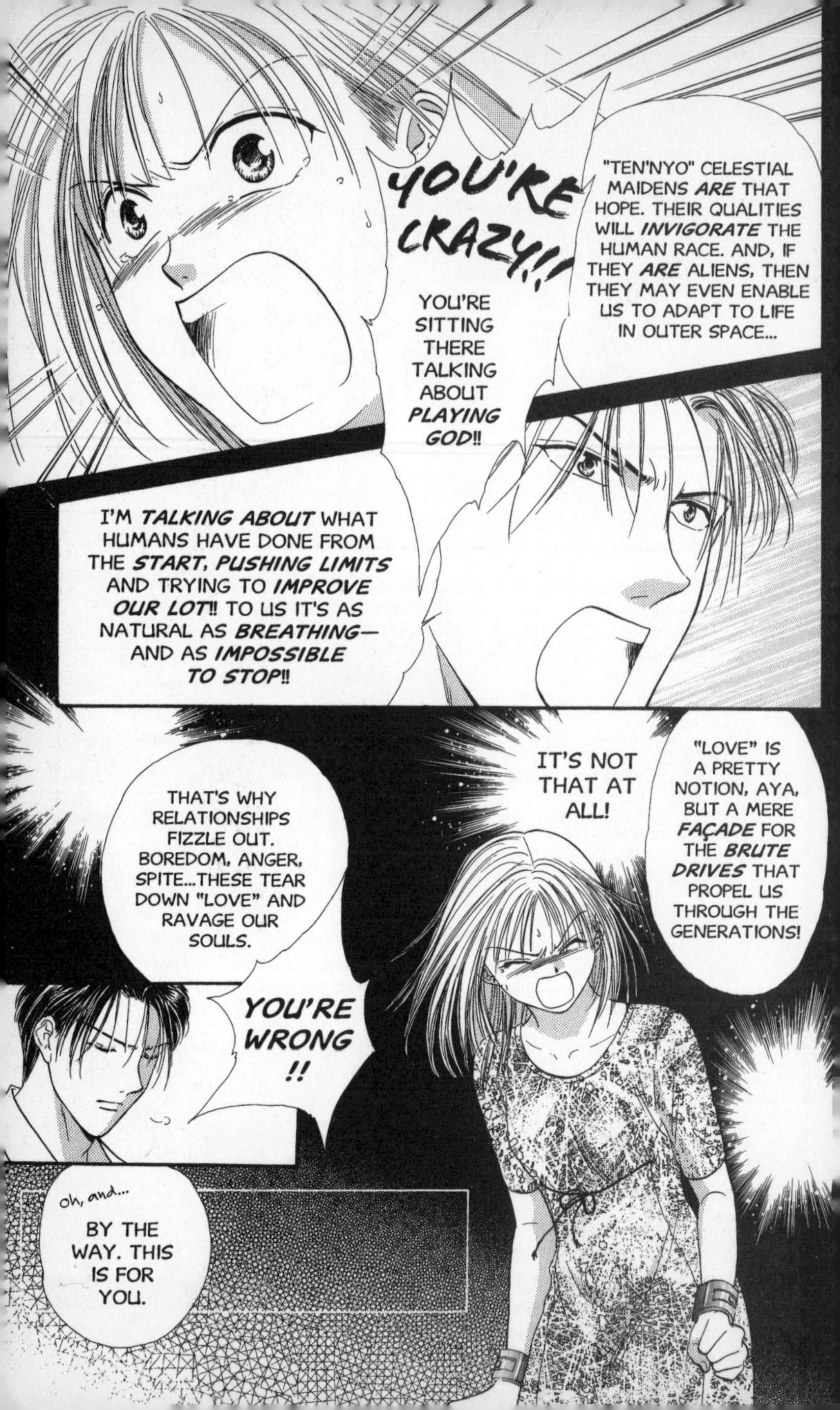
"TEN'NYO" CELESTIAL MAIDENS *ARE* THAT HOPE. THEIR QUALITIES WILL *INVIGORATE* THE HUMAN RACE. AND, IF THEY *ARE* ALIENS, THEN THEY MAY EVEN ENABLE US TO ADAPT TO LIFE IN OUTER SPACE...
YOU'RE CRAZY!!
YOU'RE SITTING THERE TALKING ABOUT *PLAYING GOD*!!
I'M *TALKING ABOUT* WHAT HUMANS HAVE DONE FROM THE *START, PUSHING LIMITS* AND TRYING TO *IMPROVE OUR LOT*!! TO US IT'S AS NATURAL AS *BREATHING*—AND AS *IMPOSSIBLE TO STOP*!!
"LOVE" IS A PRETTY NOTION, AYA, BUT A MERE *FAÇADE* FOR THE *BRUTE DRIVES* THAT PROPEL US THROUGH THE GENERATIONS!
IT'S NOT THAT AT ALL!
THAT'S WHY RELATIONSHIPS FIZZLE OUT. BOREDOM, ANGER, SPITE...THESE TEAR DOWN "LOVE" AND RAVAGE OUR SOULS.
YOU'RE WRONG !!
oh, and...
BY THE WAY. THIS IS FOR YOU.

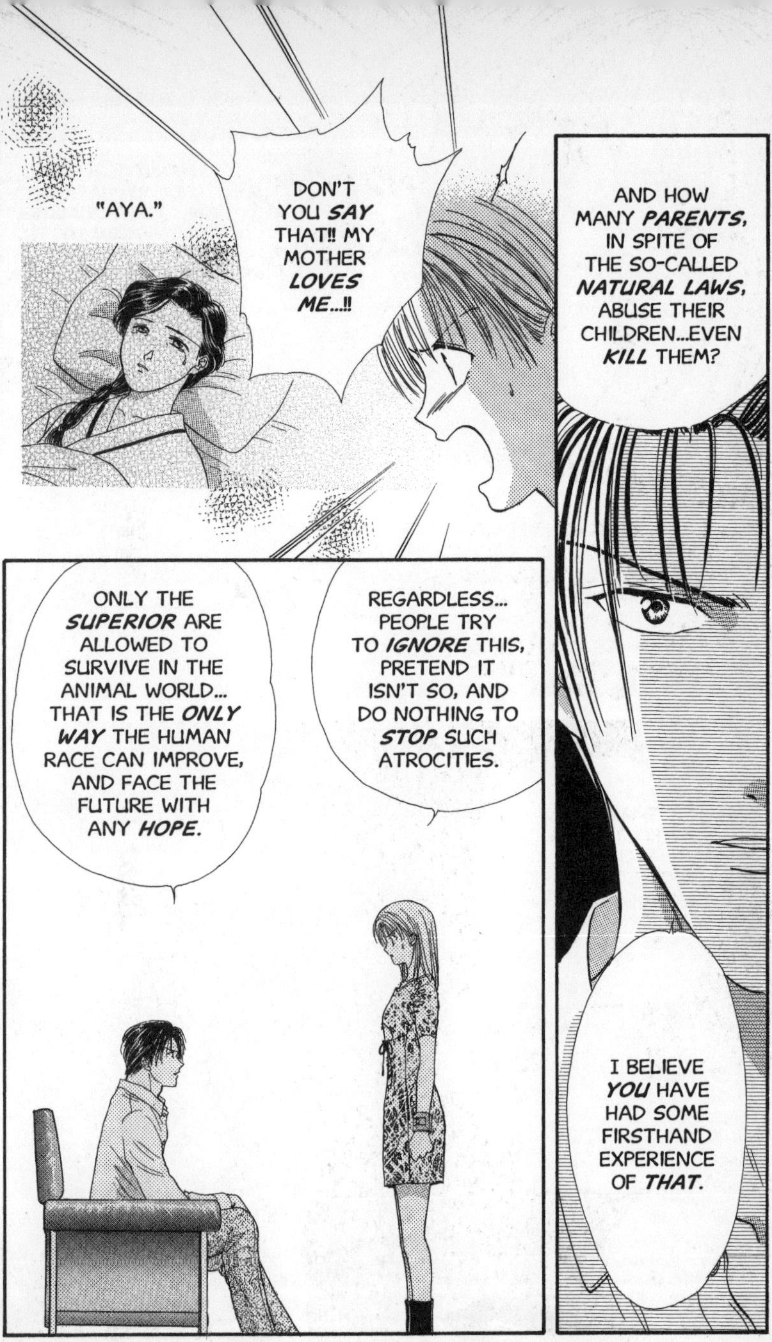
DON'T YOU SAY THAT!! MY MOTHER LOVES ME...!!
"AYA."
AND HOW MANY PARENTS, IN SPITE OF THE SO-CALLED NATURAL LAWS, ABUSE THEIR CHILDREN...EVEN KILL THEM?
I BELIEVE YOU HAVE HAD SOME FIRSTHAND EXPERIENCE OF THAT.
REGARDLESS... PEOPLE TRY TO IGNORE THIS, PRETEND IT ISN'T SO, AND DO NOTHING TO STOP SUCH ATROCITIES.
ONLY THE SUPERIOR ARE ALLOWED TO SURVIVE IN THE ANIMAL WORLD... THAT IS THE ONLY WAY THE HUMAN RACE CAN IMPROVE, AND FACE THE FUTURE WITH ANY HOPE.

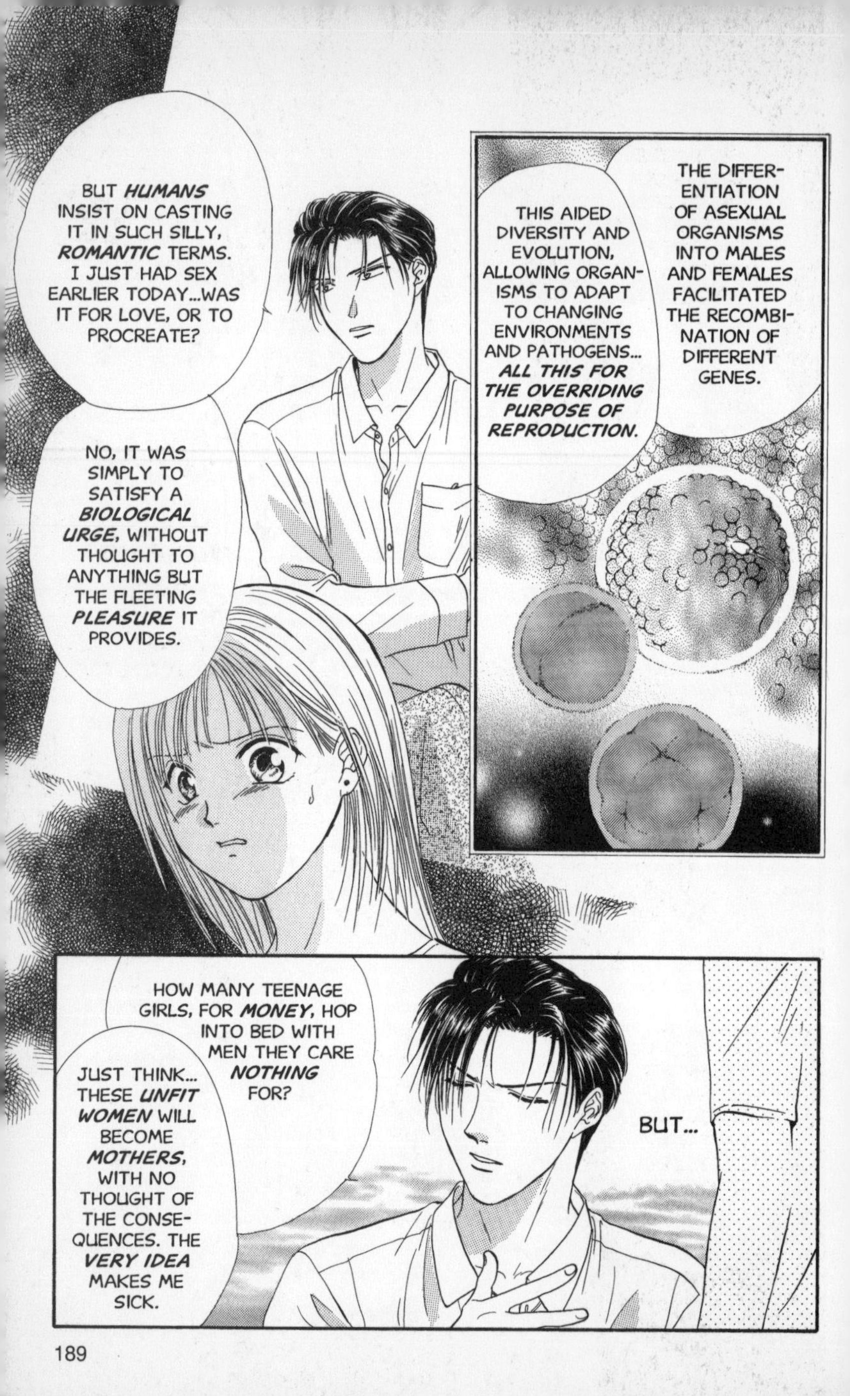
THE DIFFERENTIATION OF ASEXUAL ORGANISMS INTO MALES AND FEMALES FACILITATED THE RECOMBINATION OF DIFFERENT GENES.
THIS AIDED DIVERSITY AND EVOLUTION, ALLOWING ORGANISMS TO ADAPT TO CHANGING ENVIRONMENTS AND PATHOGENS... ***ALL THIS FOR THE OVERRIDING PURPOSE OF REPRODUCTION.***
BUT ***HUMANS*** INSIST ON CASTING IT IN SUCH SILLY, ***ROMANTIC*** TERMS. I JUST HAD SEX EARLIER TODAY...WAS IT FOR LOVE, OR TO PROCREATE?
NO, IT WAS SIMPLY TO SATISFY A ***BIOLOGICAL URGE,*** WITHOUT THOUGHT TO ANYTHING BUT THE FLEETING ***PLEASURE*** IT PROVIDES.
BUT...
HOW MANY TEENAGE GIRLS, FOR ***MONEY,*** HOP INTO BED WITH MEN THEY CARE ***NOTHING*** FOR?
JUST THINK... THESE ***UNFIT WOMEN*** WILL BECOME ***MOTHERS,*** WITH NO THOUGHT OF THE CONSEQUENCES. THE ***VERY IDEA*** MAKES ME SICK.

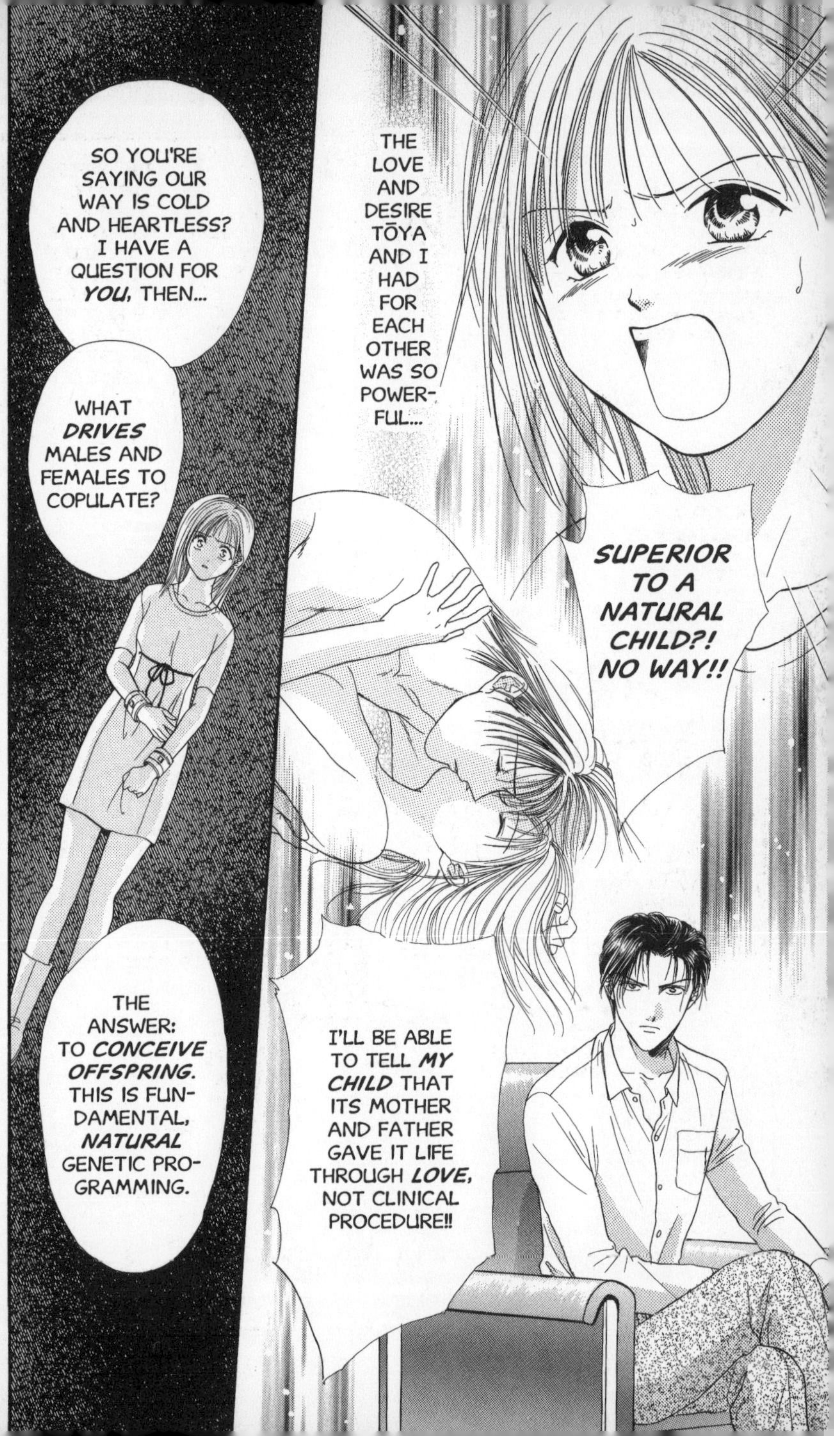
THE LOVE AND DESIRE TŌYA AND I HAD FOR EACH OTHER WAS SO POWER-FUL...
SUPERIOR TO A NATURAL CHILD?! NO WAY!!
I'LL BE ABLE TO TELL *MY CHILD* THAT ITS MOTHER AND FATHER GAVE IT LIFE THROUGH *LOVE,* NOT CLINICAL PROCEDURE!!
SO YOU'RE SAYING OUR WAY IS COLD AND HEARTLESS? I HAVE A QUESTION FOR *YOU*, THEN...
WHAT *DRIVES* MALES AND FEMALES TO COPULATE?
THE ANSWER: TO *CONCEIVE OFFSPRING.* THIS IS FUN-DAMENTAL, *NATURAL* GENETIC PRO-GRAMMING.

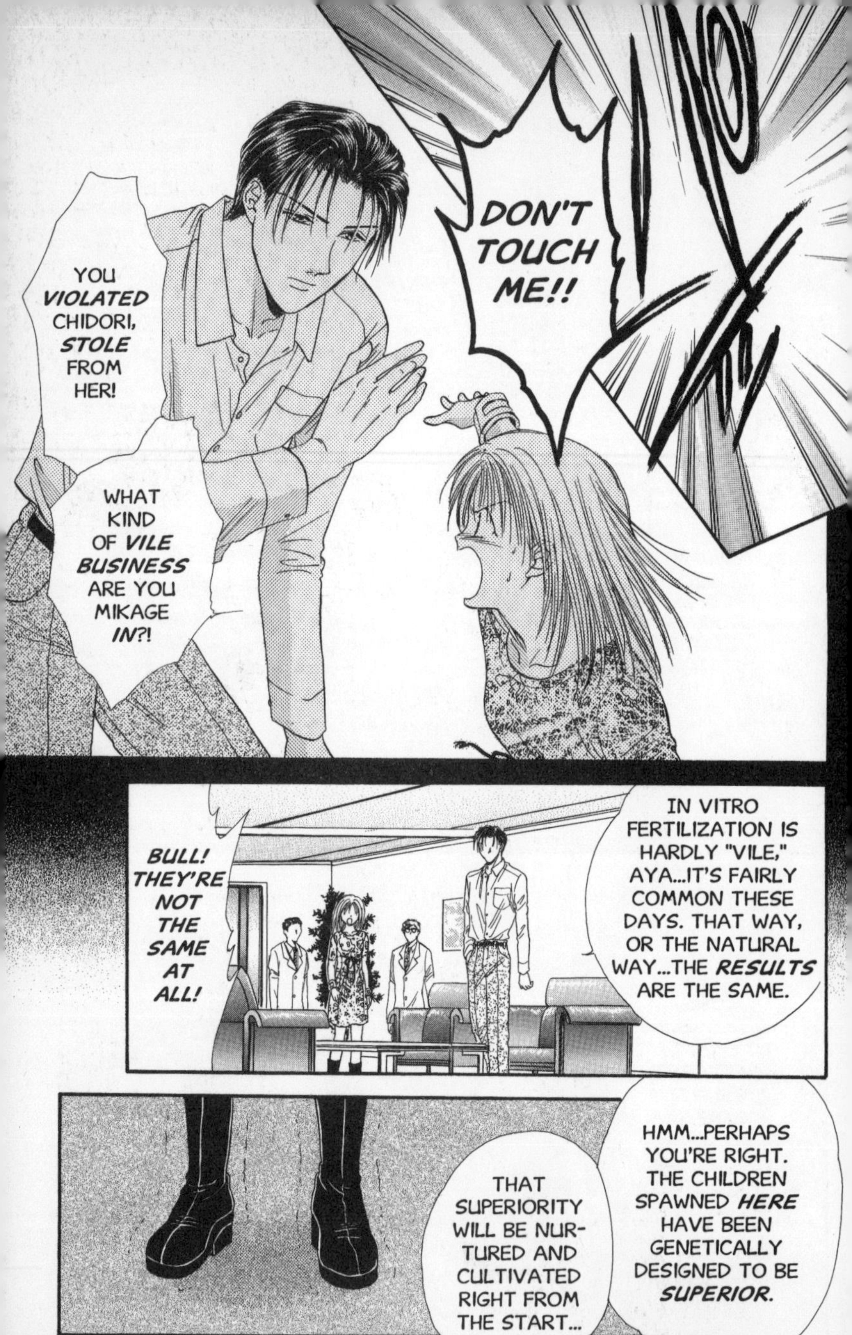
NO
DON'T TOUCH ME!!
YOU VIOLATED CHIDORI, STOLE FROM HER!
WHAT KIND OF VILE BUSINESS ARE YOU MIKAGE IN?!
IN VITRO FERTILIZATION IS HARDLY "VILE," AYA...IT'S FAIRLY COMMON THESE DAYS. THAT WAY, OR THE NATURAL WAY...THE RESULTS ARE THE SAME.
BULL! THEY'RE NOT THE SAME AT ALL!
HMM...PERHAPS YOU'RE RIGHT. THE CHILDREN SPAWNED HERE HAVE BEEN GENETICALLY DESIGNED TO BE SUPERIOR.
THAT SUPERIORITY WILL BE NURTURED AND CULTIVATED RIGHT FROM THE START...

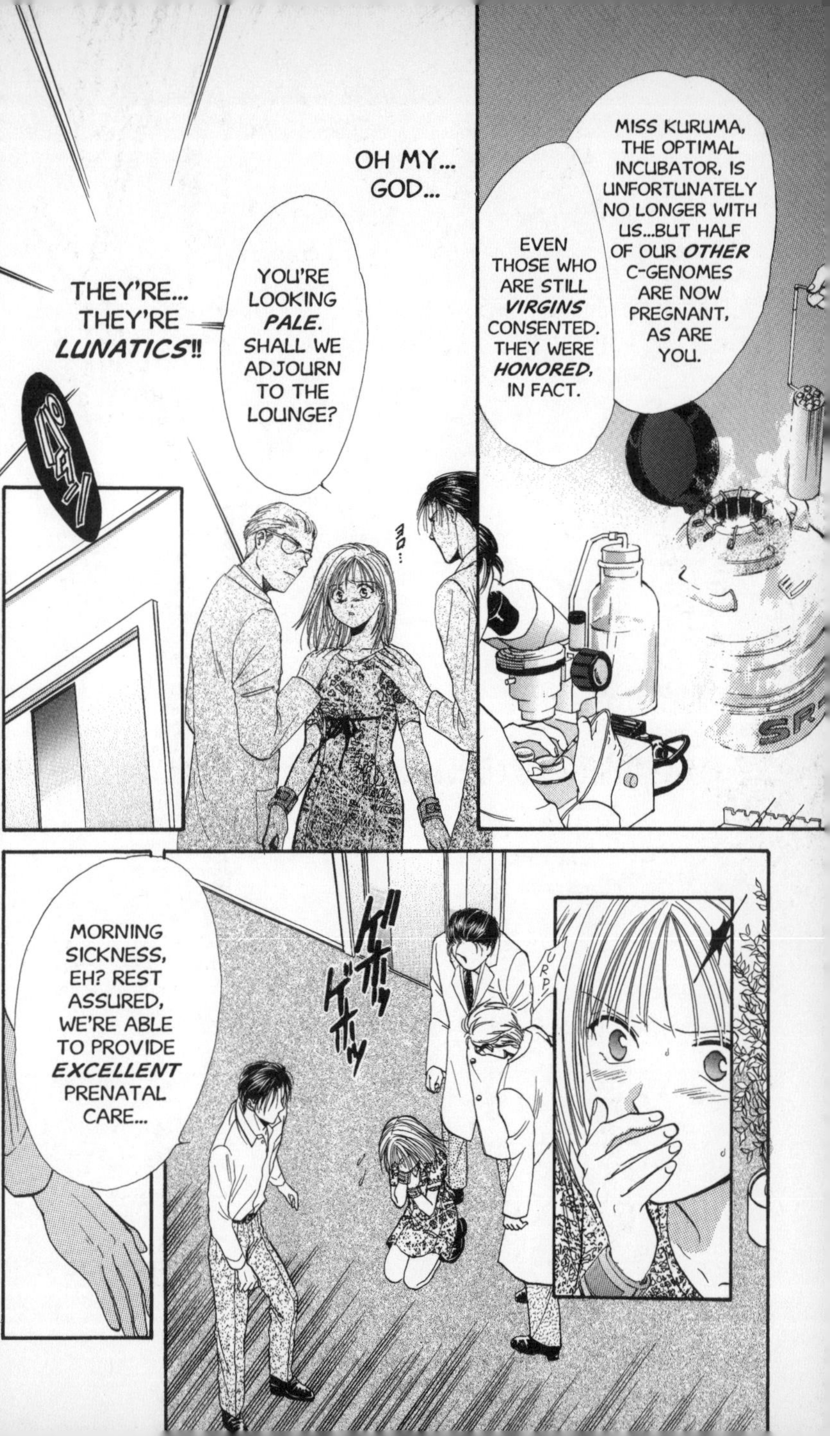
MISS KURUMA, THE OPTIMAL INCUBATOR, IS UNFORTUNATELY NO LONGER WITH US...BUT HALF OF OUR *OTHER* C-GENOMES ARE NOW PREGNANT, AS ARE YOU.
EVEN THOSE WHO ARE STILL *VIRGINS* CONSENTED. THEY WERE *HONORED,* IN FACT.
OH MY... GOD...
YOU'RE LOOKING *PALE.* SHALL WE ADJOURN TO THE LOUNGE?
THEY'RE... THEY'RE *LUNATICS*!!
URP!
MORNING SICKNESS, EH? REST ASSURED, WE'RE ABLE TO PROVIDE *EXCELLENT* PRENATAL CARE...

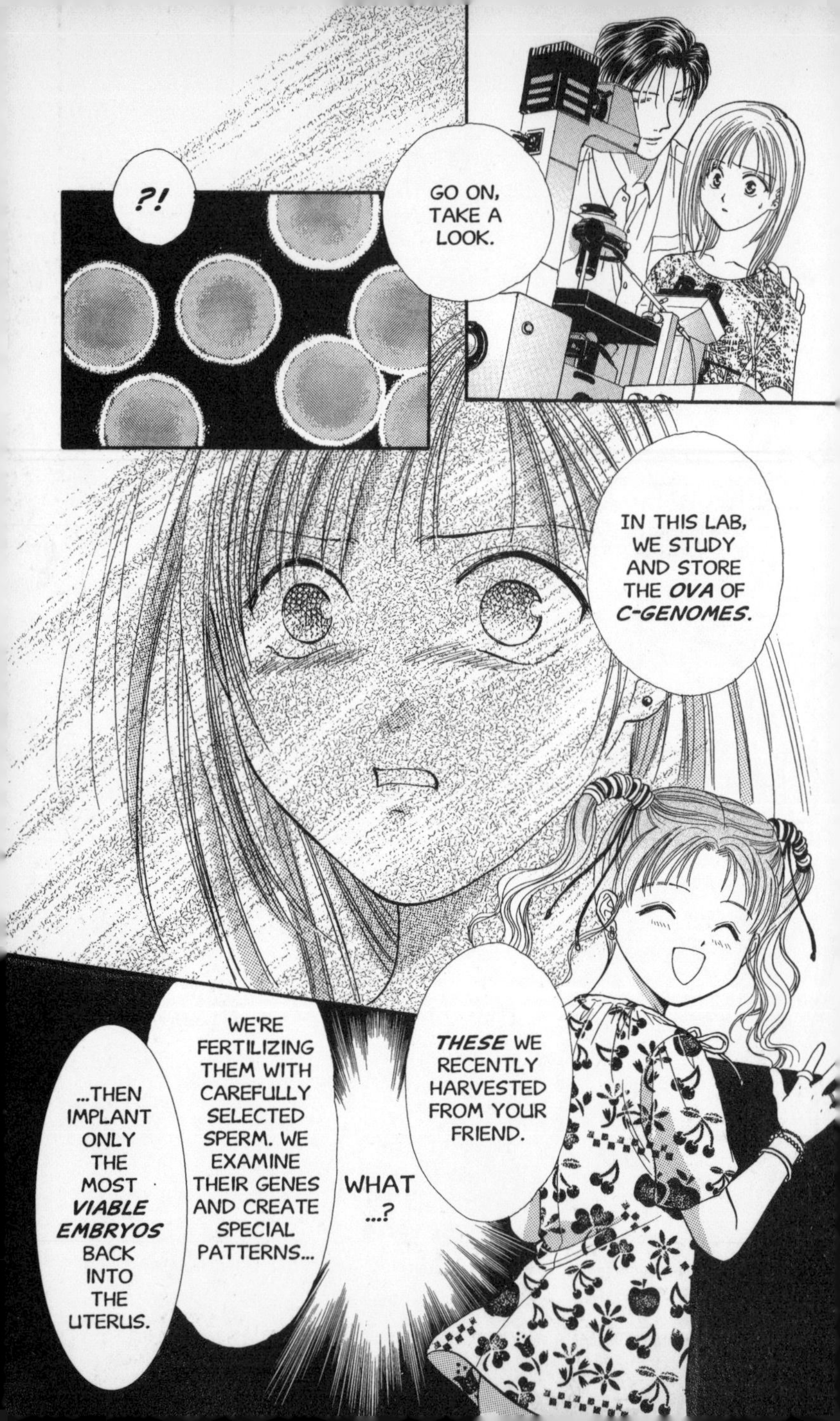
GO ON, TAKE A LOOK.
?!
IN THIS LAB, WE STUDY AND STORE THE *OVA* OF ***C-GENOMES.***
THESE WE RECENTLY HARVESTED FROM YOUR FRIEND.
WHAT ...?
WE'RE FERTILIZING THEM WITH CAREFULLY SELECTED SPERM. WE EXAMINE THEIR GENES AND CREATE SPECIAL PATTERNS...
...THEN IMPLANT ONLY THE MOST ***VIABLE EMBRYOS*** BACK INTO THE UTERUS.

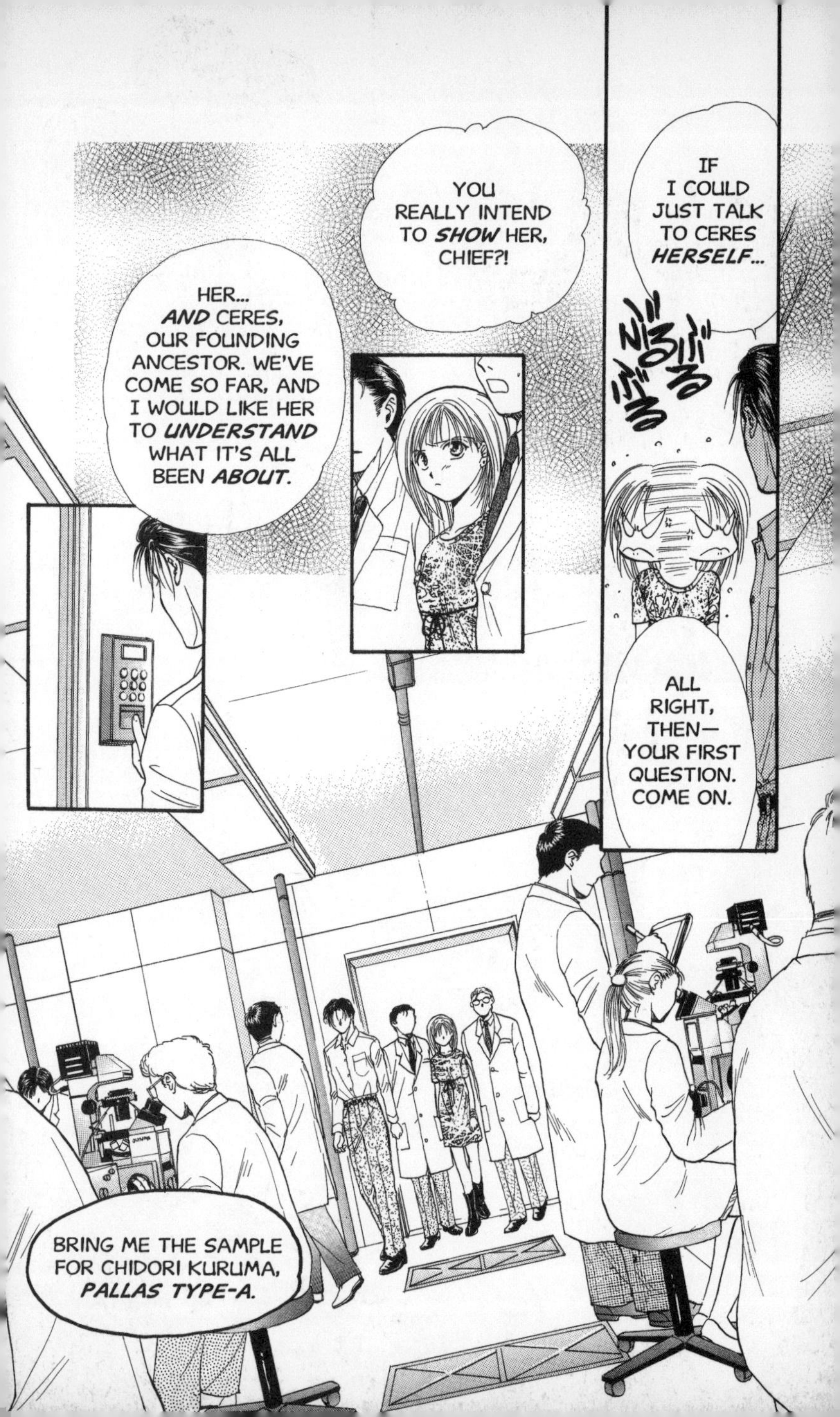
IF I COULD JUST TALK TO CERES *HERSELF*...
ぶるぶるぶるぶる
ALL RIGHT, THEN— YOUR FIRST QUESTION. COME ON.
YOU REALLY INTEND TO *SHOW* HER, CHIEF?!
HER... *AND* CERES, OUR FOUNDING ANCESTOR. WE'VE COME SO FAR, AND I WOULD LIKE HER TO *UNDERSTAND* WHAT IT'S ALL BEEN *ABOUT*.
BRING ME THE SAMPLE FOR CHIDORI KURUMA, *PALLAS TYPE-A*.

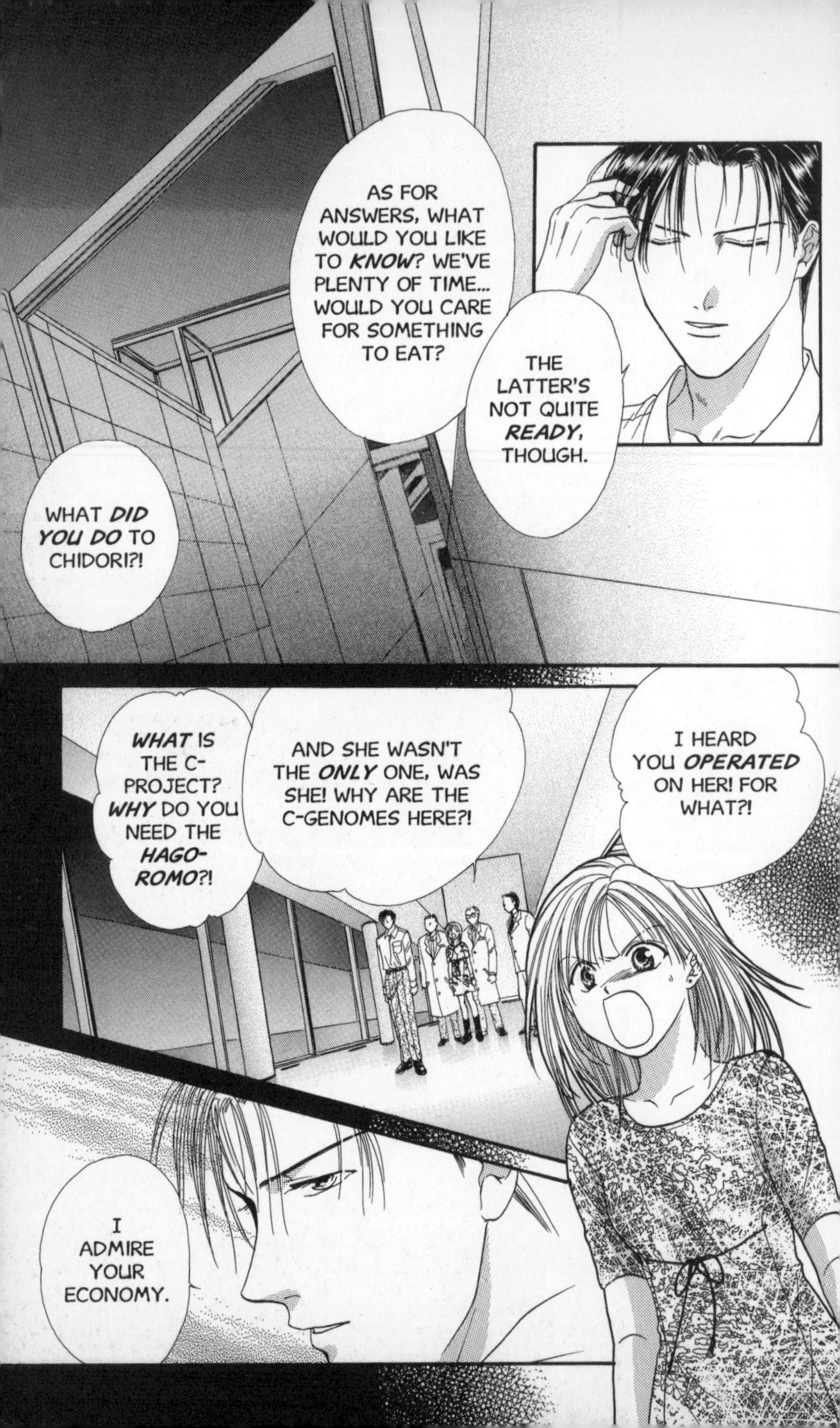
AS FOR ANSWERS, WHAT WOULD YOU LIKE TO *KNOW*? WE'VE PLENTY OF TIME... WOULD YOU CARE FOR SOMETHING TO EAT?
THE LATTER'S NOT QUITE *READY*, THOUGH.
WHAT *DID YOU DO* TO CHIDORI?!
I HEARD YOU *OPERATED* ON HER! FOR WHAT?!
AND SHE WASN'T THE *ONLY* ONE, WAS SHE! WHY ARE THE C-GENOMES HERE?!
WHAT IS THE C-PROJECT? *WHY* DO YOU NEED THE *HAGO-ROMO*?!
I ADMIRE YOUR ECONOMY.

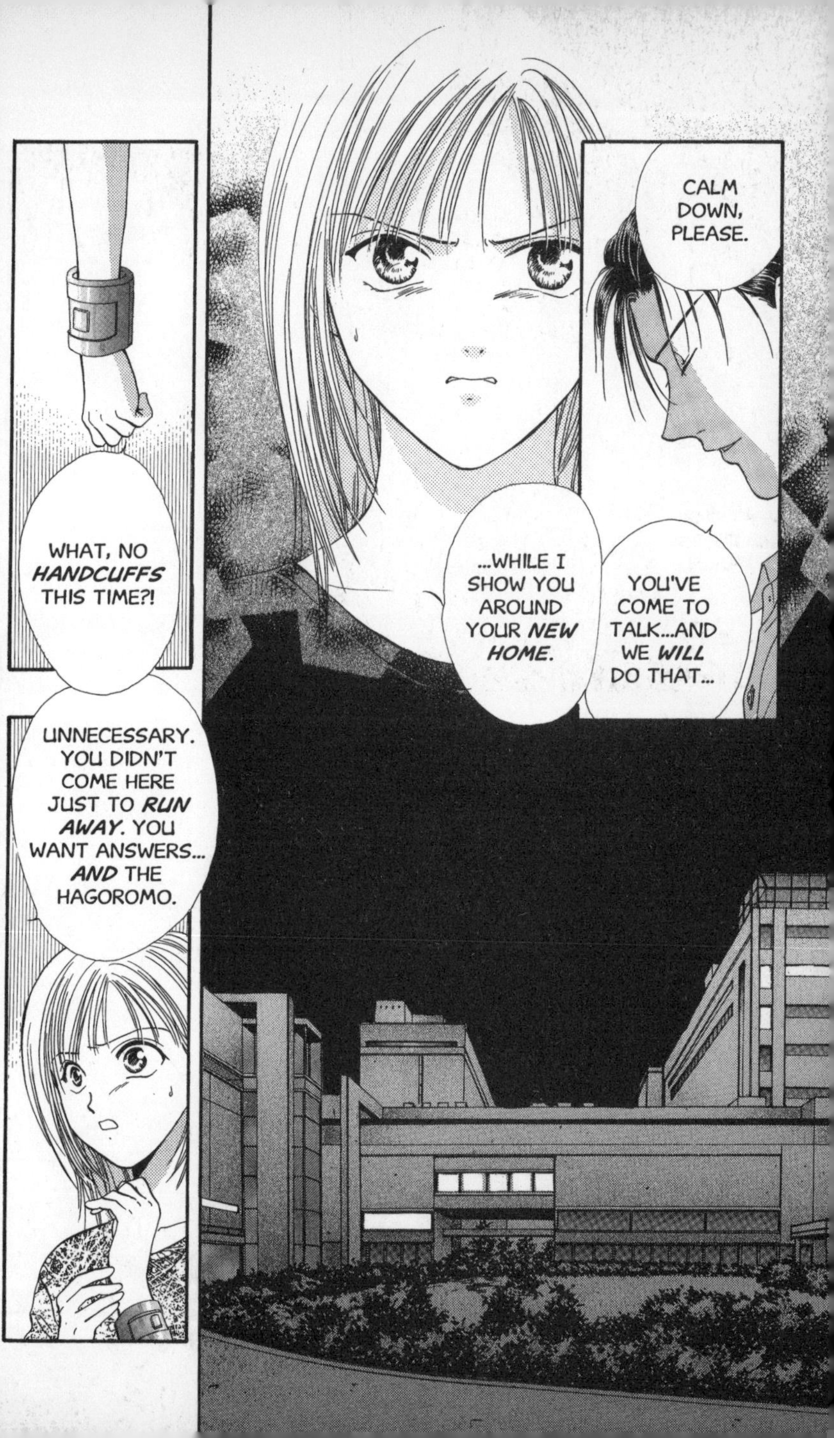
CALM DOWN, PLEASE.
YOU'VE COME TO TALK...AND WE *WILL* DO THAT...
...WHILE I SHOW YOU AROUND YOUR *NEW HOME*.
WHAT, NO *HANDCUFFS* THIS TIME?!
UNNECESSARY. YOU DIDN'T COME HERE JUST TO *RUN AWAY*. YOU WANT ANSWERS... *AND* THE HAGOROMO.

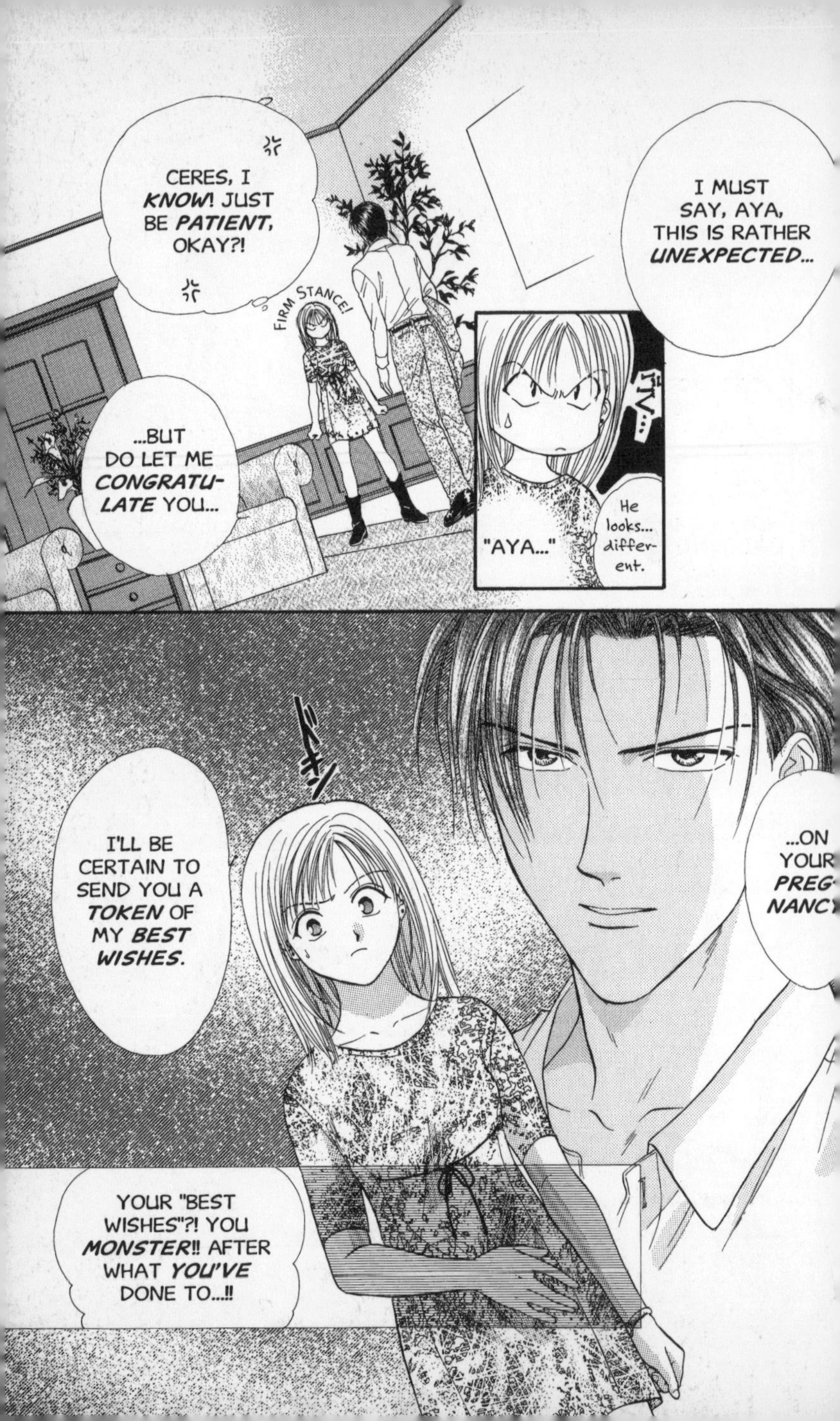
I MUST SAY, AYA, THIS IS RATHER ***UNEXPECTED...***
"AYA..."
He looks... differ- ent.
CERES, I ***KNOW!*** JUST BE ***PATIENT,*** OKAY?!
FIRM STANCE!
...BUT DO LET ME ***CONGRATU- LATE*** YOU...
...ON YOUR ***PREG- NANC***
I'LL BE CERTAIN TO SEND YOU A ***TOKEN*** OF MY ***BEST WISHES.***
YOUR "BEST WISHES"?! YOU ***MONSTER!!*** AFTER WHAT ***YOU'VE*** DONE TO...!!

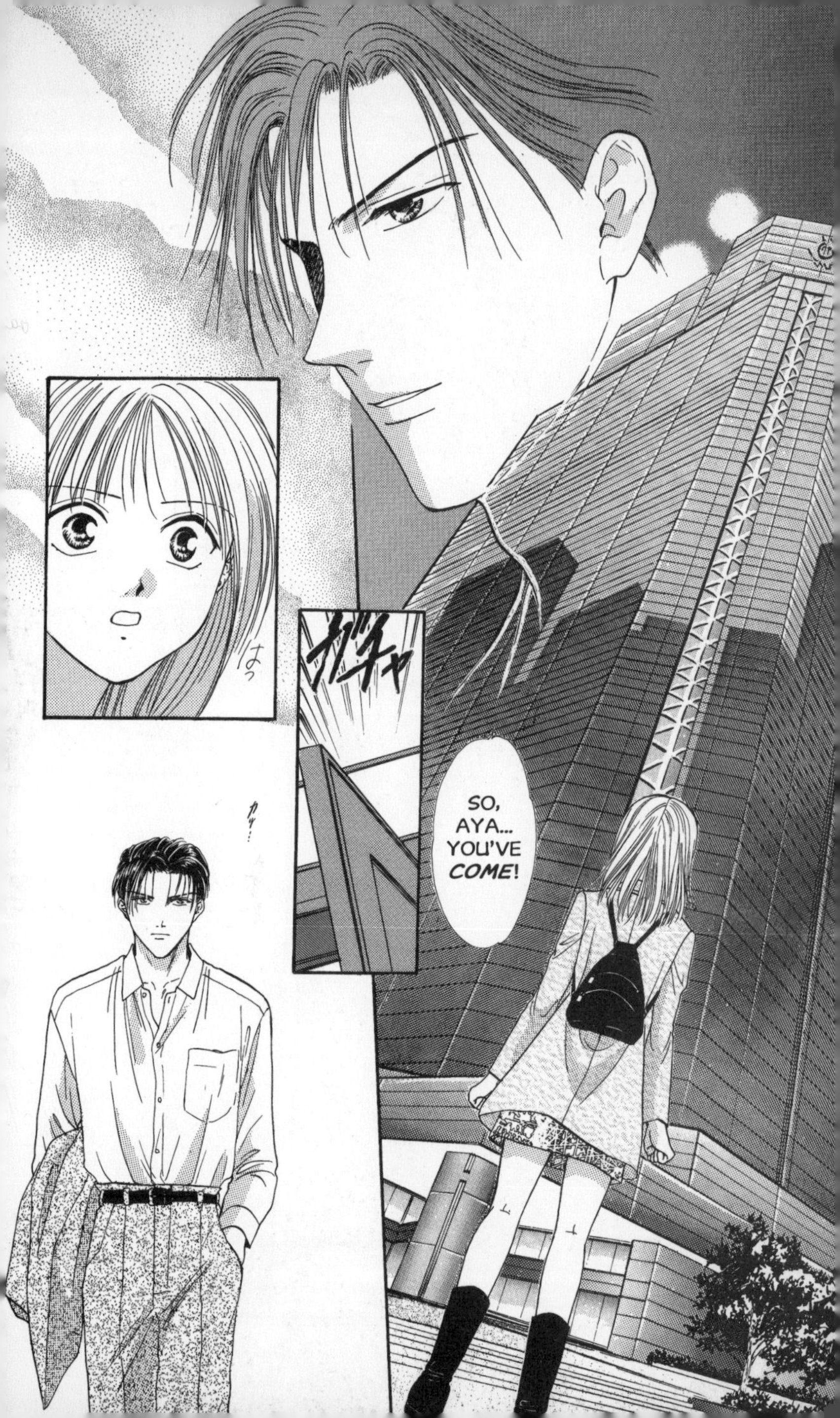
SO, AYA... YOU'VE *COME*!
ガチャ
はっ
カッ…

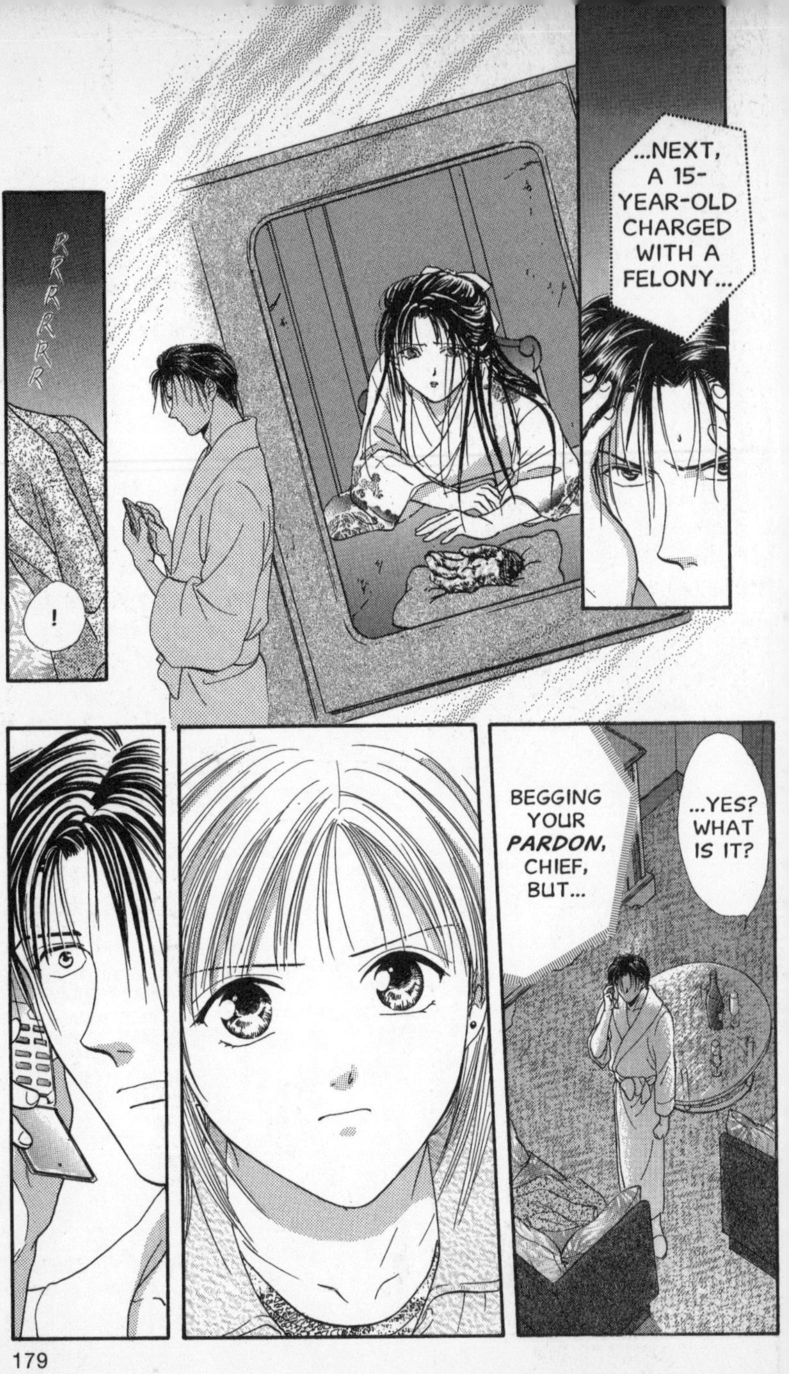
...NEXT, A 15-YEAR-OLD CHARGED WITH A FELONY...
RRRRRR
!
...YES? WHAT IS IT?
BEGGING YOUR ***PARDON,*** CHIEF, BUT...

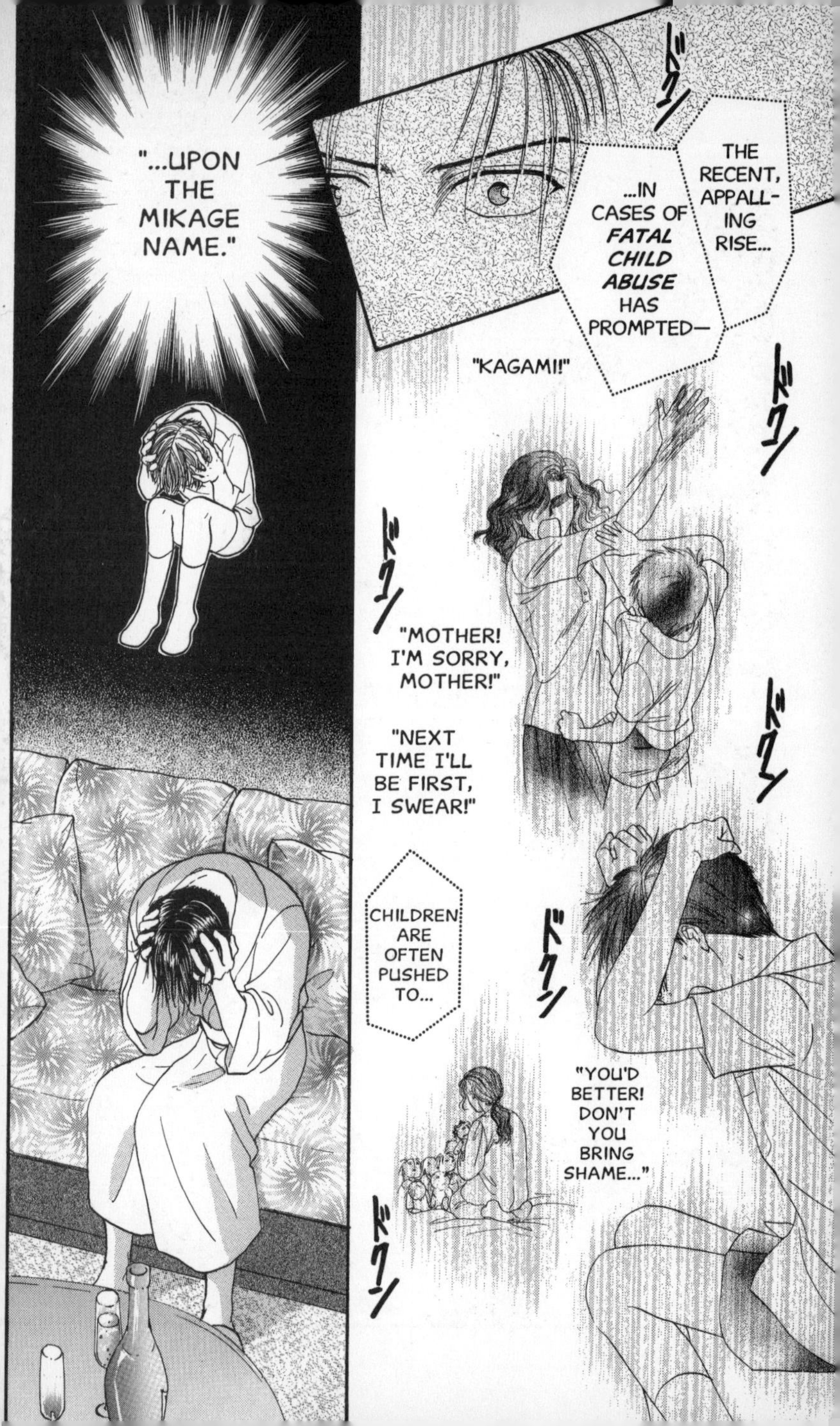
ドクン
THE RECENT, APPALL-ING RISE...
...IN CASES OF *FATAL CHILD ABUSE* HAS PROMPTED—
"KAGAMI!"
ドクン
ドクン
"MOTHER! I'M SORRY, MOTHER!"
"NEXT TIME I'LL BE FIRST, I SWEAR!"
ドクン
ドクン
CHILDREN ARE OFTEN PUSHED TO...
"YOU'D BETTER! DON'T YOU BRING SHAME..."
ドクン
"...UPON THE MIKAGE NAME."

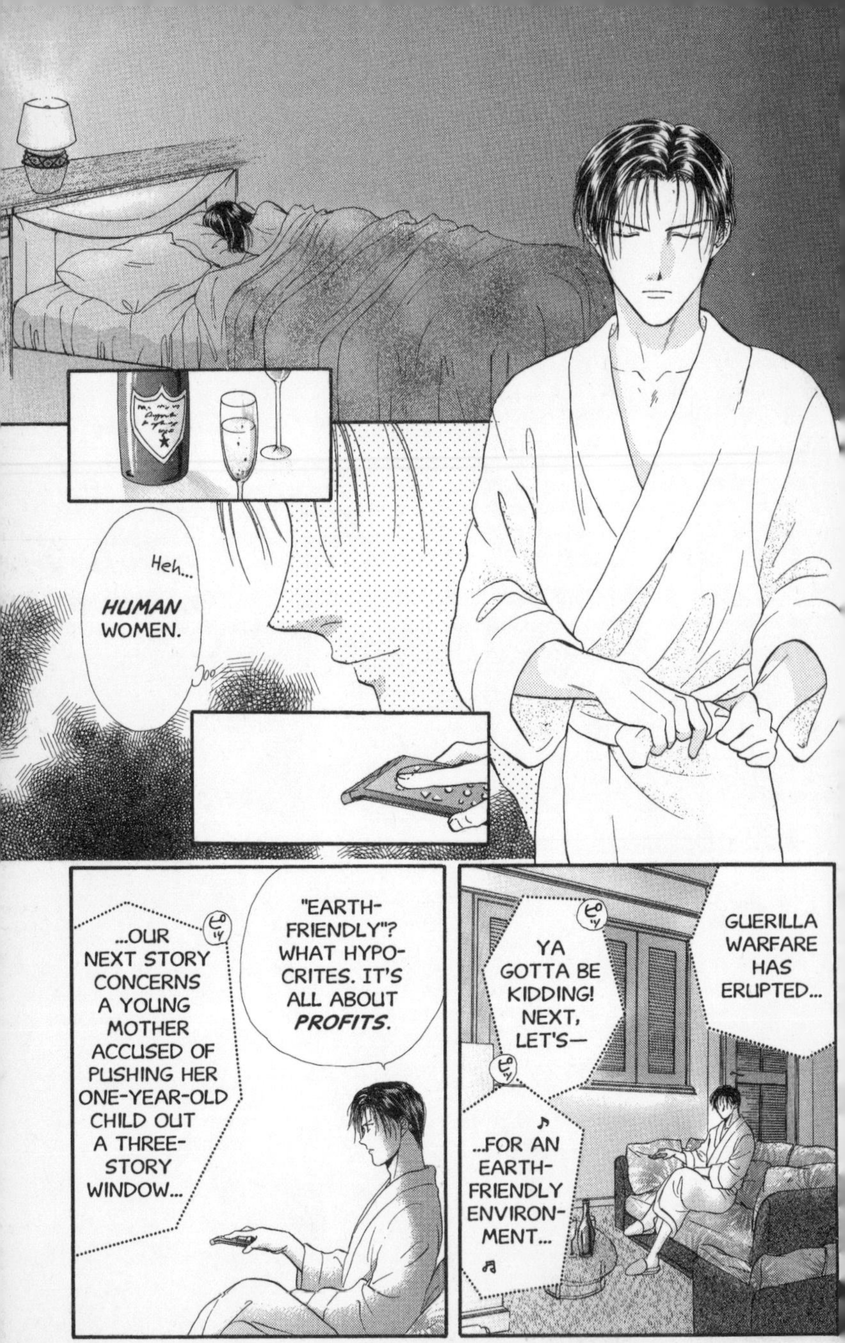
Heh... HUMAN WOMEN.
GUERILLA WARFARE HAS ERUPTED...
YA GOTTA BE KIDDING! NEXT, LET'S—
...FOR AN EARTH-FRIENDLY ENVIRONMENT...
"EARTH-FRIENDLY"? WHAT HYPOCRITES. IT'S ALL ABOUT PROFITS.
...OUR NEXT STORY CONCERNS A YOUNG MOTHER ACCUSED OF PUSHING HER ONE-YEAR-OLD CHILD OUT A THREE-STORY WINDOW...

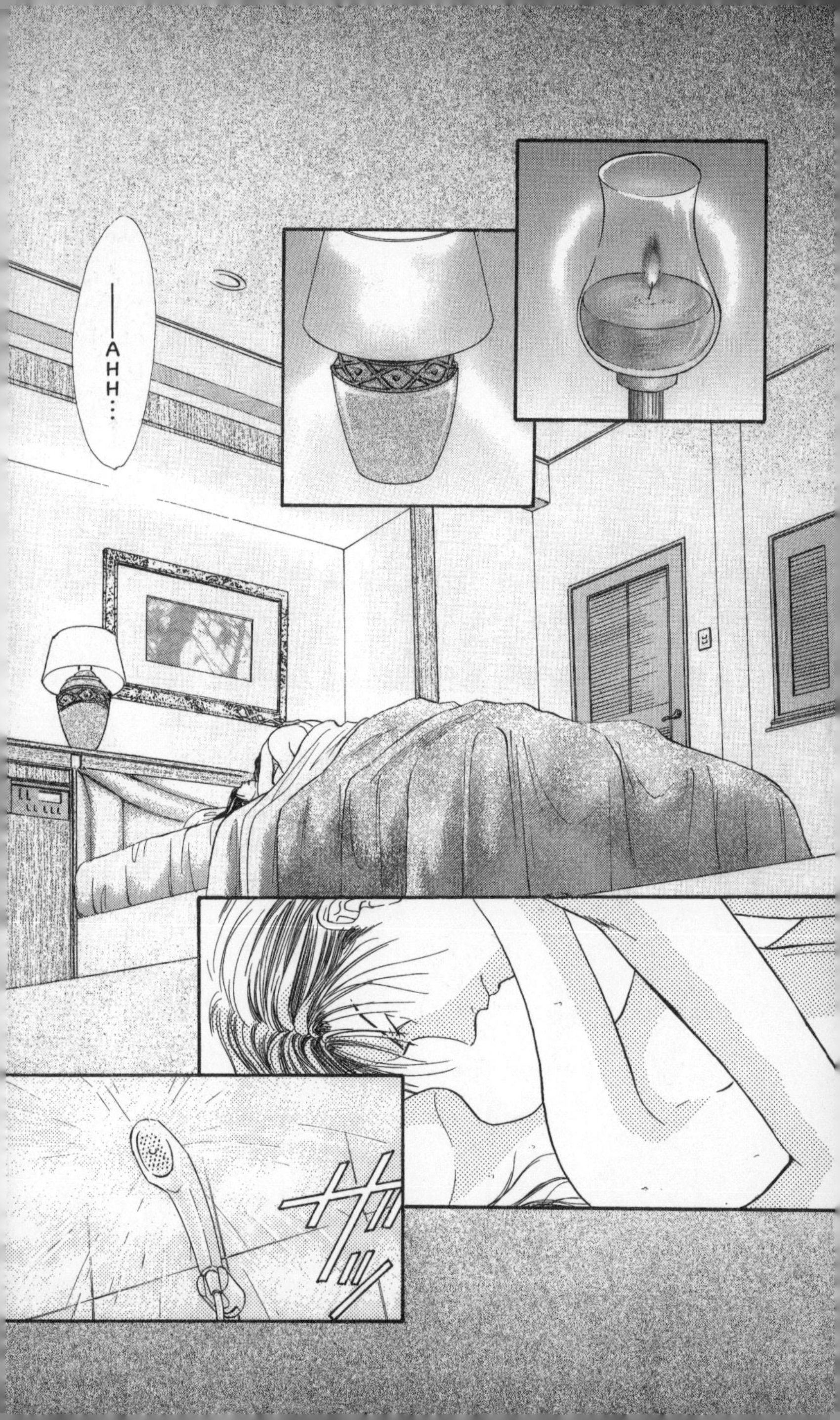
—AHH...

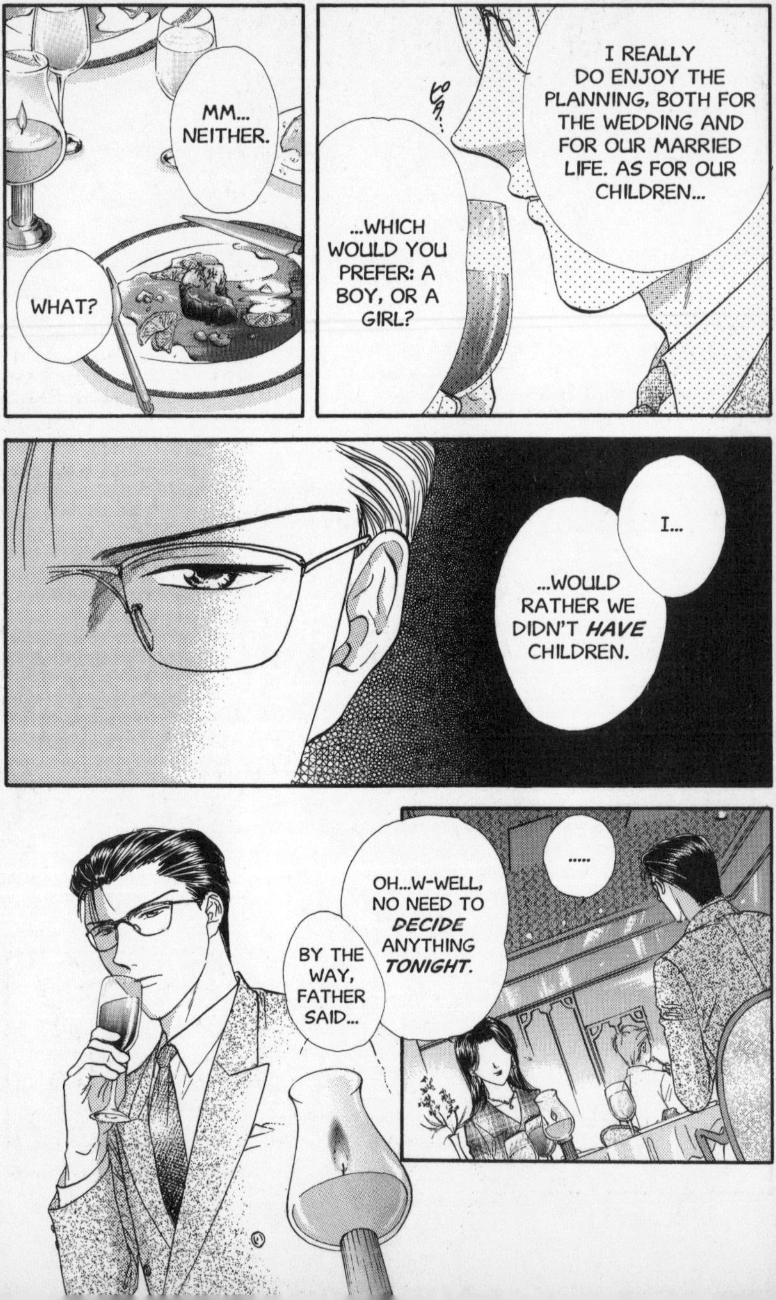
I REALLY DO ENJOY THE PLANNING, BOTH FOR THE WEDDING AND FOR OUR MARRIED LIFE. AS FOR OUR CHILDREN...
...WHICH WOULD YOU PREFER: A BOY, OR A GIRL?
MM... NEITHER.
WHAT?
I...
...WOULD RATHER WE DIDN'T *HAVE* CHILDREN.
.....
OH...W-WELL, NO NEED TO *DECIDE* ANYTHING *TONIGHT*.
BY THE WAY, FATHER SAID...

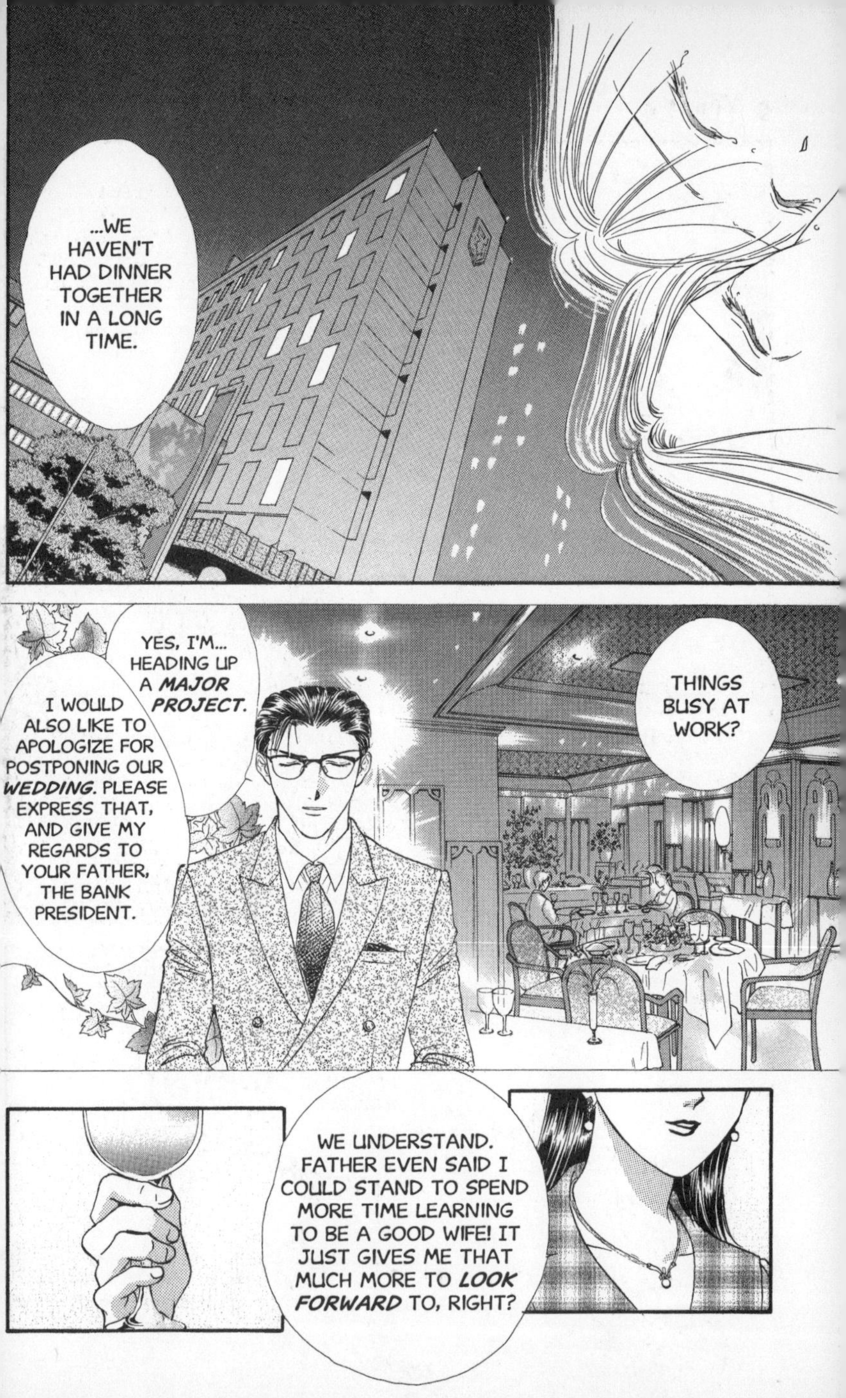
...WE HAVEN'T HAD DINNER TOGETHER IN A LONG TIME.
THINGS BUSY AT WORK?
YES, I'M... HEADING UP A ***MAJOR PROJECT***.
I WOULD ALSO LIKE TO APOLOGIZE FOR POSTPONING OUR ***WEDDING***. PLEASE EXPRESS THAT, AND GIVE MY REGARDS TO YOUR FATHER, THE BANK PRESIDENT.
WE UNDERSTAND. FATHER EVEN SAID I COULD STAND TO SPEND MORE TIME LEARNING TO BE A GOOD WIFE! IT JUST GIVES ME THAT MUCH MORE TO ***LOOK FORWARD*** TO, RIGHT?

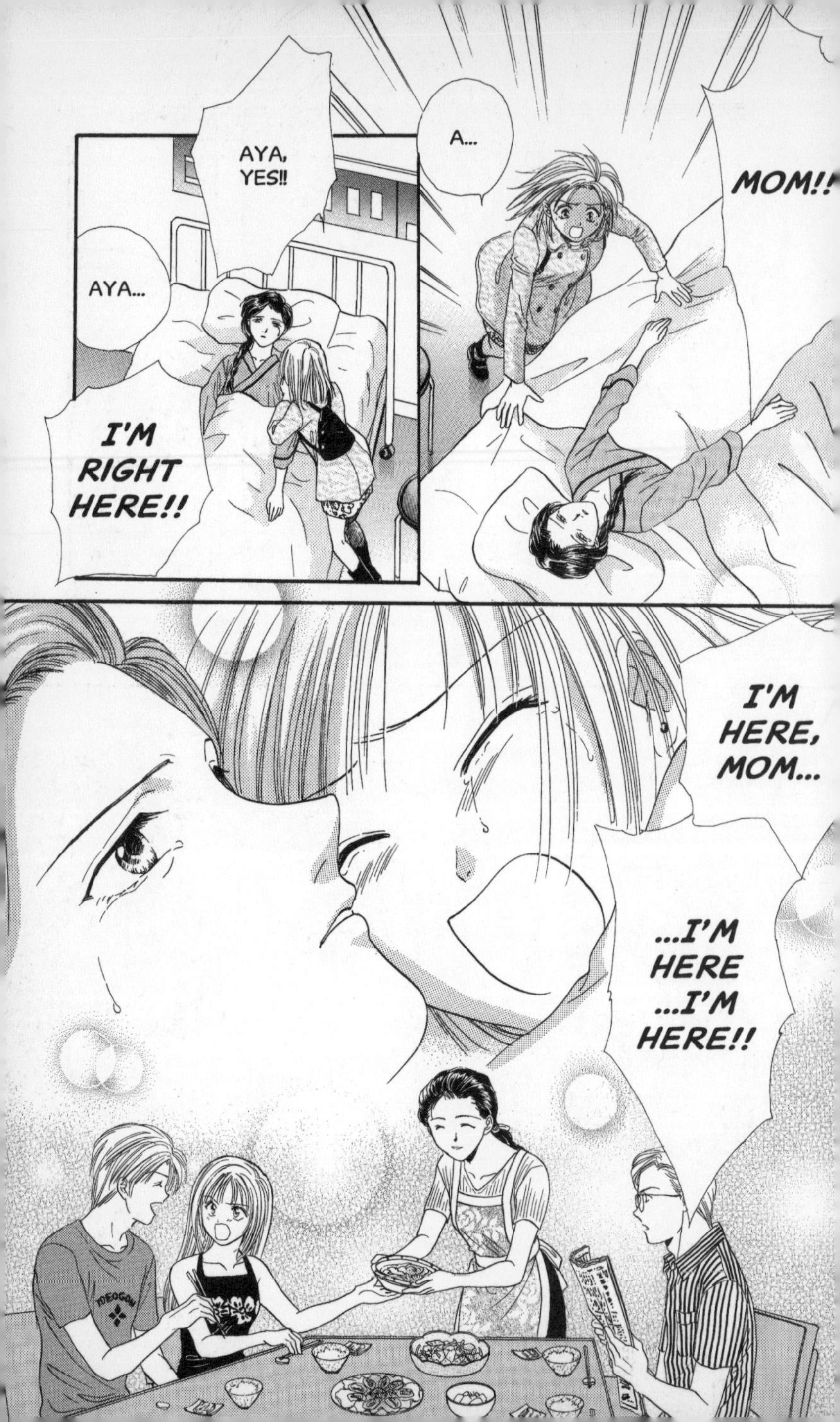
MOM!!
A...
AYA, YES!!
AYA...
I'M RIGHT HERE!!
I'M HERE, MOM...
...I'M HERE ...I'M HERE!!

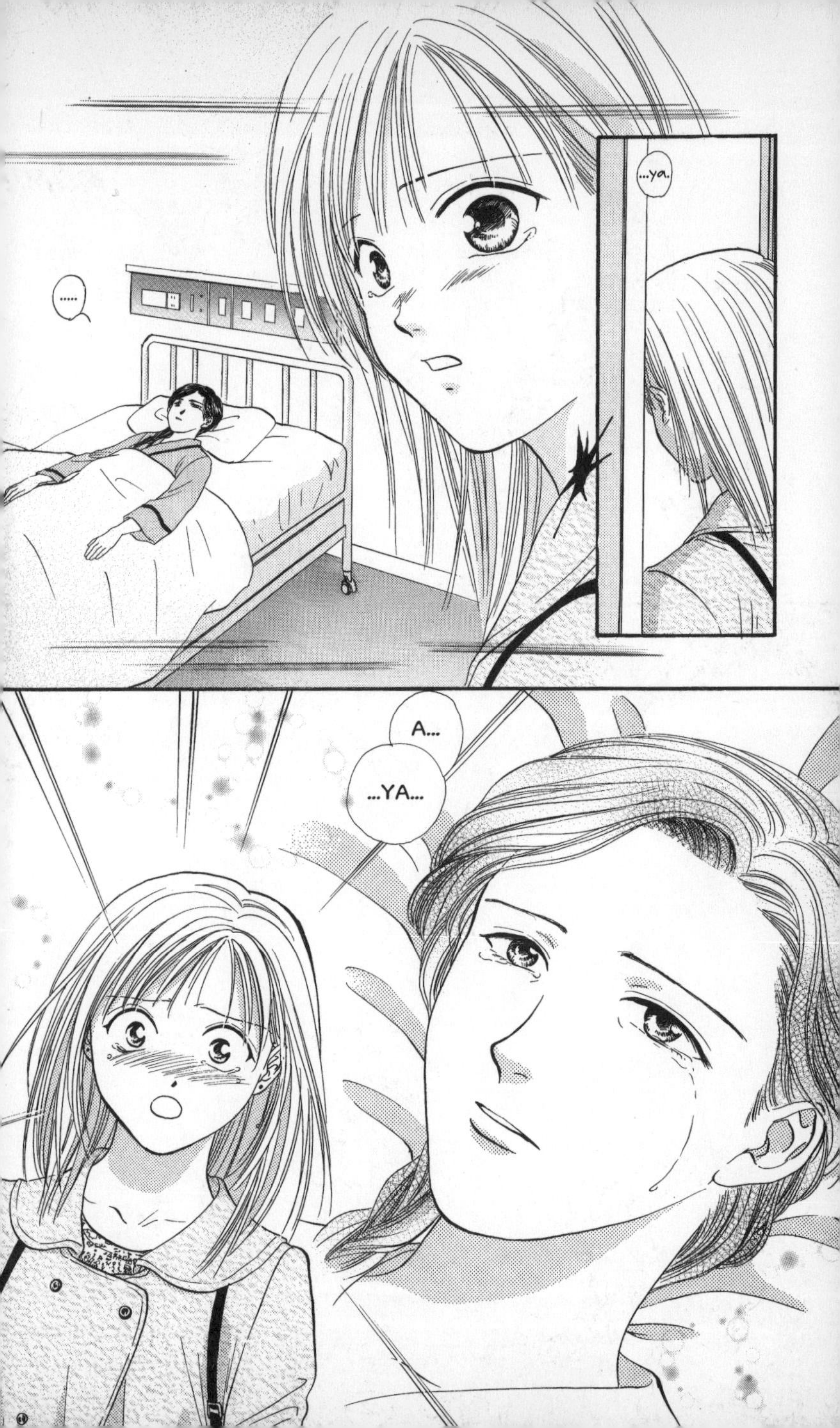
...ya.
......
A...
...YA...

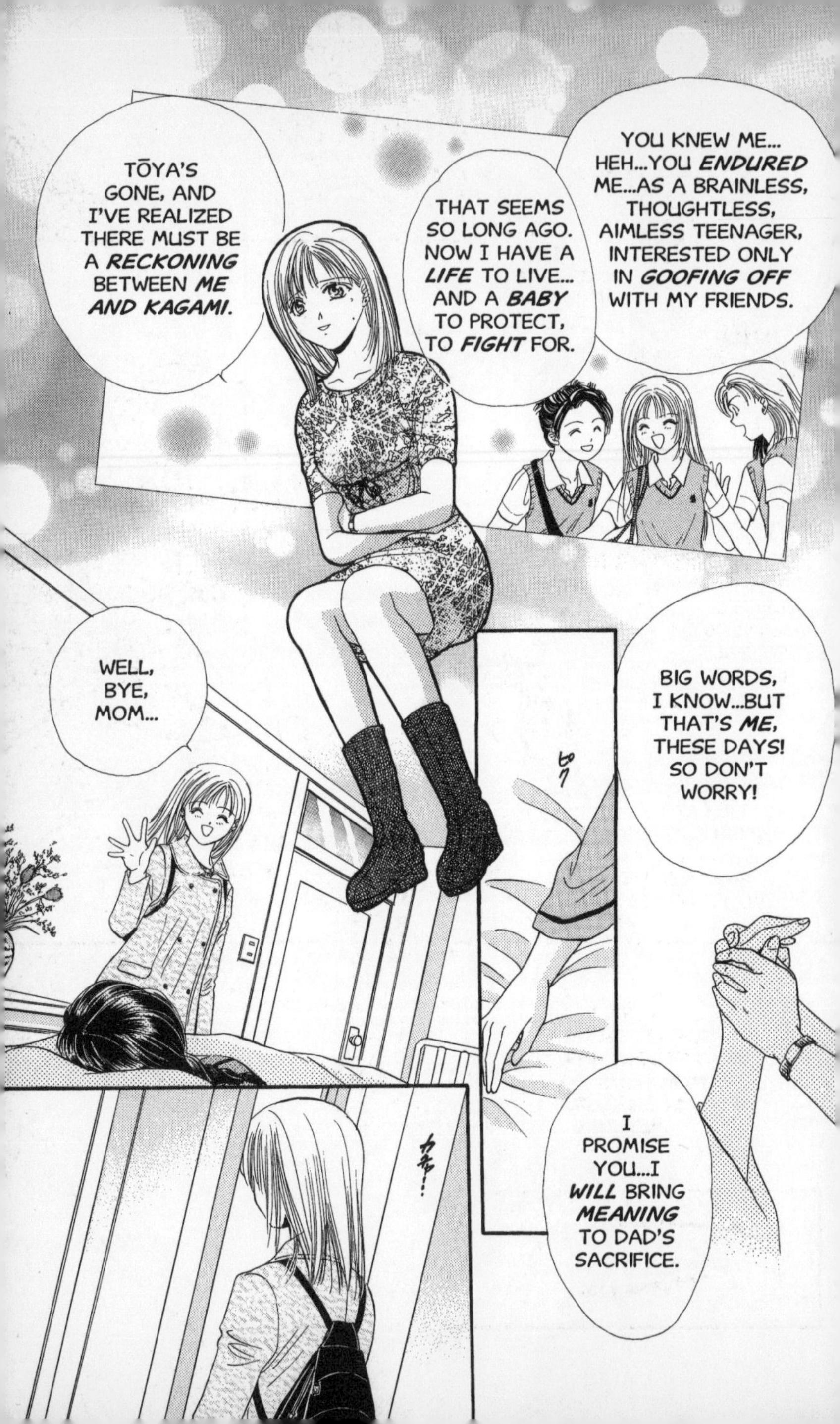
YOU KNEW ME... HEH...YOU *ENDURED* ME...AS A BRAINLESS, THOUGHTLESS, AIMLESS TEENAGER, INTERESTED ONLY IN *GOOFING OFF* WITH MY FRIENDS.
THAT SEEMS SO LONG AGO. NOW I HAVE A *LIFE* TO LIVE... AND A *BABY* TO PROTECT, TO *FIGHT* FOR.
TŌYA'S GONE, AND I'VE REALIZED THERE MUST BE A *RECKONING* BETWEEN *ME AND KAGAMI*.
BIG WORDS, I KNOW...BUT THAT'S *ME*, THESE DAYS! SO DON'T WORRY!
WELL, BYE, MOM...
I PROMISE YOU...I *WILL* BRING *MEANING* TO DAD'S SACRIFICE.

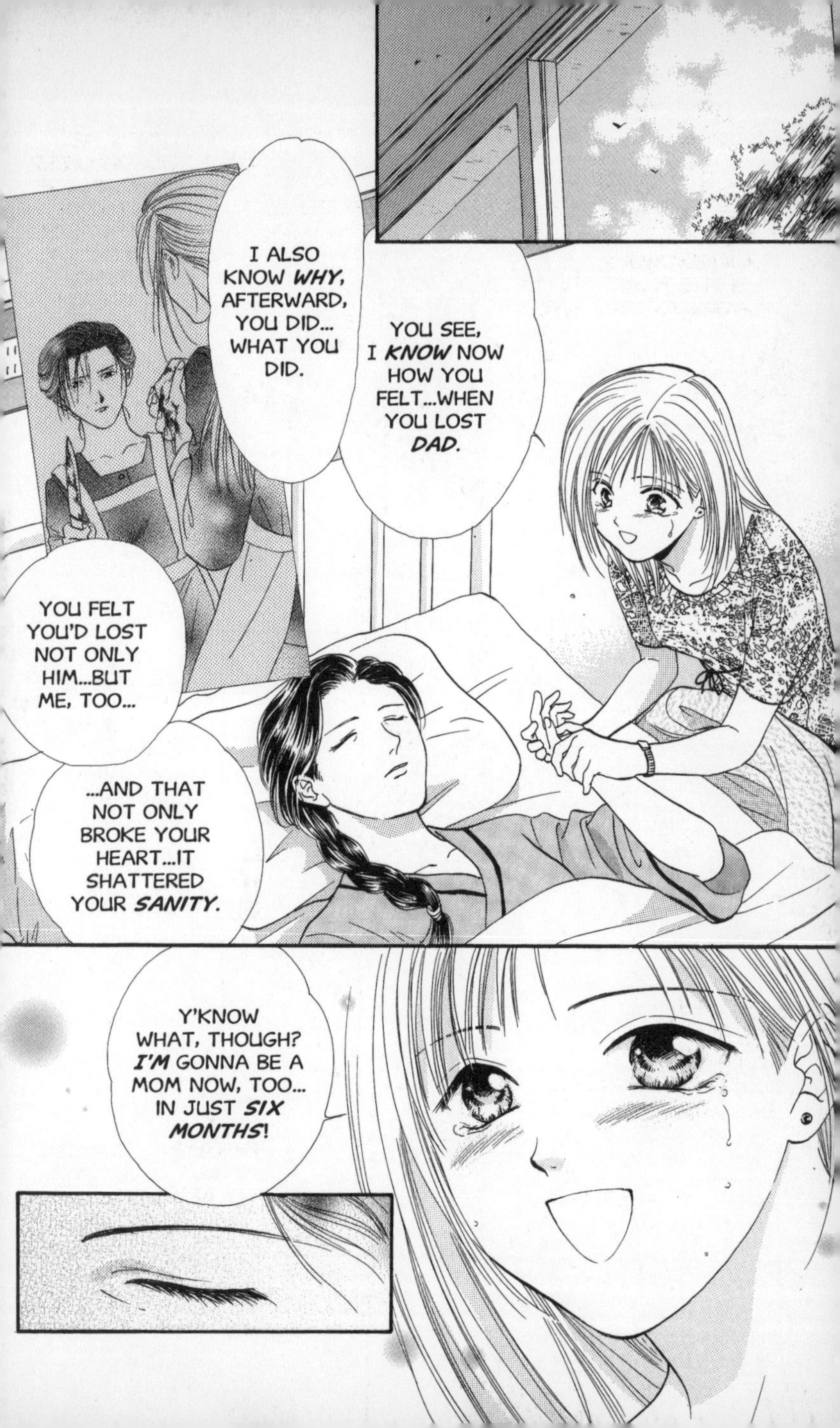
YOU SEE, I *KNOW* NOW HOW YOU FELT...WHEN YOU LOST *DAD*.
I ALSO KNOW *WHY*, AFTERWARD, YOU DID... WHAT YOU DID.
YOU FELT YOU'D LOST NOT ONLY HIM...BUT ME, TOO...
...AND THAT NOT ONLY BROKE YOUR HEART...IT SHATTERED YOUR *SANITY*.
Y'KNOW WHAT, THOUGH? *I'M* GONNA BE A MOM NOW, TOO... IN JUST *SIX MONTHS*!

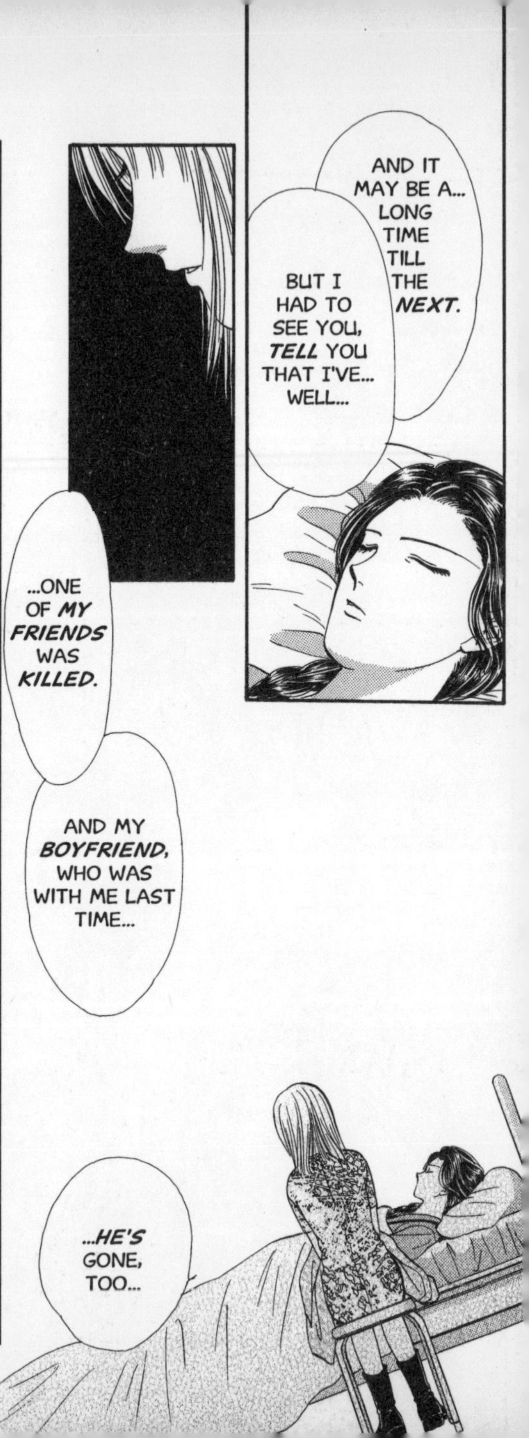
AND IT MAY BE A... LONG TIME TILL THE ***NEXT.***
BUT I HAD TO SEE YOU, ***TELL*** YOU THAT I'VE... WELL...
...ONE OF ***MY FRIENDS*** WAS ***KILLED.***
AND MY ***BOYFRIEND,*** WHO WAS WITH ME LAST TIME...
...***HE'S*** GONE, TOO...

Ceres: 12

(...Allow me to pull myself together.)
Now then, the question of Tōya aside, rest assured that various mysteries will soon be resolved. The end's in sight—keep reading! Will Aya get back the hagoromo and her life? Will Ceres allow herself to disappear? Okay, I bet the only question that's **really** on everyone's mind is, "What about Tōya?!"

Now, now. Now, now, now...

(Retreating again...)

So, let's see, **FY**! The fifth **Fūshigi Yugi** novel, "Suzaku Hiden (The Legend of the Suzaku Tragedy)" is now out from Palette Books! This one's mainly about Hotohori...but it also covers quite a bit of the entire **FY** backstory. If there aren't any copies in stock at your local (Japan) bookstore, special-ordering may take a while, so you might want to consider contacting the Shogakukan Sales Dept. directly: (03)3230-5749. More novels **will** be forthcoming (though the next won't be till December), so stay up to date!

What I need to do is make time to practice drawing on my computer. My "Post Pet" is a turtle, by the way; my assistants named it "Navona"—try and guess the reference! ^o^ I really gotta get back to work.

All right, then. Be ready for the next volume, and in the meantime, send me your comments. I won't be able to answer them individually, of course, but.... ^^;

Later!
'99.8

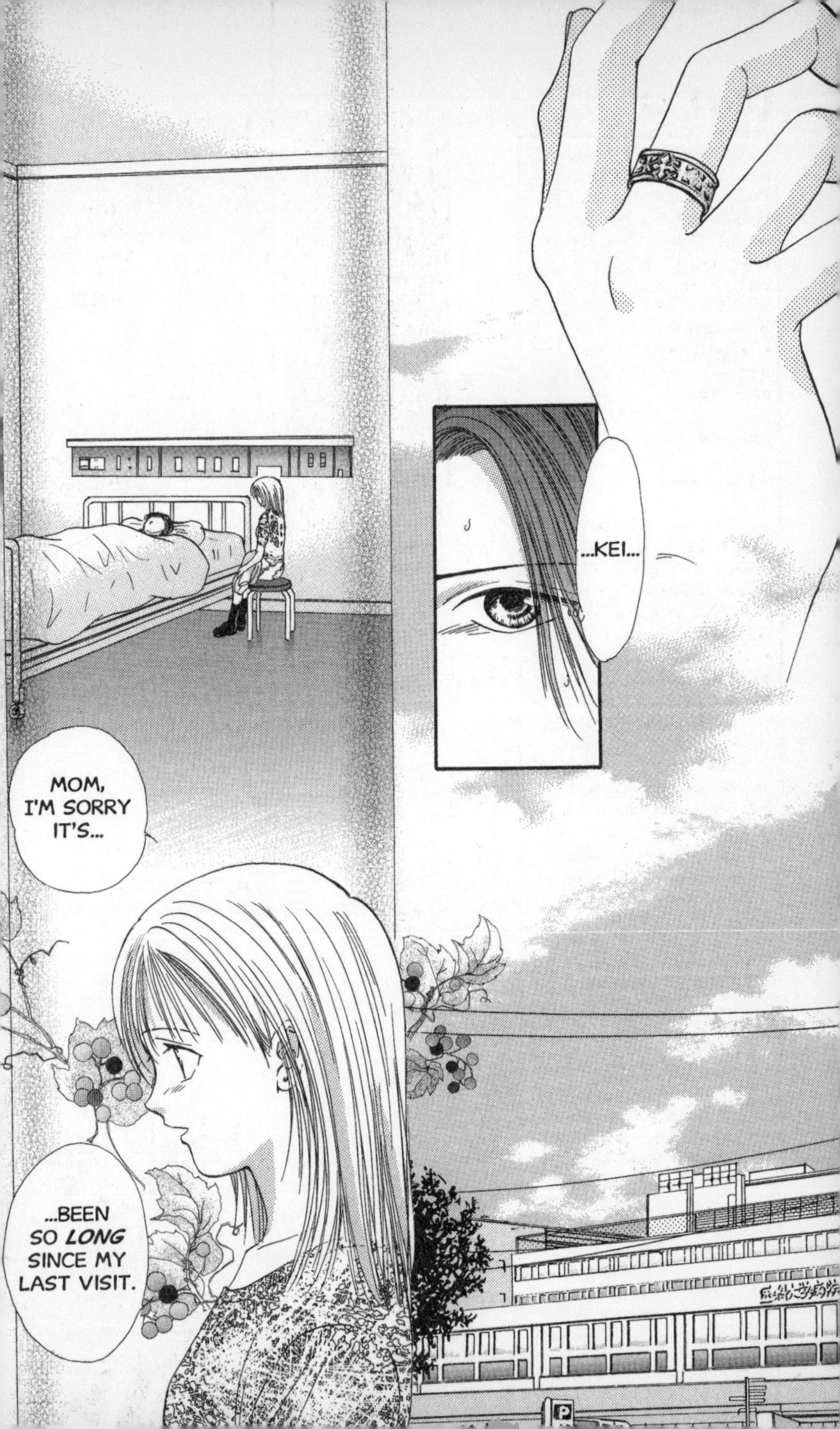
...KEI...
MOM, I'M SORRY IT'S...
...BEEN SO **LONG** SINCE MY LAST VISIT.

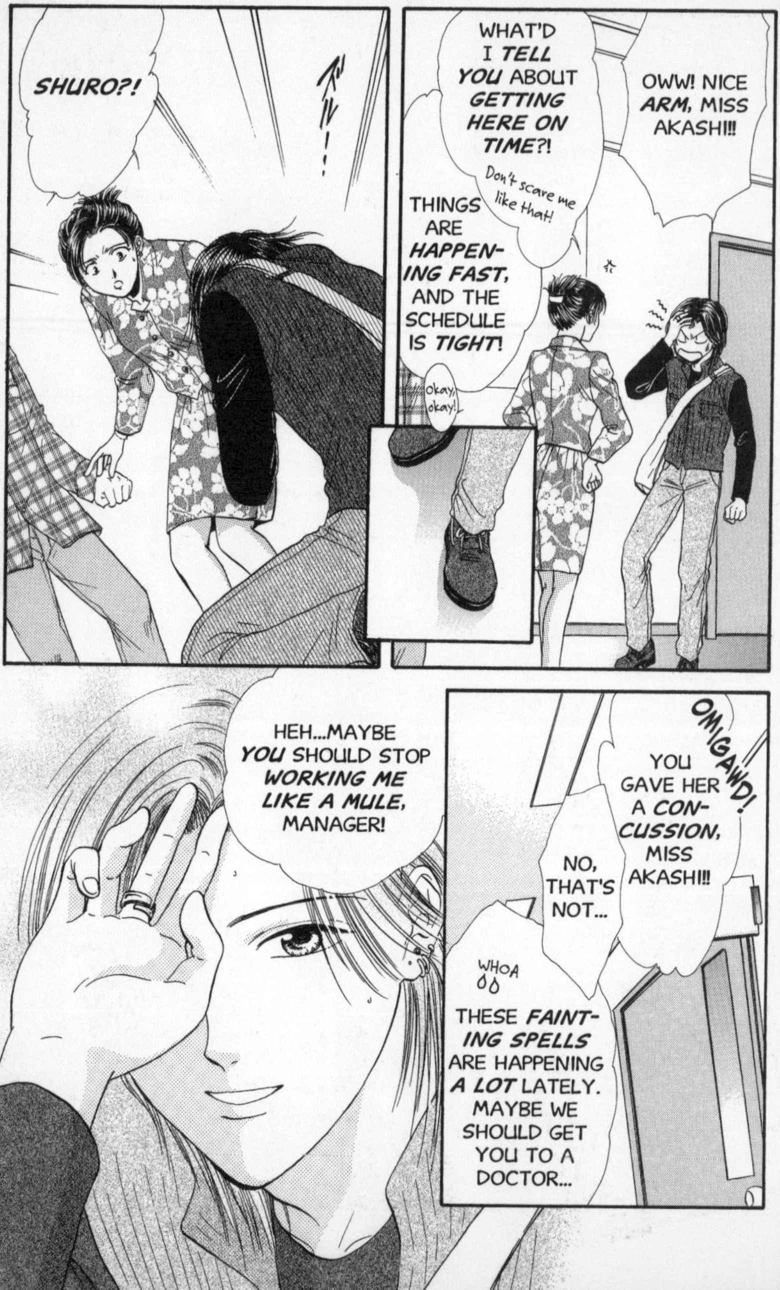
OWW! NICE ARM, MISS AKASHI!!
WHAT'D I TELL YOU ABOUT GETTING HERE ON TIME?!
Don't scare me like that!
THINGS ARE HAPPENING FAST, AND THE SCHEDULE IS TIGHT!
Okay, okay!
SHURO?!
OMIGAWD!
YOU GAVE HER A CONCUSSION, MISS AKASHI!!
NO, THAT'S NOT...
WHOA
THESE FAINTING SPELLS ARE HAPPENING A LOT LATELY. MAYBE WE SHOULD GET YOU TO A DOCTOR...
HEH...MAYBE YOU SHOULD STOP WORKING ME LIKE A MULE, MANAGER!

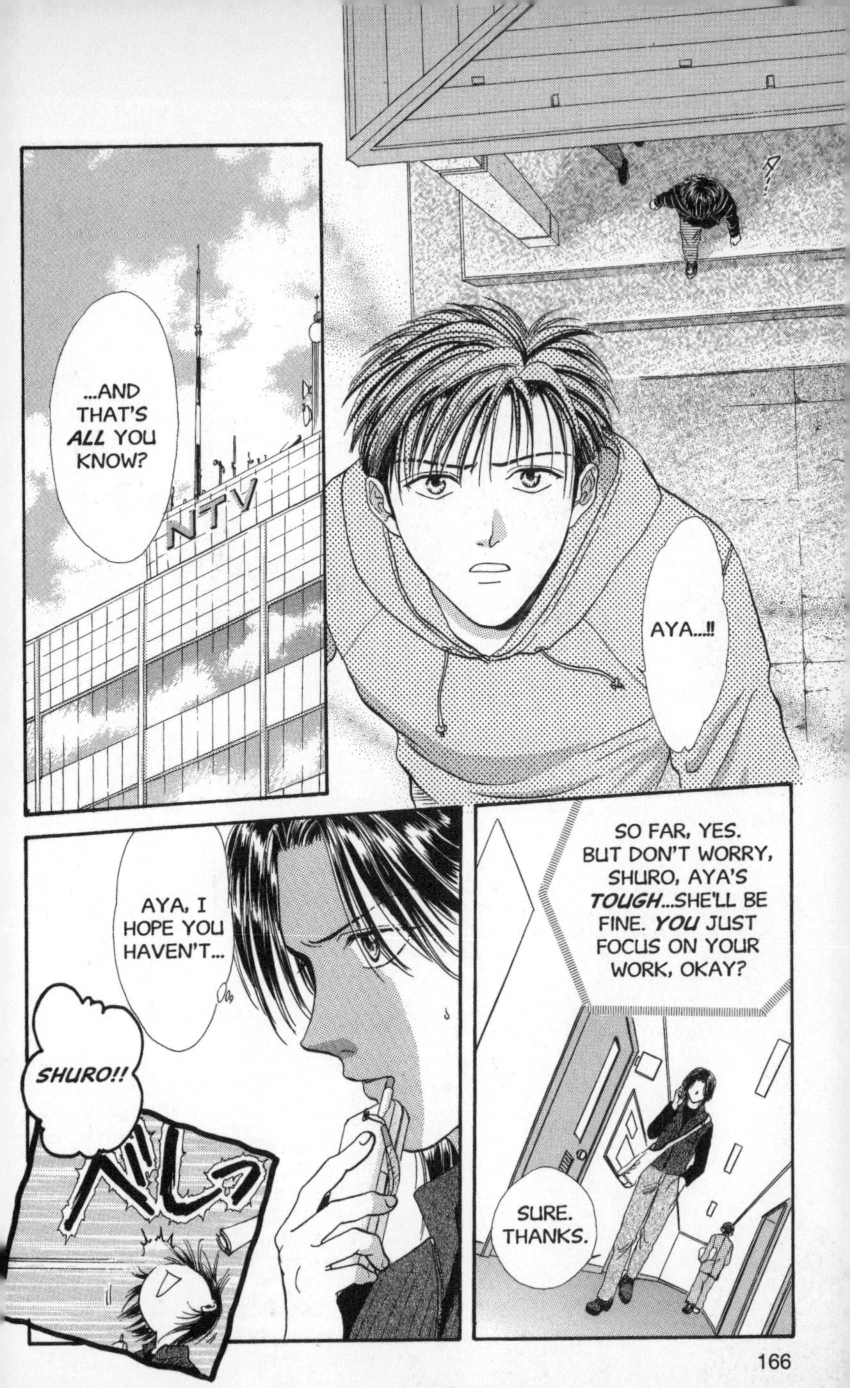
AYA...!!
...AND THAT'S ALL YOU KNOW?
SO FAR, YES. BUT DON'T WORRY, SHURO, AYA'S TOUGH...SHE'LL BE FINE. YOU JUST FOCUS ON YOUR WORK, OKAY?
SURE. THANKS.
AYA, I HOPE YOU HAVEN'T...
SHURO!!

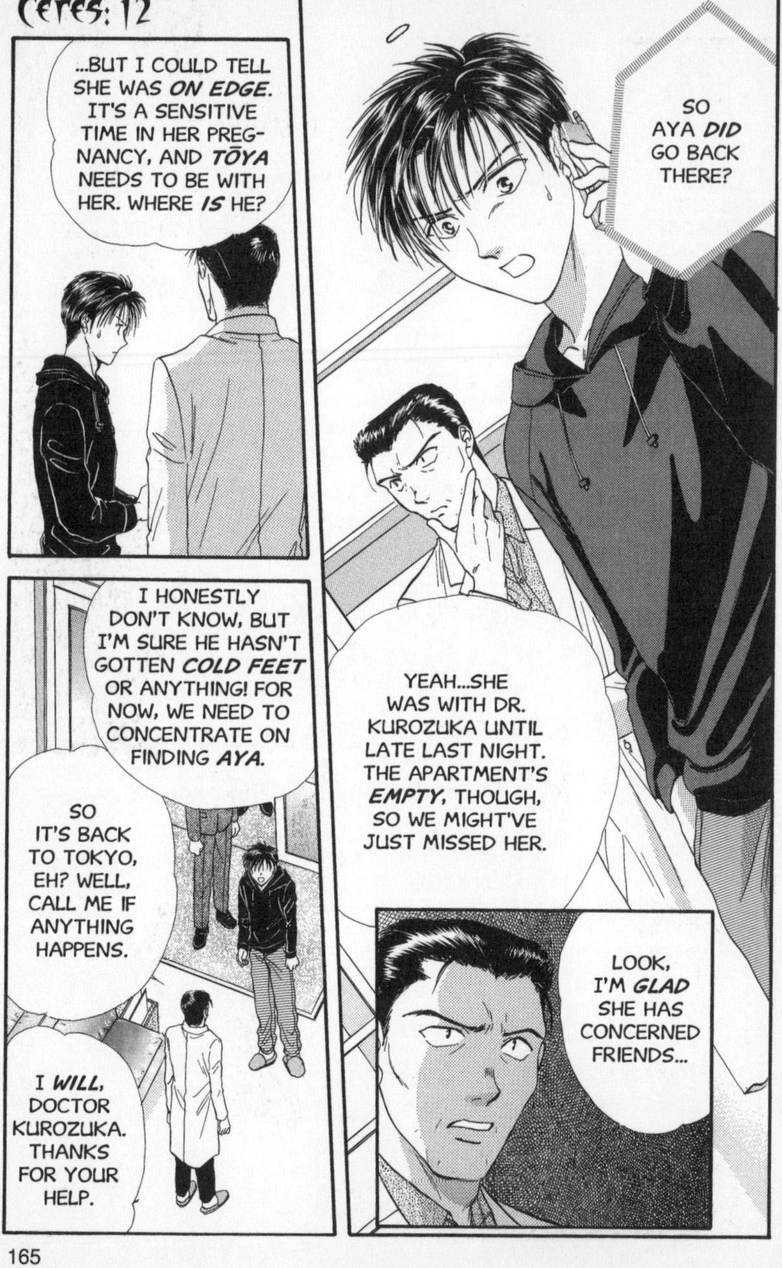
SO AYA *DID* GO BACK THERE?
YEAH...SHE WAS WITH DR. KUROZUKA UNTIL LATE LAST NIGHT. THE APARTMENT'S *EMPTY*, THOUGH, SO WE MIGHT'VE JUST MISSED HER.
LOOK, I'M *GLAD* SHE HAS CONCERNED FRIENDS...
...BUT I COULD TELL SHE WAS *ON EDGE*. IT'S A SENSITIVE TIME IN HER PREG-NANCY, AND *TŌYA* NEEDS TO BE WITH HER. WHERE *IS* HE?
I HONESTLY DON'T KNOW, BUT I'M SURE HE HASN'T GOTTEN *COLD FEET* OR ANYTHING! FOR NOW, WE NEED TO CONCENTRATE ON FINDING *AYA*.
SO IT'S BACK TO TOKYO, EH? WELL, CALL ME IF ANYTHING HAPPENS.
I *WILL*, DOCTOR KUROZUKA. THANKS FOR YOUR HELP.

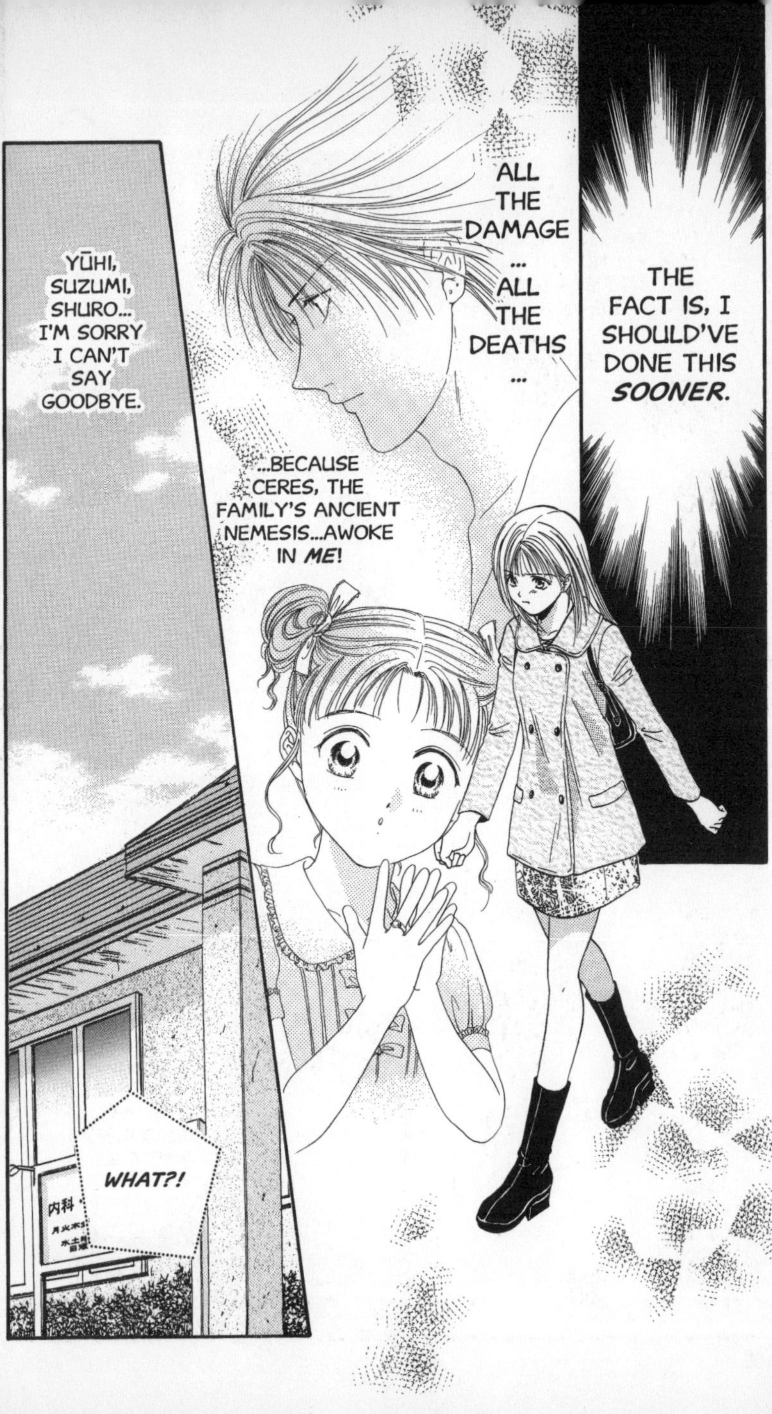
THE FACT IS, I SHOULD'VE DONE THIS SOONER.
ALL THE DAMAGE ... ALL THE DEATHS ...
...BECAUSE CERES, THE FAMILY'S ANCIENT NEMESIS...AWOKE IN ME!
YŪHI, SUZUMI, SHURO... I'M SORRY I CAN'T SAY GOODBYE.
WHAT?!
内科

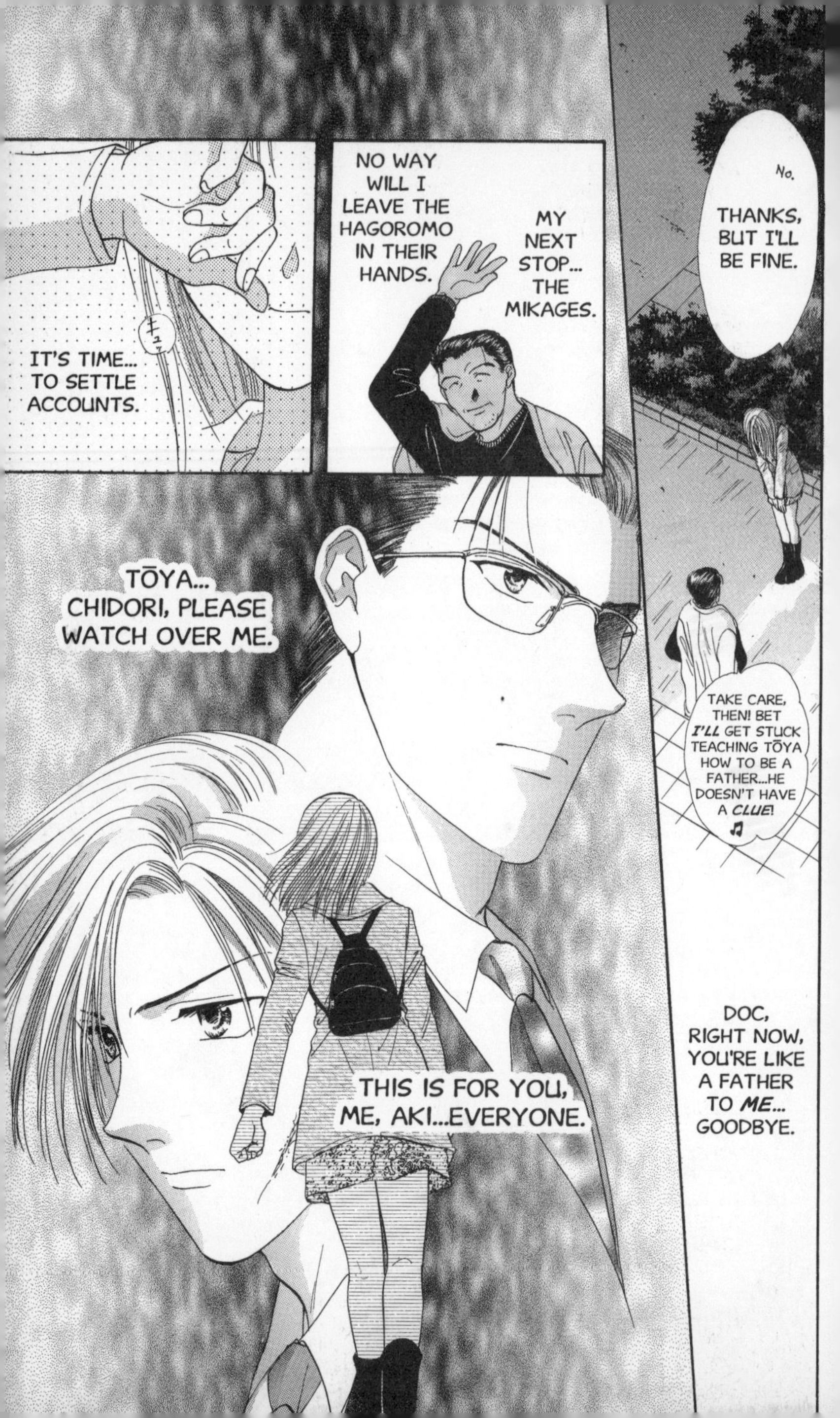
No.
THANKS, BUT I'LL BE FINE.
TAKE CARE, THEN! BET *I'LL* GET STUCK TEACHING TŌYA HOW TO BE A FATHER...HE DOESN'T HAVE A *CLUE*! ♫
DOC, RIGHT NOW, YOU'RE LIKE A FATHER TO *ME*... GOODBYE.
NO WAY WILL I LEAVE THE HAGOROMO IN THEIR HANDS.
MY NEXT STOP... THE MIKAGES.
IT'S TIME... TO SETTLE ACCOUNTS.
TŌYA... CHIDORI, PLEASE WATCH OVER ME.
THIS IS FOR YOU, ME, AKI...EVERYONE.